The Making of a Modern Quaker

Roger and Margery at their cottage in the Wye Valley, early 1960s

Fred Brown

The Making of a Modern Quaker

Roger Cowan Wilson

1906–1991

EPWORTH PRESS

0 7162 0502 5

First published 1996
by Epworth Press
1 Central Buildings, Westminster
London SW1H 9NR

Typeset at The Spartan Press Ltd,
Lymington, Hants
and printed in Great Britain by
Mackays of Chatham PLC, Chatham, Kent

For Margery,

Roger's wife, friend and confidant
in their sixty-year partnership of
mutual enrichment

During and after the 1939–45 war, civilian relief workers going abroad used to borrow some personal equipment from the Army. One of the items the Army insisted on giving us was an identity disc, and when the ordnance sergeant asked what religion he should put on it for me, I of course said *Quaker*.

'Quaker?' he said. 'Yes,' I said, 'Quaker.' 'Quaker?' he said again and paused . . . 'but that ain't a religion; that's a trade mark!'

Roger Cowan Wilson

Contents

Acknowledgments

My thanks are due to a number of people:

Most of all to Roger's family – Margery, Anthony and Elizabeth – for placing his massive archive at my disposal unconditionally, and their cheerful tolerance of my persistent questioning.

To the countless individuals I interviewed or with whom I corresponded, notably Marie Taylor, Roger's secretary during the whole of his twenty professorial years at Bristol university, whose generosity of time, hospitality and general helpfulness often cheered me on my way.

To the Joseph Rowntree Charitable Trust for covering my incidental expenses during the two years I was researching and writing the biography, in particular to Steven Burkeman, the Trust's Secretary.

To Harry and Margaret Dean for reading the manuscript as I wrote it – the final chapters on the day after their arrival by post on Christmas Eve!

Finally to my wife for assisting to decipher Roger's hand-writing, and her objectivity as I reduced the manuscript to publishable proportions. A copy of the full manuscript is in the library at Friends House.

F. B.

Prologue

Shortly after three o'clock on Wednesday afternoon, 5 January 1916, Prime Minister Herbert Asquith, not doubting the bitter controversy he was about to provoke, rose to address a packed House of Commons.

He proposed – *that leave be given to bring in a Bill to make provision with respect to Military Service in connection with the present war.*

Lamenting the failure of the latest national appeal for volunteers, he spoke of heavy casualties in France, of the depressing news of the Gallipoli campaign, and emphasized the importance of rapid victories. Conscription was not, he underlined, what he himself would have wished. If it could have been avoided no one would have been more relieved or grateful. In all the circumstances, however, national security left him with no other choice . . .

Both inside and outside the House resistance to the motion was vigorous and sustained, spearheaded by the Non-Conscription Fellowship whose members, ridiculed by the press, were described as the save-their-skins brigade, and presented with white feathers by young women. Nevertheless, despite enthusiastic mass rallies addressed by such powerful advocates as Philip Snowton, Clifford Allen, Doctor John Clifford, and Bertrand Russell, dismissed from his Cambridge post because of such anti-war activities, the Conscription Bill was passed – from 2 March all single men resident in Great Britain between the ages of eighteen and forty-one were liable for call-up.

An assurance of exemption was guaranteed for those opposed to war on grounds of conscience, but a gathering tide of narrow and soon nasty patriotism subjected such objectors not only to public humiliation and imprisonment, but persecution amounting to torture – regimes of bread and water frequently with prolonged solitary confinement, foot manacles, and strait-jackets for the forced feeding of hunger-strikers or to punish the unco-operative by leaving them hanging, feet barely off the floor, until, wracked with cramp and blue from restricted circulation, they either cried out in agony or mercifully lost consciousness.

Added to all this misery was the unofficial 'cat and mouse' policy associated with the completion of sentences; within hours or days of their release the COs were re-arrested and subjected to the same inhuman treadmill. Some died in prison or shortly after being hurriedly discharged to avoid official embarrassment. A few committed suicide. Still others lost their reason.

A Quaker man and wife were caught up in this wretchedness on a different front altogether. Though himself aged fifty and therefore not likely to be called up, he openly declared his opposition to the war, and persisted in referring to the enemy no less than to his own countrymen and their allies as sons and daughters of God. Soon he was being pointed out in the street as a probable spy, and figure of hatred. His home was stoned, windows smashed, the stonework daubed with accusations of treachery. During long interrogations by detectives he was searched, deprived of notebooks and peace leaflets, and eventually released with manifest reluctance. Such was the level of public hysteria and aggression, he was advised to leave the district, and did so out of consideration for the safety of his wife and their four children, the youngest aged six, the eldest twelve.

There was, however, another urgent factor in this gentle couple's decision to move from Birkenhead to Manchester. By now the imprisonment of C Os was widespread; Manchester prison seemed full of none other, many of them miles removed from their loved ones, and needing regular visits, help with personal and family anxieties, and somewhere to stay if only briefly on their release. So these Quakers opened their house to them as a haven, a place of total acceptance and support.

The four children silently watched and listened as the visitors talked of their own prison experiences and of other C Os far worse off than themselves – of thirty-one taken to France and forcibly dressed in military uniform; of seventeen of these placed in the front line and consequently court-martialled for refusing to obey orders; of their being paraded before thousands of soldiers to hear the outcome – death by firing squad, each sentence shouted out by the Commanding Officer before (after a long pause and barely audibly) he added: 'commuted to ten years penal servitude'.

Such details of the same kind captivated the children over the next three years as young men came or went, from or to jail. If they were heroes, an assumption the wide-eyed listeners never doubted, they also silently communicated that courage was far more than the absence of fear. Even the young men's irrepressible sense of fun could not hide the price they were paying for their refusal to support the war. Drained faces and eyes of apprehension spoke volumes to the children's minds.

A near life-time later the second-born of the quartet, Roger Cowan Wilson, recalled the lasting influence of those early days. Yet even he could hardly have realized the extent to which they were contributing to a process summed up at the end of his brilliant career as 'the making of a modern Fox'.

This allusion to the Founder of Quakerism, George Fox, was, as we shall see, amply justified.

I

Growing Up with a Radical Heritage
1866-1925

The children's father, Alexander Cowan Wilson, emulated his own father's fearless support of unpopular causes. Henry T. Wilson was a wealthy industrialist and Member of Parliament for Holmfirth in the West Riding of whom John Morley expressed the judgment: 'I don't agree with all his opinions, but he is one of the men who are as the salt of the earth, because he holds his opinions without fear of majorities or numbers.'

Some of Alex's earliest memories centred upon his ebullient father's campaigning for free education, adult suffrage, home rule for Ireland, Mrs Josephine Butler's morality crusade against what she saw as Parliament's tacit approval of prostitution, and, even more bitterly unpopular, opposition to the Boar War.

Both parents were motivated by a strong religious faith. Alex's mother, daughter of a Scottish Member of Parliament, was a staunch Presbyterian, as uncompromising in her religious dissent as her husband in his political radicalism. He, however, never completely overcame his suspicion that the institutional Church was more a hindrance than help in propagating Christian values and aims. If his devotion to Christ as Lord and Saviour was never less than boldly declared, his feelings for organized religion were never more than lukewarm.

Nevertheless Alex, like his two brothers and two sisters, was unaware of any fundamental difference between his parents in their profession of faith. Family prayers were observed daily, attended naturally by the ubiquitous domestic servants; and his mother's strong advocacy of church-going was in no way dimmed by his father's only occasional attendance at chapel or Quaker meeting.

The atmosphere at home was harmonious, both warm and loving, with lots of discussion about the latest cause thought worthy of the MP's considerable influence and his wife's eager endorsement, an insight into the nature of their relationship. Feminists would doubtless call him a bully and find his behaviour intolerable. In his own generation he simply reflected the authoritarianism accepted as desirable and necessary in husbands and fathers.

Certainly his devoted wife never complained or gave any evidence of feeling hard done by. She loved and admired her husband. He was a good man, an excellent provider, and his enviable reputation granted her social standing. No one could argue that by comparison with many of her contemporaries she was liberated.

From this home of fatherly authoritarianism tinged with liberalism, undoubtedly a progressive family for the second half of the nineteenth century, emerged five children who had taken on board not only their father's high moral principles and mother's devout non-conformity but both parents' commitment to public service. Cecil, the eldest, became a local councillor before winning election as Labour MP for the Attercliffe division of Sheffield. Doctor Helen never stopped serving the sick and numerous good causes. Gertrude's religious and social work in the East End of London typified her life-long concern for the under-privileged. Oliver, the youngest, qualified as an accountant and served the family business, at the same time working as a Liberal councillor for many years before becoming Lord Mayor of Sheffield in 1914, the year of his father's death.

Which leaves Alex, born between his sisters, and in some ways lacking the prominence achieved by his siblings. But this, given the shy nature of the man, was probably of his own choosing. Another reason was his health which at crucial periods in his life failed to match his rugged character. In his teens he was stricken with typhoid fever, necessitating a lengthy convalescence and interrupting his engineering apprenticeship. Having overcome these setbacks, his health still precarious, he readily fell in with his parents' wish to protect him from another harsh northern winter by going to South Africa, first to soak up the sun working on a farm, and then to seek gainful employment as an engineer.

He might have remained in South Africa for much longer but for a summons in his twenty-seventh year from his father to join him in India where he was fulfilling his duties as a member of the Royal Commission on the Opium Traffic. Fortuitously for Alex's whole future, another member of the Royal Commission was J.G. Alexander, secretary of the Anti-Opium Society, a Quaker who merited his reputation for statesmanship and sanctity. He it was who induced in Alex, serving as his father's secretary as the Commission travelled the country, an interest in India that lasted for the rest of his life, and a renewed interest in the Society of Friends; renewed because of Alex's once involvement with the Friends First Day Schools Association, started in 1847 to give working class men, women and children the chance to learn to read and write, and study not only the Bible but some of the classics of English literature.

On his return home, having been advised for the sake of his health to work in the open, Alex added to his engineering skills by training as a surveyor, and secured employment on an extension of the railway then being built from Nottingham to London via Leicester. Here he found lodgings and sought out the nearest meeting of the Friends First Day Schools Association which proved to be lively and open to his rather dour enthusiasm.

Now, he was fully aware, an essential aim of the Movement was 'to share a religious experience with the poor and ignorant in the inner cities by offering biblical and literary instruction', but this earnest man, far from being ablaze to share a religious experience he wasn't even sure about himself, still reflected his father's disregard for the institutional Church. In addition he was inclined, if not to repudiate, openly to criticize the whole set-up while at the same time ardently adhering to Christian standards of behaviour.

He was attracted by Fabian socialism. Unitarianism was not without its appeal. He hoped his involvement with Friends would help him to make up his mind about matters of faith. In the event he made himself thoroughly unpopular with persistent questions of implied criticism! When eventually – a mere five years later – he brought himself to apply for membership of the Society he made no attempt to hide the main reasons for his conspicuous half-heartedness.

First of all, he explained in his letter of application, he objected to senior Friends wanting to use the First Day Schools as a recruiting agency for the Society of Friends. Next, he complained that these two parts of Quakerism were not brought together enough in terms of scholars receiving from Meeting the acknowledgment they merited.

Furthermore, the exclusion of boys from the women's meeting house and lavatory was, he thought, 'a great pity'; if artisans and labourers were to be refined, or at least helped in that direction, Friends must sacrifice something. If, on the other hand, the reason for this exclusion was because the boys had abused their privileges, then surely 'some pleasant doctor could be invited to give a short address on personal and moral cleanliness'.

Finally, he felt constrained to point out the unfortunate impression being created by the many hansom cabs and the like arriving at Sunday Meeting. And it was more than the impression of wealth and social superiority they gave. 'I gladly recognize,' he conceded, 'that they are hardly used except by those who suffer from the infirmities of age, but for all that I am afraid their presence may do harm to those who have never heard or understood Friends' views on the *Observance of days*.'

Actually, he wasn't quite finished yet. 'I am young,' this thirty-three-year-old asserted, 'and may modify my views and I hope my readiness for criticism as I grow older. But I would rather not be admitted to membership than have any misunderstanding as to my feeling that the Society is in need of improvements in many directions, and that in Leicester it is in some danger from undemocratic and exclusive tendencies.'

The reaction of the elders reading this diatribe was understandable! Notwithstanding that the writer's father was a well-known Member of

Parliament of high moral repute, they wondered about the applicant's apparent lack of humility. Where was his sense of unworthiness in seeking membership? Never mind that his uprightness was self-evident and indeed winsome, were his comments, justified or not, indicative of a carping self-righteousness incompatible with Quakerism?

Fortunately they knew their man, how his hatred of falsehood in whatever form could so easily be misinterpreted as intolerant Puritanism or prickly piety. Here was a character whose wish to be diplomatic, not to offend, was always superseded by his love of truth as he saw it. Not for a moment did they seriously hesitate.

He was welcomed into membership, and – typically taking his new status to heart – attended the next Yearly Meeting in 1900, an event of profound significance for this newcomer for reasons other than the weighty matters under consideration. For also present was Edith Jane Brayshaw whose brother Shipley, an acquaintance of Alex's, was a natural bridge to bring these two shy strangers together.

She was a born Quaker, well educated, with a love of the arts which were, it must be said, largely a closed book to him. Whereas she knew classical English literature like the back of her hand, he was more interested in the likes of John Stuart Mill's *Essay on Liberty*, Charles Darwin's *Origin of Species*, and Samuel Smiles' *Self Help*, books published in the mid-1850s, and influencing the intellectual climate in which he was nourished.

In other ways they appeared to have little in common. She was an able public speaker, impressively articulate in arguing for her strong opinions. He whose views were no less positive fell over words in public debate, giving a false impression of his clarity of mind. She was introverted and insular. He was outgoing and enjoyed the company of all social classes.

The fact remains, this somewhat reticent and self-conscious man in affairs of the heart found her irresistible, and she responded with eager restraint. Within two years they were married, setting up home in Birkenhead where he was employed to supervise the building of dock walls on each side of the Mersey.

Their first child Stephen was born in 1904, and the next three, Roger, Margaret and Geoffrey, in that order, followed at two-yearly intervals.

At an early age the second-born was giving intimations of the sense of humour for which he became notorious if not famous. 'Roger,' Edith wrote to her mother, 'is growing steadily more and more rumbustical, and seems to act on the maxim of the Irishman – *when you see a head hit it*. His unprovoked assaults on Stephen are rather funny, but they are not always received in the same spirit, as Stephen's sense of humour has not yet grasped the point of the joke which consists in a sound whack delivered in the middle of the back by Roger's spade!'

Happily Margaret escaped such expressions of humour though at the approach of her second birthday Roger saw no reason why he should not share her much discussed anticipated bonanza of gifts. Overhearing his mother talking with her mother about what to get for Margaret he demanded a present too. Told he would have to wait for his own birthday he reacted: 'But it will make me snappy every day if I have to wait that long!'

Despite this evidence of a lively personality, Roger was a delicate youngster, and looked upon as such by his brothers and sister. If he alone was given cream on his porridge at breakfast, plus extra milk, they felt neither surprised nor resentful, viewing such favouritism as no more than part of the cosseting his frailty required. Just occasionally they suspected he might be trying it on, exploiting his need for coddling, but generally never doubted that his rumbustious sense of humour wasn't matched by his health.

At Birkenhead Preparatory School he was top for scripture, history, geography, English grammar and reading. The one area offering room for improvement was summed up in a gentle understatement by his headmaster: ' . . . he is not the best writer in the class'.

At his next school he was described as 'an intelligent, thoughtful worker, and a very interesting member of the class', but recipients of his adult voluminous correspondence won't be surprised to learn that his writing was dismissed with the misleading euphemism *weak*! The only other negative observation also applied throughout his life: 'He cannot sing in tune.'

Round about this time a transformation, significantly barely noticed by the children, took place in their parents' finances and, consequently, daily routine. Each came into an inheritance which coupled to their own savings guaranteed them an unearned income of £1000 a year. Bearing in mind that many working class families were living on twelve to fifteen shillings a week, this gentle Quaker couple felt indecently rich and not a little guilty.

Alex especially had uncomfortable feelings about ownership of property, and was embarrassed by income not earned by his own labours. It is highly unlikely he ever attempted to provide a religious or philosophical basis for his attitude. It was more an intuitive conviction about right and wrong as revealed in his understanding of the New Testament.

He found himself in sympathy, too, with the writings of R.H. Tawney who argued that wealth had a social purpose, that inequality of income was not necessarily wrong but that wealth should be re-distributed through progressive taxation.

After much heart searching, Alex, encouraged by his wife, came to the conclusion that he should resign from his job on the Mersey, and immerse himself full-time in a combination of Quaker concerns, mobilizing the Non-conformist witness for temperance and Christian morality in the life of the nation, and service as a Liberal councillor on the Police, Highways, and Education Committees.

At home nothing changed. Both parents rose just as early, a life-time habit granted religious sanction, and instilled into the children as essential to success. The customary Quaker grace of silence preceded breakfast which was followed less consistently by a family reading. Alex's original intention was to use these occasions systematically to read the Bible from cover to cover, but – bogged down in Leviticus beyond his own interest, never mind the children's – he increasingly turned to favourite passages or his beloved North American poets Walt Whitman and John Greenleaf Whittier.

Before rushing off to school or play the children were expected to make their own beds, and generally lend a hand in the home, supplementing the couple of domestic servants who were treated as members of the family and would have been happy to do everything. Pampering of any kind, like an undue reliance on help from others, was thought to undermine moral fibre. If the children were to stand on their own feet, make something of their life, they couldn't embrace the philosophy of self-help too soon, an outlook perhaps too exaggerated by their father's belief that success in life related to nothing more than personal discipline and hard work.

His wife clearly shared this belief though the children could hardly fail to notice a fundamental difference of attitude. Their Mother, in her ideas and life-style, was unbending. Feeling secure and at ease within Quakerism she lacked the slightest wish to step beyond its beloved parameters for either worship or personal friendships.

Her reasoning was simple – everything beyond Quakerism was necessarily inferior! If at times this attitude gave the impression of intolerance and condescension she would argue that the Quakerism she had known all her life had led her to the conclusion that it *was* superior.

Persons outside this inner circle receiving the impression she was shunning their wish for closer association, was even suspicious of them, were probably right. Not for a moment did she look down on them, and where compassion was needed to help the oppressed she was never found wanting, but none of this could hide the reality that between her and the non-Quaker world was a great gulf – fixed by her total satisfaction within the Society of Friends.

Her husband, on the other hand, was naturally outgoing with a genius for evoking trust and often deep affection. Initially his strong convictions and direct approach might give offence, but once friend or foe alike came to know him they recognized that, agreeing with him or not, here was a man who was good because he loved goodness, as free of pomposity as of Pharisaism.

Despite all the love and warmth generated within their home by both parents, something never doubted by the children, hugs and kisses were virtually non-existent; typical of parent-child relationships in many middle and upper class families of those generations.

What one of the children, however, wondered in retrospect was about the nature of his mother's interest. 'She was sort of interested in us as a family,' he remembered, 'but her interest was more intellectual and religious than personal and individual.' The comment wasn't remotely intended as a criticism, but rather as an attempt to analyse the core element of a rich maternal love he never felt the need to question.

No less self-evident was her preoccupation to protect her family from all alien – meaning basically non-Quaker – influences. The children had few if any friends beyond two groups of five and four cousins, but never felt this a privation. In their limited free time they always found plenty to do with each other – hockey in the drive at home, feeding their mother's half dozen hens and collecting the eggs, a daily excitement recalled with relish a near lifetime later, playing cards as a family though never on Sunday, a day strictly observed for spiritual renewal, and the usual pastimes of collecting stamps, specimens of natural history, and the like. But their primary leisure engrossment was reading, each of them, all of them, book after book, guided by their mother's love of literature, and their father's promptings in the direction of current affairs and social history, plus of course Quaker publications in all parts of the house.

Their mother also painted and sang seriously, recreations she encouraged in the children; encouraged if not always with consequent pleasure, for Roger's hearty tunelessness persisted, an ongoing problem for innocent bystanders no less than the family. The only real disharmony, however, was the inability of the children's father to get home for meals on time. His gentle wife would remonstrate, he would apologize and promise to do better, but the endless meetings of indeterminant length he attended about Quakerism and wider social concerns frustrated his every sincere resolve.

Eventually she became more understanding, but not, indeed never, about the other major irritation in their domestic round – his aptitude for leaving his work table littered with papers, a reminder of her losing battle to make him tidy or tidier.

No less problematic for the pair of them was how to cope with the children's abundance of energy at holiday time. Having married late, he was now in his mid-forties, she only three years younger, they found a fortnight or so by the sea a euphemism for purgatory. So, in concern for the children as much as themselves, they took to inviting an unsuspecting guest with the essential requirement of having the energy of an elephant.

One such victim who surprisingly remained a friend for life was Fenner Brockway, admitted to the inner sanctum despite not being a Quaker because of his peace witness. In his autobiography he recalled those balmy days of long ago:

> I had known Sir Geoffrey Wilson, the chairman of the Board (Race Relations), as a boy. He is the son of A. C. Wilson, a Quaker who was of great help to conscientious objectors in the First World War, and with whom I had spent a seaside summer holiday. Happy recollections remain of playing on the sands with Geoffrey and the children.[1]

Whatever these games, Roger would probably have been no more than an enthusiastic bystander. He wasn't interested in sport or ball games generally, not as a participant. Only much later in life did he watch football, cricket and rugby on TV, and through the same medium become addicted to snooker in his final years.

Almost from the start his first love was books, adventure stories, of course, but more particularly books of information to match his endless questions and wish to learn. More than this, he was early captivated by ideas, the great concepts and beliefs of man's search for meaning, a search quickened for the entire household by the outbreak of war in 1914.

The Wilson children, though largely protected from its consequences, could hardly fail to notice the grave reaction of their parents; and when to this was added the move to Manchester and the resultant coming and going of COs at the new family home each of the four children felt part of a campaign the significance of which was as exciting to them as their inability to understand little beyond the price being paid for a moral principle. They took for granted that Quakerism meant opposing the war, no less axiomatic than their assumption that every prisoner in Manchester jail was there for no other reason.

With such ideas firmly in mind, fostered needless to say by the children's love and admiration of their brave father's peace witness in the prison itself, the eldest of the quartet became a boarder at Leighton Park Quaker School, winning a scholarship but still making demands of the family budget. In the fullness of time Roger was offered the same opportunity; he hesitated – a letter from his mother a few years later suggested – out of concern, largely misplaced, not to add to his parents' financial burdens.

Finally he went to Manchester Grammar School, a choice for which he remained forever grateful, and quickly responded to the intellectual vitality

---

[1] *Towards Tomorrow*, Granada 1977, p.237.

nurtured from the High Master, J. L. Paton, down to the humblest member of staff. By the end of Michaelmas term, 1920, Roger was placed fourth in his form; by Easter term of the following year second; and by summer term of that same year first.

As a sixth-former Roger's sights were set on a history scholarship or exhibition at Oxford. Stephen was already there. Geoffrey and Margaret also made no secret of their wish to follow. Competition between them never crossed their minds. If from their early years their brilliance had been recognized, such an assessment passed them by. The nearest they came to any such awareness or comparison among themselves of their achievements at school was Margaret's unjustified assumption of her brothers' superiority. Whatever her own distinction she felt the odd one out, tagging along in the wake of their (to her) unreachable standards. Any pressure she felt to emulate them came not from her parents but the modesty of her self-evaluation.

By the time Roger travelled to Oxford to sit his exhibition examination he was reasonably confident, having worked hard and feeling he could have done no more. Eventually the result was received. No scholarship or exhibition. But then the High Master at school received a wholly unexpected hand-written letter from K.K.M. Leys, one of the examiners at University College:

> Last vacation a member of your staff wrote to me about R.C. Wilson, a candidate for our History Scholarship. In a short viva he impressed us very favourably. I felt bound, when I found out I couldn't take him for my own college, to direct the attention of others to his work . . .
>
> If he is offered a sufficient exhibition now, I think he ought to take it.
>
> I wish we could have had him for I liked his work very much.

The offer duly arrived from Queen's College, a centre of learning famous for brewing its own beer, and notorious for the amount consumed by its own undergraduates, hardly conducive, it might be thought, for a total abstainer's peace of mind!

The new exhibitioner, on the contrary, apart from seeing the funny side of the situation, didn't doubt that the best place for temperance witness was not some haven of prohibition. In any case, his attitude to alcohol, though uncompromising, was incidental to his major concern – to get the best degree possible in history.

His departure from Manchester Grammar School was not inauspicious, coinciding as it did with the farewell of the High Master, J. L. Paton, on Speech Day at the end of Michaelmas term, 1924. Roger was invited to contribute one of his marathon recitations for which he was well-known both within and far beyond the boundaries of the School, on this occasion from Tennyson's *The Passing of Arthur*:

The old order changeth, yielding place to new,
And God fulfils himself in many ways . . .

A major influence during these formative years was the great William Temple, then Bishop of Manchester, and destined to be Primate of all England. His enthronement as bishop occurred when Roger was in his sixteenth year.

Temple's decision to join the Labour Party, announced to the Lower House of Canterbury Convocation, in early 1918, had fired a national debate about the church and politics – should a bishop of the Established Church be identified with a political party? The Wilson household was not immune to such considerations, especially the parents in their genuine fear of Socialism.

For some years, Temple explained, he had questioned whether the clergy should openly support any political group, but that doubt now resolved he felt free to declare his own allegiance:

> Now the Labour Movement is essentially an effort to organize society on the basis of freedom and fellowship. As such it has a right to claim the sympathy of the Church . . . We must not support it simply because we sympathize with the motives behind it: but if we believe that these motives are, on the whole, applied with wisdom, we have no right to stand aside. We must go in and help.[2]

For as long as he could remember, Roger had watched his father as Quaker and Liberal councillor 'go in and help', translating his concerns for peace and social justice into costly involvement with the neediest members of society. So what challenged the young Roger's thinking about Temple's decision was not the priority it implied for the social gospel, reaching out a helping hand to the hungry, the thirsty, the stranger, the sick, the prisoner, emphases inseparable from Quakerism, but the nature of the best political means of changing the structures of society itself.

The Manchester Grammar Schoolboy wasn't a bit surprised at the furore created by Temple's bold move, the outrage expressed by many clergy and laymen alike, the wringing of ecclesiastical hands at such political partisanship, surely anathema, the very voice of the devil, but what could not be refuted by any of them, and of far greater appeal to Roger, was Temple's identification with the underdog from his early childhood.

During his Manchester bishopric Temple and the young Quaker became

---

[2] F. A. Iremonger *William Temple – His Life and Letters*, Oxford paperback 1963, p. 153.

known to each other, the one still continuing to ruffle feathers of both Church and State, the other altruistic and sharing his father's moral concerns. How often they met is uncertain. There is a note from the bishop saying how much he regretted missing Roger on one occasion, and expressing the hope of a get-together during next vacation; but Temple's deep and continuing influence cannot be doubted, an influence in no way undermining the younger man's commitment to Quakerism but making impossible an unthinking assumption of his father's Liberal Party allegiance.

During his final eighteen months or so at Manchester Grammar School Roger found himself drawn more and more to Socialism, not, needless to say, as a secular philosophy but rather as the natural corollary of Christianity, the latter inspiring and guiding the former. J. L. Paton would be at least sympathetic, for he and Temple, apart from being old Rugbeians, were personal friends, frequently sharing the same public platform. But the High Master's major influence was infinitely more related to Roger's academic promise than any political realignment. He pushed for the young man's exhibition at Oxford, and – despite the initial setback – never doubted his own judgment of potential greatness in his pupil's character and achievements.

By the time he arrived at Oxford for the new academic year, 1925, Roger was no less an uncompromising Quaker pacifist as militant Socialist, formidable in argument on both fronts, unnervingly courteous in disagreements either religious or political, the possessor of a wit as much appreciated as feared, and bursting to make his mark.

He didn't have long to wait.

2

Wearer of Many Hats at Oxford

1925-1928

Before going up to Oxford, Roger visited Geneva, drawn by his interest in The League of Nations and a hope of improving his French and German. It proved to be a mixed bag of sight-seeing, socializing and work. Apart from familiarizing himself as intended with the activities of the Society of Friends International Committee he was progressively caught up in preparations for an International Older Boys' Camp in Finland within the auspices of the World's Alliance of the YMCA. By the time he moved on to Germany early in the New Year, he was keenly anticipating his own attendance at the Camp but first of getting acquainted with Berlin, Munich, the Black Forest and wherever else his fancy took him. Intoxicated by travel, he was not a little alarmed by the seething political cauldron, an undercurrent of resentment at the Treaty of Versailles.

The year, remember, was 1925. Life in Germany continued to seethe with resentment over conditions of the armistice, fostering political anarchy, and setting the stage for a National Socialist dictatorship. Hitler was barely known but the country's drift toward the philosophy and policies he came to epitomize didn't escape the notice of the young nomad from England.

His fears were compounded by the charm and kindness of the German people themselves. Their hospitality was matched by their almost unnerving courtesy. On a basis of one to one Roger could hardly have been more encouraged to believe that peace was their wish for both personal and international relationships. But these other signs of drift were ominous. Despite a wonderful summer, and the excitement of returning home for Oxford, he couldn't escape a sense of menace. Whatever else he didn't do at his new seat of learning, he must support as never before Quakerism's witness for peace.

Oxford was a painful contrast to the freedom of his travels. Some aspects of undergraduate life were less than congenial, a view he didn't hesitate to express in forthright terms to his old history teacher. A reply within days was equally pungent:

The first week or so at Oxford is like looking into a series of lavatories, and finding each one more repulsive than the rest. But things settle quickly if you gang your gait. The great thing is to fix on what you want to do.

Dull tutoring is intolerable, but if I were you I'd take a high hand with the lectures, and not attend them, unless stimulating. You will find dons very sensitive to criticism and inclined to grovel immediately . . .

Whatever Roger's early disillusionment he was delighted to be at Oxford, and soon too immersed to care about minor irritants. Nevertheless he saw the danger of this privileged institution coming to represent a pseudo-exclusivity unrelated to the real world, the world he had just left in Germany, the world of festering industrial relationships in his own country, the world as he saw it of blatant social injustice heaped on the poor.

One of his first moves was to join the University Labour Club where his genius for friendship, militant idealism, and debating skills quickly made him an obvious candidate for election to the committee. Part of his appeal was inseparable from his northern wit and humour typified by Charlotte Bronte's story of a smallbusinessman and speculator she knew who had done rather well for himself. Past middle age, now very rich, he thought it judicious to insure his own life, and had just taken out the policy when he became gravely ill. The doctor was called and searching for words admitted the hopelessness of the condition. 'By jingo,' the man reacted, 'I shall *do* the insurance company! I always was a lucky fellow.'

Though possessed of a fund of such stories, Roger never remotely used any of them to rough up or ridicule opponents in debate. Likewise he was quite incapable of not greeting their retaliatory humour with gales of laughter howbeit at his own expense. His merriment was infectious, taking the sting out of possibly explosive situations. He hated deceit, despised sophistry, and – no matter how soft his tone – exposed muddled thinking for what it was worth. Unlike his father he was articulate to the point of eloquence, holding an audience, even playing on an audience, with consummate ease. What on his own admission he sometimes lacked was the ability to think on his feet, recognizing his most telling points only on reflection *after* the debate was over. Not that the people on the other side noticed! But it was such fierce criticism of himself that saved an outstandingly talented man from ego-centricity and the pit of arrogance.

It would be claiming too much, however, to say that he unfailingly conformed to the conventions of humility or at times wasn't impatient to be the focal point of attention. It was so frequently expected and demanded of him. People at meetings large or small looked to him for leadership, imposed upon him the role of spokesman, leaned on him noticeably in committee to produce a statement both representative and crystal clear. It all became so habitual that, like it or not, and on balance he preferred it, he was compelled to accept what even before Oxford was a pattern and finally inescapable.

Undermining any suggestion of place or prominence seeking was his integrity, as transparent as it was utterly free of self-righteousness. The worst evils in the world were not done, his own heart told him, by evil men but sometimes by good men who did not know they were not doing good. He didn't doubt that lack of imagination far more than naked selfishness made humans indifferent or half-hearted to their suffering international brothers and sisters. People needed to *see* and *feel*. In no better terms could he understand individuals loudly protesting their love for the world while lacking compassion for the solitary needy on their own doorstep.

One of Roger's closest friends during this first year at Oxford was William Francis Hare, son of Lord Listowell, a high Tory who demanded from the heir to his hereditary peerage early signs of the same political extremism. 'I liked and respected Roger enormously,' Billy reminisced in his old age, 'he was a sort of second conscience. I could always go to him for advice about any troublesome problems.'

And Billy had problems aplenty, having joined the Fabian Society! His father was apoplectic. Like Roger's Socialism, Billy's grew out of his personal observations of what he called 'the gross injustice in the distribution of wealth, and lack of opportunity to anyone born into a working class family compared to anyone born into a family like mine'. This political conversion guided the rest of his life. Inheriting his father's title, in 1931, he took his seat on the Labour benches at the House of Lords, served as Labour whip during the war, and went on to fill with distinction the posts of Under Secretary of State for India, the last one before Independence; Minister of State for Colonial Affairs, and Governor General of Ghana for three years from 1957.

But at the time of his friendship with Roger at Oxford, his new political allegiance caused him to be prohibited by his father from the family home. He was saved from having nowhere to go during vacations only by the secret intervention of his mother who – having money of her own – found him a tiny flat in London.

As their friendship blossomed during their shared political activities and discussions on walks by the river it was inevitable that the subject of religion, or the search for meaning, should present itself. Billy made no secret of his agnosticism, any more than Roger of his Quakerism. Usually their minds met, their views overlapped, but not in this one crucial area which while bespeaking the motivation and direction of Roger's whole life left Billy no more than respectfully sceptical.

Billy was happy to accompany Roger to the Friends Meeting House on Sunday morning, both of them relishing the silence, one for worship, the other for wonder, one no less grateful for spoken ministry than the other.

'I had always felt,' Billy said, 'that Quakers were the best Christians, the most honest Christians. I admired Roger all the more for being a Quaker.'

Later he amplified his views about religion in a letter to Roger: 'I have read your book on the Society of Friends, and I am impressed by the faith and the actions of the Quakers; as, indeed, I have always been, but I was glad to see the picture at closer quarters. I think that, whereas your mind gravitates naturally towards religion, mine gravitates with almost equal force towards science and art, so that, although we are both idealists, mine is a philosophical, yours a religious, idealism . . . There is much we might talk about.'

And talk endlessly they did, not primarily however about this shared on-going interest but the deteriorating industrial situation throughout the country, focussed on the gathering unrest in the coal fields.

The issues were clear-cut. In May 1924 the miners won a favourable wage settlement, thanks largely to promptings from the Labour government. But when shortly afterwards Polish and German coal knocked the bottom out of the European market, British mines again began to lose money.

The owners reacted instinctively – more work for less pay. After twelve months of divisive argument they gave notice to the miners' leaders of their intention to cancel all existing agreements and to reduce wages. The showdown was only averted by the government setting up a Royal Commission which spent the winter of 1925 preparing its report of some 300 pages. In essence it recommended measures to improve working conditions, like the provision of pithead baths, as soon as possible, coupled to an immediate reduction in wages.

The owners, rejecting the improvements proposals out of hand, demanded not only lower wages but longer working hours. The miners responded with what became their battle cry – *Not a penny off the pay, not a minute on the day*. On 1 May they were locked out. A special trade union conference on that same day voted by more than 3,000,000 to 50,000 for a General Strike on 3 May. It brought the nation virtually to a standstill.

The government, claiming the British Constitution was under threat, appealed to people's patriotism to volunteer for work left undone by the strikers.

At Oxford the University Labour Club promptly marshalled its forces to counter what they saw as government propaganda. Roger, with an idealist's faith that if only people were better informed they would surely see the justice of the miners' cause, was mainly responsible for compiling a series of information sheets for distribution by Club members and sympathizers. Their style and tone are better interpreted in the light of the young Quaker's diary kept over the first few days of the strike:

Friday, April 30th John Strachey at Labour Club says strike would be no catastrophe . . . now or never the fight for Socialism etc. Most cheerful. Did not agree. God give the miners strength to hold out in a struggle involving more than mere wages, but impossible to feel happy about General Strike. Danger of things getting out of hand too great. Moved insincere vote of thanks to Strachey.

Sunday, May 2nd A good Meeting (Quaker) in the morning centring wholly on industrial dispute. After Hall, Franks (don at Queen's) explains to College meeting Govt. application for volunteers. Extraordinary clear and unbiased statement, and brilliantly cutting replies to silly and fractious questions. The dispute is essentially one between two principles, and to help Govt. capture position legitimately held by trade unions (i.e. organization of supply services) is to become party to cause which we do not support.

Monday, May 3rd Study papers over breakfast. D. Herald jubilant and cocksure – perhaps inevitable in its position, but to be regretted . . . Times very hard and unsympathetic . . . M.G. pacific and moderate in main leader but futile and silly – at this time – on 'Bargaining by Threat' . . . Midday papers hopeless, ditto tea-time.

Trying to read hard for tutorial, but impossible to concentrate. Was to do nothing best policy? . . . receive ten leaflets issued by Oxford Trades and Labour Council, rabid – very – but straightforward and full, begging University men not to blackleg. Distributed mine, with fear and trembling, at bottom of staircases.

Tuesday, May 4th Go out for paper . . . On way back down High, 25 or 30 transports full of soldiers go by – going west to Wales? That explained heavy rumbling all night. Hundreds of loads had been going by since midnight. Some, but not great deal, of cheering. It looks bad . . . This afternoon to Lab. Club Executive Committee meeting . . . 18 present including G.D.H. Cole, as the man in the know. Decide to commit Club to anti-blacklegging and offer services to local action committee (Trade and Labour Council). Also to condemn colleges permitting undergraduates to blackleg at home . . .

Tuesday, 11.30 p.m. Just back from emergency meeting of Labour club. Attended by large number of rowdies. After letting some in, tried to keep others out. Light scuffle followed but no damage – beyond watches including my own done . . . Resolutions declaring against blacklegging and pledging Club to aid local Action Ctte. passed without fuss. Considering badness of speaking and chairman, meeting surprisingly good, especially after the row at the beginning. There did seem to be some sort of conversion which was encouraging.

On return to College (Queen's) distribution of first Oxford University Labour Club leaflet on wages.

Having kept abreast of developments in the mining industry, and no less concerned about the plight of men at the coal face and their families, Roger saw no reason at the end of his long life to change the essential emphasis of his views in 1926. He would have seen the closing down of so many pits in 1993 as the inevitable outcome of people being sacrificed for profit; common sense to the economist, but to this Quaker a denial of 'that of God in every man'.

Michael Stewart, appointed Foreign Secretary in Harold Wilson's government, in 1966, recalled those days in his autobiography published in 1980: 'The Club, until the impact of the General Strike, was very small. At its outset we called a meeting to rally its supporters; before we could hold it we had to eject a number of hearty undergraduates who wanted to break it up, and the meeting became known as "The Battle of Hannington Hall". Clashes of this kind did not recur because the great majority of undergraduates went away strike breaking. We Labourites remained, helping the local Council of Action to organize meetings, and bicycling round Oxfordshire villages distributing leaflets which were not always well received. The membership of the Club rose to three hundred, and grew steadily thereafter.'[1]

Stewart also made reference to the 'Cole Group' which met regularly in the rooms of G.D.H. Cole, University Reader in Economics: 'Occasionally we discussed Socialist theory but usually we were asked to consider such practical problems as the preparation of departmental estimates or the reform of local government. Undergraduate enthusiasms were harnessed to serious political work; it was significant,' Stewart noted, 'that Hugh Gaitskill, not otherwise very active in the Club (except during the General Strike) was a regular attender. Cole was very critical of many aspects of the Labour Party, but he knew very well that Leftist zeal outside the Party runs to waste.'[2]

Decidedly not running to waste was the uncompromising support of the strike by Roger and Billy. The reaction of their respective families was, however, somewhat different though for Roger no less worrying.

Lord Listowell summoned his son to demonstrate his family loyalty by returning to London to serve as a substitute policeman! Billy found it not only impossible to respond but remained at Oxford helping with the distribution of a newsheet – *The British Independent* – produced by students at his own college Balliol, and as ardent in support of the strikers as the University Labour Club leaflets. Also, being one of a minority group of car owners – his

---

[1] *Life and Labour*, Sidgwick & Jackson 1980, p.22.

[2] Ibid., p. 23.

was an Austen 7 – he transported patients to and from hospital. This further defiance of his father did not go unnoticed! Retribution was only a matter of time.

As for Roger's father, his attitude was revealed in a letter dated 9 May 1926:

> We want the miners to have decent wages, and are sure the Government was wrong on the Friday night and Sunday night – and I am not opposed to the TUC having had a General Strike for 2 or 3 days to show their backing in the country. But I cannot support 'a fight to the finish' or 'Peace by Victory'. We were for Peace by Negotiation 1916–18 and against 'Peace by Victory' then. It is not that we want Churchill and his Government to win, but the longer it goes on the more they are likely to, it seems to us.
>
> We are sure you are doing what you think right, very likely in a small minority, and perhaps risking your career. But you are still our dear son.

A letter of the same date from Roger's mother underlined her uncertainties:

> This is a time when each can only do what they feel right. I hope there will not be rioting at Oxford but there will be hotheads here [Manchester]. Fenner Brockway is up here superintending the dissemination of the TUC side of the case in answer to the Government Statement. We have not seen him yet but we have spoken to him on the phone. We are not able to see clearly enough to come down definitely on one side or the other in the latest developments of this week, so have to content ourselves with helping all round in appealing to each side to get into human touch with the other side and see what can be done . . .

Meantime at Oxford Roger continued to do his best to clarify the 'issues of the struggle', lending what he himself described as 'a large hand' in churning out a stream of Labour Club leaflets.

But he wasn't merely involved in this war of words, vital though he believed this to be. Like members of the Labour Club as a whole he was desperate to give practical help to the miners themselves and their families, an empathy sustained long after the General Strike was over, for the coal fields remained idle and mining communities were reduced to inhuman levels of subsistence.

Apart from this practical concern for the miners, Roger was also battling away on another front round the corner from his own college. He had learned that Ye Olde North Gate Tea House had excluded Indian students. The Oxford University Peace Union protested, and Roger wrote the following letter:

Dear Madam,

The members of the Oxford branch of the No More War Movement regret to hear reports that Indians have been refused admission to the North Gate Tea House. They feel that already international relations are dangerously strained, and they cannot but view with alarm any action of such a nature as may increase that strain. To encourage the feeling of racial antagonism in Oxford seems to us a serious mistake, and we should be very glad to hear from you that the reports are untrue.

Yours faithfully,

R. C. Wilson
(Hon. Sec.)

Immediately term ended Roger and others of the University Labour Club hastened to the Rhondda Valley to offer any help possible in what was reputedly by far the most socially deprived coalfield of all. His early impressions were given in a lengthy letter to his parents:

> The distress is appalling but it is very hard to deal with it. The trouble is to get the people, as individuals, to admit that they are on their beam-ends.
>
> The wife of a locked-out miner can, if she likes to apply for it, get ten shillings a week from the Poor Law, though this is only a loan; in addition she can get two shillings a week for children not receiving school meals or instead of this a pint of milk per day for babies. The only thing the men can get is one meal per day from the Federation, so long as the Russian money holds out. But to get this meal they have to line up in public with a plate and mug which a good many men would rather starve than do. Somehow or other one has got to get them fed without damaging this spirit of self-respect which is incredibly powerful here . . .
>
> Of course everything we do is prolonging the strike; there is no getting away from that. But it is impossible to think of the strike being brought to an end by the sheer breakdown through misery of the miners, as fine a set of men as one could wish to come across . . .
>
> There is here an extremely fine Wesleyan minister called Barker with whom we have been staying. He is worshipped by the people and has been working himself to death in the last few weeks. Every Friday night he has a sort of open discussion class where the men go and talk about anything under the sun.

> Among the men last night there is no sign of weakening. They know that they are beaten, but they will not admit it until they can do nothing else, which is not yet by a long way. Strikes here have no special terror; they know them too much for that. I don't believe a single month passes but that one or more of the pits has a row resulting in a stoppage. Why it is I don't know for the people are not violently red and are very highly Cultured in the real sense of the word . . .

Working through the Society of Friends Industrial Crisis Committee Roger remained in the Rhondda for a month, and left with great reluctance to fulfil other commitments including a League of Nations speaking tour. New branches were being set up in many parts of the country, and wanted to hear about and discuss not only international issues but the relevance of the peace witness to the continuing miners' strike. Roger was also keen to disabuse widespread misunderstanding about the miners themselves. The more he had come to know them the greater his respect and admiration had grown.

Billy his friend whole-heartedly shared this regard, and – despite his father's unrelenting opposition – himself remained wonderfully cheerful in the thick of his support for the strike. But another bitter personal blow was about to fall. His Lordship, having looked in vain for signs of his independently-minded son coming to his senses, and doubtless needing someone to blame, decided that this filial defiance was due to the politically corrupting influence of A.D. Lindsay, Master of Balliol, Billy's college. The answer, his Lordship felt driven to conclude, was to take his son beyond the reach of this ranting Socialist academic by the simple means of refusing to pay any more of Billy's college fees.

Furthermore, as though to add insult to injury, Lord Listowell made it clear that the only way his son and heir could continue his university education was by transferring to Cambridge, admittedly, Billy was the first to agree, hardly a disaster in itself; but made humiliating and shameful for the family prodigal by his knowledge that his admission to Magdalene College had resulted from his father pulling strings with the Master, Billy's old tutor at Eton.

Roger's university career, too, was proving problematic relative to parental intervention, though in a different way altogether. Earlier in the year, the beginning of his second term at Oxford, he had written to them about what he saw as the disproportionate amount of time demanded by his studies compared with surely the more important matters of his wish to save the world from self-destruction.

Coupled to this, he further explained, seeing he had no interest in making lots of money, wouldn't it be sensible to modify his educational aspirations, take an ordinary rather than an honour's degree, and use the time saved in

Quaker, social and political activities? To his clear-thinking mind the only logical answer was axiomatic. But not to his parents! The reply written by his mother was prompt, and revealing of this Quaker family's evaluations and priorities:

> We feel strongly against your view about an honours degree at Oxford. We feel that you may easily let down your character somewhat by acquiescing in less. We feel that your immediate work is to get at Oxford the best degree that you can. It would create all round a sense of disappointment in you if you only got a pass. Cox and everyone of that sort would say, 'Oh yes, Roger Wilson was a failure at Oxford, and we had thought better of him. He has gone off on some crank etc. etc.'
>
> Then again, you say in your letter that you are not going to make money. That precludes you from going into commerce if I understand the remark aright . . . if you are thinking of going into commerce without the money-making instinct you will not make a success of it. Of course I mean money-making in a reasonable sense.
>
> The instinct will come strongly before many years to marry and start a home, and a good Oxford degree will help you to manage things. Of course I do not want to say that we should not be satisfied if you did the best you could and yet got a pass degree, but we do feel uneasy at your acquiescing in the thought of that alone.
>
> And now in conclusion I want to say how much we appreciate your willingness to help and take your share in the effort for righteousness. It is you only who can judge of the right proportion of your time and energy that can be given to outside concerns while you are at Oxford, but take a long view and, as far as you can, think of your life as a whole – middle-age and old-age as well as youth – and try to adjust it so that throughout it shall have a message of better things for humanity than we have at present.

Roger found no easy answer to a balanced apportioning of his time, his ambivalence compounded by the miners' strike and all the suffering he witnessed as it dragged on. There were times when the very idea of university at all seemed akin to fiddling while Rome burned. How could he justify not plunging straight into the fray and using every moment to meet urgent human need?

Part of his problem of never having enough time for everything was of his own making, the voluminous private correspondence to which he remained addicted – or rather saw as part of his obligations – to the end of his days. People mattered. They couldn't simply be fobbed off with a cursory acknowledgment or forgotten because not seen.

When a donor, for instance, sent money, clothes, boots or food for distribution among mining families his reply, written often deep into the night, included a resumé of the appalling need generally followed by case histories to illustrate how the gift would be used. The final paragraph of one such lengthy letter explains why he thought this so important:

> I must apologize for this long exposition, and yet it seems only fair both to those who give and those who receive to make some sort of apology for such a horrible affair as begging [and] that you should understand as fully as I can explain them the conditions in which your gift will be spent.

Having left the Rhondda, his pen was barely out of his hand to encourage and reassure the people still there, relief workers and miners alike. A long letter from a miners' leader warrants unhurried attention in full not only because it typifies the affection and admiration Roger evoked in so many of his personal relationships but also because it reveals a miner's perspective on the strike and the essential pride, dignity and unbreakable spirit of the men and their wives against overwhelming odds:

> Dear Friend,
>
> We received your kind letter safe and were very pleased to have it. We have been talking about you many times, wondering how you were getting on, and wondering whether we would ever hear from you again.
>
> We cannot yet fully realize your great kindness to us, total strangers to you all. We feel as I have told you before that we can never repay you for what you have done for us. We are still in the middle of this crisis, and as you know things have not improved since the time you left, but although the outlook is as black as it has ever been the spirit of the men is still unbroken.
>
> As you say there is something 'rotten in the state of Denmark' that men, women and children must suffer and are prepared to suffer so much for the sake of a fuller life. The wages offered in South Wales especially are such that it would be impossible for people to live at all after working hard every day of the week. The general feeling here at the end of the twenty-fourth week is that they may as well live in a semi-starvation state idle as live in that state working.
>
> You saw the actual coal seams, and know according to the price lists I gave you what the coal hewer gets per ton for his work. There is a Minimum Wage Act in force today which enables the actual coal hewer to demand a certain wage if he can prove that his working place is an abnormal one. This is a matter of contention between him and the official

in charge weekly, and in nine cases out of ten he has to fight for his legal right under this particular Act of Parliament.

What I am coming to is this, there are hundreds of us respectable men in South Wales weekly working a great deal harder than they ought to, trying to earn their wages according to the price lists in working places that are abnormal where the price list was never intended to apply. They are so independent in spirit that they half kill themselves rather than approach the official and be charged with malingering. It is a common phrase used here always that the actual coal getter half murders himself to keep himself alive.

Mr Wilson, I have spent a quarter of a century at the coal face and I say it in cold blood, there is more injustice done underground in a day than is done anywhere else in years. The miner has endeavoured to rise above his circumstances. He does not ask for anything else now. All the improvements he has been able to obtain during the past thirty or forty years have been obtained in spite of the coal owners.

They say that there is a political object behind this crisis. I say definitely that there is not. The Welsh miner after all is said is not very particular in his political creed. He belongs to the Labour Party because that is the Party that will reach the goal he longs to reach first. Now this letter must come to an end or else you will never write another one to us if I keep on troubling you like this.

We have a tendency to despair when fighting for a lifetime against such great great odds, still we must believe as Lowell says, that although –

> Careless seems the great Avenger, history's pages but record
> One death-grapple in the darkness, twixt old systems and the Word.
> Truth for ever on the scaffold, Wrong for ever on the throne.
> Yet that scaffold sways the future, and behind the dim unknown,
> Standeth God within the shadow, keeping watch above His own.

If the miner loses this fight the hopes of thousands will be dashed to the ground, and progress delayed for another generation.

Kindly accept our thanks once more, and through all your studies believe that Right must triumph in the end.

We are hoping that when this cloud passes away that we shall meet again before you are much older. Remember always that we shall be pleased to see you.

Yours faithfully,
E. E. Johns
Sec., Cwmaman Lodge,
S. Wales Miners' Federation

It is hardly surprising that such a letter reinforced Roger's temptation to abandon his studies for what he conceived to be more urgent concerns. The fact that he didn't added paradoxically to his misery – to share the miners' plight at first hand was anguish enough yet to separate himself from them for the indulgence of book learning proved at times to be almost unbearable.

'Don't let the sufferings of others make you suffer,' Roger was counselled by his friend Billy writing from Cambridge, 'that is not the way to help them.'

Maybe. But Roger was haunted by the faces of the miners and their families, haunted by them and infuriated by the blatant injustice to which he believed they were exposed. Small wonder that Billy felt the need to add in his letter: 'Be careful of your health as on it depends successful work.'

The mystery was, how could this twenty-one year-old, with his record of childhood frailty and sickness, now appear to have the constitution of an ox, capable of working all day and half the night, apparently never tired, a characteristic retained for the rest of his life? And, with the strike still continuing, the new academic year brought with it not only renewed support for the miners by the University Labour Club but for Roger himself the added responsibility of officiating as the Club's chairman.

His election, coinciding with the early days of the General Strike, had been one of the last things Billy had been able to share before being uprooted for Cambridge. Certain Roger was the best possible candidate, never mind their friendship, Billy had wanted to canvas support, but had been sternly instructed otherwise.

'If we can't win in a straight fight,' Roger made clear, 'let's oppose without intriguing. In the end it will prove the honest thing, the decent thing, and the right thing.'

Recalling the incident nearly seventy years later Billy smiled approvingly. 'Roger said on no account; leave it to them, the members. I don't want it to be thought . . .' The old man paused, reflecting. 'That was typical of him about anything that seemed to him not extremely ethical.'

It was this element in his fundamental make-up that saved Roger always from bigotry and expediency whilst driving him on to embrace unpopular causes and make decisions seemingly inconsistent with his reputation for uncompromising righteousness. To such matters we shall return in detail at the appropriate time. Meanwhile, as Chairman of the University Labour Club, he was wrestling with the deepening conviction that social injustice of the kind witnessed during his visit to the Rhondda could only be destroyed root and branch in relation to social justice on an international scale.

It was, of course, still necessary to attack racism locally, as the continuing boycott of the Ye Olde Tea House illustrated, but such a narrow vision led to palliative rather than decisive action. If before the strike his Quaker peace witness and his internationalism joined hands, each a natural corollary of the other, he now perceived that justice for the coalfields of Britain could never be achieved in isolation from the rest of the world. Despite the approaching new term and his added responsibilities as Labour Club Chairman, he gave expression to this quickened understanding in another of his lengthy letters, this time to a foreigner overseas. Much of it reiterates his letter about the Rhondda to his parents, but the following extract, apart from its subjective evaluations of the coal field's social environment, culminates in what was, on this occasion, a broader concern:

> The valley itself is about twelve miles long, ending against a steep mountain wall. It is very narrow – from the top of the mountains on one side to the top on the other side is less than a mile in many places – and as the valley is a thousand feet deep, you can imagine the sides are pretty steep. A hundred years ago, before coal was discovered there, the valley was one of the most beautiful in Wales, so thickly wooded that a squirrel could go from one end to the other on the tree tops. Now, the people tell you, a cat can go the same journey on the roof-tops! All the natural beauty is gone, except in one or two places, where just enough remains to make the utter ugliness and horror of the rest worse by contrast.
>
> From one end of the valley to the other there is one unbroken ribbon of what we call industrial civilization. Anything more utterly hellish is impossible to imagine. The valley is so narrow that there is only room for the railway, river and about two narrow, unending streets on each side. There is no room for any dignity – all is squalid, dirty, and huddled together, for mining populations increase fast, and there is no room to expand outwards here. Dwellings, pits, and dirt tips are mixed up anyhow, and hardly for a moment can you get away from the horrible whirr of the fan engines. And the utter impossibility of getting away from the thing and all its complications is the most horrible of all.
>
> The miner has to work, in some cases, in conditions almost inconceivably bad. At the best of times, mining is not pleasant, but we saw some places underground which made one shudder. The worst was a seam only eighteen inches high, so low that you couldn't go on hands and knees, but had to be on your front and wriggle along by your elbows, and lie on your side six and a half hours a day, swinging a pick. It is suggested by some people that longer hours will provide the solution to our coal problem.
>
> Such a solution would be intolerable, in fact we are morally in the wrong to let such conditions exist at all, but economies say it must be. In other words our economies and our moral convictions won't square. That's the dilemma we're in. One of the standards has got to be adjusted. I think it must be the economies.

> It is the seriousness of industrial problems which makes some of us keen on internationalism. For this western form of civilization is built on an industrial basis after all, and unless our nations are built on sound foundations all internationalism can go for nought. But on the other hand, modern industry is the most international thing the world has ever known, and unless we tackle it internationally it will be hopeless to seek for a better national life.

Internationalism and how best he could work for it, like the apportioning of his time for study and active campaigning, was still an anxiety. Should he be satisfied with whatever degree he could get or heed the advice of Gordon Cox, his old history master, who, hearing of his dilemma, promptly wrote with a positive suggestion: 'Modern greats (Philosophy, Politics and Economics) is essentially a four-year course, and those who have attempted it in three have generally complained of pressure. A First', Cox dangled the carrot, 'is a definite advantage.' Billy, now ensconced at Cambridge, didn't hesitate to chip in with his advice: 'I hear your tutor has ordered *work*; don't let that weigh on your conscience. A change of that kind is recuperation, not confinement.'

The tutor was Oliver Franks, only a few years older than Roger, and clearly destined for a brilliant career. In fact, after what was described as a good war (1939–45) at the Ministry of Supply, he went on to become British Embassador in Washington, followed by a series of Top Jobs, and a Life Peerage.

No less impressive were the jobs he was reputedly offered and turned down – Head of Nato, of the Treasury, of the Coal Board; Director-General of the BBC; Chairman of British Rail; Headmaster at Harrow . . . An exceptional man!

He and Roger had much in common but perhaps their fundamental difference of approach to a whole gamut of tricky situations pin-points why they got on so well together from their first meeting and became life-long friends.

Franks was excellent at guiding studies, but showed little interest in his students' personal problems and anxieties. Whether in fact he wasn't interested or conceived that this was not part of his responsibilities is debatable, but in terms of the tutor-student relationship this was precisely what Roger wanted. His good fortune in being free from most of the worries that menace and sometimes destroy undergraduates made his tutor's strictly cerebral attitude ideal.

Then again, Franks for all his intellectual brilliance was not an original thinker. He had exceptional capacity for seeing into the core of conflicting opinions, analysing and clarifying them, and finally formulating a statement or minute that was acceptable to all parties and interests. The securing of diplomatic consensus was the measure of his considerable negotiating skills. Perhaps this was why his most ardent admirers found it difficult to get closer to the man himself beneath his scintillating talents whose very brilliance constantly exposed him to the danger of mistaking sterile bureaucracy for fundamental progress.

Roger on the other hand was an innovator; competent as an administrator but with sufficient imagination and daring to step out of line and pioneer the initially unwelcome. The central aim of his life was to be a reconciler and peace-maker, but never at the price of barren agreement.

These two young men, separated in age by a mere one or two years, with affinity yet distinctive dissimilarities adding spice to their tutor-student relationship, developed a mutual respect that, as already mentioned, blossomed into life-long friendship. Which was just as well, for only weeks after receiving an order from his tutor for more work Roger stumbled across another mighty diversion.

Her name was Margery Emmet.

3

Romance and the Oxford Union

1928–1929

Roger and Margery met through the good offices of Canon B.H. Streeter, though a romantic liaison between them was the last thing on his mind when inviting them, along with a dozen or so other undergraduates, to one of his regular reading weeks at Jordan's Quaker Conference Centre. His contact with Margery was her father, a close friend over many years, the two clerics being early members of the Modern Churchmen's Union, thought at the time to be a hotbed of heresy. His contact with Roger was through another of his friends, the Rev. Frank Lenwood, a Free Church leader whose wife was a sister of Roger's father.

Margery was encouraged to attend by her sister Dorothy, in her final year at Oxford, and unable to share Margery's excitement at the prospect of a week of combined study and recreation.

Roger read a paper on pacifism. Margery was impressed, not initially by the speaker so much as his subject. She *thought* she was a pacifist, her mind turned in that direction by a student lodger saying she could not imagine Jesus Christ firing a gun. But this whole area bristled with imponderables, not least the absolutism advocated by Roger!

They talked about it during the rest of the week, Roger himself increasingly aware that, no matter how circumspect his behaviour, far more than his Quaker peace witness was uppermost in his mind. Following their return to Oxford he kept in touch. In returning a book he loaned her about pacifism she set out her reservations about his absolutism:

Dear Mr Wilson,

I am returning *Disenchantment*[1] for which many thanks; I'm so sorry I've kept it so long, but one of the girls in the house wanted to read it. I hope you don't mind? I think it is quite Montague's best thing that I have read, and quite the best thing on war too.

---

[1] C. E. Montague's bitter account of the First World War in which he served as a private soldier.

You know, I've got a hopeless kind of head! Having been quite convinced about China the other day, I don't think I am any longer. What on earth am I to do with myself? Can you re-convince me? If it won't bore you too much, may I say what I think, and if you find it full of fallacies I shall be delighted.

To begin with, all force is immoral, but I believe also that simple inaction is immoral too.

There are three possibilities in China – a spiritual way, inaction, or troops. The danger as far as I can gather seems to be entirely from mob violence (is that true?). The first possibility is obviously the perfect one, but can it be done? That's to say, is there anyone at present who could do it? It would mean swaying a crowd of thousands and bringing them under the influence of the Spirit. There doesn't seem much chance of this, though.

There are left then inaction and troops. The first would probably mean the death of thousands at the hands of the mob, especially as the evacuation of Shanghai does not seem possible. But if the danger is only from mob violence troops will probably prevent any bloodshed at all as it isn't likely that they, the mob, would attack a strongly defended place. They are there as policemen only. I do feel that if we do nothing we are as responsible for our people's death as if we had killed them ourselves.

One can do what one likes with oneself but not with others. So if we aren't using the spiritual force, troops seem inevitable. I don't say it is absolutely right but more right than doing nothing.

Am I talking nonsense? This will probably make you see red, and, as I say, if you can disprove me, I shall be most grateful. Excuse me writing all this.

Yours ever,
Margery L. Emmet

With so much to discuss, long walks by the river and into the countryside round Oxford seemed eminently sensible, and it was during these meanderings that Roger made the astonishing discovery that wild flowers also grew in Britain. A city man to his finger tips, he'd noticed them first in Germany, a riot of spring loveliness, and lamented there was nothing of the sort in England! Now, with Margery, brought up in the country, he repeatedly not only had the flowers pointed out to him but actually named; and learning their names, he discovered, enhanced his appreciation and pleasure.

Margery and Roger had much in common – religion, pacifism, Socialism, and cultural background. But – as we have seen in Margery's questions about war and peace – there was not always agreement between them. Indeed the very strength of their unity sometimes led to the opposite of unanimity, for instance, in the area of religion. He was a Quaker, she an Anglican, devoted to the traditions, not to mention the music, of the Established Church. This originated in her love and respect for her parents, notably her father, biblical scholar and theologian, an earlier-day John Robinson or David Jenkins, subjected to the same condemnation and abuse when publishing his radical thinking about the nature of God, arguing that judgment, divine wrath, punishment, eternal damnation, the horrors of hell and the like were utterly inconsistent with the revelation centred in Jesus of Nazareth.

As vicar at a small village under the Berkshire downs – West Hendred – and vice-principal of Ripon Hall, the Modern Churchmen's theological college near Oxford, he had become a symbol of hope for Christians disaffected by the orthodox teaching of the church. Of course, much of this had passed Margery by. She was only a teenager when he unexpectedly died during a preaching and lecturing visit to New York, in 1921, two years after his appointment as Dean and Chaplain to University College, Oxford. She remembered him primarily as a loving father, always caring and courteous in any company – family, theological college or crowded railway compartment of weary mothers, whimpering children, and a couple of drunks who, like the other passengers, responded to his down-to-earth helpfulness.

Canon Streeter summed him up as a man who did good simply because he saw life through the eyes of his Master. Understandably his love for the Anglican Church was buried deep in Margery, too, not only because of his influence but her own imperceptible endorsement over the years. So, early in her relationship with Roger, realizing that he was too ardent a Quaker to be happy as anything else, she confronted the issue of her allegiance to the church into which she had been baptized and confirmed. Roger fully acknowledged and respected her right to remain an Anglican; no problem. But Margery didn't hesitate. She knew that being the sort of people they were they would wish to worship together; and that, this granted, it made more sense for her to accompany him to Meeting than to plunge him into a sacramental church foreign not only to his background but more importantly his temperament.

With a couple of reservations she found the transition easier than anticipated. She missed the choral and congregrational singing of the church; and at times, for all the enrichment of Quaker silent worship and spoken ministry, she particularly missed the sacrament of the Lord's Supper. But never for a moment during the next sixty-odd years, sixty of them as Roger's wife, did she regret her decision.

Fortuitously the miners' strike had brought them closer together politically. Knowing nothing of Roger or the University Labour Club, she had gone to the Rhondda with a religious group called the Knighthood to assist welfare relief, hardly interested in politics at all; but after what she'd experienced living with a mining family and seeing working conditions at the coal face, she'd returned to her studies smarting with indignation, admittedly a demure Socialist but passionate nonetheless.

This new and exciting romantic development wasn't the only thing eating into Roger's over-crowded time-table. His facility with words was winning him growing admiration and respect at the Oxford Union. His sister Margaret approvingly described his contributions as more sermons than speeches, emphasizing the urgency and feeling with which he argued his case. Not that his style was emotional or remotely tinged with emotionalism, anathema in any case to sophisticated undergraduates.

Billy attributed Roger's effectiveness to his icy logic and fiery presentation, a unity conveying that here was a man with a message more concerned to win votes than make a personal impression. His support of any proposition consistent with his Socialism, pacifism, and advocacy of total abstinance was hardly likely to win him many friends, superficially confirmed when he was nominated for the Union Presidency in Trinity term, 1928, and beaten. But in Michaelmas term he was nominated again, this time to face opposition from Quintin Hogg, later Lord Hailsham, son of the Lord Chancellor. The result of the voting surprised everybody, not so much the result itself (though some were frankly astonished), as the size of Roger's majority – sixty-eight.

His opponent was gracious in defeat. 'I must congratulate you,' he wrote, 'although I thought your margin much too large. I had expected about 15. Q.'

Harold Laski wrote from London: 'Dear Wilson, I congratulate you warmly on a remarkable victory; it was a real pleasure to see you at the top of the poll. Almost you persuade me of the value of an interest in the Union. Good luck to you!'

The Bishop of Manchester, in sending his congratulations, expressed the regret that because of his visit to Jerusalem for a conference he would miss Roger during the Christmas vacation.

Significantly Roger's election as President of the Union brought a letter from the coal fields of South Wales: 'May we send our congratulations on your latest honour. Many of your friends at Aberdare are most happy to think that the Union has singled you out as President. There would be too many names to mention all who wish to be remembered to you . . .'

Finals in Modern Greats still had to be faced. Then Roger planned to enter the cotton industry after a meeting with J.W. Armitage, part mill owner of Armitage and Rigby, who had offered him a job on the spot. Billy heard the news of his acceptance with incredulity and foreboding.

Some of the newly elected President's admirers, thinking of him as a future Prime Minister or at least member of the Cabinet, made no secret of their disappointment. What of course they could not know was Roger's motivation and aim.

Like his paternal grandfather and father, he wanted to devote himself not exclusively to politics but to a goodly measure of voluntary public service. His father had managed it through a family inheritance, his grandfather by earning enough in three days of each week to leave himself free for three days, with Sundays naturally reserved for rest and spiritual renewal.

Roger, having no private funds, with little prospect of any, decided that his best chance of following what he saw as this worthy family tradition was his earning capacity in business, against the grain really, for his interest in money was almost irresponsibly moderate.

But first his finals loomed. Oliver Franks was again emphasizing the indispensability of work. The Dean of his college was fearful 'when we remember all your other activities' of the inevitable retribution.

Roger himself was bright enough to heed the warnings, but as usual somewhat preoccupied with his other, to him, inescapable commitments. On top of his many university activities, he was also in demand as a scheduled or standby speaker, typified by a postcard from the Secretary of the Society of Friends Coalfields Distress Committee, received shortly after his election as President of the Union:

> My warm congratulations to you! I fear however that you would not have got them, unless I had wanted to ask whether you are going out to Geneva in time to speak at this Coal Distress Meeting at Montreux. Your Father has been asking if any of our people are likely to be there, and I can't give him any names, so I hope you are going. If you want latest details, do come in here on your way through.
>
> Yours, Joan Mary Fry

Apart from wanting to oblige, Roger was keen to see his parents who by now – having discovered that the cost of living in Geneva was cheaper than in Manchester – were living there and continuing to support Quakerism's international peace witness. He would welcome too the opportunity to share with them his wish to become engaged. Margery had already intimated her agreement, but, conforming to the custom of those now seemingly antediluvian days, he wanted to seek their approval of the match.

His mother was enthusiastic, reflecting the response within Margery's family, but, aware of all the pressure he was under following his election and his concurrent Chairmanship of the University Labour Club, plus the required intensification of his studies, she advised him to 'get through schools' *first*, and then, not wasting a moment, to proceed not only with his engagement but marriage too.

Mrs Wilson appeared to have a penchant for getting her children married, most of all Margaret, who now wonders, her eyes mischievous, whether this was because either she had so many boyfriends or her mother's fear that finally nobody would be prepared to take her on. Whatever the reason Margaret didn't keep her mother in too much suspense, marrying James Meade, an academic who went on to win a Nobel Prize for economics, and with whom she joyfully shared the celebration of her parents' diamond wedding.

As far as Roger and Margery were concerned, they decided to keep their engagement *secret* until he had sat his finals. Meanwhile he continued to give the impression of a man rushing off in all directions at once, struggling not always successfully enough to find time for his books.

Part of the trouble was lack of co-operation from national and international figures with sufficient clout to address the Union or the Labour Club. Bernard Shaw replied: 'Mr Shaw does not open exhibitions or bazaars, take the chair, speak at public dinners, give his name as vice-president or patron, nor do any ceremonial public work; and he begs his correspondents to excuse him accordingly.'

But even when big names did respond and pack the house, this very success was hardly likely to give the President of the Union more time for private study! Not that Roger complained. He welcomed the honour and revelled in every moment of fulfilling his duties. Understandably nevertheless the Jeremiahs among his political friends and foes alike told him, his finals in mind, that he was surely cutting the ground from beneath his own feet.

Conspicuously not of their number was his old adversary for the Presidency, Quintin Hogg. Immediately the finals lists were pinned up he wrote to Roger: 'No one is more detestable than the man who says "I told you so" – except when what he foretold is good. I foretold your First.' No less impressed was his eldest brother Stephen who admitted, ' . . . quite honestly I thought that you had not an earthly'.

John Parker, elected Labour member for Romford in 1935, was cock-a-hoop: 'The Labour Club seem to have done well with Michael, Escott Reid, Durbin and yourself . . . You and Michael, I see, are mentioned in the "D.H." today; you are indeed two "lights".' (The Michael referred to was Michael Stewart, himself elected as a Labour MP in 1945, for East Fulham.) This success of leading lights in the Labour Club prompted one commentator to observe: ' . . . no doubt we will expect a Morning Post campaign to cancel the school on the grounds that it is a Socialist breeding ground under the sinister influence of the Master of Balliol.'

Roger's father's delight was as irrepressible as his humour: ' . . . Only a *step* now to the Premiership or the Dictatorship of the Workers' Cotton Trust or any other prize you may covet . . .' His mother was more concerned that he and Margery should recognize 'all the wonderful things that come to you as calls to opportunities for the service of your fellows. You can just imagine,' she concluded, 'how our thoughts go out in thankfulness for the wonderful future that surely lies ahead of you. Love, love and love again, E.J.W.'

Warmest double congratulations were also received from Aubrey Herbert who beat him for the University College scholarship in 1924. But of all the many greetings none was more sincere than the one from A. Alec Clifton Taylor, a shy and reticent man, apolitical, non-pacifist, not averse to a glass of wine, who as an undergraduate himself had shared little of Roger's hectic activities outside their common interest in books and scholarship. Their friendship, superficially surprising, had blossomed into a sort of David and Jonathan relationship that continued throughout their long lives constantly to reveal depths of mutual affection and loyalty born and nourished by nothing more than the simple pleasure of each other's company.

Alec who, like Billy, referred to Roger as his conscience now wrote from his post-graduate studies in Paris lamenting he did not really know Margery Emmet which made him feel 'how far I am from my friends and that other life which I led only a year ago!' He also made the confession: 'I hardly have the brazenness to tell you, but after all one must follow one's convictions, even when they expose one to the charge of being a chameleon; therefore I will – I am thinking of joining the Labour Party.' Only those aware of Alec's background and disinclination to join anything could fully appreciate why and how he made this proposed step sound like a shameful secret.

Anyhow, knowing of Roger's plans immediately on going down to spend six weeks or so in Russia, accompanied by Oliver Franks, Alec inquired whether Margery was going too? If not, he suggested, 'you are either going to be very brave or very unhappy or both'.

In the event, barely having slipped the engagement ring on Margery's finger, and his old tutor finding it necessary to withdraw, he set off. Alone.

4

Love Letters and Marriage

1930-1931

Roger left for Leningrad on a Soviet steamer berthed at Hays Wharf, London Bridge, an area known to him as a centre of undergraduate activity during the General Strike. By this, as he called it, 'curious bit of irony' he now found himself eating off crockery decorated with the Communist hammer and sickle, national symbols for which 'millions of Russians would willingly die'.

The voyage lasted five days on a ship, roomy and beautifully clean, newly built at Leningrad. The only serious drawback he mentioned was the lack of adequate deck space for walking or playing off the 'exceedingly good and plentiful food!'.

The ship's company was attractive, too, from the captain down. There was a pleasing lack of formality; nobody bothered about uniform, and the stewardesses, instead of stiff black clothes, looked bright and cheerful in their own tasteful jumpers and skirts.

The crew appeared disciplined, but were certainly not servile. When the cook's boy brought out his ukelele and the first mate his mouth organ, the doctor danced with a stewardess, and the fat and jolly cook cut the nimblest of capers. On three of the afternoons three of the Russian-speaking passengers were invited by the crew to talk to them or ask questions on any subjects of their own choosing. Each session lasted for at least an hour and a half.

There were fourteen passengers on board, and it took numerous officials at Leningrad two and a half hours to get them ashore. First, terrific passport formalities; then a list of personal possessions had to be made, followed by what Roger called the real fun, every item of luggage meticulously examined. Luxury goods were confiscated. One woman was allowed to keep twelve pairs of silk stockings, and the remainder taken. When she protested she was informed there was no point, was there, in passing through customs unless something was removed, pending of course its return when she left the country.

All books, manuscripts and writing materials were scutinized by the political police. At Roger's turn a man looking no more than a teenager, and not knowing a word of English, gravely stared at a small edition of William Blake 'to see if he could detect anything counter-revolutionary'.

Roger's first impressions ashore were happier. 'The bristly haired, grim looking ruffian usually presented to us as a typical Bolshevik was,' he said, 'a myth.' Except for the grubby old cab drivers, the men were a clean shaven lot, tall and well built, and the crowd, apart from its very homely clothing, looked far more like an English crowd than a group of Frenchmen, Italians or Germans.

Nevertheless he found the city itself slowly slowly rotting away and lifeless, in contrast to Moscow which impressed him as 'brim-full of energy'. Not that the streets and buildings were any less drab, but there was a feeling of vitality in distinction, he emphasized, to a feeling of exhilaration claimed by some visitors.

Despite his Socialism making him sympathetic to the Bolsheviks and happy to applaud every evidence of progress his observations were still objective. Public transport was hopelessly inadequate; seventy passengers in a tram made for forty with still many people left waiting. Restaurants were numerous and fairly cheap, but the food, though admirably cooked, was very plain and crudely served. Phones were rarely available not least because of 'the Russian's capacity to talk'.

The churches, contrary to popular belief in the Western world, were not closed, and there appeared to be no interference with those wishing to attend. But there could be no doubting the new regime's 'anti-religious' attitude, an understandable reaction to the church in Russia having been used as 'an instrument in the hands of the reactionaries'. The Communists, however, failed to distinguish between religion and ecclesiastical institutions, meaning they might eventually undermine the latter without necessarily uprooting living faith.

He expressed surprise at the equal status of men and women in society at large, an equality not only manifested in women working on road and railway repairs but just as likely doing key jobs in any profession. Consequently places of employment had creches and nursery schools attached, giving the authorities, he noted, 'greater control over the education of children of the country, with what results we shall see in thirty years time'.

More immediately startling was the way, right in the middle of Moscow, anywhere along the river, people bathed with nothing on. At Yalta the beach was well populated with both sexes sun and sea bathing in their 'birthday suits', all with the most perfect unselfconsciousness. 'It was,' he wrote, 'rather a lovely sight to see all the naked brown bodies leaping about, but rather pathetic to see a most beautiful nude female figure busy powdering her nose and painting her lips!'

Summing up the visit he said there was much human kindness and yet a curious streak of appalling cruelty.

On his homeward journey he called at Constantinople, Athens, Marseilles and then Geneva to see his parents before rendezvousing with Margery at Rouen Cathedral. But he never stopped scribbling his impressions of Russia, some of them in the form of commissioned articles, all making an earnest plea: 'My main concern is to beg that people should refrain from judging Russia. Everything there is different, and the more you see of it the less do you feel that you understand it. Explanations might be found in history, in the Russian character and in communist philosophy, but it is impossible for the stranger to disentangle the influences let alone understand them. And in any case, it is a long experiment, and not before two generations have passed shall we begin to know whether it has succeeded or failed.'

Fifty-five years later the winds of perestroika began to blow!

In accepting his job in the cotton trade Roger made clear that he wanted to be a useful business man but more than a 'mere' business man. He also desired to remain human, on top of his job and at the same time maintaining his interest in what he called 'non-purely business affairs'.

In the event his employer, startled, he said, by such frankness, requested further details! Roger explained he wanted contact with the mill workers, with other executives, and responsibilities with international implications, the first two, he admitted, not easily compatible but still desirable. His employer saw the point, and further requested that Roger should incorporate in his first twelve months of managerial training a course of study on three half days a week at Manchester Technical College, a centre geared to the requirements of the Lancashire Cotton Industry.

Part of the way he kept his 'humanity' alive was by living at Dalton Hall, a hostel run by Friends for students who frequently involved themselves in social and educational activities related to the needs of the very poor. And with the gathering Depression of the early 1930s throwing more and more people out of work the maintenance of even shameful subsistent levels was proving increasingly problematic. Roger, appalled at the misery and degradation of it all, early decided that his best contribution was to produce a detailed analysis of the deteriorating situation in the cotton trade, and within months of completing his college course it was on the managing director's desk.

What he and his fellow directors with a life-time in the business made of this newcomer's sweeping suggestions is not reported, apart from the fact that they took his report very seriously, seeing in it confirmation of his ability to fix a goal and formulate a programme to reach it. Typically he pulled no punches:

'There is hardly a single function in the mills which is in the hands of a specialist whose job it is to deal with it. The purchase of raw material is about the only function which is not duplicated. Selling, production, maintenance, costing, labour, general administration – in all these functions two or more responsible persons, each with full knowledge, act only over a portion of the field. To exaggerate, the place is run as a series of one man businesses, and this is not ideal . . .'

There was much more, all of it delivered with courteous pungency, and focussing the exposure of what he saw as furious activity serving as a cover for lack of direction.

The background to all this at the Warrington mill and his continuing involvement at the Quaker hostel for students was the stream of letters, sometimes a torrent, between himself and Margery, still at home in Oxford, and working for the League of Nations Union, pushing the message of pacifism for all she was worth. Many of the letters are undated, but cover the period from September 1929, to the time of their wedding, on 4 August, 1931.

' . . . whatever we do,' Margery wrote shortly after Roger's return from Russia, 'we must never degenerate into luxury, anything near it.' She was responding to *his* reminder of something Canon Charles Raven had said at Westminster, that 'the rich were a far more difficult problem than the poor'. The congregation had smiled, and this, Roger went on, 'did rather worry me because it's true I believe and it *is* the biggest problem of the lot. Most of the people there could, I suppose, be put down as at least comfortable, if not rich, and I don't believe that they realized it's because our social arrangements make people like us comfortable at the expense of the miners that, however much our individual lives may be directed toward real fellowship and a realization of the meaning of God, our social institutions do nothing to reflect that spirit, so we're left with a contradiction that just means muddle . . . I feel the whole thing most damnably. For most of the last year I've felt pretty lifeless spiritually, and the fact is that what is generally known as success has come fairly easily without me doing anything particularly about it, and there's been an absolute absence of hardship or giving of anything up, and one becomes just spineless, however much one would like to be pulling one's whole weight.'

'I think,' Margery replied, 'the Discipline of Religion is quite a good thing . . . I do agree with you that we do need a measure of asceticism in our own lives, but the kind that comes from leading a simple life, and putting first things first, not the kind that comes from a deliberate stunting of one side of one's personality.'

'About asceticism,' he responded, 'you're right of course; but it's so much easier to bully people into some sort of moderation than it is to put it to them as honest-to-God human beings!'

The following week he told her about 'an old boy called Standing, aged 70 something and looking 55, talking most thrillingly about biology' at an after-supper meeting at the students' hostel. The lesson of evolution, the old man claimed, was 'the demonstration of how God is behind all growth and how the end is spiritual. The whole thing,' Roger concluded, 'was most ingenious and he certainly knew his stuff from A to Z, but it seemed just a bit too easy to be true. But I'd run a mile to hear him again.'

Margery, however, was apparently more concerned about asceticism. *She* reminded *him* of something else Canon Raven had said, that conflict, the world being in the state it was, was inevitable, the natural outcome of leading a Christian life; but that we were going the wrong way about it if we went looking for it for itself. 'And I think,' she continued, 'in the same way the hard things will come along as the natural sequence to the kind of life you always do lead – I don't think you will have to look for them long. They come as a result of what you are more than what you do.'

On her own admission Margery was no good at talking, explaining her thoughts and feelings face to face. She much preferred writing, arguing for her point of view on paper. And especially, the evidence suggests, with Roger whose facility with words made him a formidable opponent in any diversion of opinion. Open-minded he was, ready to acknowledge he was mistaken and modify his thinking accordingly, but his ability to win arguments, to carry the day in debate, exposed him, he early realized, to the danger of winning any verbal duel but possibly losing the truth. Face to face few people could withstand his logic and fluency. Far from feeding his ego, or making him regret this gift, he remained alive to its potential pitfalls, never forgetting that to silence anyone by force of words was not necessarily to change a single mind.

So this correspondence with Margery was good for them both, giving one time to marshall her thoughts, the other to ponder unhurriedly. The result was a mutual clarification of big issues sprinkled with endearments, probing questions and not a little humour.

'You seem to be discovering,' Margery wrote only weeks after he had started work at the mill, 'there is no peace for the wicked, but much less for the good.'

'I'm not so much worried,' he replied, 'that I'm not doing anything hard as that I'm not doing anything at all. I wouldn't mind slacking forever if I felt I was ruminating healthily or using what grey matter I may have systematically. My quarrel with myself is that I'm being scrappy – doing no work and not even getting myself into a state of mind, by systematically using it, to do anything . . . In my spare time I've been contemplating quantities. Armitage and Rigby have 70,000 spindles (spinning units) and 2000 looms. We spin about 85 thousand million yards of yarn a year (not so much when one considers that there are from 4 to 6000 yards of yarn in a square yard of pyjamas). This is about 4½ million lbs weight. And I reckon that we weave about 10,000,000 yards length of cloth – mostly dirt cheap stuff that'll fall to bits as soon as it's bought. We only make the most worthless of stuff. Still we do seem to make up for it in quantity!'

Margery tried to lift his eyes as well as his spirits from the immediate: 'I feel that some day – before we get too old – we must go to California and camp in the Rockies. I don't quite know how we shall get there, but we can always hope! And until then we will camp on Dartmoor which probably in its own way is quite as lovely. But think of going to places where men have scarcely been before, and the absolute unspoiltness of it all – or perhaps we shall have to be like John Smith of Harrow who, asked what would be the first thing he would do in heaven, said he would take a holiday in Switzerland – only we'll make it California.'

Despite an underlying seriousness she had been no less light-hearted when he had turned down a lucrative position by refusing to be involved in the making of shirts for the army.

'It's a moot point about the shirts,' Margery wrote, 'but they are certainly an essential part of an army! I'm glad though that there is no immediate prospect of your becoming a millionaire and dying of gout . . . you must have known it was spoiling your chance – I only hope we shall all do as much. Though I suppose if the country insists on having an army they must have shirts, poor dears . . . I don't know if you were right or wrong, but hope when it comes to a practical point we'll keep as near to our principles as you did.'

Sometimes questions of principle and its practical implications became for her personally both inescapable and confusing. We've already seen how her very first letter to Roger shortly after they were introduced concerned pacifism; yet again she found herself writing on the same theme, having, as she said, been *shocked* on hearing at a public meeting the pacifist's supposed attitude to nursing and the Red Cross in war time. 'It had never entered my head,' she made no attempt to hide her indignation, 'that a pacifist could object to that, and I can't see why . . . I think there must be a lot behind it I haven't realized, as so many people felt they couldn't do it. It rather upsets all my ideas on pacifism. I'll try to explain what I mean. By the time a soldier is wounded, he isn't a principle, only a man. One may say, I suppose, that if you cure him he may fight again, but it seems to me that the reconstructive good quite outweighs that. Didn't you feel *that* when you went to the Rhondda in the strike? In one sense you might have been said to be prolonging the strike which you couldn't have approved of morally, being force. But I imagine the stronger reasons outweighed that objection. Do you see what I mean? I feel standing entirely on moral grounds may save your soul, but it seems selfish, and not constructive.'

Having assuring her that her 'awkward questions' were 'very good for us bigots!', he then sought to meet her objections: 'I can't think it right to compromise in the pacifist attitude when war has broken out. Mending soldiers seems to me to be that, for you can't do it without becoming part of the military machine. If somebody says we're going to have an army for fighting purposes, somebody else says, these days, we must have a Red Cross. The pacifist position is your army is all wrong and your Red Cross is only an essential attribute of a wrong thing. An army's just as wrong fighting as in peace time and therefore its essential attribute is also impossible for me to support.

'Intellectually there is no case for humanitarianism. Just before going to S. Wales I spoke in the Union against humanitarianism and shocked all my friends, but I would do it again. Humanitarian work is simply relieving suffering, making the underlying conditions more tolerable and hindering the frank facing of the fact that as long as you persist in those conditions you will have suffering to relieve.

'Were the only chance of doing constructive work in wartime that of helping the military wounded the choice would be even more difficult than it is. From a practical point of view I think the pacifist might do other work, and it seems to me that he (or she) can only decide what is the right thing when they have considered the possibilities of war work and their attitude to war. For instance, until they went to prison a number of Quakers were working in connection with German prisoners of war and even more with the wives and children of Germans who had lived in England but were now interned. If you ask what the difference is, I don't know except that that work is not part of the military machine, and that, though it's humanitarian, it's more nearly tackling the problem by the roots in its effort to show international goodwill than is the nursing of soldiers of either side quite apart from the fact that all patriots would do the latter, and that only the pro-Germans would do the former very necessary work . . .'

After such a lengthy preliminary exposition of his position he now came to the hub of Margery's shocked protest – the pacifist's attitude to the nursing of wounded soldiers: 'It's not because we don't care about the suffering of the combatants that we can't undertake Red Cross work. It's because we believe our action of another kind cuts even deeper. We may be wrong; it may be right to deal with suffering here and now rather than pass it by, not without sympathy, but without pausing, because you believe you can, by going further, stop more suffering.'

In another letter on the same theme he felt constrained to add, 'The point that worries me most is that it is very difficult for any pacifist to undergo the suffering of the combatants. I wish I could feel that the whole business was hurting pacifists as much physically and mentally as war does the rank and file soldier.'

To what extent this immediately satisfied Margery in her understanding of Roger's absolutist pacifism, never mind to what degree her judgment was carried, is doubtful. All the evidence suggests that they never did wholly see eye to eye about nursing military casualties of war! Beyond peradventure she persisted in her interrogation, evoking from him the cheerful confession that she had so 'bullied' him about aspects of his pacifism he had been compelled constantly to re-examine the principle itself and its practical implications, apart from putting steel girders into his obedience to its demands.

Such obedience was, of course, still to be tested on the anvil of a war situation. When it was the sparks really began to fly, revealing his freedom from narrow dogmatism no less than the measure of his conviction.

Testing of another sort sprang to mind when he described what he called 'an interesting week-end at the Manchester University Settlement hut', a back-of-beyond oasis and recreational centre for, among others, slum children in the city. 'I think I can understand now,' he told Margery, 'why some people with no stamina, physique or persistence could stand trenches without apparently turning a hair.' Only three boys turned up, and they hadn't a whole boot sole between them, despite having walked five miles to get there from Ancoats. They had no kit, just the rags they stood up in, prepared to lie down in a tent on wet grass, no ground sheet or blankets, relying on each other's body heat to provide warmth. They had brought very little but bread and margarine for the whole week-end, and during the whole time would not normally take off any clothing except jackets, even their wet shoes.

Into the bargain, Saturday night, said Roger, was a *stinker*; and their tent, not a sturdy one at the best of times, was inescapably exposed to the elements. Yet the boys were clamouring to return next week, survivors of twenty-four hours that would have put most people in bed for days. Physically they were in a frightful condition; kicking a football for fifteen minutes exhausted them for a few minutes. They had no persistence; half an hour of one thing was as much as they could stand. Nevertheless, their ability to cope with such deprivation and sparsity left the likes of 'us' standing. He concluded that 'physical discomfort must be so much a part of their life that it is no longer discomfort'.

Maybe. But he still hated the poverty they suffered, poverty he saw every day in the faces of people either thrown out of work by the deepening Depression or hounded by the thought of losing their jobs. His reaction was twofold – guilt that his personal circumstances were free of hardship, and determination to play whatever part he could in changing the social structures of society.

Earlier in the Rhondda, facing what he called the 'problem of all the blood and sweat and ugliness of life', he quickly realized the danger of people like himself, doing commendable and necessary relief work, not appreciating that 'this sort of thing goes on because some of us are not prepared to throw over a social organization which makes *us* uncomfortable'. The reason wasn't hypocrisy, dishonesty or anything of that sort, but lack of the practical and intellectual insight to see the enormous difficulty of shifting the burden and misery – lock, stock and barrel. And until this was realized, he wondered whether the often sacrificial helping hand to the poor was not 'an awful tragedy of wasted effort'; not that it was *all* wasted, but 'there is a striving after the Kingdom of God to a point where some fundamental conditions are wrong and are not being changed'.

Part of his own efforts to change society was inseparable in his own mind from his peace witness. At the local branch of the League of Nations Union, where he was due to speak, he set out in deep snow hoping, he admitted to Margery, to find nobody there. 'Unfortunately there were lots, and I was put completely out of my stride just before the meeting by a woman whom I'd never seen before producing a photograph taken over twenty years ago and libellously accusing me of being the bellowing baby on my grandmother's knee. She uttered the pious hope that my vocal style had changed since then!

'The chairman introduced me to the meeting as the grandson of my grandfather, and when I'd finished the world's worst speech said that I had spoken just as the said grandfather would have spoken. My grandfather was an admirable man but he was a Liberal, and he passed on to a better world fifteen years ago; so it was disappointing to find oneself branded a Liberal of fifteen years ago! Then the vicar was asked to move a vote of thanks, and began by apologizing for coming half an hour late saying that as a matter of fact he had been in *blissful* ignorance of the time of the meeting! So now I know what the world really thinks of me, and maybe I shall shake depression off and return to normality.'

Meanwhile Margery was happily telling him that her mother, knowing that they were looking out for field glasses, had seen a second-hand pair, good ones, and was now suggesting she gave them to him for Christmas; then she remembered she'd given him nothing for his birthday so he could have them for that. 'As you wear old army breeches,' Margery concluded this item of good tidings, 'I suppose you'll have no objection to army glasses! It's a good example of beating one's swords into ploughshares!'

It wasn't long before inevitably this question of *principle* cropped up again. 'Wing Commander G.,' wrote Margery, 'gave a dance for the Air Squadron (of which Margery's brother, Maitland, then at university, was a member) and I went – should it have been against my principles? I'm afraid it wasn't . . . an added attraction was three full-size aeroplanes in the hangar which we got into and had their workings explained by various partners, obviously very proud of their knowledge! There was also an arrangement with lights connected with the joy stick and feet pieces which is supposed to show if you'll ever be any good as a pilot. I tried that too and was told I was very good. You'll see me a fully fledged pilot one of these days!'

Roger's response was to share his own problem of being a Christian with uncompromising principles and a responsible person in his current working situation: 'In commerce, refuse to do recognized but beastly practices and it's not you but your 1600 staff who suffer because you're knocked out of trade. The same is true of war, and there one has made up one's own mind that it is right to risk everything and everybody but somehow this question of ordinary life seems different. There is', he continued, 'a difference between theory and practice, as anti-socialists say, and go on to assume that practice is right. I believe the theory is right, but it's frightfully hard to see it in practice, and sometimes it's awfully hard to be patient with people who don't realize the difficulty.'

Well, Margery was not of this number. She understood perfectly well what Roger meant when he wondered whether by the age of forty he would be a slightly stout, very respectable, thoroughly conventional cotton merchant wearing a watch chain and a bowler hat, or perhaps a cadaverous bankrupt who had ruined a business and deprived the army of the wherewithal to blow its nose, all because of a happy-go-lucky and enthusiastic belief that the world's all wrong, and that it might be all right. He saw no third alternative and wasn't sure which of the two was the least attractive.

To this was added another concern, with him all his life: 'I do feel,' he told her, 'there's an awful danger in taking up the attitude: "We know that we've got to be thoughtful and therefore we're free to do what we consider right", for unless one has previously set some standard it's so terribly easy to consider right just what one wants to do.'

The problem was, of course, the practical implications of that 'standard', focussed by a question that haunted him: Could Jesus let anybody down by himself refusing to compromise? Searching his heart in the light of that scrutiny he was saved from both fundamentalism and arrogance without becoming one wit less a man of principle. What we need to discover is the precise nature of what 'principle' meant to Roger.

More immediately straight-forward was his long anticipation of the ideas of feminism. 'You do know,' he wrote to Margery, 'or at least I hope you do, how much I hate the thought of the traditional dependence of women. "Giving away" at weddings is one of the most loathsome ceremonies I can conceive; I should rather like you to keep the Emmet in your name, at least as an initial; I hope to heaven that you'll have some other interest in life in addition to the purely domestic one and a friendly interest in what I do; and I think it will be all the better if you have a certain amount of money at your disposal about which I need know nothing. I suppose it's usual for a man to give his wife a certain amount and ask no questions, but even this stinks of dependence; and if you've got something that I've had nothing whatsoever to do with, you will be so much more like a person and not a chattel!'

Margery liked the idea though, she protested, 'I don't think I'm likely to feel a chattel with you, whether I have independent means or not. What I do feel is that the wife ought if possible to earn a certain amount for herself, especially for her personal things, and I hope to do so by coaching etc . . . I wish all wives had husbands with views like yours; it would make a very different world for women if they did.'

About children, they nearly saw eye to eye! He said that the importance of children was terrific but not absolute. 'It differs for different people. Jesus and St Francis couldn't have done their work if they'd had families. My own headmaster Paton whom I always imagine to be one of those lonely people almost too big to be understood by anybody was able to do so much for Manchester's boyhood because he never married and could go all out for his boys. Some people are right, I think, to keep clear of family responsibility because they are themselves so valuable to the world. But in general I agree that it is supremely important to try to beget children who'll be more valuable than anything one can do oneself.'

The question of children cropped up again almost in passing when he appealed to Margery for her opinion about his job and their future together. The gloom of the Depression was deepening, and his own situation was no longer guaranteed. 'Quite frankly, then,' he wrote, 'shall we run the risk of sticking to Armitage and Rigby or would you prefer that I begin right away to look for some other job which might be quite as interesting, and be rather safer? If I stick to A. and R. I may get no rise in screw [= salary]; it might be a further all-round reduction for the whole staff (some firms have cut all screws 2/3); it might go phut in five years and I should be thirty, relying on my wits for a job. Dare you trust my wits? As I say, I'm in your hands, so you must be perfectly honest. The future of a lot of kids may be at stake.'

She didn't hesitate. It *was*, she said, rather a blow, but everything was insecure these days; clearly one couldn't depend on keeping a job one was once certain of lasting one's whole life. So if he felt it was right for him to stay she was perfectly willing. However, there was something else worthy of comment! 'You talk about lots of kids in five years,' she wrote, 'whose future may be at stake. I don't know how many you intend to have, but I don't bargain for more than two in that time!'

Not surprised but reassured by Margery's positive attitude, Roger further revealed himself as a precursor of women's lib with a proposal – an incredible proposal for its time – of how they might cope if he lost his job: 'What I was wondering was whether you would not be doing a really useful thing by learning shorthand. With a knowledge of French and some knowledge of German, you might be able to be very useful as a secretary or journalist's assistant if you have shorthand as well as your typing.' As though this wasn't revolutionary – lots of husbands would have said *shameful* – enough (wives going out to work!) he added, doubtless with a characteristic twinkle in his eye, 'If I get booted out I can live on you a good bit . . .'

Just so. The fact was, he felt so carefree about the whole precarious situation that he was burdened by feeling unburdened. 'I find it almost impossible these days,' he confessed to Margery, 'to work up any aching concern for people or things – nothing lies on my mind at nights to keep me awake as it has done in the past – everything slips off as soon as it's done. I'm a bit concerned by this failure to *feel* things, as it means I don't think properly; and it means I find life all great fun.'

One reason might have been that despite the general austerity he was as a consequence of his position at the mill occasionally brushing against the fleshpots of privilege, with apparent relish. 'On Wednesday afternoon,' he told Margery, 'I went to Liverpool for a Management Group meeting. It was dull. I came back with several people one of whom paid the excess for me to travel first class for the first time in my life! He's a big wig in the financial world . . .'

He went on, again revealingly: 'Meeting this morning, then preaching in a local Anglican pulpit this afternoon. One tells too many half-truths to be a Christian when propaganding. Yet you can't be a Christian propagandist and tell the whole truth!'

Precisely what he meant is difficult to ascertain. Hypocrisy was out of the question; he was too straight up and down for that. Was it the dawning realization that Christian leaders sometimes had a public and a private point of view, the former not always entirely consistent with the latter out of genuine concern for the supposed vulnerability of people in the pew if exposed to an overdose of radicalism? Was Roger beginning to feel that on occasion the wind must be tempered to the lamb?

As a Quaker he would find such ideas obnoxious. As a man's man who instinctively led with his chin he would dismiss such rationalizations as cowardice, tinkering with the truth posing as diplomacy. All his life, in acknowledging 'that of God in every man', he sought to keep in touch with 'that of God' within himself. And once persuaded of the way forward he countenanced neither compromise nor mealy-mouthed utterances, all needless to say in the spirit of courtesy though not always without the inner suffering of exasperation.

'I'm not proposing,' he told Margery on one occasion, 'that anyone should compel the Society (of Friends) as a group of individuals to be Socialist but I don't see how anyone can consistently be religiously Quaker without being politically Socialist which does not necessarily mean joining the Labour Party.'

Not that he saw politics through rose coloured spectacles. 'I believe,' he commented on the deteriorating situation at the mill, 'that trade unions are not making things any easier. They have borrowed the capitalist garment of self-righteousness and are hideously unadaptable. I don't blame them but I wish they weren't . . .'

But at what point did adaptability become compromise, the question often lurking somewhere in the background of this heavy correspondence, heavy yet also bubbling with love and humour? 'On Friday,' wrote Margery, 'I went out to Y village for a first League of Nations Union meeting there . . . the vicar is an odd bird; he says he wouldn't have a German in his house for anything. Oh, these vicars, what is to be done about them?'

The same light-heartedness was evident when she told Roger about six Plymouth Brethren aunts – or some of them – of Mr S.'s who had tried to convert Maitland and the family. They made no secret of their horror at the modern-day fashion of short sleeves; and were likewise shocked as they watched tennis for the first time, until it was explained to them that when the scorer said 'deuce' he was not swearing. This granted, they were content to give their *ex cathedra* approval to this 'quite harmless form of exercise'.

'It seems to me,' wrote Roger, 'that there's nothing quite so lovely as people who are so wholly and unself-consciously conscious of God that they are wholly and perfectly human; so many of us are at best only half of each, and very pitiable objects as a consequence . . . I can't tell you how thankful I am that we shall have, through you, that sort of life behind us all along.'

Throughout this early correspondence he was particularly interested to hear of any light she might receive on what he called 'the guts of Quakerism'. On one occasion he requested that she let him know 'before Saturday' as he was committed to give a lecture at an ecumenical gathering the following day. 'At the moment I have revolution on the brain,' he told her, 'and I tend towards the line that Quakerism at its best has been revolutionary because it pinned its faith on God, when the world's faith was, at best, qualified. Not only in social matters,' he added, 'but in theology, politics and international relations.'

'I think I feel like you,' she replied, 'that a Friend should be able to be known by his face, and one puts a terrifically high standard, and it's rather hard to expect them all to be saints and heroes straight away! Please don't think I mean to be disparaging to the young Friends because they seemed an awfully nice lot, and I'm probably just talking rot.' Roger didn't think so, confirmed by his constant asking for her opinion, not least about his own failings. His grouse was that she was too gentle, not forthright enough.

His more robust approach was epitomized when they exchanged views about the arts and religion: 'To Friends it has always seemed there is one great danger about artistic values – you may mistake aesthetic exaltation for worship. That is why we distrust a cathedral service!' Insisting that living is itself an artistic experience, he went on: 'My feeling is that some of us are trying to shove too much into our work of art, and consequently there is no particular significance about our lives. What I feel about myself is that I do a lot of things which are neither here nor there. I like them and that is why I do them. Incidentally they make it easier for me to converse with people, and personally I regard conversation as one of the supreme arts of civilization – this may be because I read Modern Greats which teaches one to do nothing else – but it is not a necessity. Life is more difficult if one's range of talk is limited, but one's life in itself may well be more significant if one gets one's emphases right.'

'On the question of art,' she responded, 'it may be necessary as you say for the artistic side of you to go overboard, but I hope it won't have to. There's a rather nice Chinese proverb: "If you have two loaves, sell one and buy a lily", and it's awfully true.'

The same quiet assertiveness was evident when they exchanged ideas about a central issue of theology. 'You once said,' she reminded him, 'you thought it was wrong to say "Come to Jesus"; you ought to say "Come to God". I'm not sure that I agree with that.'

'I suppose,' Roger replied, 'that we'll quarrel about Jesus and God till we're dead! . . . but I can't help feeling that there's a terrific danger in approaching Jesus as many do. In the first place there's a tendency to live on the experience of Jesus instead of personal experience of God. People say, "What would Jesus have done in this case?"; but that is not really the question, is it? The real question seems to me to be, "What is the way of God for me, in so far as I know God through the lives of Jesus and other great people?" It is not good enough to shove it off on to Jesus: the thought of Jesus as the man who showed us and still shows us the way to God so that we may approach God for ourselves seems to me to have more of inspiration about it than the thought of Jesus as making up our minds for us.'

Days later he wrote again with a sort of postscript: 'About theology – yes, you beat me every time, mostly because you know what you talk about and I merely argue for my own assumptions.' 'I wish I knew what to do about my tongue,' he earlier lamented, 'for I'm beginning to substitute a glibness about a lot of things for a capacity to feel about anything. I think this is really so and not just the result of morbid thinking.' To illustrate this desirability to feel as well as to think, he referred to reading in bed a volume of Churchill's war memoirs. 'My word,' he summed up, 'he's a blood-thirsty little beast, but he writes awfully well and convincingly. His heart was certainly in it.'

The new year, 1931, was greeted with another related aspiration: 'I wish, too, that I was a witty or good talker,' he confessed to Margery; 'we're so heavy as a family.'

Actually, no family could have been more characterized by humour, leg-pulling and fun, but it must also be admitted that an underlying concern about the world and its needs generated an earnestness that could easily be mistaken for habitual solemnity bordering at times on morbidity. Certainly Roger saw little to lift his spirits in the cotton industry. The two sides of management and trade unions were being as 'stupid' as ever, and deserved to lose all they would lose, if the result would not be so 'damnable', he told Margery.

What infuriated him was the obduracy of people on both sides of negotiations who thought winning more important than justice; or even more important than a settlement tipped either way if it meant the mills could remain open and the workers continue to receive their pay, no matter how derisory. The threatened lock-out would be catastrophic, leading to a deeper level of deprivation and misery for countless innocent bystanders in the form of wives and children, already, many of them, emaciated and diseased.

'Cotton,' he wrote to Margery, 'may begin to rise in price any day, especially if the lock-out and strike drag on indefinitely. The whole business is too fatuous for words.'

There were happier thoughts between them, not least about their wedding day, now clearly in sight and occupying both their minds about the arrangements. Roger would have preferred a Quaker wedding but was fully understanding of Margery's wish for a traditional Anglican service. By now she was herself a Quaker in all but official membership, wholly committed to the move but still exploring and adjusting to the different style of worship – no sacraments, no ritual, no music. To her, no less than her mother and family, the ease and indeed enrichment of the transition had been barely believable.

But other factors tugged at her heart, one centred in her love for her father. Not for a moment did she doubt that he would have been delighted she was marrying a Quaker, but – remembering his last appointment as Dean and Chaplain of University College – she thought that somehow he would be present if the marriage ceremony took place in the university church of St Mary the Virgin. But once such a decision had been made with the unanimous agreement of both families the grandiose corollaries formed a lengthening queue. Roger plumped for simplicity in all things, most of all when a suggestion wafted over from Margery's side that perhaps top hats and tails might be appropriate.

Roger's inclination was for a working suit – obviously a pressed suit, even a new suit, but as for dressing up in anything so alien to his Quaker background, never mind his love for the informal and casual, top hat and tails or anything even remotely moving in that direction was unthinkable.

Then there was the question of Margery's dress. Roger again wanted simplicity which he found hard to reconcile to the traditional bridal gown and veil. Margery herself was sympathetic to and indeed excited at the prospect of wearing a gown made by her mother from the material of her own wedding gown, plus the lace veil she had also worn.

Roger gallantly conceded this though he was not always so accommodating. The date itself of the wedding had to be negotiated. 'So far as I can see,' he wrote to Margery, 'the only snag of a June wedding is that I shall be nominally as well as really your inferior.' Being nine months Margery's junior, he wanted a date on which they would appear the same age! She celebrated her twenty-fifth birthday on 21 November of the previous year; he turned twenty-five on 3 August of the following year. The date was fixed for 4 August.

Another minor bone of contention as they anticipated setting up their own home was what books they should either discard, keep or acquire; some, suggested Roger, for reading together. 'I don't mean anything improving,' he explained, 'but something that isn't a sheer waste of time and doesn't after ten minutes send one off into contemplation or daydreams! *Three Men in a Boat*, Shakespeare, the *Iliad*, anything.'

'What about,' Margery responded, 'Whitehead's new book of *Science and the Modern World* which I imagine would be much on the lines of Eddington. I believe *Process and Reality* is really good, and we can get Dorothy to explain it to us! Then I should suggest Dante; and what about Blake instead of two Hardy novels? . . . Still, as you say, you'll get what you want anyhow, though it's good for me to say what I think which is how democracy works in Russia, isn't it?'

Less problematic, despite the splendour of St Mary's University Church, and a choral service to go with it, was the choice of preacher for the wedding sermon. Roger commended him as a cleric who 'doesn't wear a dog collar, doesn't wear robes, doesn't use the pulpit so that he doesn't preach *at* the congregation but is part of it, uses a blackboard to illustrate the sermon, and yesterday preached with his coat off because it was so hot! He keeps up a running commentary on everything he says and does so that nothing degenerates into mere formalism.'

This unusual Free Churchman, Rev. Frank Lenwood, Roger's uncle, was already known to Margery through his theological writings, not least his exposition of why, years into his ministry, he had abandoned his belief in the divinity of Christ without thinking of him as any less significant and central. She'd read the book in manuscript chapter by chapter as he'd written it. 'I liked it,' she wrote to Roger, 'where he said his theology had changed, but his religion hadn't; it's a good way of expressing it, and it's just what I feel too.'

Anyhow, wholly unconcerned by Uncle Frank's radicalism because of her Father's explorations into new conceptualizations of God, an openness she maintained all her life, Margery was more than happy with the choice of preacher for her wedding day though it has to be admitted that certain members of her wider family would have been more content with an orthodox Anglican priest.

Possibly they changed their minds on the day itself, for the sermon proved to be compulsive listening, revealing too of the spirit in which Roger and Margery approached their union. If his words now sound dated this simply reflects changing social mores about marriage!

'Remember first of all,' he addressed the newly-weds immediately after they had exchanged their vows, 'that your wills are given you to keep love burning with a fire that's never put out. You will sometimes hear the phrase, "He ceased to love her" or "She found she no longer cared for him". When those phrases are used there has been something wrong – I do not apportion blame but one or both must have forgotten that love began as devotion is nourished and fed by the will. Even marriages unmistakably made in heaven are not always kept there.'

So far the well-heeled congregation including Lady Harcourt Smith, Sir Alban and Lady Young, Lady Mary Murray, Sir Benjamin and Lady Lindsay, the President of Corpus, and countless professors, doctors, other dons and clerics felt content with the dignified flamboyance of the preacher; but then he turned to other matters.

'You have both felt the call to comradeship with those working people for whom our unhappy social divisions so often separate men and women from the class represented by us gathered here . . . I am sure that one great cure for this social problem of our time is that families should live downwards, not upwards; that instead of climbing into a higher social position and measuring success in that way they should aim at special comradeship with those a little less advantaged than themselves. But to maintain it needs a deep conviction – a mere sentiment of sympathy and discontent is not sufficient.'

Once more he addressed Roger and Margery directly: 'Don't be afraid of talking to each other about your spiritual aspirations. If at the end of thirty years each can say to the other, I never made any proposal that meant fuller service for God and man but my comrade gave me eager support, your marriage will be as near perfect as the earth can show. To make a home, a beautiful marriage,' he concluded, 'there is nothing so productive for the Kingdom of God on earth.'

On such a note, after a reception again in the delightful surroundings of University College during which the best man, Roger's eldest brother Stephen, had spoken for all in wishing them *bon voyage*, Mr and Mrs Roger Cowan Wilson set off for their honeymoon in Skye climbing the Cuillins; Margery, at Roger's suggestion, armed with a substantial book in case the weather wasn't co-operative and they had nothing else to do.

5

The Cotton Mills and Living with the Workers 1931-1935

The Wilsons' first home consisted of two rooms at Manchester University Settlement while details were finalized for the lease of a house on one of the new council housing estates springing up in the outskirts of city, the idea being that the newly-weds should develop Roger's already extensive voluntary service among the poor. In agreeing to this proposal he was not unmindful of the contrast facing Margery after the quiet dignity of Oxford with the peace of its surrounding countryside, but even the prospect of Ancoats, formerly a notorious slum with air guaranteed to clog the healthiest of lungs, failed to put her off.

Eventually the Settlement was granted not one but two houses, semi-detached, adjacent to each other, at Newton Heath, the second for a couple of women social workers. So while Roger continued his work at Warrington cotton mill, Margery during the day and the pair of them every night set about establishing a community centre in their own home – soon a veritable thoroughfare for all sorts and conditions of human need. In no time at all, it seemed, new activities were bursting out all over the place, all of them centred on their creaking lounge.

Margery concentrated on wives' fellowships, girls' clubs, children's recreations; Roger initiated lecture series and discussion groups, most popular with the men though no part of the programme was exclusive to either sex. Within a matter of months the numbers attending, never mind Margery's longing for a bit of privacy, made additional accommodation essential.

The Settlement had no money. The council couldn't help further. If anything was to be done, the people on the estate, now proudly calling themselves a Guild, would have to do it. They made a bargain. If the council would grant them a little bit of land they would themselves rebuild and renovate an old army hut. Cost – with hordes of unemployed men happy to provide free labour and also repair furniture and equipment – £15, the lot. And a superb job they made of it, too, facilitating a giant extension of the weekly programme, and making the new building the heart of the whole estate.

Nothing was more popular than the discussion group which – with the cotton mills fighting for their very existence, and poverty decimating more and more families – provided relief for the men's bitterness and the opportunity to interrogate visiting authorities. Roger revelled in the give and take of this open forum, gratified that some of the near illiterate victims of the Depression proved more than capable, given the chance, of speaking up for themselves. No one on the Newton Heath estate doubted his commitment to their comprehensive welfare, manifested not least in the extent to which he and Margery thought of their home as also a haven for the worst victims of the Depression.

These hard-pressed individuals knew that this young couple, though *different* – in social background, education, culture, refinement, ability to take on the authorities and get things done – were at the same time *one of them*, a development (for it didn't happen overnight) only unappreciated by people who have never sought to bridge social barriers downwards. Hence the sense of family rejoicing throughout the Guild at the birth of Roger's and Margery's first child, Anthony, in 1933. Margery was overwhelmed with motherly advice and the offer of too many hands wanting to nurse, cradle, rock, bounce, and pass round for admiring inspection; Roger, proud as a peacock, took fatherhood in his stride, only regretting that the obligations of his non-stop activities somewhat circumscribed his practical involvement in baby care.

From Gothenburg, on a selling tour of Scandinavia for Armitage and Rigby, he wrote to Margery: 'This is a fairly luxurious hotel. I have a small private bathroom decorated with tiles of somewhat angular naked women. The bathroom bristles with nobs and switches but I dare not exercise them as there appears to be a Swedish custom whereby a chambermaid comes in to bath and scrub you in a most unbourgeois way, and I fear one of the nobs may be the signal.'

During this absence Margery took Anthony to Oxford. 'Hordes of people are coming to tea to see Anthony,' she told Roger. 'He is much admired. I am glad he is approved of in Sweden, but I'm sorry his charm doesn't help you to sell things . . . I think your bathroom sounds superb! I should experiment if I were you; you can always barricade the door.'

Business apart, both Roger and Margery were progressively caught up in what many saw as a significant new movement within Quakerism. 'Simpler Standards of Living' called upon Friends to examine their life-style with particular reference to wealth and poverty. Gatherings were called in various parts of the country to thrash out the nitty-gritty of income, both the upper limit 'which it would seem wrong to exceed as long as there are others below the poverty line' and the lower limit below which 'we believe most people cannot be expected to live a reasonably full and happy life in the modern world'.

Not surprisingly 'Simpler Standards of Living' was not universally popular, and in fact petered out probably destroyed by its own idealism and the diverting political uncertainties resulting in the gathering threat of war, but it merits attention here if only because its key ideas were advocated by Roger, then Chairman of the Young Friends Committee, in a memorable address at Yearly Meeting in 1934, and continued to be the standard by which he sought to govern his life: 'We know that all men are brothers, and that the pictures of unemployment, based on the experiences of Friends in various parts of the country, are a ghastly blot, not to be sorry for, but to be ashamed of. We know that charity, love, decency – call it what you will – is the only ultimate guarantee of a right social life . . . the immediate task, I think, is not to wait till we know more, but to do something about what we do know.

'Let us make that personal. A former Clerk of Yearly Meeting has called our attention to the fact that there are more hot-water bottles per foot in the Society of Friends than in any other religious body. How much is our worship of God conditioned by a very homely appreciation of the comfort which so many of us Quakers know?'

Now he shared the heart of his concern: 'We speak of the need for freedom, but we know that men cannot be free so long as they are in the grip of industrial and financial arrangements which cannot work save by disregarding the needs of real individual men and women. Part of my job is to think how the labour staff of the firm with which I am connected may be reduced – how men can be displaced – in order that the firm may continue to keep going and continue to employ the 1700 workers who remain. Which of us is free in positions like that? Do we ever consider by what right we hold that authority? And if we do, and find that we cannot honestly contract out of it, how many of us try to create safeguards which will at least prevent us exercising authority in the interests of our own comfort or convenience, or according to the condition of our temper or the sort of night we have had? We speak of equality, but know men cannot be equal so long as it is largely personal finance that determines whether education shall stop at fourteen or twenty-two . . .'

Then, this man of peace confronted head-on the rumblings of war echoing from Nazi Germany: 'To think that if catastrophe comes we have been deserted by God, or that success which we thought almost predestined has somehow gone wrong, is crude self-centredness; it is sheer ego-centricity to think that God should grant physical salvation to this of all generations. Until men are spiritually ready to live God-led lives, we shall go on crucifying Christ in the person of our fellows, and it may well be that our ceaseless crucifixions will bring the world to unimaginable destruction . . .'

Shortly afterwards Margery went to Vienna for a few days, staying at the Friends International Centre, charmed by the gaiety of the people and the lovely setting, but too perceptive not also to feel apprehensive. 'We then walked on to Mittenwald,' she wrote to Roger, 'a lovely little village in the woods, and where they made violins. Every house on Sunday almost had flags and pictures of Hitler; posters everywhere and loudspeakers in the streets holding forth . . .'

This was in August 1934, a time also for Roger of apprehension for a reason not remotely anticipated. He was valued in his job; the Newton Heath Guild was booming; his witness for peace and social justice was, he had no reason to doubt, needed in the north to which he felt he belonged and where he was most at home. As far as he could see, whatever his reservations about the cotton industry, he saw his future as a business man, eventually sufficiently senior and prosperous to fulfil his dream of devoting three days of each week to voluntary public service. Then, out of the blue, came an invitation from the BBC for an interview in London about an opening in the Talks Department. Apparently somebody there had heard of the eminently successful discussion and lecture series at the Guild, and was wondering whether the man mainly responsible might like to transfer his talents to Broadcasting House.

He would, and he did, starting in the New Year; but first there was another mighty upheaval to face, no less unexpected, and this time the opposite of his choosing. Early on the morning of 6 September his beloved uncle Frank, the man who had preached at his wedding, was leading three young climbers up a steep ice slope in the Alps. By cutting steps he had almost reached the top when his foot had slipped, sending him and the two climbers immediately behind him slithering down the ice; and though the last man had made a herculean effort to hold the party he too had been pulled off, and all four had slid some hundreds of feet. The Rev. Frank Lenwood's skull had been fractured on a projecting rock, and death had been instantaneous. Two of the others had escaped with bruises, and though the anchor man had been badly hurt he subsequently recovered.

Only once before, two years earlier, had Roger been confronted by the death of someone he cared about deeply. Indeed the funeral of Gordon Cox, his old teacher and friend, was the first funeral he had ever attended. He had gone expecting, as he put it, 'to be perfectly impassive by the formality of the thing', but the formality had appalled him intellectually, and he had experienced for the first time what it was, quite literally, to have a lump in his throat. 'It was a melancholy and – it seemed to me – a morbid business;' he reported to Margery, 'if I only believed in cremation before for hygenic reasons, give it me now for mental health as well.'

Now he was grieving over someone much closer, someone a month short of his sixtieth birthday at the time of his death. The obituary written by Roger not only captured the measure of the man, an obituary incidentally he later amplified into a full-length biography,[1] but the extent to which the values by which he lived represented the touchstone of Roger's own aspirations: 'As an Oxford don he had influenced the religious life of the whole university as, in the opinion of at least one competent observer, no other don has done in this century. As a missionary in India he had in a short stay marked himself as a powerful and imaginative worker in the field; as a missionary administrator he had been the leader of more than one big development in mission policy, and was a missionary statesman of international authority. And yet it was as the pastor at Plaistow of a little tin church of eighty members or so that Frank Lenwood seemed to those who knew him best to testify *most* convincingly to the power and beauty of the Christian experience of God.'

All this and much more paid in heartfelt tribute, Roger was surely speaking of his own experience when he claimed that after this death the people most within its influence because of their love and respect 'were braver not more frightened, truer not weaker, more imaginative not less confident followers of Jesus than they had been before. The Christian triumph over death,' he continued, 'is often enough recited in words which do their brave best, but how rarely are the words illuminated by any real glow of triumph! When the spirit is indeed triumphant it is because death is felt to be but a natural stage in the happy spiritual life – the real life – of the friend which he or she has long been living. It was because Frank Lenwood's life had for so long shown men something of the glory of living in the power of God under the leadership of Jesus that his death revealed to them a still greater glory.'

Nearly sixty years later Roger would seal his own testimony to the glory of living in the power of God under the leadership of Jesus not only by unconsciously demonstrating day after day that this was the way but – more persuasively still – showing us all how to die, how to face death, confront it not in a moment of accident but over months of triumphant waiting for the terminal prognosis to run its course.

At the time of the mountaineering fatality, however, he barely had a chance to grieve. What with his transfer to London, a prospect about which – despite his enthusiasm for the BBC – he was less than whole-hearted; and leaving an orderly desk at the cotton mill; and – in many ways most difficult of all – extricating himself from the running of the Guild, he appeared even more to be sprinting up an escalator coming down. Yet incredibly, notwithstanding an impression of turmoil, he and Margery were at peace about the move, a peace invulnerable to teasing doubt and worry about all the upheaval.

---

[1] *Frank Lenwood*, SCM Press 1936.

Roger's friend Alec Clifton-Taylor, never having believed that Roger's gifts were meant for industry, was delighted at the news. At the same time he requested a frank assessment of the work he himself was researching in Paris, an interest in art and architecture that eventually made him a TV personally in numerous series of programmes about the design and structure of ancient English villages and towns.

In sending to Roger his early writings, and anticipating the worst – 'it won't be the first time you have pulled me to pieces!' – he demonstrated his own ability to be forthright: 'You know, I cannot conceive why you are not a better talker, Roger. Your gift for speaking in public might have been expected to have led you to write letters a little like public speeches written down, but instead your letters are delicious compounds of wit, humour and intimacy, with all little human touches added. Yet, except occasionally when we have been alone, I have never heard you transfer this into living conversation. You simply cannot claim shyness the reason, or how is it you can jump up and make a speech without any apparent signs of nervousness?! Yet, as much as I love coming to stay with you, I always leave feeling I have talked far too much. If only you would talk me down sometimes! Tell Margery she has got to, too.'

Roger's style wasn't to shut anybody up with verbosity of his own. His usual line was to keep any disapproval or hurtful criticism to himself. About Alec, he told Margery: 'He is a marvellous conversationalist though his matter is thin. I get angry with him for he either can't or won't understand; I expect the latter, just to see me angry. Unfortunately he can't stand his own leg being pulled.'

No question, Roger could be angry, sometimes for no other reason than his own impatience, or tiredness, or disappointment with himself. But Margery alone was privy to these outbursts which she accepted as necessary relief for him and confirmation of their mutual understanding within a never doubted loving partnership. To a degree not always appreciated by outsiders – and occasionally, it must be said, not always by Roger himself – he needed her, an adored wife and tower of strength, often obscured behind his robust leadership and delight in other people's company, as a sort of verbal punchbag.

On the threshold of starting at the BBC, alone in London until family accommodation could be found, he wrote to her: 'I've been thinking a good bit about how to make the best of the next few months. It'll be none too easy, but it may be a good chance for us to get some practice in prayer. So let's try to pray hard . . . I would like enormously that you should keep a diary of Anthony that I can see whenever we meet – of his doings, sayings, health and anything that will help to give a lively picture of him; not just a sentence a day from duty but something as vivid as you can make it. I know of no one who can say so much in fewer words than you.'

His other request to her was also revealing of the nature of their relationship. Anticipating that his new job at least initially would be all consuming and continue to occupy his mind away from the office, he appealed to her: 'So it will be you who will have to make up *both* our minds what to do when we are free together.' Aware of his tendency to be obsessive about every responsibility, he went on: 'I shall probably take every chance of refusing to do anything except work unless you make me do something else by having plans already laid. So you will have to see that we don't waste a lot of time. Incidentally,' he concluded, 'this should be good training for both of us, as hitherto I think perhaps I have been too insistent on knowing what must be done next, and you have allowed yourself too little scope for starting things or lines of thought. If this is true it is a BAD THING.'

6

Success at the BBC

1935-1941

In August 1934 a new General Talks Department had been formed at the BBC by the amalgamation of the old General Talks Department and the Adult Education Department. The aim was simple though precarious: to permit maximum freedom of expression without abusing the Corporation's wish to maintain a policy of impartiality and the upholding of standards. To this end a Director of Talks was appointed with four General Assistants and two part-time assistants.

Earlier that year an excellent series called 'Whither Britain' had featured such speakers as H. G. Wells, Ernest Bevin, Bernard Shaw and Lloyd George, followed shortly afterwards by another series on 'The Causes of War'. Interest had been sufficiently widespread to suggest that this was an essential element in the way forward. But, as Asa Briggs also noted in his history of the BBC, 'the way of the Talks Branch was never smooth'.[1] Norman Luker who joined the Talks Department shortly before Roger and eventually became the Head of Talks referred to this time as 'a period of anarchy'. Much of the controversy centred upon Members of Parliament anxious to speak for themselves on the BBC without the nomination or necessary approval of their respective parties.

Into this lingering atmosphere of 'anarchy' arrived the new member of staff from the north, bursting with enthusiasm and ideas, believing implicitly in the role of the BBC as a disseminator of enlightenment through the spoken word. Rarely could an idealist communicator and the facilities of a national institution have appeared better matched.

One of the first things he noticed was the preponderance of middle and upper class broadcasters, an imbalance his experiences at Newton Heath community centre of first-rate working-class speakers and debaters made him determined to correct.

Margery, staying with her mother while he tried to find suitable family accommodation in London, did her best with the diary of Anthony's doings

---

[1] See *The Golden Age of Wireless*, Oxford University Press 1965, p.148.

and sayings. 'When I took him out in the morning,' she wrote, 'we met several coal carts, and he pointed to every one and said "Dadda". As he only did it to coal carts I thought he must have spotted some similarity between you and a coal heaver, but I think now it was the horse he was referring to. It'll be a bit awkward if he insists on the same name for you and horses, but I dare say we shall avoid confusion.' Her excitement at the news of a possible house at Gloucester Crescent, with an open-air school not far away, was almost unconstrained. 'But do,' she added, 'have a look at the Kensington house; it may be cheaper.'

The Capital itself held little appeal for either of them, a fact charmingly revealed when Margery broke the news of her longed-for second pregnancy. 'Welcome though she (I hope) will be, I can't help being a bit sorry it's just now, as November or December is a rotton time to be born, especially in London, and I would rather have got all the sweat of moving over first.'

Gloucester Place it proved to be, and soon typically their home was often a haven for overseas students, some of them from Germany bringing alarming reports of gathering anti-Semitism, reports corroborated by a tickle of refugees beginning to make their way to Britain through the assistance of among others the Society of Friends or individual members. An occasional girl would live with the Wilsons as a member of the family in exchange for domestic help, grateful for the opportunity to improve her English and otherwise prepare for an uncertain future. Such associations led to a network of contacts on the continent which provided essential information of dangers facing refugees from growing Nazi tyranny, and quickened the establishment of rescue operations.

At the BBC Roger was finding his feet, learning how to cope within a fiercely bureaucratic organization, revelling in the challenge of the work and the enormous possibilities it offered. Fundamentally a happy man, he nevertheless was aware of something tugging at his heart strings, a home sickness for the north shared to a lesser extent by Margery. What Manchester thinks today, he used to tell her, England thinks tomorrow.

So when, after some eighteen months, a vacancy in the Talks Department of the BBC in that very city came up he didn't hesitate. His London bosses were incredulous. 'You don't want to go to Manchester!' they said. 'I want to go to Manchester,' he affirmed. 'Have you no ambition?' they sought to advise. 'Yes,' he said, 'my ambition is to go to Manchester.' Shaking their heads they agreed to the transfer.

There was, even so, an element of sadness as he and Margery packed their bags and – with Anthony triumphantly the self-appointed protector of his baby sister Elizabeth – finalized plans to return north. To leave so many new friends both inside and out the BBC wasn't easy. Roger's only consolation was the prospect of his personal correspondence growing even more voluminous as he maintained links, many of them as it proved, for the rest of his life. As for Margery, she was content to exchange the grime of one city for another. Admittedly Manchester wasn't Oxford; but to return to the open-hearted people of the north was just like going home.

What cannot be gainsaid is that Roger found his new working environment both more congenial and uninhibited. There was an openness to new ideas not always apparent in London, a readiness to venture with well-argued if unproven aims. 'It is important to note,' wrote Asa Briggs, 'that among the significant broadcasting developments of the years just before the war, developments within the Regions were as interesting – and in some cases more interesting – than developments at the centre. It is in Manchester, Birmingham, and Bristol that changes in talks policy were most clear and most striking. Agricultural talks from the Midlands and West Region, "Midland Parliament" and "Northern Cockpit" programmes from the Midlands and North, and, above all, two series of programmes from the north, planned by Donald Boyd and Roger Wilson, broke entirely new ground.'

'In 1937,' Professor Briggs continued, 'Wilson had paid a visit to the United States to study "serious broadcasting", and in the course of his trip he made acquaintance with the Chicago Round Table programmes, a serious unscripted discussion series sponsored by the University. With the help of Boyd he determined on his return "to use the idea better" than the Americans had done, in the North Region. *Why Do We Believe That?* was the first of two series of programmes he devised. In it J.H. Sprott of Nottingham University conducted a Socratic dialogue with three "partners in discussion", one of them a steelworker from Scunthorpe. This programme ran into difficulties with Iremonger, the BBC's Director of Religion, who listened zealously to all programmes on "moral themes", not only on Sundays.'[2]

Iremonger wasn't the only objector. Spontaneity on the air – now called *live* broadcasts – were viewed with grave suspicion. Sometimes sounding self-righteous in its role of custodian of the nation's moral standards, the BBC appeared to act on the assumption that broadcasters of the spoken word could be trusted only if the script had been submitted in good time, finally approved, and read without the slightest deviation. No less concerned about the BBC's standards and reputation, Roger also focussed on the key word 'spontaneity', convinced that, first, speakers could be trusted to keep within their terms of reference, and, secondly, that unscripted broadcasts would add a new dimension of both authenticity and excitement to the proceedings.

For the second series of programmes under the general title of *Public*

---

[2] Asa Briggs, *Golden Age*, p. 152.

Enquiry an audience of two hundred was assembled in Manchester – where else! – to listen to two speakers of opposing views discussing issues in local government. Questions were asked by members of the audience who genuinely participated, no planted questions or steps taken to eliminate awkward customers by earlier selection. It really was a free for all, the only problem a technical one – in the absence of an omni-directional microphone – of picking up voices in any part of the hall. However, it proved so successful that plans were made for it to be included in the National Programme, due to go out in the autumn of 1939.

It wasn't the North Region's only success from within the Talks Department. A series called *Burbleton* after the name of an imaginery borough with a mayor called Alderman Wool had such realism that a Staffordshire town clerk wrote to the Burbleton Town Planning Officer to ask for his advice, and prompted a Cheshire town councillor to accuse the BBC of having copied a speech he had just delivered to his own council. 'It is interesting,' Asa Briggs observed, 'to speculate what would have happened to this genre of broadcast had not war intervened.'[3]

Indeed, but for the intervention of war, what would have happened to the 'Live Wire' helping to pioneer these new, some thought, risky and potentially dangerous wireless programmes? Roger himself always dismissed such speculation as futile, dismissed it without trying to hide his disappointment at what happened to his relationship with the BBC from the outbreak of war in 1939.

From the moment he joined the Corporation no one associated with him could mistake his whole-hearted commitment to peace. But his pacifism, though as absolutist as his father's, was still sufficiently free of dogmatism to demand of both himself and Quakers generally that they face with attention to detail the implications of their uncompromising witness. Following the return of Prime Minister Chamberlain from Munich waving the statement signed by himself and Hitler, an agreement 'symbolic of the desire of our two peoples never to go to war with one another again', Roger though sharing the nation's relief found little fundamental reassurance. He expressed his forebodings in a letter to *The Friend* dated 4 November 1938:

> My pacifist convictions have been strengthened rather than weakened by recent events. With most of the material in *The Friend* in recent weeks dealing both with long term policy and with training for service, I find myself in deep agreement. But I should welcome guidance on an even more pressing question, because until we have an answer we are evading

---

[3] Briggs, p. 152.

the chief issue which our countrymen are facing. And that question is: How do you propose to deal with Hitler here and now?

The common point of view of ordinary decent people is something like this:

'There is nothing wrong with the German people; they've had a raw deal and we'd like to give them fair play. But Hitler's another matter. It was the concrete threat of war implied by the mobilisation of the British Navy, and no sudden conversion to even the forms of civilised negotiation, that led to the Munich conference. He may perfectly well go on to march into Denmark, Lithuania or Poland. He may extend his dominion down the Danube, across the Rhine, across the Channel even, not by invasion but by blackmail, rigging Cabinets, stifling criticism, circumscribing the citizenship of Jews. We don't want to fight any more than the pacifists, but what's going to stop Hitler except the *threat* of force? All the evidence suggests that Hitler will lie, deceive, repress, bully and blackmail in the interests of "Germanhood". Nobody has yet seen any signs of reasonableness, but he has been frightened once or twice. So long as Hitler is about we must be able to frighten him. When he's gone we'll be able to settle down and work out a reasonable way of living with the Germans, but not until. While he's here, it's just a question of who can frighten whom, and we're going to do the frightening.'

Now I couldn't see any flaws in the premises of that argument. I believe Hitler was stopped by threat of war and that his vision of 'Germanhood' is by no means fulfilled. I do not believe people in this country want rearmament because they want to fight or even because they are willing to fight. I think all that most of them think they are doing is to call Hitler's bluff. We do not approve of all this, but have we any convincing evidence or faith that Hitler can be treated successfully in any other way? I am as heartily in favour of a far-reaching conference as anybody and maybe through that we could get at the German people. But what if Hitler were adamant or agreed to a policy which he failed to implement subsequently?

We believe that all men can be reached by searching for that of God within them. But we can only help some people with the assistance of a mental home. What happens when the head of a great State is as impervious to ordinary reason as mental patients?

I ask this question because it is the one to which so many non-pacifists want the pacifist answer, and I can only give the long term answer.

At about the same time a committee concerned about Friends Community Service issued a lengthy report advocating an intensification of peace propaganda by pacifist groups throughout the country together with a greater emphasis upon the use of Meeting Houses as centres of Quaker service reaching out into local communities. The suggested programme could hardly have been more down-to-earth – working in aged and sick people's allotments and gardens; bringing of waste land under cultivation, the produce to be given to hospitals and old-age pensioners; making of garments for war refugees; the running of play centres; the provision of substitute labour to enable unskilled workers not qualifying for holidays with pay to have a break; the list was endless, all geared to 'the expression of Christian love which may be a standing witness to our faith'.

No one was more supportive than Roger, but the efficacy of Christian love in the face of Nazism and Fascism continued to throw up searching questions he had no wish to dodge. He wasn't the only one! Mary Stocks, Principal at Westfield College, London, wrote to him shortly after the outbreak of war: 'Very strange, I too find the war puzzling. Goodness knows what has happened to my pacifism. I think that Chamberlain is really something worse than a fool, but I am convinced that we must eliminate Germany in its present mood before we deal with the Home Front. But we *must* deal with it or we shall have fought another war in vain.'

There should be no misunderstanding. Roger remained utterly convinced that pacifism was personally the only way forward, but this did not hide from him at all that there were equally committed Christians who, sharing his detestation of war, nevertheless saw no other way of confronting the evil personified by Hitler; and also that the emphasis of Christian love even of one's enemies neither resolved this dilemma nor clarified the nature of love's practical manifestations in time of war.

Again he shared his concern through the pages of *The Friend*: 'It may be that too many of us Friends do not give ourselves any chance of strenuous Christian living. If we live, work and play among people who are like-minded with ourselves, perhaps we never come into contact with bullies, blusterers, stupidity, meanness, deceit, carelessness or vicious vested interests. If we don't know these trials as part of our own experience, what is the good of giving up all our spare time to the most selfless propaganda, preaching in big terms of how these evils should be dealt with by others?'

That was his problem. *How* were these evils to be dealt with? In the *immediate*, with tyranny on the march? Britain's answer was an ultimatum delivered at 9 a.m. on 3 September 1939. The Germans made no reply, and, the ultimatum expired at 11 a.m., Chamberlain broadcast that a state of war existed between the two countries.

Roger was almost immediately affected by an upheaval both at home and at work. With plans for the early evacuation of children from urban areas likely to be bombed, Quakers in the north, even before the declaration of war, decided to keep as many of their children as possible together, and secured accommodation to this end at Yealand Conyers, taking over what hitherto had been a Quaker guest house. Up to a hundred children between the ages of three and ten years, including German Jewish refugees, burst the seams of the place, beds everywhere, privacy of any sort out of the question for children and any accompanying mothers alike.

A school programme was quickly established under the guidance of Elfrida Foulds, with teaching provided by the mothers themselves, some of them qualified, others like Margery, an Oxford graduate in French, filling in wherever possible teaching such subjects as painting, natural history and French. 'We were very fortunate,' Margery recalled, 'in having Arthur and Winifred Percival. He was deputy leader of the Halle Orchestra, and she an accomplished pianist. He started a remarkable children's orchestra; I remember him saying if a child could only play two notes on a violin he wrote a part for two notes. We also had George Seddon from the *Manchester Guardian* as our gardener; he learned his gardening through growing vegetables in the Manor's walled garden, and after the war became a well-known writer of gardening books.'

But in the early days of the move triumphant chaos was rarely far away, not least when love-sick fathers paid a week-end visit. Roger, it must be said, sometimes found the experience less than endearing though in retrospect he never lost his wonderment that the whole place pulsated with laughter and happiness – most of the time!

This apart, his work at the BBC was beginning to present problems which looked as ominous as insoluble. The dilemma facing the Corporation could hardly have been more stark. The nation was at war. Everyone therefore associated with broadcasting with its access to virtually every home in the land must beyond doubt be wholly in support of the war, synonymous at the BBC with patriotism. Pacifists were not wholly in support of the war so *ipso facto* they were not patriotic or at least not sufficiently committed to the war effort to be trustworthy in any dealings on the wireless. Roger deplored the logic but recognized the force of the argument. He was, after all, commissioning talks or editing them or supervising their delivery on the air. In such a position an unscrupulous individual could do untold harm. Everybody at the BBC agreed that Roger was the extreme opposite of unscrupulous; that he was a man of integrity and judgment and fidelity to the highest traditions of the Corporation, but this wasn't the point. It was the general principle that counted. Whoever you were, if you were not prepared to sign a statement of unreserved support of the war then you disqualified yourself from access to the air waves in any shape or form. So touchy were the authorities in the higher echelons at the BBC that Roger was asked to report immediately if he was approached by a member of the fifth column!

In the meantime, though still working from his office at the BBC, he was seconded to Manchester and Salford Council of Social Service to pioneer the establishment of Citizens Advice Bureaux in the region. Selections from his personal diary which he kept from the outbreak of war provide details not only of this work but the sometimes militant impulses within his pacifism:

September 4th The most difficult of Ancoats problems at the moment is what to do with evacuees who return for good or bad reasons, e.g. mother and eight children back from Edale farm because it is too quiet; mother and children back because hosts declined to give her a cup of tea on arrival . . . a hostess who suggested that her guest should have a bath; the guest regarded this as an insult and came back! There are scores of such stories which gain in the telling, I don't doubt . . . if there's no air-raid before the week is up half Ancoats will be back.

September 7th J.W. doing CAB work for experience told grim stories of men left to fend for themselves by evacuated wives, and of invalids sent home from empty hospitals . . . read Liddle Hart's history of 1914–18 war. Military affairs fascinate me.

September 9th Last night the Js (German refugees) were very distressed because they had heard at the Mtg. Hse. that she could not now begin work till she had a permit and this would not be available for some time. They seem quite incapable of grasping the situation that we are at war and that the H. Office has more to do than attend to alien permits. I have tried to make it clear that I am glad to put them up for as long as necessary. They seem a little comforted. Poor beggars, it's bad enough to be English and have nothing to do. It's awful for them . . .

People have courage; three came in who'd lost their work – dancer, musician, and money raiser. All cheerful and sensible. A fourth girl, policeman's wife, will work vol. as long as husband remains in police but will have to work when he is called up. S. has been offeredb £5 p.w. as asst. to billeting officer at Ch. Hulme. She was put on to sort out its difficulties and pointed out to folks that if you give children 5 gl. of lemonade for supper they're bound to wet their beds, while they'll always eat fish and chips if they won't eat anything else. This seems to have gone down well.

September 10th A poor night on the floor of the Yealand school, and a beastly wet morning . . . The whole programme is admirable as a temporary expedient but I don't know about it as a long term thing. For the staff the worst feature is the complete lack of privacy (I never saw M. alone except in the drive last night).

September 11th . . . Physical infirmity is a frightful handicap in days like these. F.M. tends to adopt pomposity as a compensation and the result is unsatisfactory . . . There is virtually no news tonight. What *is* happening? It's all very well to say that it'll be a long war and that we're not going to make a peace with Poland annihilated, but why doesn't the RAF again bomb the fleet or blow up the Rhine bridges or even bomb the Siegfried line? If Hitler has 70 divisions in Poland, one would think that militarily now was the time to go for the West. And there can't be a paucity of purely military targets.

September 12th M.M. came to see me in the evening. She was a bit more cheerful herself but has gloomy stories of the growing anti-German feeling in the factory. This is bad and shows what an artificial world I live in, for I have not heard a word of bitterness yet . . . M. was full of funny stories about evacuees, and bitter about the second raters who won't fight because it's uncomfortable but aren't pacifists . . . Another obscure and vital problem is what will happen to family life if evacuation lasts for three years? Which will break down first, monogamy or evacuation?

September 17th L.M. asked if I knew whether it was true that Russia had invaded Poland. I said I couldn't believe it. But 4 o'clock news confirmed it. It gave me the same sick feeling as the German-Russian pact of 2½ weeks ago. Not I think rational fear so much as moral revulsion at the duplicity of it all. I wish I'd kept a diary of how I felt at Munich.

September 18th I was wrong yesterday. It's not moral revulsion but vague physical fear; for after being shivery all day I got a lot more so after hearing of the sinking of the aircraft carrier. What cards Hitler has; to get two strokes like this on successive days is terrific. How ought a pacifist to feel under the circumstances?

September 22nd The country's problem is how to win the war and lose the Empire. Our problem is how to midwife the new world rather than prop up the old, or even sick nurse it.

September 29th For almost the first time the 8 a.m. radio news had something new in the Russo-German get together, telling GB and France to call the war off, and the Russian terms to Estonia. I've shivered all day in just the sort of funk I was in after the Russian invasion of Poland. It looks as if my supposition of a solid European block east of the Rhine was lamentably near the truth. And the thing is that I don't know that I want the war calling off at this stage; yet Chamberlain, the old fool, can't win and doesn't really know what he's fighting for.

October 2nd The Archbishop of York spoke on spirit and aims of war – no peace with Hitler and gang, but a far-reaching and co-operative peace – very good if you rule out the point of view that it is better to suffer redemptively under Hitler than to fight him out of existence. But again, can you win a war in that spirit? Or yet, can you lose?

October 7th A message from Mrs S. set me ringing her up. I had asked if her husband (on the tribunal for aliens) could push forward E.'s case. She had written a nice letter saying he couldn't, but had now consulted further and thought he might be able to help. I hate pulling strings, but the cause is a good one, and people are very nice.

Apart from such happenings, part of his day-to-day routine of helping people with problems thrown up by the war, Roger's three preoccupations were his family at Yealand, the credibility of his pacifism, and the manoeuvrings at the BBC about his future. The diary is peppered with often amusing references to Yealand visits, though – despite the humour – he remained concerned that the crowded conditions were subjecting the children no less than the staff to intolerable stress. He wrote of sleeping reasonably well with Margery and four children in five beds in one room. There was honey for breakfast after which the children were invited to clean their own shoes, not a good idea, he thought, for Sunday clothes. The outcome justified his reservations.

He noted that Elizabeth had a 'huge appetite', Anthony was becoming more independent, and Margery was thoroughly enjoying looking after the youngest children to the extent of saying 'she wouldn't mind another brace of her own'. She and Roger agreed that 'the job of pacifists is to co-operate when possible'. Unanimity was not always so readily achieved, as, for instance, when talking together about the greater evil of war or Britain being occupied by Hitler and his gang. Roger thought the latter might lead to a spiritual renaissance; Margery that the consequent physical suffering was too awful to contemplate. The peaceful setting of a hillock overlooking the splendours of Morecambe Bay did nothing to reconcile their differences.

Having heard Winston Churchill saying on the wireless that he regarded Russia as a bulwark against Nazidom in the East, and Italy as a secret friend, Roger wondered whether this was 'wishful thinking'. About the effectiveness of the broadcast itself, however, Roger was in no doubt. 'If he can keep this up he'll be prime minister in a remarkably short time. I'd trust him to win the war, but he'll have to be kept out of the peace.'

The peace, its achievement and post-war aims, was for Roger the corollary of pacifism, a corollary bristling with dangers no less than offering a glorious new beginning. Not for him to sit on the sidelines sniping at warmongers and hugging ever closer to himself garments of self-justifying passivity. If he couldn't support the war, he wanted to work for a just peace. And this affected his attitude no more than at the BBC.

Once again his position was seriously in doubt, not least about the continued payment of his 'screw'. His boss, seeking to retain Roger, admitted his fear he was going to lose this battle. What would he do? his boss inquired. Join the Quaker ambulance unit? Roger explained that he'd thought about it, but had rejected the idea as a 'waste of what wits and training I'd had'. He went on to explain that as the war was running at present he was more concerned to co-operate in rebuilding than in being obstructive and that he wouldn't necessarily feel obliged to decline all BBC or government jobs. His boss appeared delighted. But on reflection Roger wondered whether the BBC could find him enough to do, if his return was in any way conditional. 'I don't see any need,' he reiterated in his diary, 'to be non-co-operative at present, and if leaders go on talking in the terms they do of the new world I want to be in on its creation.'

Meanwhile, his colleagues sympathetic and wanting him back, he was left to develop the rapidly growing number of Citizens Advice Bureaux and recruit by careful selection the army of voluntary workers to staff them.

Doing the rounds he picked up innumerable stories about evacuees. One lad was billeted in a home where the husband and wife were somewhat quieter than was habitual in his own home and neighbourhood. He stood it for a week but finally reached a stage when he had to say something. At supper on Sunday night he burst out, 'Hey, don't you two buggers ever quarrel?'

A major problem was the fruit of his own success. More and more people sought advice at the bureaux, pressurizing voluntary staff who weren't always available when needed. One Saturday morning, for instance, he learned that four bureaux within library buildings looked like being unmanned. He phoned the first to cancel, only to be told there was already a queue. Having resolved that problem by appealing to a friend to step into the breach, he pleaded with staff at one of the other libraries to officiate at their bureau, while at another he was again able to appeal to a friend for help. The fourth bureau simply didn't open that day! 'I fear,' Roger castigated himself, 'my inability to organize tidily and infallibly may be a weakness.'

Others didn't see it this way which explained why, having attended a meeting of CAB organizers, he accepted that in the end he might well have to take on the job of Field Officer for the whole of the North-West Region. 'It'd be fun in some ways,' he reacted, 'but I'd be appalled at the inefficiency I'd find.'

Something much more unexpected alarmed him. Learning of increasing RAF reconnaissance flights over Germany he was shocked to find himself 'almost anxious to hear the first news that they have actually hit a whacking big military objective'.

Constantly he wrestled not only with the self-evident impotence of non-violence to halt the march of evil but also with his own impulses to hit out in retaliation or even revenge at the perpetrators of so much misery and suffering. Inspired by the uncompromising pacifism of the likes of Bishop George Bell of Chichester and Pastor Martin Niemöller of Germany, Roger was also not unmindful of other spiritual giants like Archbishop William Temple and Pastor Dietrich Bonhoeffer who – hating violence – saw it as the only option in confronting Nazism. Small wonder, then, that his own commitment to pacifism was saved from dogmatism and constantly subjected to fierce re-examination.

But such introspection prompted rather than hindered his concern to find suitable employment for young pacifists granted unconditional exemption from military service. One of his suggestions was to create 'maintenance squads' to help with war damage, the proviso being that the members were willing, and no attempt was made to force them. He also appealed to the Chief Education Inspector to use them as teachers, only to be told that despite the massive upheaval of evacuation the educational services were coping at the moment, and there was no money anyway.

More successful was his ever deepening involvement with the CABs and the welfare of refugees, victims of Nazi tyranny. The former brought him a fund of funny stories, the latter both heartache and exasperation. One day at breakfast he asked the wife of the refugee couple staying with him about the possible job at Winchester. 'She produced first a doubt on the question of fares and then a doubt about the possibility of doing anything with her husband. This negativeness and apparent willingness to go on living on other people's contributions make me wild. One's glad to support refugees when they must depend on others, but some of them are damned particular about what they do, and they're as fertile as I am in producing reasons why they shouldn't do what's inconvenient.'

His indignation was no less pronounced when a couple of days later he read the White Paper about Nazi brutality in concentration camps. 'I don't think it is good enough for its purpose; and anyway I don't like it being published now. Many of the documents are pro-Munich. What a humbug it shows Chamberlain to have been if he knew this. And if he didn't, what a state of affairs. "Consult General Small-bones" is a superb appellation, fit only for comic opera.'

Another tragedy for which there was no relief or comfort was his mother's loss of memory in middle-age, consequence of head injuries in a road accident. Discussing it with his brother Geoffrey who had come from London to say goodbye before leaving for Russia as civil service assistant to Sir Stafford Cripps, they recalled 'the grand stuff she wrote' during the First World War, and her 'quite first-rate mind'.

'But she was never objective about herself', Roger commented in his diary. 'We all suffered a great deal of spiritual bullying as youngsters, and when we reacted Mother's reply was an expression of personal pain – very unfair. And she had an unlimited capacity to fool herself into a belief that she was being disinterested when in fact she was acting primarily in her own interests. She had a gloriously keen wit but a good deal less of a sense of humour. And now in old age it's all the weaknesses that are coming out, and all her children avoid being left alone with her because of the sentimental gush about our souls that she feels obliged to pour out – I wonder why. If only she'd aged as well as Daddy has done!'

7

Dismissed for being a Pacifist

1941

By mid-November – ten weeks after the declaration of war – Roger's BBC situation was demanding decisions from both sides. He was informed that the Treasury wouldn't recognize CABs and that therefore he must make up his mind either to return to the BBC on their terms or go on loan to a government department. 'So long as I'm not asked to do Churchillian stuff at the BBC,' he said, 'I shall be glad to go back provided that when I'm not broadcasting I am free to do other things.' Among these 'other things' was of course his witness for peace. Even so, the North Regional Director, John Coatman, expressed his personal agreement and suggested that the arrangement could be purely informal. Roger requested a letter asking him to go back to which he would reply stating his position.

News of his apparently impending return to the BBC was regretted at the Manchester and Salford Council of Social Service, for an idea was already being floated that the Council should become a major force with Roger as secretary. 'I'd like that in many ways,' he reacted, 'if the money was secure; but I haven't the courage to tackle a job when a quarter of the work is raising one's own salary. And anyway,' he was typically realistic, 'I doubt very much whether I've a creative enough mind to be top dog of any show – or the patience and pertinacity.'

Within a week of his interview at the BBC about his possible return he was engaged in one of the 'other things' he insisted upon being free to continue – a talk to a men's meeting on the pacifist in wartime: the dilemma of co-operating with people whose purposes 'were as honest as our own, whose humility and repentance were as great or greater, but whose methods reluctantly differed,' plus the danger of 'being a positive negativist and so being kept outside'.

These uncertain days were difficult and emotionally draining, taxing his patience and tolerance at the office. He relieved his irritation in his diary, writing of a 'long and rather silly row' with a woman colleague who couldn't understand why parents were miserable without their evacuated children! 'It was,' he recorded, 'the most mechanistic explosion I've ever heard from an intelligent woman. She has absolutely no conception of the rigidity of pattern of dull lives. She went so far as to admit that women might be lost for a month, but after that, what with meetings, guilds and other interests, they should be easily able to settle down. She has no glimmering of sympathy for the father who took his child away because he found him calling his foster-parent "Daddy"; true, the father ought if an intelligent man to know better, but God knows we're not all intelligent. And she entirely failed to comprehend the point of a case history of a woman with five children – one a year – evacuated to Derbyshire. Within forty-eight hours she was home again – too lonely. A month later she applied to the court for a separation order on the ground of persistent cruelty that took the form of nightly importuning for intercourse. Yet when given the chance of living her own life she couldn't stand it.' The colleague, he lamented, 'doesn't go further than treat the woman as a fool who doesn't know her own mind. I shouldn't have thought a woman of her experience could have lived so long without allowing something for the emotional complexity of even the most reasonable of us.'

On 29 November he was once more called to the BBC for an interview with the North Regional Director who informed him that he, Coatman, saw no reason why Roger should not be allowed to continue his working association with CABs after his return to the BBC – 11 December was the suggested date – and was recommending that he be permitted to officiate as chairman of this growing service to the community. The proposal was less trouble free than immediately met the eye.

For a start the controversy about pacifism and patriotism rumbled on for months, if anything turning the Corporation into a hotbed of suspicion. The atmosphere within the BBC, not to mention the Ministry of Information, was forcefully indicated at a Ministry meeting on 22 April, attended by among others the BBC's Director General (F.W. Ogilvie), and the Lord Privy Seal (Sir Kingsley Wood) who chose the occasion to attack 'pacifist sermons' broadcast in the Home Service and raised the general question of 'whether all our (BBC) officials were sufficiently charged with patriotism and wisdom in dealing with the output of news and talks'. The matter was duly taken up by the Governors at the BBC at their meeting two days later.[1]

It was hardly surprising therefore that the BBC, lambasted at such a government level for its reputed dangerous incompetence if not disloyalty, should agonize over what to do with pacifist members of staff.

Coupled to this was of course the precise nature of the work to which Roger was possibly being invited to return. The Talks Department was manifestly out of bounds. If he was to take up other responsibilities they would have to be cleared of all security risks. Knowing his man, Coatman was

---

[1] Asa Briggs, *The War of Words*, Oxford University Press 1970, pp. 197–8.

impatient to sweep such an irrelevance aside and continued to push for all he was worth in recommending that an opening be found.

In all this mayhem, starting at the outbreak of war and only intensifying as the weeks and months slipped by, Roger was, as he recorded in his diary, encouraged by the BBC broadcasting prayers 'for the faithfulness of COs as well as for men who fight and hate it with all their souls. That's good anyway and worth going back for'.

In the interim there was still the Citizens' Advice Bureaux plus the Manchester and Salford Council of Social Service plus his Secretaryship of the University Settlement which somehow continued to maintain and develop its extensive outreach programme plus, his Quaker commitment at local and national level, the latter undergirding everything else.

Another uppermost concern never far from his mind was the situation at Yealand Manor School – the self-evident need of staff/mothers and children for a break from their cramped and crowded living conditions. Without some sort of respite, he reiterated, health would surely suffer possibly to the point of serious break-down.

During one of his week-end visits, juggling with too many bodies in too little space to find a comfortable bed – even an uncomfortable bed – for himself let alone to share with Margery, he listened to the four-to-six-year-olds having a discussion about Father Christmas. One of them claimed that Father Christmas was the most important person in the world. The others disagreed and finally settled on the correct order – (1) God; (2) Jesus; (3) Father Christmas. Days later he received a letter from Margery saying that Anthony had been speculating on the parenthood of Jesus, and concluded that they were Joseph Christ and Mrs Christ.

Such innocence and happiness within his own family, sustained despite his living apart and the lack of privacy when they were together, did nothing to save him from a haunting background to his life of the plight of his parents. 'It's a terrible picture of old age,' he recorded. 'I suggested to Daddy that the strain of Mother might be relieved if she went into some sort of home. He was surprised and, I think, shocked. I am sure he does not realize how difficult she is for outside folk, since he talked of getting some young person to brighten them up in the evening. I had to say that no young person would consider it for a moment. He then said that he thought for Mother to be in a home would be unpleasant for us children. So it would, but not so undoing as this all round wear and tear, which is breaking up Daddy fast. He is getting terribly fussy and uncertain in his judgments.'

But not remotely uncertain about the absolutism of his pacifism! Never for a moment since his brave peace witness of the First World War had he doubted that, quite apart from his religious convictions, love for his country demanded uncompromising opposition to the support of the war in any shape or form. This alone must have added poignancy to any conversation between father and son as they picked over their common commitment, for Roger found it impossible to share his father's certainty.

Shortly afterwards one major uncertainty in his life was resolved; on 25 January (1940) he was summoned to the office of John Coatman, still the BBC's North Regional Director, to be shown a memo from Stephen Tallents, Controller (Public Relations) cracking him up as *the* sort of man for Listener Research! 'Coatman says the North won't see me again. I said I'd like to come back – to do Talks if I can, to be Programme Director if possible. I did not go on,' his diary recorded, 'to say that I should like to be Regional Director, but I should! We agreed that the future set-up was so odd that neither of us could predict. We talked a good deal about the sickness of the world, the validity of religion, and the capacity to face disaster. Coatman has still not adequately grasped the shortcomings of liberal optimism.'

Ironically the Listener Research Section was rapidly expanding and gaining critical authority as a result of the war! Indeed it wasn't long before the Ministry of Information sought to take it over and recruit the staff to its own Intelligence Branch.

One of the first to react to the news of Roger's new assignment was the Vice Chancellor of Manchester University, John S.B. Stopford: 'My dear Wilson, this is a terrible blow to hear that you are to leave us and I feel completely floored by the fact. What we shall do without you at the present time I really do not know but I quite understand that it is inevitable and that you must go to London. May I thank you most warmly for the valiant and valuable work you have done for the Settlement. I am more than grateful.'

Significantly none of this 'valiant and valuable work' was mentioned in his diary.

Two entries, however, at the time of his departure point to what was never far from his thinking. Saying farewell to his parents, his father gave him a letter expressing his trouble at the thought of Roger doing a job which would bring him into closer touch with the military and might involve a uniform. 'He is, I am afraid,' Roger observed, 'an inveterate liberal humanitarian. It's a grand type but I think its work is finished for the present. My conscience is quite clear and I'm quite ready to defend it to Friends.'

Days later, on 23 February, he talked shop and conscientious objection over lunch with a BBC colleague and fellow pacifist, the pair of them again asking: 'Can we be COs? We're convinced of the wrongness of war; but so is everybody else. *We* would be prepared to make a politically humiliating peace. But if the country won't (or can't) what then? The sentimental "Make peace now for the sake of the children" is nauseating slop. How far should one take advantage of the machinery of conscientious objection in order to keep it functioning? Not at all, I think, if that is your only motive. What motives *are* good enough in the face of one's enormous obligations to society? It's a terrible problem. And Daddy disapproves of even mixing with soldiers. I wish I had as undisturbed a mind.'

By the time Roger arrived in London the Listener Research Section had already dug out details of the 'listening day' of different social classes.[2] Each stratum clearly posed different problems for broadcasters, a situation compounded by a congestion of programmes and only one outlet from the outbreak of war. As listener research gathered momentum so pressure grew for wider opportunities to reach people at all levels.

Roger knew that one of the BBC's primary concerns was British Forces serving overseas, but even before the Dunkirk evacuation he was pointing out that there were more servicemen at home in Britain than elsewhere. 'Sentimentally our first obligation,' he acknowledged, 'is to those serving overseas; practically the matter does not appear to be as simple as that.' Many troops in Britain were scattered in small isolated Anti-Aircraft posts and 'living in unrelieved contact with an unchanging group' or concentrated in bigger units in small towns 'with only the most limited recreational opportunities'.

He went on to argue that these very differences of Service conditions between groups at home and abroad surely had significance from a programme point of view and merited attention.

Even though it had meant leaving his beloved Manchester for London, he was glad to be back to a job within the Corporation, both excited by and soon contributing to the new bold thinking and enterprise of the Listener Research Section. Inevitably usually polite flare-ups about whether BBC employees could be pacifists and not thereby unpatriotic continued, but he was saved from this often empty noisiness not only by his preoccupation in learning new skills for his job, but his almost constant involvement with individuals at the sharp end of war. Within Quaker circles his long sustained efforts on behalf of victims of Nazi tyranny meant that wherever he found himself he was likely to be approached by someone soliciting help.

Shortly after his return to London, as he cleaned windows at the home of his brother Stephen with whom he was staying, he was recognized by a refugee desperate to unburden herself about her fears for her Jewish parents in Vienna. Against the security and comfort following her own escape, she felt guilty, she explained, thinking of their danger and hunger. Her inability to help them was unbearable.

At other times, often on the train visiting Yealand, his obvious interest led total strangers to share their anxieties, encouraged by his non-judgmental

[2] Asa Briggs, *The War of Words*, pp. 123–4.

capacity to listen. He used to say that most people simply needed someone to listen to sort out their own problems. For an inveterate talker like himself who loved nothing more than the cut and thrust of debate, this insight was an exercise in self-discipline.

An almost bizarre arrangement resulted from the BBC's wish to accommodate Roger's pacifism and *his* wish to affirm his patriotism. He was made liaison officer to two Anti-Aircraft (AA) Batteries, his task to find out by personal visitation to the gun sites what the Service personnel thought of existing programmes and crucially what types of programmes they wished to hear. Roger was, of course, aware that some pacifists including his father saw these latest responsibilities as inconsistent with his witness for peace, but he himself accepted them as an opportunity for face to face listener research on a level normally not possible. Equally to the point, if the BBC was inclined to give priority to troops serving overseas, and he was emphasizing the claims of the far greater number based in Britain, it behoved him to support the new Forces programme for all he was worth. Typically he recorded his early impressions with a frankness intimating his disappointment with officials in uniform or not who failed to share the seriousness of his purpose:

April 14th To Salisbury to see Southern Command people about b'casting for the Forces. Saw the Welfare Officer who seemed a self-important little snob, the Asst. Chaplain General who seemed pleasant but not very able, and the Education Officer who looked as if alcohol was his only love. I talked with one or two chaplains over the phone, and may get some results that way, but altogether it was very disappointing and we shan't win the war if these are a fair sample of staff officers.

Some of these forthright not to say aggressive remarks, apart from their possible objective justification, might appear strange coming from a man dedicated to non-violence, verbal no less than physical. But this would be to underestimate not only human frailty in the most worthy among us but to ignore the stress and uncertainty to which Roger found himself inescapably subjected – separation from his wife and children, the precarious nature of his work at the BBC, and the doubts that continued to surface about the precise nature of his pacifism. Even his 'very pacifist' father admitted to 'fleshly weakness' in hoping that the Germans would be chucked out of Belgium and that the USA would come in, though such thoughts were promptly deplored as 'not Christian'.

Roger also confessed to waking in the middle of the night 'furiously angry' with Margery for what he described as her failure to write 'proper letters'. 'My impression is that I almost wept with rage. This seems unreasonable in my waking moments, though I must say I find her lack of interest in letter-writing pretty disappointing, and I am sure it makes it harder for me to keep abreast of either her or the children.'

Margery was of course still struggling with her own situation of cramped space and no privacy, not to mention her own longings for her and the children to be with Roger. But even this, the one thing they both wanted most, created problems between them, she emphasizing the physical dangers to the children of leaving Yealand, and he more concerned to balance the risk of air raids against the psychological damage resulting from the loss of home life for the four of them as a family.

To this uncertainty was shortly added another dilemma, initiated by a colleague of Roger's receiving the offer of a safe haven for his children on the other side of the Atlantic. Should he accept? Roger felt it wasn't a question on which he could advise, though talking that night with Stephen, who with his American wife was facing the same situation, he expressed the view that if the children 'can survive the next three months physically in England one would feel very sick for the next three years if one's own had gone to the USA. And if,' he added, 'we're beaten we shall still have to make our lives here somehow. But should I feel the same if I had the chance of sending mine?'.

Soon he was to know. Within a matter of weeks, out of the blue, Margery received an offer from relatives in Canada to care for her and the children for as long as necessary. At the first possible moment, the following week-end, Roger caught the Friday night train for Yealand. The weather was glorious; and enveloped in the peace of their favourite spot on summer-house hill overlooking Morecambe Bay he and Margery found discussing 'chances of life' unreal, little short of crazy. Nevertheless they decided that '*probably* we should not want to send the children, but if they go it should be with Margery's mother'; as much as Margery hated the thought of being parted from the children she felt constrained, whatever the tune, to face the music with Roger. And at the time the tune sounded decidedly discordant. The British Expeditionary Force had been, as Roger put it, 'chucked out of France' and saved from total annihilation by the 'miracle' of the evacuation of 225,000 soldiers plus 110,000 of their French allies from Dunkirk in a host mostly of small boats. A German invasion was expected daily. So fears of defeat and starvation as a serious threat were anything but an indulgence in hyperbole.

To add to his personal problems, Roger was seeking to negotiate at the BBC not only about his future but now about a new instruction that men employees should help to form an *armed* guard of the building. His proposal that he should be an unarmed guard was at first ridiculed, thought to be a contradiction in terms, but eventually this was agreed. Of his first duty watch – 7–9 p.m., 11–1 a.m., 3–5 a.m. – he commented: 'It's a dreary job which, like the barrage balloons, may have some deterrent effect! We sat about in most of the high-up rooms and spent some time on the roof; light enough at 3.45 to see St Paul's. Lovely morning'.

For Roger the new arrangement was not without its funny side. During the day a 'bayonetted sentry' guarded the corridor entrance to the outbuildings. Returning from lunch one day Roger found himself walking behind the relief guard – bandy legged and a dot and carry. 'I got up to him just as I heard him say to his pal, "Come on, give us yer gun and get back to yer bloody 'utch in the 'all" – changing the guard at Buckingham Palace.'

But if his impish wit and capacity to see the funny side intimated his fundamentally cheerful outlook, his sensitivity to human need especially of the underdog often found him more inclined to weep. One of his colleagues requested him to take out to lunch a sixty-year-old naturalized Russian. He had, Roger learned, done research on housing and population which would now not get published; he had no money and wanted a job. Poor beggar!

Such individuals fired Roger to move heaven and earth to help, but on the other hand he was no longer an easy touch, and, as we have had cause to notice before, he couldn't bear human buffoons in high places.

There were other more serious disappointments. Leslie Baily, a fellow Quaker, wrote to him about an official meeting at the BBC in Bristol during which staff were given to understand that there was no room 'for less than 100% patriotism'. Baily, in exactly the same position as Roger, confessed himself deeply puzzled spiritually, prompting Roger to wish that he himself was clearer and fearing that a supportive colleague was right in calling him 'a religious atheist'.

Another blow was news of the sacking of a BBC secretary because her fiancé, it had been discovered, was an interned German. 'I don't know what else you can do,' Roger saw the BBC's problem, 'this 5th column is the most devitalizing thing I know. You just can't trust anybody.'

Roger recognized that his position was, to put it no stronger, open to misunderstanding. 'For a Peace Pledge Union member to be the Corporation's liaison with two military commands was bound to be suspicious', perhaps even more if it became known that he had guaranteed 'at least three Germans of whom one is interned'!

Understandably Dunkirk and the uncertainty that followed made the BBC increasingly touchy about its staff being manifestly at least 100% patriotic. By early June Roger was making what proved to be his last visit to a Royal Artillery site, at Runcorn; his reception was 'stiff at first and then very friendly'. From there he took the opportunity for a weekend at Yealand during which, despite the tranquillity of their favourite view from summerhouse hill, he and Margery found themselves caught up in a 'violent argument on how much worse a German victory would be than an allied one'. Margery thought infinitely worse; Roger 'not so much because democracies will have no policy for victory and Europe will sink back into complete anarchy from which authoritarianism of the worse sort will spring, probably under German spiritual leadership. A gloomy business either way, for a German victory will be dreadful physically and politically, even if it does throw the church back into a state of more health – heaven knows there's scope'.

Returning to London he was soon confronted by the BBC's final decision that all pacifists on the staff, once officially registered as COs, were to be given a month to find a job and go into C category, clear evidence that a question mark hung over their whole-hearted patriotism. 'It's reasonable enough, I think,' Roger reacted. 'The Corporation can't spend its time defending its employment policy when it has other things to do. At present I am quite clear that I must stick to my Conscientious Objection. But it will be tough on the family, and I don't see what else I can do'. He also accepted his banning from military sites as 'awkward', seemingly an insuperable barrier to his researching military personnel's opinions of BBC programmes.

However, within a week, as his diary for 18 June makes clear, he was given reason to believe a reprieve might be coming his way. The Director of Staff Administration (W. St J. Pym) sent for him with the news that MI5 had granted him security clearance provided he didn't propagate his pacifist views at military installations. Roger confirmed the undertaking the Director had already given. He was also informed that the new BBC ruling applied only to men under reserved age which excluded him for the time being. 'But I'm glad,' Roger declared, 'to have had to face the position.'

The reprieve was short lived. By the end of July it became known that *all* COs at the BBC were to be sacked with three months' notice. Only days later it emerged that the sackings would come sooner than ever, though what angered Roger was what he described as the 'furtive way in which the Corporation acts – no general statement either internally or externally'.

He talked over the matter with Harold Laski who promised to talk to Clement Attlee, Leader of the Labour Party. John Parker, a friend from Oxford days, and still a Member of Parliament, advised him to write to Creech Jones, Ernest Bevin's Parliamentary Secretary. Within the BBC everyone to whom he spoke shared his anger and was 'awfully kind'.

His interview with the Director General (F.W. Ogilvie) was restricted to a few minutes, described by Roger as 'an unfair dodge which he played with more skill than I expected'. All he promised was to consult with the governors.

Roger immediately set about trying to write his tribunal statement, and discovered that from all he wanted to say it was hard to select the bits that were neither 'priggish nor soapy'. Then he went to register as a CO at Camden Town. 'I haven't any doubts it's the right thing to do, but it's not *absolutely* right, and I hate the dislocation and break it's going to cause. And it'll be hard on Margery and the children before it's finished. Is it,' he wondered, 'the end or the beginning of things?'

By this time the idea of sending the children to Canada had fallen through. Their grandmother wasn't well enough to accompany them, and for them to travel on their own was for both Roger and Margery out of the question. But fundamentally the reason was an unwillingness to break up the family, and the absence of any clear conviction that to do so in these circumstances was either wise or justifiable for children and parents alike.

Apart from his tribunal statement Roger was also having difficulty with a follow-up memo to the Director General. Initially he put in 'all the bitter bits I could think of', but eventually took them out and 'got as much satisfaction as I did in putting them in'. It remained 'still fairly strong, possibly insolent'. This draft of his tribunal statement he showed to Oliver Franks who 'made a lot of good suggestions for making it less argumentative and rhetorical and more simple and dignified. He is a genius'.

Margery's reaction to all these consequences of Roger's registration as a CO was typical of her support throughout: 'So the deed is done and I hope having done it you feel it was the right thing. I'm sure it was for you, and I'm sure too that a useful job will turn up for you to do – too many people know your capacity for you to be left long. Do try to take a holiday before the job though. It'll probably be the hell of a winter, and you need a holiday.'

No less supportive was his old boss, John Coatman. 'I confess, I don't see what else you can do,' he wrote, 'but I have always drawn a very clear distinction between Quakers and other conscientious objectors, nine-tenths of whom are either exhibitionist would-be intellectuals or merely cowards. I wish Ogilvie had had the strength to make a stand on behalf of genuine religious conviction as opposed to personal views and idiosyncracies. However, it is no good chasing that hare now. He is as God and the Chairman have made him, and there is neither strength nor honesty at the head of the BBC now. At any rate, I hope you will come back after the war. Of course, I knew nothing of this new decision about COs. Nobody ever does hear anything now – even Ogilvie doesn't – until the Treasury announce their orders.'

In the light of all this upheaval it might seem surprising that Roger in a letter to Margery was still expressing the wish 'that being a CO was *absolutely* right instead of being just the right thing to do'. Such a wish doubtless stemmed from or was reinforced at Quaker Yearly Meeting a few weeks before, when Professor H.G. Wood, a Quaker revered for his sanctity and scholarship, made a statement that Roger himself feared he also 'should have to make at some time' – that war was better morally than a Munich and that though it is wholly wrong, the country cannot either withdraw with honour or not wage it efficiently; the alternative to that *is* German domination. In the face of either situation we must do what unbelievers think negatively or positively right, but we have no right to embarrass our fellow citizens.

'He did it well,' Roger commented, 'and the meeting was not as shocked as I thought it should be.' But if not the meeting, individual well-known Friends were, accusing the Quaker scholar of asking support of the war. Afterwards he was surrounded by a crowd either thanking or reviling him. Roger's father said he disagreed; Roger followed at once with his agreement. 'So there we are,' he left the matter.

Paradoxically, at the end of that day his pacifism felt 'a good deal stronger', for the prospect of having to bear the burden of German oppression 'makes me feel that pacifism may be dynamic after all. It's an odd possibility,' he went on, 'that only in some form of suffering – fighting or not fighting – can one feel that one is doing one's job. Just to be happy seems useless.'

If such open honesty gives the impression that his attitude to war was tinged with ambivalence, one has only to recall the price he was paying to be true to the inner light as he perceived it. No man of his integrity places the job he loves on the line with the corollary of possible unemployment and risk to the welfare of his family without an overwhelming and inescapable conviction he could do no other. If being a CO wasn't *absolutely* right, he never seriously doubted that for him 'it was the right thing to do'.

He was still frequently in London, but increasingly from September his work in the Listener Research Section was centred in Bristol where his total freedom from self-pity and pompous self-justification at the way things were developing reinforced both his popularity and the respect he'd won throughout the Corporation. But as with God's mills, the BBC's were grinding exceeding slow, and as late as the end of October, five months after the initial threat of dismissal, Roger was writing to Margery: 'There's no further word about my departure or about other jobs . . . If I saw an actual job that I could do properly, I'd ask to be sacked on the spot. But whether to be asked to be sacked and then begin to look for the job I don't know. All I know is how much I hate *this* bloody war!'

Within days the BBC axe fell at last, marking his instant departure though strangely not his formal dismissal. Such fine distinctions were lost on Margery who promptly responded in a letter dated 3 November 1940: 'It's a horrid feeling being sacked, whatever the reason, and as you say not feeling indispensable. But I've no doubt they'll miss you a lot. I wish you could hear of the right job preferably in Manchester!' Equally revealing, having referred to a colleague moving into a cottage with her own bits and pieces, she went on: 'It made me rather homesick for our own furniture and pleasant things which is bad for one. In a way I feel it's rather good for us to be separated from them as we have acquired quite a lot, and I always thought one was only justified in having them if one could give them up again and didn't get too attached to them; having nothing is probably good for the soul though I must say I hope they don't get bombed, and we get them back afterwards!'.

Concurrent with this development on the BBC front, Meeting for Sufferings (the executive committee of the Society of Friends in Great Britain) decided on 1 November to establish a Friends War Victims Relief Committee whose aim would be to co-ordinate the relief services of existing Quaker groups, to investigate new openings, to raise and allocate funds, to support local efforts, and to consider training workers.

It met on 7 November, and among much other business set up a sub-committee to consider the appointment of a Secretary. Within a week Roger was invited to accept this undertaking 'as soon as his forthcoming dismissal from the BBC as a conscientious objector would permit'. He took up the post on 25 November.

Two days later the North Regional Director sent a handwritten letter from Broadcasting House, Manchester: 'It was a shock to find that you had already left the Corporation by the time your letter reached me. I had hoped that, in the usual BBC fashion, nothing would be done and you would just stay on. I can appreciate your feelings because I know your feeling for your work. Of course, it is no use wasting time and energy in vain regrets or recriminations. I suppose there is nothing for you to do at the present moment except take up some such employment as you mention. I don't for a minute decry the importance of such work, but it is not the work you ought to be doing now . . . I feel so strongly that you ought to be somewhere much nearer the centre of things because you have much to contribute. I sincerely hope that you will come back to Broadcasting after the War or, perhaps, even before it ends.'

Whether or not the Secretaryship of the War Victims Relief Committee was the work Roger 'ought to be doing now' was yet to be tested, but of one thing he could have no doubt – his ability to continue depended upon the outcome of his still long awaited CO's tribunal. It finally took place on 1 May 1941. Roger's statement declared:

> I apply for unconditional registration as a conscientious objector on religious grounds. I have held pacifist convictions for many years. I come of a long line of Quaker ancestry and myself joined the Society of Friends in 1929 at the conclusion of my university career during which I took a prominent part in pacifist activity in Oxford . . .
>
> The ultimate basis of my claim for unconditional registration is my personal religious conviction that it is wrong for me to try to achieve any object by methods of war. I would much rather not feel obliged to come to this decision, for I am in complete sympathy with the majority of my fellow countrymen in believing that Nazism is a monstrous evil, and I should be

freer, in a physical sense, to fight against it with all my strength if my convictions did not lead me to be at variance with the community on the question of method. The difference between us is how and where the evils of Nazism shall be fought. I believe that its symptoms must be fought wherever they occur by the methods of Christian suffering and love.

I am not an expert in these methods and I do not see with complete clarity how to practise them in a country whose people are fighting and dying among other things for my right to be a conscientious objector. But I cannot escape the obligation to try to rely on these methods alone, even though the methods of the Christian pacifist are not necessarily successful.

Christianity, as I understand it, does not guarantee men success in this world; it teaches them that evil and suffering and love and happiness are inextricably mixed and that only through the peace of God can men overcome the world.

The other side of my conviction that I cannot take part in war is the obligation to do all I can in the constructive work of the community in war as in peace. It is not possible to be entirely logical about one's form of work in wartime, and what I can most usefully do is a matter on which I am glad to have the advice of anybody qualified to give it, but the ultimate decision must be taken before God and by my own conscience . . .

My concern is not to escape military service but to serve the community in accordance with my conscience and to the best of my ability at this time of war.

The hearing lasting five minutes did not appear to Roger to give any consideration to his application for unconditional registration, asked no questions, and refused him permission to submit letters of support or present a witness. On learning the tribunal's decision 'that you shall be conditionally registered in the Register of Conscientious Objectors until the end of the present emergency, that condition being that you continue in your present occupation (Secretary, Friends War Victims Relief Committee) or undertake full-time APR (air-raid precaution) work, AFS (auxiliary fire service) work or work in connection with the land', Roger immediately appealed, and was granted a further opportunity to present his case, before an Appellate Tribunal, on 11 July 1941: ' . . . I do not wish in any way to offer obstruction to the military methods which my fellows believe to be their obligation', he explained, 'but I do ask to be free to serve the country with what training and imagination I have in things that seem to need doing, at present as Secretary of Friends War Victims Relief Committee – a Quaker organization for relief of civilian war suffering – but as war develops there may be new openings – who knows? I hope the Tribunal will regard me not primarily as a CO, but as a conscientious person. There is, I am aware, a danger of arrogance, but whatever the Tribunal decides cannot make any difference to what I do. I have no present intention, or future, as far as I can see, of changing my present service, but if I do feel it right to change I shall do so regardless of consequences. But I hope that in the interests of effective work the Tribunal will leave me free to follow what some would regard as my own choice but which I venture to claim is the leading of God. I think I can honestly say that so far he has led me into neither easy ways nor exotic ways.'

The three letters of support he was able to provide illustrated the consistency of his commitment during three phases of his life.

The first was from William Noble in South Wales, the Maes-yr-haf Educational Settlement; the second from the Vice-Chancellor of the University of Manchester. But perhaps the most persuasive, certainly the most interesting and revealing of the nature of Roger's pacifism, was from his old BBC boss in Manchester. Doubtless its length tested the patience of the members of the Tribunal, but it stands as a clear critique and endorsement of Roger's attitude to war from someone not sharing his conviction:

> I can best support Mr Wilson's application for unconditional registration as a Conscientious Objector by giving some account of my own relations with him. I met him first in 1935 when he joined the BBC in London where I was then Senior News Editor . . . It was not long before I discovered his views on Pacifism. They did not surprise me, because I knew that he belonged to the Society of Friends and that he came, as he himself says, of a long line of Quaker ancestry. I must admit, however, that at first there was a good deal of incredulity and, I must confess it, a certain tinge of contempt in my view of his pacifism. I hasten to state that the tinge of contempt quickly disappeared and has been replaced by admiration. It was inevitable, however, that I should regard pacifism in this way at first, because I myself hold diametrically opposite views on this subject. I am an Imperialist and I hold to the perhaps old-fashioned view that my duty is to support my country right or wrong . . .
>
> The change in my view came about through long and serious discussions with Mr Wilson. I found him fully alive to the logical difficulties of his position and I was able to force his assent to many of my arguments. Nevertheless, in the end, I found myself up against the unshakable rock of his moral conviction that the use of force so far from being any solution to any of our problems can only aggravate and perpetuate the unhappy conditions in the world which produce these terrible wars from time to time . . .
>
> When war became inevitable I assumed without any further argument or discussion that Mr Wilson would not serve in any organization which could be regarded as directly concerned with the war. For a time he ceased

to be an active member of the BBC but then, happily, one branch of the Corporation's activities to which he has referred complied with the stringent conditions which he laid down for himself and, to the benefit of the BBC and the country, he was able to return to service. He left the service as he has stated owing to no wish of his own. Since then he has been doing work which I regard as fully as important as any work that any one man can do in these days. I, therefore, with a full sense of responsibility state that from my own personal knowledge Mr Wilson is a genuine religious Conscientious Objector.

My own experience of him assures me that it is literally impossible to shake him in his views, and that if he were disturbed in his present employment the country would be the sufferer. Therefore, as a patriotic citizen, I personally request that what I have said be taken seriously into consideration. Every word in this note represents what I believe to be the truth, and I think I have given good reasons for believing that I have understood the truth about Mr Wilson's convictions.

J. Coatman

Doubtless such an authoritative testimonial was 'taken seriously into consideration' but it made no difference to the outcome. The Appellate Tribunal endorsed the earlier Tribunal's decision to grant only conditional registration, the conditions themselves precisely the same as before.

So Roger returned to his work with the Quaker War Victims Relief Committee, happy to do so, but no less committed to the dictates of his own conscience under, as he put it, 'the leading of God'.

The hectic six months since he had taken up his post had long fully persuaded him that these Quaker responsibilities, as fiercely demanding as any he had faced, were to test his courage no less than his competence.

He was soon to discover that the action had barely started.

8

A Pacifist Goes to War

1941–1943

Roger's first week-end in his new job set the pattern for what proved to be at least physically the most hectic and probably the most demanding years of his life. He stayed the night on Friday at Gerbeston, arriving there at ten o'clock having cycled through country lanes from the station which pleased him incidentally because his new dynamo lamp justified itself.

On Saturday morning he cycled the ten miles to Spiceland, a Quaker training centre near Cullompton in Devonshire for young men and women pacifists preparing for relief work, hospital work, work on the land, and so on. Having acquainted himself with staff and trainees there, he left early on Sunday morning to cycle the six miles to Cullompton for a train to Weston from where he cycled seven miles to Sidcot to talk with Friends about various evacuation schemes which nation-wide centred upon children, children and mothers, and old people made homeless by the bombing.

Among those consulted was a married couple living in 'a very sizable old manor house on a pretty generous scale'. With six children already billeted on them they responded to the start of the blitz by turning their squash court into accommodation for twenty-five more, and 'got three Spiceland men to come and handle the little toughs'.

Later that day he cycled the fifteen miles back to Bristol and experienced the city's first blitz of the war. 'The noise wasn't as bad as I've heard in London,' he noted in his diary, 'but the fires were so huge as to make one shiver all over.' In the flat above where he was staying for a couple of nights was an old lady who was so terrified she came down and had to be kept quiet. He finally got to a makeshift bed at 1 a.m.

The city centre was still burning on Monday night, but this did nothing to curb Roger's appetite to fulfil his crowded itinerary which included the happy duty of attending a get-together of BBC colleagues anxious to mark his departure with a corporate expression of respect and affection. They packed a pub near Broadcasting House in Bristol, a setting in which, it must be said, Roger was never more than uncomfortable. He wasn't a total abstainer on principle though the long tradition of the Society of Friend's attitude to alcohol made him virtually a non-partaker. At his Bristol farewell he was content to circulate holding a glass of sherry, and sipping it very occasionally with evident distaste.

Back in London late on Tuesday night he was typically one of the first to arrive for work at Friends House on Wednesday morning. Much of the afternoon was taken up by the first meeting of the FWVRC with its full-time Secretary during which it was agreed that relief work must never be attempted unless it was believed that it could be done efficiently. As Roger later explained, this was really the Secretary's charter 'for trying to put salt on the tails of the unpromising inherited schemes'.

Significantly immediately after this meeting he rushed off to see for himself the relief work being done at Whitechapel and Wapping in the tube stations now serving at night as air-raid shelters. Underground, he said, 'the air was pretty foul; and how the devil one lives like that I don't know'. But beggars couldn't be choosers, for, as he noted, his arrival at a shelter coincided with a hell of a row overhead. 'Not much trouble really,' he was typically sanguine, evidence not of bravado or a man whistling in the dark but of an attitude to danger both realistic yet free of self-concern. 'I can't say I feel much nervousness in general,' he commented after one heavy raid, 'though the whistle (of the descending bombs) is a little disturbing.' His problems were on a different front altogether. 'I lack somebody with wide knowledge to talk to. I'd rather be a number 2 than number 1; and if I have to be number 1 I want a good number 2!'

He was by now living at the relief headquarters of the FAU in the student hostel of the London Hospital in Stepney, a move for which he suffered a concerted attack from his brother Stephen and Oliver Franks out of concern for his safety and general well-being. One of the few compromises he accepted was to visit Stephen's home to luxuriate in a good bath. The first time he went – his first good bath for months! – he was no sooner in than he heard the familiar swish of falling bombs from nowhere at all followed by an explosion which rocked the house and cracked the bathroom plaster. 'I rapidly washed my feet, half dried myself and bolted for the cellar, an unhappy end especially as the siren went five minutes later, and the all-clear, without another sound, fifteen minutes later still. Not a very good night though quite quiet.'

The next morning, Sunday, he attended Meeting at Hampstead before cycling to Friends Hall at Barnet Grove where wardens and eight youngsters 'hold the fort in local shelters'. He was appalled at the conditions under which they lived – no privacy, no tidiness, overcrowding and perpetual tiredness, the worst situation he had so far come across. 'Something must be done about it quickly. Our people can't be efficient in those conditions. I slept fairly well in dirty blankets on a horrible mattress on the floor. The place will fall down if a good bomb lands within a hundred yards.'

His comments about 'the great Columbia Market shelter' were similarly robust: 'Seven to eight hundred people in pens, like a cattle market. Fairly good air and room but damp. No bunks yet. The shelter marshall is a cynical but desperately concerned bricklayer.'

Roger always saw the danger of frantic activity being confidently identified as progress. But this did nothing to modify the pace of his own self-imposed programme, illustrated by his diary entry for 5 December, the eleventh day into his new job:

December 5th Up at 6.30 yesterday morning and left London Hospital at 7.40 for Birmingham via Euston; found train warm and empty. Filled to normal and left on time; had to get out 4 or 5 miles from centre of Birmingham and finish off by bus. Some of Birmingham's suburbs and semi-suburbs through which we passed looked v. bad; the centre not so bad as I'd expected . . . conferred with a group of Friends who accept my view that we must work officially through local Friends. It remains to be seen how far we can translate the intention of order into the fact of order . . . got train from New Street to Derby, and Derby to Bakewell . . . by bus to Sheffield. What a relief to go to a town when one was not frightened of the damage one might find round the next corner . . . train to York which ran on time and in which I did quite a bit of useful typing. It's a method of using interminable train times usefully, but doesn't make you popular with fellow travellers and isn't much good when it's full.

Meeting for Sufferings next day. P. opened up well by putting the difficulties involved in saying anything but was convinced that something must be said. Neither he nor anybody else faced the dilemma of pacifists in such a war or had the courage or the humility to say that they didn't know the answer and must wait quietly till they find one. They think that politics can be Christianized in the simple sense . . . After the interval I talked for 15 instead of 10 minutes on War Vics.[1] No very intelligent questions but I got a laugh or two. Then a discussion on a demolition squad for Conscientious Objectors at Army pay. I'm doubtful about it in practice but see no objection in principle. Meeting continued till 2. Caught train back at 3, not too full and did a bit of typing. Back at 8.45 – 1½ hrs late.

So it went on, day after day, though his only comment about it in his diary was: 'I must get down to harder work'! What cheered him was, of course,

---

[1] A colloquial term used indiscriminately in the organization to designate either the whole corporate enterprise or individual members of it, since the full title of the organization was impossibly long for ordinary use.

any news of his family. 'I show Anthony's letters to everybody,' he wrote to Margery. 'They are much impressed as they ought to be.' Typically he confined to his diary that visiting his brother Stephen at Hampstead he went for a walk on the Heath 'and saw the large hole made by the bomb that blew me out of the bath last Saturday'.

He was cheered as on so many occasions by a letter from Margery who seemed however, 'more worried about me than she need be. Out of London we all like to think of ourselves as the front line. In London nothing feels less like the front line. It's a lot less dangerous than rock-climbing; at least I'm not nearly so frightened.'

His diary covering this period reveals his determination to acquaint himself with the growing number of pockets of Quaker relief service spontaneously breaking out in many places, to which he travelled by cold trains that frequently arrived late. Consequently by the time he reached Yealand late on Christmas Eve for a few days with his family, he was afflicted with 'an awful cold'.

December 26th Elizabeth woke up as we were filling stockings and was glad to see me. Margery says that after telling Elizabeth the rhyme about 'Please put a penny in the old man's hat', Elizabeth forthwith improvised a 3rd verse:

> If you haven't got a God
> Another will do;
> If you haven't got another God,
> Then God help you.

Kids up at 7 on Christmas Day and pretty pleased with themselves. Anthony delighted with stamps and Elizabeth with a stuffed panda and a puppet. I stayed in bed v. miserable till lunch. Anthony left me his stamps to play with while he went to Meeting. A very good dinner indeed and then back to bed till tea. No mean tea and then the children played round till Father Christmas came up the drive by spotlight. Anthony still a complete believer. He asked how Father Christmas's sledge went when no snow and completely satisfied by M.'s explanation about wheels for occasions of that sort! Nine o'clock news says no bombing on either side last night. I hope this is based on some generous feeling and not on technical disability or thought for political good looks.

December 27th It turned out a very nice day and Margery and I had a turn up the hill before lunch. We had to return abruptly to avoid T. whose dreary righteousness in an extraordinarily small setting is unnerving. He's worse than he was, but he's got a wife now who I gather is Yealand's heaviest cross.

After lunch I read to the kids, slept, dressed Elizabeth in her best, and went down to a play which Margery had been busily dressing. Where the stuff comes from heaven only knows, but it seemed to me about the most finished part of the show. Dressing up may please the brats, but if that's the line, the thing should frankly be charades of some sort. But the play is meant to have some significance, and if so it should be tidier. Fundamentally I believe it may encourage the sentimentality of sloppy ideas. Perhaps this feeling arises from my own dislike of not finishing off a job properly, which irritates me though I do nothing about it!

After tea I played draughts with Anthony. He's pretty quick off the mark . . . Before supper there was a discussion in the common room on the shortcomings of non-pacifists – awful arrogant thinking . . . Felt pretty tired at the end of the day though I'd done nothing.

Finance was, at the time and often subsequently, his own biggest headache. He never doubted that the cash would come, but to spend it economically and with the right priority left him less confident. What both pleased and alarmed him most was the excellent work being done, his central criterion of success, but often without an eye to the future. Any evidence of muddled planning and bad administration infuriated him. Clearly he was a man of high standards and robust opinions but never as an expression of rigidity of mind or reluctance to admit the vindication of contrary views. Visiting evacuation schemes at Banbury and Adderbury, he reflected about the latter: 'I should say that it could never work, except that the village – a rather pretty one – is said to be full of evacuees and some of the men who might come have got jobs. I feel justified in all that I've said about half-baked schemes, but this must now go through.'

On other occasions he was less accommodating, exasperated – almost! – beyond words. 'Either I'm getting middle-aged or this war is getting me down, for I get drearily tired o' nights and waste time in all sorts of dreary idle ways. It's hard work in the office. Without the pretty efficient help of the present team I couldn't begin to cope. With the right people I could delegate a lot more, but I must break my committee in slowly and not spring too large a staff on them before we have any money at all.'

But the 'slowly' approach was not always, he thought, appropriate. Hearing that the Friends Ambulance Unit family evacuation centre, referred to for months by the Ministry of Health as a model scheme, was to be closed by that same authority, he attended a meeting with a government representative. 'It wasn't exactly the row I should choose,' he reflected. The Ministry of Health man arrived at 10.15 to see the evacuees and ask them if they wouldn't like to go. Instead of the quiet chat he'd confidently anticipated he suddenly found himself surrounded by eight angry young men, Roger vociferously among them, and for seventy-five minutes they gave him hell. 'He has the power,' Roger conceded, 'and I think we shall lose, but at least he had to work for his insults. It's a terrific example of the danger of going ahead without anything in writing from a Ministry.'

That afternoon he went to Golders Green – 'how forlorn the suburb looks with its poor battered little houses' – to meet first two 'remarkable old women' who were running five allotments as part of the Friends war relief programme, and then for a second time a Friend 'who wanted my advice on whether he should marry again to a woman a bit older than himself who would really be his housekeeper. A man of his age shouldn't marry for the sake of housekeeping, but he may need the ballast. My general advice was "No" but I'm probably wrong.'

This double-sided approach to life – leading the group for which he was responsible and quietly ministering to individuals of all sorts – was characteristic. Yet surprisingly for so perceptive a man it seemed not to have occurred to him that his growing weariness was related to sixteen-plus-hour days. 'This tiredness,' he wrote to Margery, 'is probably only lack of sunshine. Anyway I hope so. I have now to make myself run upstairs; nonetheless I managed to run all the way up the Bank escalator, two at a time, which doesn't seem to me so bad. It's a slow 'un, too.'

Apart from the length of his working day, usually seven days a week, his energy was dissipated by his unrelieved anxiety about money. 'Finance does worry me,' he admitted after a less than satisfactory Finance Committee which had budgeted for every penny available. 'I wish we'd got £5000 behind us! I'm still messing about with too much detail to be able to get about and see people and ideas and work. How to devolve I don't know, but it'll come.'

But how? He saw part of the answer in the Society of Friends in the USA to whom an appeal for funds was dispatched, but instead of the money they replied by saying they would send a deputation! He accepted that, though 'annoying' in the first place, this was not 'unreasonable' particularly as much of their own relief activities were geared to the feeding of children war victims in Europe. 'Which needs available money most? Child feeding in Europe or work here? In that there is no doubt. On the other hand, a corps of workers has got to be in training here if we are to take European responsibility at the end of the war and if it ends like that.'

Such an assessment could hardly have been more balanced, but this did nothing for his own peace of mind. Only eight days later he wrote to Margery: 'Last week was utterly quiet in the skies, but furiously busy in the office. It's beginning to get me down in the way that I write snappy letters to people who mean well, and am getting bad-tempered. If I had more time or more money at my disposal I'd be nicer, but I haven't! Not yet anyway. On Friday the two Americans turned up, unexpectedly soon. They'll be here for 2 or 3 weeks; I hope they'll believe in our work adequately to produce 10,000 dollars a month.'

Meanwhile he took steps to raise funds nearer home, he and a colleague presenting themselves at the Mansion House to be examined by the Lord Mayor's Committee on Grants. The twenty or so members asked what Roger called 'fairly pertinent questions' and it so happened, he gleefully recorded, 'we knew all the answers'. This doubtless helped, but more influentially, the pair of Friends surmised, was the 'modesty' of their request, a modesty evoking surprise from the Committee.

'We left thinking we might get £250 or even £500. When I got back to the office on Tuesday I found £2000. Whether it was us, or our friends in the City, or both I don't know, but it was certainly the most profitable half-hour I've ever spent! I hope to improve with practice.'

Perhaps improvement wasn't necessary, for within three weeks he was cheered by a cable from America promising 10,000 dollars a month. '*That*,' he indulged in euphemism, 'will lighten our burden quite a bit!'

But only lighten it. As within all embyronic administrations attempting the impossible in half the time, there came moments when, Roger confided to his diary, he was inclined to chuck up War Vics and begin again as a humble member of FAU. Key members of his committee seemed concerned to do as little as possible rather than to tackle the job with imagination and faith. 'If it were not a Quaker organization from which, I gather, one does not resign, I should put the issue straight – either I go or the Chairman goes. As a matter of fact,' he did apparently put the issue straight, 'he will be willing to go if we can find the right successor. So it's really up to me.'

The clash was between caution and enterprise; between making a job small and thereby saving money, and Roger's approach of doing the job and hoping the money would be found. If he carried the day it still left him emotionally drained and inclined to irritability. One outlet brought him immense satisfaction, something, he said, he had always wanted to do. It happened during a heavy raid when he was fire watching. Incendiaries in the immediate area for a couple of hours caused innumerable blazes, some inside buildings and houses. At one house he kicked in the front door only to discover that the bomb was next door. So he kicked in that one, too, enjoying every moment, aware of the therapy of legitimate destructiveness!

Perhaps the best way of sharing this pacifist's war, with its tensions of administration, and field situations fraught with moral dilemmas, is through extracts from his correspondence with his wife. Apart from vivid cameos of how ordinary people handled the daily hazards of war, the many letters also contain robust opinions of civic authorities and colleagues alike:

28.4.41 To Cheveley where we have a rectory with 30 mothers and children, and the married wardens; he is very trying. She is 10 years older and to show that she isn't the boss allows him to boss her and everything else. He's a gas-bag, and both guests and neighbourhood are finding it out . . .

Then 3½ miles away is the Wood Ditton vicarage where A. and M.P. run a hostel on very different lines – all love and no authority, rather like us at Newton Heath, I think. So the women fight and knock one another's teeth out. And now we're going to have to tackle a house in between which is used by its evacuee residents as a brothel. So nobody can say that we lack enterprise! To cap it all, M.L. has been appointed welfare officer by the Rural District Council – a very enlightened but foolish appointment in an area where invasion dominates everything and where a racing tradition does not mean that liberal traditions are well established. The area is already suspicious of COs and if we get co-operating with Austrians (which Newmarket thinks exactly the equivalent of Germans) there'll be hell.

M.L. was extremely pleasant, friendly and sensible. I wish I knew what to do with her. She is not a good co-operator and nobody in the Society wants to have her – but I'd as soon talk straight to her as to anybody I know.

10.5.41 I wish I were a better judge of people and leader of them so as to get the best that they can do. I can work longer than most without tiring unduly and I can get a lot out of them that way, but there is a lot of wasted effort.

22.6.41 My relations with the central office of the Society are not good. They were awfully offended on Friday when we had the first of a series of fortnightly lunches to get office and field workers together. We had 40 of them and were very happy. But the Central Office just didn't like it. Jack Cadbury[2] and I covered ourselves with glory – he by making a speech and eating his lunch at the same time, and I by remembering 39 out of the 40 names right off and putting the right job to them.

13.9.41 . . . and now we've got registration for fire watching on top. I'm quite clear that I have no objection to registration for this as such, but I have an objection to the very sweeping forms which one signs, and I shall alter mine in the signing, for I am not prepared to fire watch war factories nor to fire watch other premises to the detriment of my major concern.

But a good many of our chaps don't feel free to register at all, which is reasonable enough, and want us or the FAU or the Society or somebody to refuse as a body. This, of course, we refuse to do, but the argument rumbles

---

[2] One of the two-man deputation sent by the American Friends Service Council to investigate financial help for War Vics, in February, 1941.

on, with them thinking we old folks timid and we thinking them young! Actually I believe what is biting them, though they don't know it, is the popularity and security which they now enjoy as Quaker relief workers.

When they registered as COs they expected to have to *witness* under conditions of difficulty. This hasn't happened and they are uneasy. So the opportunity to object is irresistible. I doubt if anybody will bother with them. There are more important things to do, and they all do fire watch or equivalent night work.

The bright spot of the week is that one of our chaps who has had two courts martial has had a further appeal allowed and he will now be able to rejoin the Relief Service. We still have two chaps in gaol for refusing medical exam. so they won't get out so finally.

5.10.41 Jack Cadbury and I got to a Ministry very high-up on Wednesday evening, helped by junior friends in the Min. but hindered by a middling high-up. And after an hour's talk, the first half pretty sticky, we came away with Min. permission to rebuild on or near the site,[3] provided we found the necessary money and provided we did *not* say to America that the Govt. could not cope with its homeless, but that we were engaged in a social experiment with Govt. goodwill. We kept our faces straight and accepted this compromise.

We have been saying for a long time that we want to build a village; now we can. The only troubles are that we are not ready and that the huts will have to be what we can get which is far from ideal. We shall have a good many poorish nights before P'field is an established success, but so far so good . . .

On Thursday morning I went out to our market garden at Pinner, with our Treasurer and a card called John D. of Leicester. The latter is a market gardener whose expert opinion we wanted. I imagine that he's a man of great natural shrewdness, but his most obvious characteristic is his utter unusualness. He says it's no good being a Christian unless you are obviously different; so he is, partly in what he wears but even more in what he says which is a mixture of the profoundest simplicity and hardest sense.

Absurdly generous in the ordinary scale of estimation yet none of it pointless. He sold his tomatoes in Leicester mining villages this year because they wouldn't have got any otherwise. I asked whether he wouldn't get into trouble for retailing without a licence, to which he replied that if he did he'd print a placard: John D–goes to jail for selling tomatoes to miners.

He's exactly the sort of man the authorities would do well to leave alone. He's Quaker chaplain at Leicester goal. He was most refreshing.

---

[3] At Petersfield, where a fire had destroyed their hut.

15.11.41 When I got back I found a letter from Buckingham Palace offering us a quarter of a ton of honey for our 'nurseries'. It was said to be in 56 lb tins so I distributed the ten tins to seven hostels by giving two to three of them, or at least I wrote what I thought was a charming note to the Queen telling her where to send the things. However, it turns out that they are packed in twos so they've sent 7 cwt instead of a mere 5, with an equally charming note back . . .

23.11.41 To Petersfield again. The proposition bristles with difficulties; 120 evacuees living communally without privacy *is* a sticky proposition which we should refuse to touch in cold blood but the fire has thrust it on us. The wardens are good and resourceful improvisers working on their own but they have no natural sense of organizing or of leading colleagues . . . things are a bit chaotic.

Dorothy S.'s assurance that 'they have been living so near to the heart of God that they can't go far wrong' may be true, but a very little wrong can be very irritating when the ridge on which the thing balanced is so Skye-line. However, I think we shall pull through in the end.

Living with the very poor is an exhausting business. I slept pretty well with six other men on the staff in a piggy dormitory. They prefer it piggy apparently . . .

14.2.42 Thursday's real smack came late in the day. A woman (Mrs D.) had written offering her services together with her husband for running a nursery group on v. generous terms. Her letter and some previous correspondence suggested that she was a v. vigorous but not very sensitive and a rather dominating personality. In her letter she mentioned a Friend, J.P., under whose chairmanship she had run a hostel. I know J.P. well; so I wrote a letter saying that we had had this v. generous offer, but was Mrs D. the powerful bully we feared? J.P. wrote back to say that I had not perhaps realized that Mrs D. was his sister. He was v. nice about it, but you can't be too careful in the Society.

This afternoon we have had a conference 140 strong of relief workers on post-war service. What we shall do after the war I don't know, do you? I don't want to be a professional Quaker. Somehow, though, we must live closer to people than we did at Moorfield Road or Gloucester Crescent. Newton Heath was physically too much, but that was the kind of relationship that we ought to have with neighbours. It's tougher on you than on me.

14.3.42 One of our girls by the way has gone to live as the wife of another woman's – not one of our women – husband, not one of our men. What do we do now? It's not a case of flightiness or lack of thought or of two young people – the ages are about 30–40 I think. So far as I can judge there's a good deal to be said for the decision. The girl came to see me to ask if she should resign. She's a first-class worker and enjoys the dreary job she does (old clothes) hugely. I told her that I thought she'd better carry on and we'd see if the thing had any bad repercussions on the work. Is that just hoping to avoid trouble and evading any sort of principle? I don't know, but I think it was the right thing to do anyway.

We've fallen very foul of the B'ham lot about organization and personnel; my view is that they lack judgment, insight and competence but have complete devotion – a difficult combination. I imagine they think we domineer, and doubt if they analyse us further. But it means that our relations do not hinge on differences of opinion but on feelings, and that is difficult.

I have also had to tell several people this week that we shall have to send them away sooner or later. It's very unpleasant, but I think people know how I dislike it.

It's three years tomorrow since Hitler marched into Prague, 3½ years since Munich. I must say that I hadn't in the least foreseen the shape that personal events have taken and I continually feel surprised that war for me should mean week-ends at Bournemouth, occasional first-class travel, and telephone conversations about birthday honours for members of the FAU; and for you school, teaching in painting . . . The separation, break-up of family life and general weariness I had, I think, foreseen, and they aren't any better in fact than in prospect.

9.5.42 On Monday we were in the depths of despair about our Cambs. nursery because the Ministry [of Health] were insisting on rehousing it in an unsuitable house in Cambridge itself. In the middle of our gloom came £1000 from the Queen for some constructive project. So we quickly got cracking on the ideal house for a nursery which we had had to turn down for want of the £200 to put in hot water, drains and electric light. Is this sort of thing coincidence or is it a real coming together for good?

One of my hostel colleagues, Bert Wills, a simple soul full of goodness and faith, made a fine plea that it must be regarded as the outcome of the united religious concern of a lot of people, even if it wasn't the sort of thing they prayed for nightly. I'm not sure that he's not right. There seems to me to have been a remarkable number of instances recently in which a solution has come at the moment of apparent despair – many more than the usual run of coincidences leads one to expect.

31.5.42 At Huggate we have the Rectory; the warden is a 7th Day Adventist known to us all as the Mouse. She's a most extraordinarily courageous little woman, with all the Christian virtues including humour but excluding imagination. The guests are Hull mothers and children – a very difficult lot . . ..

We encouraged the Mouse to treat them rough with the Rector's help if they won't do their whack of work. It's easy to say; I'm glad I'm not the warden . . .

Life on tour is one long conversation about people's problems. It'd be intolerable if I couldn't move on to somebody else's problems when I find the existing lot insoluble.

13.6.42 The hostel at Kidsgrove is an old pub, and all the names – vaults, bar, snug etc. – still persist on doors and frosted glass. It's for old ladies from L'pool. The two girls in charge are absolutely first-class, and it's one of the cheerfullest places I've ever been to.

I spoke at Manchester at midday; a biggish audience but I wasn't very good. I was too tired. Mother and Daddy were there, and I'm sure Daddy thinks I'd be better off in jail!

20.6.42 Supped with some of the Nat. Council of Social Service people and a woman who's in the Embassy at Washington. She's stimulating abt. Europe after the war – says it's no good Friends going into Germany if they're not prepared to tell Germans that they've done wrong, and that we didn't fight them, not because they weren't wrong, but because we didn't think that was the right way to help them to get right. She's got something there . . .

4.7.42 Brent Moor House is a hostel that we have for 15 deaf and dumb children from Plymouth. The house is at the top of an attractive valley and is very remote. The river goes by the side of the house and the woods go straight up one side and the moor the other . . .

We have a staff of 5 and there are 3 teachers; which sounds heavy, and is. The teachers strike us all as a singularly ungenerous lot. They take 4½ hours duty daily, 5 days a week! Our folk do the rest! And they were pretty irregular in their 4½ hours until our people told them to pull themselves together. Of course, tending deaf and dumb children *is* pretty exhausting, but not all that; this place is one of our successes.

19.7.42 I wish it were possible to make up one's mind about Oxford. It *is* so lovely. But the contemplation of it makes inevitably for quiescence, conservatism and all the virtues that one knows are good in moderation but are too dangerous to play with. And in the middle of it we have a conference on the peace testimony. On the whole it is very disappointing. One felt that people have come with set ideas and there is no learning of one another or of God. Carl Heath spoke well last night saying that if we have anything to say let it be out of our own experience and not a reiteration of 1660 experience.

Then H.G. Wood followed with what I thought was the best thing so far – let's realize that this war is about something and that the issues in some minds are so deep that politics won't solve them. Let's have a truce of God for 24 hours during which we may all contemplate the depth of our sin and then go back to fighting if we must and can.

It was very far-reaching; then Y must needs crash in with 10 minutes platitude on economics and free trade; and Z with his dreary boring sneers at those who think the situation more complicated than the simple *War's wrong, stop it.*

So few Friends have any idea of how much other people suffer because they can't see the light with complete clarity. It makes me feel sick at times.

6.9.42 I gathered that you are relieved to know that I didn't think it'd work anyway for you and the kids to come and live south. I was relieved to know that you were relieved. It's not an unmitigated good, of course. It's hard on you and the kids, and it means I get no rest at home. But I *do* get experience and I have been astonished at the powers of endurance which have come from somewhere. What the end of the story will be God only knows; but there can't be any turning back, I think, and one must just *not* be frightened of life.

20.9.42 The 'adultery and bigamy' hostel is giving a lot of anxiety. We've nobody quite big enough to tackle it – it needs a veritable giant. We've got three instances of chaps with wives falling in love or being fallen in love with by the girls they're working with, and one or two instances of chaps who aren't good enough at their work to hold their place in FWRS and who ought to go. But what a responsibility to put them out.

27.9.42 I left London on Thursday afternoon – stayed with E.C. and visited her slum hostels on Friday morning. The conditions are disgraceful but the folk are happy. So what?

11.10.42 Up betimes on Friday morning to go with 3 colleagues to see Ministry of Health hostels for difficult children in the Cambridge region. In the course of Friday and Saturday we saw 5 as different as could be, some terrifyingly efficient, clean, tidy and awful, some full of humanity and wisdom. The second best was run by an illiterate gardener who was vastly interested in his boys and – unafflicted by any doubts – sets about creating their self-respect. He thrills them by taking bicycles and Bren guns to pieces and making them put the bits together again. He wants a blackboard and if nobody else can provide one we will, for Bren guns, tanks or any other bloodthirsty purpose. He's got the boys moving.

The best hostel was an absolute barrack of a building in Cambridge. It has no equipment and most of the windows are boarded up; there are 24 boys from 7 to 14. I think anybody just looking at it would say it was utterly impossible. It is run by two women (resident) and three part-time women to scrub and cook in the mornings only. The children go to the local school. And then in this fourth year of war, when Meccano nuts and bolts have been unobtainable for 2 years, the kids were playing with highly elaborate and very well-kept Meccano sets. It's the biggest triumph of personality over all the lack of equipment that I've ever seen. I doubt if we've got anything comparable to show. And certainly I doubt if more than half-a-dozen of our people work as hard as any we saw. The gardener and his wife hadn't slept out of the hostel for 16 months. It makes me pretty humble . . .

Apart from the diaries and letters, all Roger's writings about this period of the war indicate that he had enough worries of his own.

Almost incidental to his daily life was the constant physical discomfort, typified by his remembrance of the folk at one air-raid shelter, a spice warehouse, sleeping on sacks of peppers and cloves. 'It was too much for me,' he laughed, 'and I found more comfort outside in a small blitz.'

Then there was the saga of the bugs! To rid himself of his own lice proved elementary enough, but – as he again laughingly recalled – 'no account of evacuation is complete without reference to bugs'. The subject was of such widespread interest within War Vics that the Midlands Regional Secretary kept a few bugs in a box with a transparent lid for the instruction of inexperienced wardens who had previously led sheltered and therefore bugless lives.

From this standpoint the biggest shock of all came from the residential hostel used by Quaker relief workers in London's East End. When bugs were discovered there two whole years after Quaker occupation commenced, everybody except the residents enjoyed the joke. But even this 'embarrassment' wasn't wasted, since a FAU member, an entomologist in civil life, found examples of a very rare sub-species!

All such irritations were trivial compared with a growing agitation within War Vic – vociferous and sometimes vehement – for a greater say in the running of the service. An element of the problem was undoubtedly a streak of anarchy in some of the young and immature conscientious objectors, but of course it frequently went much deeper than this, best illustrated, as Roger put it, by an individual's belief that his stand had a sort of divine mandate:

> A. is engaged on a shelter project in a target area. Those responsible for the allocation of duties decide that his help is even more urgently needed to deal with a crisis in the running of a country evacuation centre a hundred miles away – and he receives instructions to hand over to B. and get to the hostel as quickly as possible. But A. may say that this will not do; he has a *concern* to stay where he is. He feels as sure that this is the place for him as he was sure of his pacifist convictions when he appeared before his tribunal as a conscientious objector. And before anybody realizes what has happened he has asserted a conscientious objection to being moved.

'Now this,' Roger indulged in understatement, 'is difficult. In practice, nothing is more unsatisfactory than to send an unwilling man to join a small group on an isolated relief project. There is no reason to suppose that he will not perform his technical duties to the best of his ability; but good relief work depends at least as much on conviction about its rightness for the relief worker as on technical abilities. And secondly, if a conscientious objector in an organization whose very existence is rooted in the conviction that conscience cannot be judged by man, claims a conscience on a matter, who is to say him *nay*?'

There were times when Roger felt that *concern* was a word in danger of being debased by excessive use so that too often it covered merely a strong desire or personal preference. Yet even allowing for this devout mis-identification the majority of Quaker relief workers were not Friends. Their denominational labels varied from Roman Catholic to Seventh Day Adventist, not to mention those professing Christian agnosticism!

With such a disparity, it was hardly surprising that their motivation likewise varied considerably. Consciously or otherwise some were seeking the adventure possible in a wartime pacifist organization as in a war-like one; others wished to find out if their refusal to fight had any connections with physical cowardice; not a few welcomed the chance to do something more interesting than had been their lot as bank clerks or shorthand typists and the like; all of them sought to support relief work whose effects in human life were both obvious and immediate; and there was the by no means inconsidable number seeking, as Roger's pastoral involvement discovered, an escape from worries of their own of one sort or another. Little wonder he sometimes felt a greater affinity with those of his friends in the fighting services who, detesting war as deeply as he did, yet reluctantly believed that there was no other way in which they could share in the agony of the world.

More interesting still in seeking to understand the inner springs of his life was how he dealt with personal criticism. Being human, it hurt. But for him bigger issues were at stake than his own reputation or pride. If he was at fault he wanted to correct the matter if at all possible; if he wasn't he knew that fragile relationships or arguments about policy would not be helped by self-vindication or the harbouring of resentment, least of all by standing on his dignity, an attitude he detested at all levels of society. And if, as he believed, the greatest disabling stumbling block in any individual or group was a lust for personal power, he took good care to check any such development within himself.

Significantly, in all the voluminous letters, diaries and papers he left, there is not a trace of self-pity or criticism of others simply because they opposed or disagreed with him. If sometimes he grew angry and even lost his temper he was never slow to apologize – no matter how right he still felt about his point of view – and as for the least hint of harbouring a grudge it was totally foreign to his nature.

No less important in his coming to terms with unfair charges levelled against him of behaving like a despot or conversely of not being autocratic enough, he recognized that pacifists, by their very nature strong-minded individualists of principle, were bound to be a headache to any organization more concerned with good order and conformity than the sometimes creative eccentricity of personal enterprise. 'Penn, Woolman, Elizabeth Fry,' he made the point, 'all rendered service which Friends are proud to claim as their heritage. I doubt whether any of them would have been easily sponsored by a modern Quaker Committee.'

So Roger's response to the rumblings of 'democracy' was to initiate a week-end conference attended by twenty-four field workers chosen by their fellow-workers. The gathering discovered many things, not least that the situation it had been called to confront, far from being unique, had been known in more acute form by Quaker administration in the First World War! But altogether it proved to be, on this and similar occasions at six-monthly intervals, a turning point not only for the Service as a whole, but for Roger's own concept and feelings about the responsibility he carried. 'It was not,' he later sought to explain, 'that we all came to those gatherings in an ideal frame of mind. Some of us were irritable and had matters of complaint in the forefront of our minds; and others of us had been fiercely busy with matters of administration or personal relationships; others of us had come with plans of our own or of a group that we felt should figure prominently. We had all the weaknesses of human kind . . .'

Quoting William Penn, 'Liberty without obedience is confusion and obedience without liberty is slavery', Roger summed up: 'The Service worked hard on the matter, and in the end found a way of handling the tension between liberty and obedience, between personal concern and administrative discipline, that gave a good deal of satisfaction to all concerned'.

Part of that satisfaction was his own whole-hearted support when the Conference asked for the right regularly to review the appointment of the senior executive officer of the Service – Roger himself! – and if it thought necessary to revise it, a polite way of saying either to modify the job's terms of appointment or issue a dismissal notice.

A case of the tail wagging the dog? Hardly. Not when Roger's concept of leadership is understood on a deeper level. For he never believed that democratic administration was enough to resolve differences of opinion let alone overcome entrenched conviction. Government by majority vote could ideally be superseded as men and women waited in creative silence, waited on ministry from the least in positions of authority to the highest, all of them, professing religion or none, open to each other and the Spirit of Truth.

This belief was one of the guiding stars throughout his life, a belief quickened by his experience with War Vics. No matter how apparently intractable, nothing was beyond the wisdom of what in Quaker parlance he called 'a sense of Meeting'. He believed it. He preached it. He lived it. Yet he was the first to admit that finally this *sense* defied articulation. It was an amalgam of expectant waiting, silent openness, spontaneous ministry, creative thinking, prayerful insight, moral courage from a source beyond itself, bold enterprise, three centuries of accumulated wisdom constantly renewed and enlarged; all this but infinitely more that he simply summed up as the Quaker Way.

Some of Roger's non-Quaker friends and colleagues, not a few of them life-long and calling themselves agnostics or atheists, understandably might have been inclined to dismiss this aspect of his faith as naïve to the point of pious wishful thinking, but not after hearing him argue for its proven validity as part of Quakerism's tradition and witness, the bringing of all human schemes, divisions, foibles and selfishness to the Touchstone of Truth.

'If you're going on a family holiday,' he illustrated the extent to which he believed this applied not just to big issues but the most mundane of situations, 'and hold different views of what you should do you can easily compromise and do something which in fact pleases nobody much; but if you're lucky, as you discuss your plans there may emerge a sort of master-plan where the special interest of each builds up in such a way that everybody gets more out of his own bit than he's expected. That's the *sense of the meeting* working constructively.'

Of course, as he was quick to underline, his eyes twinkling, this didn't necessarily guarantee unconstrained happiness all round. 'It may lay on people a compelling moral obligation to do things that in themselves are difficult and distasteful, but that still make sense.'

Make sense, maybe, but this in itself, as he was also quick to concede, was no assurance of infallibility! He was too much of a Quaker historian not to know of some of the judgments of Yearly Meeting of one generation being seen as smug and pompously self-righteous – not to say mistaken! – by another. Yet none of this shifted his conviction born of long testing that 'the Quaker Way' was of God, and applicable to every situation, religious and secular alike.

He needed such an anchor of faith to sort out the inevitable stresses and strains of Friends relief operations in Britain, mushrooming at a rate to test the finest of administrations, and not always understood by older Friends on various sub-committees; but even more as, already grossly over-worked, he increasingly incorporated in his daily programme planning for post-war relief operations in Europe.

9

Quaker among International War Victims

1943–1945

As early as Christmas 1941, the outcome of the war precarious, and Quaker resources already stretched to the limit in responding to war victims in Britain, Roger issued a memorandum hoping to stimulate discussion among Friends of the Society's post-war obligations in Europe.

To avoid what he saw as self-indulgent verbosity, he asked specific questions:

> How best Germany could be helped to find her right relationship to the rest of Europe and indeed the world?
>
> How an apparently utterly demoralized France could regain her self-respect?
>
> What was the right response to authoritarianism in general and Communism in particular?
>
> What were the relief implications for movements of populations both in the repatriation of refugees and the re-drawing of frontiers?

The most important for Friends centred, he believed, on Germany, bearing in mind the isolation the detested aggressor was likely to experience in contrast to the sympathy felt for France.

By January 1943, still pressurized by the demands of work in Britain, he was regretting that 'I have not had much time recently to think carefully and discuss with those who know a great deal about it this question of the tactics of food relief in Europe'. What disturbed him was the danger he perceived of food distribution being presented by humanitarian non-Friends as an opening for 'a good piece of Allied war strategy', and his fear that Friends might get themselves identified with such a presentation, a possibility he saw as 'wrong in principle and mistaken in practice'.

It wasn't, as we shall come across on numerous subsequent occasions, that his motivation was petty concern for the good name of the Society of Friends or disparagement of humanitarian non-Friends. To make the former a primary consideration was, he believed, to stand in danger of institutional idolatry, and as for the latter he knew from within War Vics that humanitarian non-Friends were capable of serving in a spirit worthy of emulation by everybody, Friend and non-Friend alike. His preoccupation was far more basic.

'So far as we know,' he explained, 'it is not at present necessary to agitate on behalf of the children of enemy Europe, but it might become so, and I should be deeply grieved if our previous propaganda prevented us saying at some future date before the end of the war that the children of Germany and Austria and Italy must not starve in order that the Allies might best beat adult Germans, Austrians and Italians.'

In retrospect it seems hardly conceivable that malnourished children should be sacrificed on the altar of national pride or used as pawns of war, but events proved that Roger's fears in this direction were anything but groundless. Already by 1943 the idea of the Allies feeding the enemy, young or old, was largely unthinkable, assessed by war leaders as militarily counterproductive and therefore out of the question.

This apart, the general public in Britain, themselves strictly rationed and often hungry, not to mention their understandable reaction to night after night of bombing, were unlikely either to take kindly to any suggestion of further self-denial to release food supplies for Germany and her partners, children or not, or to respond with other than resentment to appeals for funds to this end. Any opposition to this understandable attitude even within the Society of Friends was by no means a foregone conclusion, not, needless to say, for crude feelings of revenge and the like but rather out of the sincere belief that not feeding the enemy was a wretched necessity for speeding up the end of the war.

In any case, military leaders remained unbending: the enemy of whatever age was not to be fed.

So what should be the response of Friends Service Council (FRS), the title under which all Quaker relief now functioned?[1]

Roger was in no doubt. 'It seems to me,' he pleaded, 'that we are in the gravest danger of allowing ourselves to be swept up into an agitation which regards food for the hungry as a political weapon, and ghastly though it is to let many children go hungry for want of willingness to use that weapon I should consider it an even greater betrayal of our responsibility to the world now and of the future if we retreated an inch from our belief that the feeding of children is an absolute obligation. The only answer to this whole business of political bargains and juggling seems to me a brief and full-hearted assertion of our belief in human values as such, quite apart from whose children are involved, and I hope that all those concerned may feel that

---

[1] See Roger C. Wilson, *Quaker Relief*, Allen and Unwin 1952, appendix 1.

immediate gains cannot be bought at the price of the universality of our convictions.'

What were those 'immediate gains'? Easy access to Europe; engaging in relief work for desperately needy people not deemed by military authority as *the enemy*; institutional acceptance; popularity in official circles; a reputation for not causing any trouble; a hail-fellow-well-met relationship at all levels of government organization. Roger wouldn't have been the first or the last to capitulate to such enticements. And of course at this distance in time, with Britain and Germany firm friends and members of the European Union, with children of whatever nation at the heart of international concern for their welfare, it's hard to believe let alone experience the passions aroused in good people who despite their common motivation couldn't easily agree about what to do for the best!

Eventually Roger and his many like-minded colleagues won the day not only within the Society generally but at the War Office too where 'the universality of our convictions' was – no matter how reluctantly – conceded.

Decidedly on Roger's side in all these things was his ten year-old son, already an avowed pacifist. In a scripture paper at school, asked to name four Quaker saints, Anthony found no reason to hesitate: Elizabeth Fry, George Fox, William Penn and 'Daddy'. He explained to his mother that his fourth choice was 'as good as the rest' so 'it was worth trying'. Passing on the news of his canonization, Margery hoped Roger felt duly honoured. He did; honoured and amused, aware that his inescapable tiredness sometimes resulted in most unsaintlike irritability.

Fortunately there arrived in mid-1943, if not exactly a let-up, at least a few days of blissful relaxation; American Friends requested that a British Friend should visit the United States to talk about British relief experience and also discuss with Americans the way in which Great Britain had handled conscientious objection to war service. There was on the British side another dimension, an assumption that American and British Friends would co-operate in post-war relief work in Europe, and this was a further reason why Roger was seen as the most suitable nominee.

He crossed the Atlantic in late July by courtesy of the British navy, grateful, never mind the lurking danger from U-boats, to laze on deck, one 'lovely evening' talking with two young lieutenants, both in minesweepers, one having been in the Arctic for three years, the other, having joined to go to sea, restricted almost entirely on shore service; both wondered how on earth it was going to be possible to settle down again in civil life, with its routine and 'its respect for staid old men'.

Almost immediately on his arrival he learned that American Friends, expecting *him* to be a staid old man as evidence of expertise and authority, were shocked by his youthful appearance, estimating his age as a mere thirty, far too junior to carry any real clout!

Anyhow, his American diary is sprinkled with cameos of his encounters with the great. In New York he had an hour with Isaiah Berlin: 'Terribly gratified when he said that as a freshman he remembered me as a senior at 'Arcy's lectures at Oxford. He belongs to the gloomy school, but talks about it with the wit of All Souls.'

Another early contact from the Old Country confessed that he and his wife were also 'awfully gloomy about American Friends' failure to know what was going on in the world' and in consequence he had ceased to call himself a pacifist, 'since such an attitude equalled retreat from all responsibility'.

It wasn't long before Roger, ceaselessly travelling with barely a night in the same bed, found it necessary to cope with 'varieties of American pacifism', prompting the comment: 'There is an outrageous pamphlet demanding *Peace Now* that has many weighty Quaker names attached to it. Every single sentence is wrong. Re-written it would be a very good case for the urgency of War/Peace Aims and could be effective.'

At the same time he was frequently confronted by anti-British attitudes, a contrast to the more usual overwhelming American hospitality. His two-hour session with a doctor and his wife whose son, in the US air force, had just gone to England proved an eye-opener in the way this was dramatized by the mother as 'giving their all *for England*' despite her unconcealed hatred for England. 'The impossibility of arguing with parents whose son stands so little chance of unhurt survival saved me from discourtesy, I think. But the self-righteous transfer of all responsibility is unbelievable.'

A further complication was that they detested and distrusted Great Britain so much that whatever he said simply made things worse.

Equally disturbing was his first real contact with racism. 'To a visiting Englishman,' he said, 'it is just staggering to see the discrimination blatantly practised . . . Obviously the issue is not simple, and where to begin to tackle it on a large scale must be a nightmare.' His conclusion was that coloured soldiers returning from abroad where there was little discrimination would not make for quiescence.

In all this variety of experiences, most of them at least as enriching as his expectations, the one thing that never varied was his sense of humour. Somewhat reluctantly he presented himself to the federated French Relief Committee of which the chairman was Anne Morgan, the daughter of Pierpont, his reticence to attend finally overcome by the assurance that it would be a 'good thing' that such a group should get some idea of British Friends as well as American. 'It was,' he recorded, 'the choicest farce ever. The great A.M., a sort of mixture of Mrs Malaprop, Lady Astor, straight

Lady Bountiful and Miss K. of Portsmouth who ran the show in the last war and has not yet discovered that this one is too big a proposition even for her, was vehement, intelligent, patronizing and irrelevant all at the same time. We talked all sorts of sense and nonsense. Her French deputy stood up for Churchill when A.M. was rude; John Judkin and I stood up for Quakerism against all belligerency; we kept up the pantomime for an hour and a half and then broke up in confusion. (Three days later H.W. who sits on their Committee reported that it had been an entirely successful interview, and that J.J. and I now have the reputation of being *those sweet young Englishmen*.) I hope,' Roger reacted to the compliment, 'we did not give too much away to earn this.'

Less than a week later there were no smiles; only inward tears and profound respect as he witnessed an entirely new expression of human need and dedication. He was taken to meet thirty-five men and some wives, members of a unit for COs working at a hospital for the mentally ill in all stages of distress. The first place he visited, for three hundred incontinent men, was, he said, awful beyond the power of description; the stench overwhelming, and the staff so short that there were never more than two attendants on duty for eight hours at a time. In the one large day room, some one hundred feet by fifty, all the patients congregated mostly naked and completely out of control of their bodily functions. The floor was concrete and never dry. 'It is,' he wrote in his diary referring to the COs who had taken over this block, 'heroic beyond belief. I came out after half-an-hour, almost dead. As one of the COs said to me – when you get through the door you will notice an unusual smell. That's fresh air.'

Shortly afterwards he went to Pendle Hill Quaker Conference Centre to address a week-end school, and doubtless still haunted by his experience at the mental hospital chose as his theme '*the importance of failure* of which Americans are even more frightened than we are'.

'Nothing fails like success,' one of his own self-created maxims, underlined his suspicion of any evaluation by outward appearances only, related in his mind to the defeat triumphant of Christ on the cross.

However, when things went wrong and seemed devoid of hope, he was able to transcend his disappointment and see life in a new perspective by his seemingly endless capacity to poke fun at himself. 'I am,' he wrote to Margery at the height of his American campaign, 'in difficulty with my trousers. I sent them to a tailor to have some belt loops put on. But in putting them on he took the braces buttons off. The trousers sit lower with a belt and drape round the ankle, and I cannot wear braces to hitch them up. And I go to Washington to see Governors, Generals and Ambassadors tomorrow.'

His adaptability was more severely tested following his acceptance of an invitation to preach at what he believed to be 'the largest Quaker church in the world!'. The choir, in gowns, led the singing virtually excluding the congregation of some three hundred from joining in. During the ten minutes or so 'without programme', four women, all on the edge of middle-age, ministered 'very shortly and acceptably'. Then Roger sermonized for about thirty-five minutes on the importance of spiritual knowledge rather than religious philosophy as the basis of far-reaching relief work, a theme to which he felt constrained to return repeatedly throughout his travels. This totally new expression of Quakerism he took in his stride simply concluding that British and American Friends, or some of them, had a different way of doing things, outward appearances yet again no reliable criteria of judgment!

It was, in fact, the ease with which he adjusted to varied manifestations of Quakerism that produced toward him a growing adulation, a development he undoubtedly enjoyed – who wouldn't! – but which he also exposed and nullified with characteristic ease by pricking the bubble of his own self-importance, evidence of his irrepressible aptitude for merriment at his own expense.

Work was, as usual, his meat and drink. Two-and-a-half months into his intinerary he confessed to Margery: 'This gets worse. I haven't written for twelve days; life itself is too interesting for comment or record, and I'm dead at the end of the day.' There was, however, a consolation – eighty hours a week on trains gave him the chance to rest and think!

With such a solid accumulation of cross-country meetings and listening and discussings coupled to sharing the toils of relief workers on the field he began seriously to talk with members of the American Friends Service Council about what he described as 'future issues', candid exchanges which revealed lots of room for misunderstanding but also any amount of common solid ground.

Initially Roger was astonished to find the Americans much less ready to assume co-operation with British relief teams, but eventually for reasons he attributed very considerably to the Americans readiness to adapt themselves to European limitations, and the high quality of American leadership, a satisfactory outcome was assured, subsequently proved in France, Germany and Poland.

'I hardly like to say how much I've enjoyed this trip,' Roger wrote to his colleagues at Friends House in London three weeks before his return. 'It seems sort of mean to those of you who have had to stick around and carry on. But I hope that in some indirect way you may all get something out of it. I think the whole thing is in right ordering and I know that Anglo-American Quaker relationships will be more valuable as a result.'

To Margery he expressed the hope that their children would be able to experience America 'for a year or two of their schooling'. Not that he was entirely enamoured. He thought that at a later age they might be inclined to irritation by 'the lack of wisdom in the community' but at an earlier age 'they'd be caught up by the vigour and interest of it all; and to have the first experience a happy one would make it easier for them to watch development of America in the second half of the century with an understanding eye'. As for Margery herself: 'You'd enjoy it, too, though not New York. I've seen too much of wealthy Friends and not enough of the simple folk.' He added, perhaps shame-facedly, 'I get on terribly well with the wealthy'.

Back home he returned to the same unrelenting routine of general administrator and field emergency fixer as his first responsibility; but increasingly, as the liberation of Europe became a realistic prospect, his mind was never entirely free of consequent FRS commitments. They centred, as far as he could see, on five main issues, all but the first potentially explosive and again by no means assured of Quaker unanimity.

Everybody agreed that relief workers for post-war Europe required specialist preparation, and with this in mind – as early as autumn 1943 – a training centre was established at Mount Waltham, a house of large open spaces near Finchley Road underground station.

After his American experience Roger was more convinced than ever that essential training for relief work was more a spiritual and social exploration in community living than formal instruction. For the relief worker's basic need was, as he perceived it, to be able with both adaptability and imagination to maintain inward balance in unforeseen circumstances of tensions and frustrations. No text book in the world could develop, let alone guarantee, a capacity for sustained purposeful commitment in the midst of degradation or a sense of confident daring in human relationships of every variety.

He was quietly insistent that *Quaker* relief work involved the whole personality, and could not be done by individuals prepared to offer technical skills and little more. This was not, he clarified, to say that the heart was all-important and skills secondary, but rather to emphasize that skills in themselves were useless unless held together in some sort of mature spiritual and social background.

In no way, as we have already seen, was this a plea for all relief workers preferably to be Quakers, and only then of the highest order. On the contrary, he was criticized, sometimes severely, for being part of a selection procedure that rejected nine of every ten offers for service, more than half of them from Friends, with the result that only about two of every five FRS workers were members of the Society. The requirement was more than to be of 'good standing' with longevity as further proof of faithfulness! What he looked for were the essential qualities of personal enterprise and daring, the capacity to act with initiative in new situations miles removed from easy consultation with authority, Quaker or otherwise.

So Mount Waltham was an experiment in corporate living in uncomfortable conditions; strenuous outdoor emergency assignments to test dealing with chaos; language instruction at various grades in Greek, Serbo-Croat, Polish, French and German; technical know-how in hygiene, organization of feeding, international refugee camps, camp management and the like; plus courses on political, social and cultural conditions in Europe. Central, however, were talks and discussions on Christian experience, an echo of Roger's reiterated theme in America, the danger of Quakers identifying or even replacing vital living faith with religious philosophy or theological polemics.

For him God was essentially irrefutable inward knowledge, mystical, mysterious, often baffling, but finally too real to be doubted or diminished by endless debate, least of all argument. He sympathized with modern theologians frustrated by traditional religious concepts, and driven to talk about the 'Ground of our Being', the 'God above God', 'Ultimate Reality' and so on. But the words of a much younger Quaker some years later perfectly reflected his own feelings about God: 'An awareness of some entity greater than ourselves is, perhaps, the chief characteristic of a religious attitude to life. It is not belief or even faith, but certainty arising from experience. It gives one a meaning to life and a source of confidence, exhilaration and joy, in spite of circumstances. It is less of an intellectual or philosophical assessment of values than an inner calling. Paradoxically it may be both certain and vague – certain emotionally and yet vague in definition. It yields a sense of aim and direction.'[2]

Certainly he made this central at Mount Waltham as lecturer, seminar leader and sharer of informal discussions often late into the night, but little gave him greater uninhibited enjoyment than the role play he contributed as part of the training programme. His portrayal of a very stupid, slightly-German-speaking Turkish sailor with a wooden box he wouldn't allow anyone near as it contained all the items he'd stolen from under the group's noses completely fooled everybody. The only consolation was, he said, that they were clueless enough to justify a thoroughly lively post-mortem.

During all this preparation for post-war Europe he was, of course, still running the FRS at home. One result was that his growing weariness made him somewhat less tolerant of procrastinators and obstructionists who – sharing neither his quickness of mind nor vision – wasted precious time in talking too much. At one committee meeting during which he found much of

---

[2] Jack H. Wallis, *Jung and the Quaker Way*, Quaker Home Service, 1992 ed., p.41.

the thinking about proposed Anglo-American co-operation 'impossibly woolly' he and the normally tranquil chairman 'nearly lost our tempers with one another'. In extenuation Roger said he was very tired; but he still maintained his opinion that the chairman 'ought to realize he's past work of this kind'.

Other trials were less fleeting or easy to resolve within himself. Gladys Kidd, his former secretary at Friends House for about a year, 'a most delightful and vital girl', died in childbirth, though the baby was well. 'Three weeks ago,' he told Margery, 'I wrote a testimonial for her husband for the Home Office as he wanted to do probation work. He is only B+ himself but I said that he'd had the wit to shift himself into the top grade by marrying Gladys. And now this. It just doesn't make sense.'

On another plane altogether, and making only too much sense in the circumstances, were the new flying bombs with which to contend; bombs which fell randomly as their engines cut. 'They have no penetrating power,' he explained to his wife, 'but great blast force, causing a lot of damage on the ground but very little above ground level. Nonetheless, when one hears them,' he wondered about his reaction, 'one hopes profoundly that they won't stop just here but will go on elsewhere. It is puzzling in relation to the command to love one's neighbour as ourselves!'

Unfortunately some committee members were proving no less difficult to love, or love enough. One inspired in Roger the fervent hope that he would never become so self-centred; another – though both, he didn't doubt, were good people in their own way – that she wasn't so touchy about her own shortcomings. Such opinions he confined to his diary, throwing light on his wish that he could write as easily as he could talk, but 'one has to be more honest in writing!'.

At this particular time especially – the approach of D-Day and its uncertain aftermath – FRS policy making appeared to be confronted by 'nothing but trouble'. First there was the relationship between the military and relief workers once the liberation of Europe was underway. For Quakers with their pacifist tradition the danger of being caught up as part of a military operation, if only in appearance, involved a lot of sorting out. Then there was the associated problem of uniform, a controversy within the Society which Roger assessed as having caused 'more strong feeling among Friends than any other issue during the organization's existence'.

Precisely what this tells us about the ordering of Quaker priorities – the relation between principle and practice in time of war – remains an open question, rightly so. In 1945, however, the debate appeared to generate more heat than light even after it was decided to make application through the Council of British Societies for Relief Abroad for FRS relief workers to wear uniform of battle-dress design in traditional Quaker grey. The War Office granted permission, but wanted khaki. The Society insisted on grey, compromise being out of the question.

Any bystander inclined to look upon the conflict as a storm in a teacup should reflect, Roger himself suggested, that for Friends, relief work was but one expression of a major concern for Christian action, and that dissociation from military operations was a large part of their religious testimony.

Views within FRS varied considerably. Some workers felt that a fundamental Quaker witness was involved and that khaki uniform, implying association with Allied forces, would hinder the primary task of reconciliation. Others, while not favouring khaki, accepted that if this was a requirement for the work to be done, it at least merited further consideration. A goodly number felt that the matter should be left to individual consciences, Roger's own position.

Two months after these views were endorsed by both committees directly responsible for FRS and additionally by Meeting for Sufferings, Yearly Meeting decided that the Society should not permit any of its representatives to wear khaki.

For Roger himself this presented a pressing practical problem. Expecting at any moment to be on the continent to explore possibilities for Quaker relief, and acting in the spirit of the relevant committees, he had already been issued with khaki uniform! As he put it to Margery: 'I went out in full fancy dress all the way from Gordon Square to Mount Waltham to address some Allied women. I managed to avoid a salute the whole way, and by the time I got back had lost most of my self-consciousness. All the same I'd sooner it wasn't khaki.'

So once more it was back to the War Office with a renewed plea for permission to wear grey, a special dispensation for FRS alone. When this was eventually granted there followed the not inconsiderable problem of finding speedily – at a time of austere clothes rationing – a couple of thousand yards of grey material! The fact that this was done largely through the Chief Clothing Adviser to the Board of Trade was, commented Roger, a further sign of respect for liberty of conscience which again and again he and his colleagues found so moving.

Even so, not everybody was happy at the outcome, doubtless not least because of Roger's vigorous advocacy of policies distressing to older Friends. One of them went so far as to suggest that within Friends House itself the FRS's General Secretary had lost the confidence of his staff. The only answer Roger knew to such a charge was the direct and open approach, first to find out if the claim was true, and next to engage in a frank exchange of views.

It wasn't in the least surprising that his style of leadership, inseparable from his emergency-stricken job, incurred the disapproval of the more cautious and backward looking who sometimes misidentified an inescapable demand for on-the-spot decisions as evidence of autocracy, little realizing how much he himself hated such apparent arbitrariness and the loneliness of the burden it imposed. He much preferred consultation and prior agreement, but in facing the latest blitz or flying bomb victims in the form of old people and mothers with children needing somewhere to stay that night he moved decisively, impatient with the niceties of protocol or anything else standing in the way of creative action.

10

Confronting the Horrors of Post-War Europe 1945-1946

By early November 1944 Roger was duly rigged out in grey uniform, and awaiting transport across the Channel, an uncertain arrangement costly in time he couldn't afford, hanging about at secret assembly points. Eventually he and some twenty passengers climbed aboard a military plane for Paris. Among them was a French professor of physics with whom he 'made friends' and who was amusing about why the Americans wouldn't accept his services while the British would. He also spoke of two of his professional colleagues who were tortured to death in an effort to get the secret of Radar from them. 'Actually,' he concluded, 'they had not got the information.'

The passengers were seated on highly uncomfortable benches on each side of the plane, but the flight was smooth until 'having landed at Paris it suddenly stuck in a mud hole while taxiing to the hanger, and threw all the passengers opposite into our laps. I received a leading wren in the pit of the stomach, and a colonel's cap under the right arm'.

The centre of Paris was much cleaner and brighter than he'd anticipated, but later in the day the extreme contrast was provided at Draney Internment Camp, packed with 6000 collaborationist suspects, 2000 more prisoners than the Germans had detained there. Rudimentary welfare services were provided by French Friends, members of *Secours Quaker*, evidence of the new France, determined to carry its own responsibility, being 'chary of admitting foreign relief workers at all'. If an exception was sometimes made for Friends from other countries it was because there was confidence that they would not exploit their power. 'This confidence,' Roger observed, 'should make us very humble and very faithful.'

At Draney, however, Roger, in the vanguard of foreign relief workers, wasn't allowed inside. Appreciating the reason behind the prohibition, he promptly initiated consultations which eventually resulted in all FRS workers, and finally American, functioning freely as members of *Secours Quaker*.

On that first night in France he listened with about thirty-five other Friends to Marias Grout reading a paper on the right attitude to Germans and Germany. 'He began by saying that he was going to say what he thought.

My reaction,' Roger recorded, 'was *What a commonplace beginning*, until halfway through the next sentence I realized that he hadn't said in public what he thought for more than four years. It then became most moving. And as he went on one realized what a small experience ours has been by the side of those who have taken this.'

After the gathering he spoke with a Dutch Friend stranded in Paris whose wife 'is in Amsterdam if she is anywhere. He takes it with courage' spending his time looking after Dutch nationals lost in France while most of his friends were 'getting lost in Holland'.

Such encounters did nothing to relieve his irritability with self-important persons unaware of their own good fortune. 'Since writing last,' he told Margery in early December, 'I have spent five days out of Paris – very exhausting since one of the party was the most infuriating woman I have ever met, and I am afraid I was terribly rude to her most of the time and she knew it'. Going on to mention endless problems of organization, and holding back the Americans from being too managerial while responding to their drive to do things properly, and not messily, he confessed: 'Unfortunately my temper is very short these days; one reason is that there was no coal for laundry last week, and I feel dirty.'

Returning to England for a few days to what he called the relative peace and quiet of Manchester, he explained why his letters to Margery, like his diary jottings, had been so sparse – the absence of opportunity, cramped accommodation, cold and damp making bed the only warm place, and of course the over-full programme. But he still thought it worth mentioning that every Frenchman to whom he had spoken had the highest regard for the accuracy of RAF bombing, even at night, and the greatest fear for the inaccuracy of American bombing!

Reflecting on this first sortie into France he was again moved by the manner – the spirit and dignity – with which the Paris Press was facing the issues of past and future moral responsibility: 'I sensed a profound effort to set long-term wisdom above straight hate, and a creative vitality trying to burst through the bonds of either bourgeois conventions or the deceits learned in resistance.'

He had been no less moved by the group of French Quakers in Paris who in their own way shared, he didn't doubt, the same tensions, hopes, fears, vitality and restraint of their compatriots. 'One quickly appreciates,' he summed up, 'the quality of their striving to be a worshipping and consequently a serving religious company. Equally it is easy to share the fear of inadequacy that exercises a small group on whom is placed the obligation to carry a relatively large piece of relief work. But Friends here will remember the words of the Epistle of France Yearly Meeting that took hold of our own Yearly Meeting last year – *We do not ask Thee to keep us safe, but to keep us loyal.*

The French would be safer if they said, "We lack strength". In fact they are moved by a sense of "that one talent which is death to hide", and in loyalty to their leading they have shouldered an immense spiritual responsibility. The quality of their loyalty will depend on the quality of our prayers no less than on the quality of their own.'[1]

For such a gentle and generous Quaker – or perhaps because he was so gentle and generous! – travel by public transport was rarely without incident. Following what he considered to be a very privileged Christmas with Margery and the children, he caught a train to return to his hostel accommodation at London Hospital, a train packed to overflowing, with four passengers standing in his compartment, one of them a woman.

Fighting the temptation not to give up his seat for such a long journey he invited her to sit on his knee. She declined, not without general amusement, so there was nothing for it, as he said, but to sit and stand alternately. Then came the real dilemma: 'I had two sandwiches left,' he wrote to Margery, 'but didn't know how to divide them between eleven companions, and failed to do anything about it which has lain on my conscience ever since.'

More problematic shortly after his arrival was a United Nations Relief and Rehabilitation Administration meeting to discuss relief work in France, a rather depressing meeting 'because of the stupidity of an American who just could not see the difference between the arrangements for 1000 tons and the possibility of a ton here and there shoved in with persistent ingenuity'.

Ah, yes, *persistent ingenuity*, the quality he saw as essential if things were to be *done* as distinct from endlessly *discussed*!

Little wonder he found himself in trouble with committee members not always familiar with the hard facts; but whatever the subsequent frank exchanges they were all, he said, spoken 'in a spirit of mutual helpfulness'.

What really bothered him was the constant danger of FRS becoming administratively so insular and inward looking that it lost touch with ideas circulating outside, and thereby not only landed itself in a mess but was left behind. And never was his ability to keep a finger on all outside developments and possibilities needed more than when Montgomery issued a *Non-fraternization Order* forbidding troops under his command from having anything but strictly impersonal relationships with Germans, an order, it soon became clear, also applying to members of civilian relief units.

With teams standing by for work in Germany among Displaced Persons, FRS promptly protested in the only way it could:

We regret that the only immediate step we can take is temporarily to

---

[1] Article in *The Friend*, 5 January 1945.

withdraw our teams. But we do not wish to make this withdrawal final without an effort to achieve some mutual understanding . . . as a Christian Society we believe in the brotherhood of all mankind. This does not mean that we are uncritical of our fellows, but we are convinced that it is wrong for us to draw distinctions on the basis of nationality alone.

More positively we believe that it is only in a spirit of brotherhood that we can play any real part in the relief of suffering.

We are fully alive to the danger that Nazis may exploit signs of friendliness. The British Society of Friends was at work in Germany up to 1939 doing what it could on the spot to rescue and succour the victims of Nazi policy, and Friends are the last people to have illusions as to the evils which have been and are rife . . . We therefore expect our members to exercise judgment, tact, courtesy, imagination and restraint in all their relationships, whether with their own or other nationals.

There was of course something else, a positive proposal to resolve the impasse:

If we may make a suggestion, it is that the members of civilian relief teams should be regarded as being in a different category from members of the Forces. They have been recruited and appointed on a different basis from that of the armed forces, and we suggest that they should be allowed to exercise some discretion in the relationships arising out of their work.

Roger had 'entirely off the record' discussions at the War Office where officials explained that if they were to comment officially 'it would mean reference to 21 Army Group Headquarters and a whole heap of discussions of increasing meaninglessness with delay. What would happen,' they asked, 'if they did not reply at all?'

Roger assured them that 'it would be all right by us' so long as this in no way compromised 'where we stood as a Christian body'; left to themselves FRS workers would be content to work out their relationships with all and sundry, Germans included, on the field. The War Office gave a tacit nod and a wink that this was acceptable. Yet Roger hesitated.

'While I am clear,' he brooded over the issue, 'that this is a right decision as far as we are concerned, and that it is through decisions such as this that the policy will, in fact, be modified, there are Friends, possibly a majority, who would take the view that without specific consent we are participating in an immoral situation.' He then admitted that for the only time he could remember he was tempted to suppress a substantial matter in order to save 'a fruitless and utterly abstract argument'. But, he resolved the temptation, 'it would be wrong to do so'.

Yet when he brought the otherwise deadlocked negotiations before the next FRS Committee meeting, he could hardly believe his ears! 'You could have dropped me through the floor with surprise,' he recorded, 'when the chairman felt that the War Office action on fraternization was OK.'

Nonetheless doubts persisted, leading to the kind of Quaker creativity in dead-end situations which Roger never doubted was part of the Society's spiritual heritage. It was decided that instead of prolonged haggling between Friends House, the War Office and Headquarters of the 21st Army Group, the outcome uncertain, the desired freedom to fraternize could best be won not in such abstract argument but in face-to-face exchanges with authority and FRS workers on the field. Two teams were therefore sent not directly to Germany but to Holland; and within weeks, their discretion amply demonstrated, they were permitted to enter Germany on acceptable terms.

Difficulties also had to be overcome when Roger was called to the War Office to discuss 'concentration camp rehabilitation' in France. Officials were initially obstructionist based on pressure of administration and the impossibility, they explained, of differentiation between FRS and Jewish relief missions, further aggravated by the reasonableness of FRS in not asking for the impossible.'

In all these matters an added dilemma for Friends, faced again and again, were the moral conundrums of war and its aftermath. Some tender consciences even agonized that the greater the success of Quaker relief operations the more this reflected advantageously on military government! To this and the like Roger argued that if military government was a step to ordered government why not help it, 'so long as you don't sell your soul in the process?'. In any case, FRS had helped the war effort from the start in one sense, if getting 'nearer to the root of people's perplexities' was considered in such terms.

Clearly these tricky negotiations of conscience were bound to generate disagreement or at least concern, and the wonder was not that Roger was sometimes criticized for walking moral tightropes he couldn't responsibly avoid, but that rather he wasn't criticized far more by sincere and good people who – removed from the action – insisted on seeing life strictly in terms of black or white. But even they must have smiled at a FAU retort to a fussy British officer's protest against wasting DDT on Germans – no order will prevent Allied and German lice from fraternizing!

Apart from these high-level consultations Roger was also facing more personal problems. Nominally he and his family were now under one roof, sharing a house at Wimbledon with the owners, a schoolmaster and his wife, but Roger was rarely there for long, and Anthony was away at boarding school, bothered like Roger in his own boyhood by a stammer, exacerbated it transpired by one of the masters publicly humiliating him for stammering!

Fortuitously Roger was at home when the consequent psychologist's report arrived. Not wasting a moment he drove to the school, Anthony said hurried farewells, and they returned to Wimbledom, impatiently awaited by Elizabeth who was desperate that her kitten after a night on the tiles should not be too sleepy to share the massive welcome she planned. Anthony himself unforgettably added to the occasion by his authoritative declaration that lipstick was part of ATS uniform. At any rate, he'd never seen one without it.

Shortly afterwards he became a day pupil at Raynes Park, and his stammer, it was generally agreed, didn't seem to trouble him much.

Unfortunately but to no one's surprise the same could not be said for Roger's crowded itinerary which, finally impossible, led to the suggestion that he should be relieved of his FRS General Secretaryship to concentrate on relief work on the other side of the Channel with the title of Travelling Commissioner. 'I'd much rather,' he reacted, 'stick at home now we've got one.'

Nevertheless he could see that the proposal made sense, with the proviso that 'Friends will trust me'. But surely he was trusted, hence the new appointment! Just so. But hard experience had already taught him that facing unpredictable and often horrendous expressions of human misery would require instant response without the luxury or back-up of committee approval. Having agreed that the assignment made sense if only because 'there isn't anybody else free and able to travel abroad', he simply recorded in his diary for 22 October 1945 – five months after the end of the war in Europe: 'Myself transferred from General Secretary to Travelling Commissioner, but I can't say it feels any different.'

Within days he was in the Ruhr where at every railway station 'some scores of kids hang around waiting for food or cigarettes' and dart off with any pickings 'like sticklebacks with breadcrumbs'. What didn't 'dart off', on the contrary crowded in everywhere, were the problems facing bewildered colleagues on the field who, appealing to him for guidance, led him to spell out what he understood by *trust*. One was a woman 'quite top-rank as a giver of personal services, but who cannot relate it to policy yet is terribly anxious to get policy to back her'. He told her that she wouldn't go far wrong if she did what she believed she ought though she must not ask for approval or call attention to her own inattention to the rules! It was the *spirit* of the rules that mattered, not slavish adherence to the letter of the law; but he thought himself not very good at explaining such matters, 'especially when one has to do all one's talking against the roar of truck engines'.

He talked with several Poles who insisted they would not go home while the Russians were there. One explained that in 1940, aged eighteen, he was out walking in the woods one Sunday morning when the Germans swooped down, pushed him and others into lorries, and brought them all to Germany to work. Not until they arrived were they able to tell their families what had happened. Now aged twenty-three, he was acting commandant of a camp of 500, many of them convinced that though Germany had concentration camps Russia was one whole concentration camp.

At the first opportunity, for a personal reason typical of the man, he made his way to Frankfurt, 'an awful mess even if not as bad as Cologne'. Apart from the devastation making it almost impossible to find his way about, the streets were virtually empty, shops were few with next to nothing to sell, and rations were even less. But uppermost in his mind was to seek out a German whose influence on Roger reached back to his boyhood and grew with the years.

Emil Fuchs, appointed before the First World War as a Lutheran clergyman to minister to a German congregation in Manchester, quickly identified himself with industrial workers in the slums of that city, and additionally appealed to the Wilson family by his outspoken pacifism. Returning to Germany he joined the Social Democratic Party, one of a handful of clergymen to do so, and bravely set his face both *for* the social betterment of the poor and *against* the militarism fostered by the government and gripping the nation.

He was Professor of Theology at a teacher training college in Kiel when the Nazis came to power but shortly afterwards was dismissed for his opposition to the new regime. No less uncompromising was his criticism of church leaders whose conservatism was, he concluded, condoning if not actively colluding with evil in high places. This led him to resign from the Lutheran Church and – in 1933 – seek membership of the Society of Friends, for him a natural progression. He was a deeply committed pacifist, numerous Friends known for many years were on his spiritual and political wavelength, and theologically – seeking a more direct relationship between God and Man not dependent upon the need to believe in a Messiah or the miracles of the New Testament – he felt at home at Quaker gatherings.

Arrested by the Nazis for his continued opposition, he was released on bail by the intervention of a Friend. At his trial a British Friend was present as an observer, one reason it was believed why the court, not wanting to offend international links, sentenced him to only a month's imprisonment.

All this would be known to Roger the internationalist, already himself in the 1930s, as we have seen, exercised by the plight of the victims of Nazi tyranny, and taking steps to facilitate possible escape routes; at that time Margery was working in Manchester for the Friends Committee getting Jews out of Germany several of whom lived in the Wilson house. But what he could do nothing about was the inescapable personal anguish suffered by Emil Fuchs because of his family. His wife, like her own mother before her, committed suicide – both were chronic depressives; of his two sons, one fled

Nazi persecution to England,[2] the other secretly left the country to seek treatment for tuberculosis, in Switzerland. His elder daughter, hounded by the Nazis, also committed suicide; his younger daughter somehow got to America and eventually was admitted to a mental asylum.

Roger often wondered about this brave man, a monument to Germanic sanity and saintliness, who by now was surely frail and more needy than most. Obtaining an address, the home of a couple with whom the old man was last known to be staying, Roger boarded a tram, miraculously already working in the devastated city, and asked to be put down at the nearest point.

He was received kindly by Emil's hosts who explained that he was out but expected back shortly. Waiting, Roger tried to comfort the couple who lamented that Germany now had nothing to look forward to. A full two hours later in walked 'a delightful old man, looking very well and emphatic that Germany *must* realize and act on the understanding that the plight of others is worse, and that she is responsible'. 'He thinks,' Roger summarized, 'the spiritual need is still greater. I am not sure how fully he realizes the economic blankness, but he certainly had the presence of God in his soul.'

In considering policy decisions which should guide the future work of FRS in Germany, Roger had been reminded of the words of Thomas Kelly that 'we cannot die on every cross. Nor are we expected to'.

But some crosses, if such they could be called, easily avoidable, were obligations amounting to what he considered *concerns*. One such was another search, this time from Berlin – described as 'the deadest thing I've seen, the place *feels* dead' – from where he set off along appalling roads through one picturesque village after another enquiring about the family of Adam von Trott, an Oxford acquaintance who was 'hanged last year for his part in the July conspiracy'.

He eventually found the house, a large manor, in rolling country, and learned that von Trott's wife and children were away in Switzerland. Roger spent some time with the dead man's mother, 'a magnificent old lady, with one of the most humanely stern senses of presence I have ever known. One was throughout intensely aware,' he went on, 'of the indestructibility of her standards, and yet I found her not frightening perhaps partly because of her great social skill in including all her guests in the circle.

'We sat in a small cold parlour in the growing gloom. She talked of Adam with courage though it hurt a lot. She told us that he had been a member of the Party because he couldn't have done his work against the Nazis and the Foreign Office otherwise. And this she used as an instance of the injustice of regarding Party membership as itself evidence against a man. That's true;

---

[2] See Norman Moss, *Klaus Fuchs – the Man who stole the Atom Bomb*, Grafton 1987.

and yet as we talked I kept wondering whether Adam was right to get involved in all the counter-trickery of meeting Nazism in that way. *If* he'd been successful the war would have been over last August. But wasn't it this feeling that Party membership could be squared with ultimate ends that starts the moral rot from which Nazism grows? And yet few of us outside Germany can ever really grasp what the pressures were within, and none of us can be sure that we should have the courage to resist noiselessly. For German public opinion never was compatible to British . . .'

They went on to talk about the relationship of eternity to the world of politics, a theme made all the more poignant by an old lady grieving over her martyr son. 'I'd like to go back and see more of the family,' was Roger's final comment.

These moral conundrums epitomized by von Trott's no less than Dietrich Bonhoeffer's part in a conspiracy of murder to achieve ultimate good confronted Roger on every hand, sometimes from unexpected sources. 'I heard a refugee say with conviction,' he reflected, 'that if she were not a Jew she would be a Nazi because she has in her bones this profound psychological sense of Fate, and a tragic one at that, that haunts so much of German thinking. I don't pretend to understand it myself, but as one talks to Germans one begins to feel that it may provide them with a sense of unity over and against other people that is stronger than the economic and class unity which unites the majority of them internationally.'

This led him, as did so much else, to a favourite theme we have already noticed, the defeat triumphant of suffering love. 'What we ought to be doing,' he said, 'is discovering how we can make that suffering creative.' What bothered him far more was on the one hand the stark distress of war victims, and on the other the crass indifference of privileged officials. 'I don't believe,' he said of a refugee from Poland to whom he gave a lift, 'she even knew that it was an Englishman in a military government car who picked her up', so great was her misery for coherence. Yet a British brigadier, 'offensive in tone and manner', a 'disloyal cad of rich vintage', concluded that most displaced persons were 'phoney' and that if he could get any of them hanged as collaborationists, at least 'they'd be off his hands'. In any case, displaced persons, he claimed, were not his business and furthermore he heartily wished they were nobody else's, and thus abandoned might be punished for their iniquities.

Relief workers of course represented the contrasting spirit of practical compassion, but even this, Roger discovered, didn't always guarantee the right sort of approach. A couple of very earnest girls whose enthusiasm appeared to eclipse their common sense demonstrated ideas about children's homes of 'an extraordinary half-baked nature'. Roger confessed his dilemma. He didn't want, any more than other Quaker leaders, to be heavy-handed, but at the same time, quite apart from the primary concern for the children's maximum welfare, he needed to ensure that the Allied military authorities, wielding absolute power, did not associate the name of Quaker with half-baked ideas!

In such situations his leadership qualities were at their best. He would listen at least as much as he talked, focus the positive elements, confront the problem head-on, gently suggest alternatives, and leave the workers concerned more encouraged than dismayed. Whatever his own feelings – anxiety, anger, indignation, impatience, capacity to empathize – he guarded against the over-emotional involvement that undermined objective judgment, recognizing the latter as essential for both understanding at depth and the fostering of harmonious relationships even if agreement proved impossible.

A quick sortie to Vienna reassured him about the British army's 'humanitarian striving'. 'I guess that, barring sheer bad luck,' he decided, 'the British and Americans will keep Vienna from starving this winter – but not much more. And if influenza comes,' his typical realism felt constrained to add, 'heaven help them.'

On a family level during a brief visit home for Christmas he was reassured too to find Anthony's stammer almost wholly gone, though it became 'heavy' as they read Shakespeare together! As for another family pastime, the serious game of spillikews, Roger observed: 'So far I win – just'. Also pleasing were the children's now 'consciously witty remarks', typified by what he called Elizabeth's winner – 'Soup isn't food for children'.

Early in the New Year – 1946 – he was back in France, the region of Toulouse, where he helped with the distribution of clothing among French and Spanish inhabitants of a village totally looted by the Germans before they withdrew. Their need was desperate, but he was still appalled by the 'eager ill-temper with which sober and respectable village women struggled for coats and frocks they wouldn't have thought of moving a yard for before the war'.

In the square outside the cathedral in Toulouse itself a totally different spirit also exploded as several hundred Catalans with many more watching danced to lively music provided by eleven players with a wonderful assortment of instruments of local type. The dancers, aged fifteen to eighty, were always led by a bunch of elderly men, all light on their feet, bursting with merriment, the whole thing 'most agreeable'. 'I gather,' Roger commented, 'it's a refugee custom which has only grown up since the liberation.'

His endless travelling was punctuated by meetings with military and civic authorities, and of course teams of relief workers whose growing tendency to organize people and administration in standard patterns disappointed him. 'It makes sense in one way, but precludes genius the other', he returned to a favourite emphasis of his about Quaker leadership and enterprise.

What also bothered him sometimes to the point of exasperation were administrative meetings both inadequately prepared and conducted incompetently. 'I find,' he bluntly lamented the dithering and waste of time, 'that the only thing which makes sense to me is for me to be chairman. In some ways I look forward to it – I've hated not being chairman of anything for years!'

Certainly time was at a premium, his constant problem of running hard to stand still, always more meetings, more problems, more journeys, more demands. After what he called a 'surprising series of Sundays – Paris, Le Havre, Jordans, Goslar, Plymouth . . .' he recorded that morning Meeting at Goslar had been attended by two Germans, one of them, he explained, Eva Hermann, who'd been imprisoned during the war for two to three years for befriending Jews. 'She spoke movingly and strikes me as being a remarkably fine person.' In the light of such encounters he found his own trials and weariness not worth a mention, particularly as, unlike Eva in her prison, he was surrounded by lively like-minded individuals who shared completely his aims and motivation.

Additionally there was the occasional social gathering, as after the Goslar Meeting when everybody stayed for lunch, joined by a local army captain who appeared very much at home with the whole FRS team and was, Roger judged, 'more or less in love with most of the girls'. 'It must be a god-send,' Roger added, 'to the army chaps to have a home to come to where girls darn their socks and men play the piano or write letters home, and nobody talks in a loud voice.'

Not surprisingly some of his visits to FRS teams were anything but so free of tension. Once more back in the Ruhr, he discovered, for instance, that at Oberhausen some of the younger members of the team 'had drifted into a number of weak positions regarding alcohol, cigarettes, staff, etc.; nothing very vicious but all sapping to the basic integrity'.

What he called 'this cigarette economy' was, he admitted, 'fearfully difficult', illustrated by a series of questions. When does giving a present stop and paying begin? You can get a good briefcase for 200 cigarettes. At what point does reasonable barter, where money has no value, become exploitation of the prostration of the country? In a set-up where theft is almost universal, how does one set out to deal with it constructively when you have large stores in your responsibility?

Only armchair critics found easy answers. As for Roger, no less sure of the ideal but compelled to function in a world of varying shades of grey, he engaged with the culprits in free-for-all discussions laced with 'bits from the Book of Discipline', some 'good bits' he'd forgotten himself and found piercingly relevant.

He knew that generally speaking outward appearances were not to be trusted, and that within circumstances of war victims' relief they were frequently misleading. Visiting a couple of barracks for refugees at Vlother still in Germany he found 'one tidy and a bit frigid' and the other 'squalid and warm in atmosphere'. So which, he asked, is the better? His own answer did not always receive universal assent. Indeed, how could it with such a variety of relief personnel facing the same inescapable areas of moral grey as a matter of routine? Roger himself, needing to catch a train to Berlin, didn't hesitate to slip aboard without any proper papers, and somehow evaded officials on arrival 'without showing papers which I hadn't got. I know of nothing easier,' he confessed, 'than unauthorized travel on army trains. It's quite incredible'.

What his own father, never mind numerous other equally committed Friends, would have made of such enterprise leaves little room for doubt. And his handling of some officials might have raised a few eyebrows too. Confronting a couple sent by London to assist the re-establishment of education and the teaching of religion in a part of Germany, he described one as 'intelligent and exactly the sort of squalid young woman whom the unrighteous would respect in such a department', and the other as 'a blightering old fool Cambridge don who called me *Dear boy*'. Recording the encounter in his diary his summing up was typically succinct: 'Both Fleming and I lost our tempers which did something to pull them together.' Fleming, too, was a gentle Quaker!

During all his travelling in Germany and France Roger kept in touch with FRS affairs in Gibraltar, Casablanca, Italy, Holland, Austria and Poland, but this proved more difficult during phases of his sorties into Greece, devastated not only by the worst horrors of war but entrenched bitter divisions within families and local communities. Extracts from his diary indicate the extent of the tragedy:

30.4.46 Solonika. After tea we walked up to the domestic Quaker school; the girls are an intelligent looking lot of a great variety of size but not much variety in age . . . They were obviously happy and much at home. As we stood and looked at them the Locks and Hilda gave us personal histories – the father of this one was thrown on to a refuse pile and eaten by dogs, the father of that one known to have murdered several of his neighbours, these ones from a village devastated by the relatives of that group, and so on. Their history epitomizes the feeling of Greece . . .

4.5.46 In the evening J. and I walked up the meadows behind the campus (of the domestic science school). It isn't dusty yet, and the meadows are covered with delicate wild flowers not quite so brilliant as alpine plants but very charming all the same . . . In the distance we watched an eagle or a vulture circling against the hills. A stork flapped down a gully below us. Altogether interesting and agreeable.

Then to UNRRA (United Nations Relief and Rehabilitation Administration) for an hour's talk with A.J. He is very pleased with FRS who have 3 merits: they get other people to work; they get on with Greeks without showing dislike or contempt; and they see a job under their nose. He has seen nothing like it before.

19.5.46 ... After lunch we sat on the roof (a small group of international relief workers) and talked about Europe till 4 o'clock. I felt it incumbent on me to lecture them on not judging Mediterranian people by Anglo-Saxon standards. If people don't *want* to work very hard, not from demoralization but because that's how life is lived, and they are happy, it's not our business to change it.

8.8.46 Salonika ... in terrific heat went to a foundling home in a Jewish school. The whole Jewish quarter has been flattened by the Germans. But the school remains, housing 140 children 0–8 in a most awful condition. Some are all right, some like the worst of famine photos. I wasn't sick quite but had doubts about myself several times. The place was obviously badly run – milk left standing in very hot kitchen, not in ice box; no qualified staff; 12 nurses' beds in rooms 21 × 30 feet, no sitting room or other accommodation for them. No toys.

18.8.46 ... I met Nomikondis the very nice public-spirited Greek who works in the Prefecture on Refugees. He took me to have a coffee. We talked about politics – his fear of Russia is unlimited. At the end he explained that he wanted to be at his home (an island village) looking after his sick wife, but that he had to make peace with his heart and see these people settled. He then paid an unsolicited and terrific tribute to Frinston, Hadley and Saunders. When UNRRA proper was in charge with M. and Miss G. there was much noise and planning, but when they went things became much easier because it was so much easier to work quietly and effectively with FRS men who discussed quietly and sensibly and never made a noise or threw things away. It's another example of the power of not seeking power

20.8.46 Athens ... A hot sticky voyage to the Perains ... on board talked a good deal with an extremely intelligent Gk. girl who happened also to be reading *War and Peace*. She warmed to the lack of formalism among Friends. We discussed whether hunger or bombing were the more demoralizing – she was in Athens in the winter of 41/42 – and agreed on hunger.

Strangely enough, he didn't refer in detail to perhaps his most agonizing experience in Greece, if not throughout the whole war, for many months. It happened on a remote island in the Aegean Sea not very far from Asia Minor. There wasn't any reliable way of getting news from the outside world, but 'I well remember,' he said, 'the sense of deep though only half-believing relief when we heard that the war with Japan was over, and how that was followed by a desolating sense of horror and fear and shame as rumours began to circulate of a new bomb that had obliterated a whole town. And while I was still trying to sort out relief and horror, the first photographs reached the island of the ghastly scenes found in the concentration camp at Belsen'.

This understandably was traumatic and haunting, but what coloured his memory of the whole occasion was its postscript. A group of mostly American relief workers belonging to UNRRA, there to repair some of the damage of war, passionately incorporated every German man, woman and children in their condemnation of such atrocities as they gazed at the photographs. Roger himself felt decidedly uneasy. It was, he thought, too simple to react like that 'with this Japanese desolation on one's conscience', yet what to say, what *ought* one to say, and in what spirit?

As he hesitated one of his relief-worker colleagues, unimpressive to look at, a Turk who had lived in England only during the war, twice a refugee herself, began to speak in broken English: what were they all doing in Greece seeking to mend shattered lives if they believed that brutality could only be met with brutality?

'Nothing she said,' Roger recorded, 'mitigated the horror of Belsen; everything she said brought right home to us that this cruelty of man to man that comes so naturally in certain circumstances is a sin which we all share and yet is one from which, in a way, we can be liberated by the grace of God, as we give ourselves up to the service of our fellows, the persecutors no less than the persecuted.'

Roger confessed he'd rarely seen a group of men and women more fundamentally challenged or so rapidly respond with so confident respect to a critic as she spoke from her own experience of suffering and forgiving and loving one's enemies. He later included the incident in a broadcast talk, describing it as 'a demonstration of the power of simple and single-minded Christian teaching' that he'd never seen equalled.

The war in both Europe and the Far East now ended, with relief operations increasingly taken over by indigenous governments anxious to assert their independence, Roger gratefully accepted that his work as Travelling Commissioner was soon to draw to a close. Like many others he was weary of separation from wife and family, physically and emotionally drained, in need of a break, ready for a change. In any case, in accordance with Quaker policy, the emergency administrative machinery and field work for war victims was to be wound up as soon as reasonable, and in fact ceased as a separate agency on 31 May 1948. But long before this Roger knew that his own contribution to FRS was done, posing the question of what he was to do in the next phase of his life?

Return to the BBC? Top executives there made no secret of their belief that he had the professionalism and capacity to guarantee a welcome, with ample scope for his distinctive gifts.

Work overseas for the under-privileged? He and Margery had discussed this possibility during the war, one no less than the other open to the challenge of costly service.

A professional appointment within the Society of Friends? Both in Britain and elsewhere the possibilities were multifarious, outcome of his Oxford first, industrial experience, and leadership of war victims' relief.

In the event, the answer chose him rather than the other way round, fixing his destiny for the rest of his working life. Initially, no one was more surprised – or reluctant! – then Roger himself.

11

Pioneering Academic
1946-1951

Referring to Roger's hectic life as a relief worker, Alec Clifton Taylor made the observation: 'It's a good job you are blessed with an iron constitution and endless enthusiasm – or are you going to tell me that it is that magnificent conscience of yours which provides the motive force for all your activity, unaided by the above?'

Roger left no record of his response about either his reputed 'magnificent conscience' or his old friend's further equally revealing insight that Roger needed work which above all allowed him an absolutely free hand, for 'you are not always a very contented horse when somebody else holds the reins, are you?'!

Alec was less perceptive or simply under a misapprehension in asking about the sort of post-war job Roger might have in mind. 'A *public* career for you is a certainty; do you still hanker after the House of Commons?'

Still hanker! There is nothing to suggest, not the merest hint, on the contrary, that Roger ever seriously thought in such terms. He was profoundly interested in politics, seeing this as part of his Christian commitment, but never in becoming a Member of Parliament. In fact, this was just about the only thing he *was* sure about as, his work as Travelling Commissioner nearing its completion, he wondered about what to do with the rest of his life.

He and Margery had reached only one conclusion – that if the overseas job they had frequently discussed must be done, it must; but certainly *he* wished it needn't! The prospect of being a career Quaker lacked all appeal.

Another possibility, a proposal turned down for the same reason, was an appointment as Director of Studies at Woodbrooke, a Quaker educational centre at Birmingham, with the wardenship of the college likely in four or five years' time. 'In many ways it would be delightful,' he reacted, 'and one would get all the freedom that a Friend can have. But it'd be very easy to drift in the job and I need tightening up by a stiff competitive job. I doubt if the Lord will lead me to Woodbrooke yet!'

He felt similarly about Hull where John Nicholson, a former BBC colleague and now installed as Vice-Chancellor and Principal of University College, was urging him to join the academic staff as Director of the Social

Studies Department. 'Everybody including me is against Hull,' summed up Roger's initial response.

Nicholson, knowing his man, was persistent, outlining what he called some of the attractions – a growing college, the chance to build an authoritative department in a relatively new academic discipline, a job at least as much in the town and countryside as in the college, and the opportunity to make something of rural as well as urban training. 'It needs,' Roger agreed, 'thinking about'.

There can be little doubt, however, that viewed strictly objectively Hull would have joined the other two rejected propositions, but as so often at the crossroads in Roger's life 'the wind bloweth where it listeth', finally leaving him and Margery in no doubt that University College, Hull, it *must* be.

As though confirming the decision they found a house almost as soon as they started looking, in the village of Cottingham, only five miles from the centre of Hull, and the owner, a doctor, though himself not a Quaker, turned out to have been a pupil at both Ackworth and Bootham Friends Schools, and knocked ten per cent off the price because, he said, 'he would like Friends to have the house'.

Beyond question the timing for both a new job and working environment was right. After six years as a relief worker he found himself becoming what he called 'case hardened to misery', a perennial danger to individuals constantly surrounded by appalling human need. Compounding this often unconscious trend was a draining of physical and emotional resources that made him at first touchy and finally – or so he thought – guilty of a 'savage ill-temper'.

Significantly this was denied by his colleagues, one of whom expressed his dismay that Roger, 'one of the most considerate of men', should accuse himself in such terms. 'I hope,' he added, 'that the new job will remove the causes of such distempers, and would myself believe that the heart-rendingly difficult job you've been doing during these years would naturally make uneasy and irritable a mind and heart as catholic as yours.'

Roger was unconvinced. In commenting on a brief report about FRS endeavours for air-raid victims in Britain, he opened on a personal note: 'I have spent the first unbroken month with my family for seven years. Within the family circle my temper is both shorter and noisier than it used to be. To the family's credit this seems to trouble them less than it troubles me. We have talked it over with Friends and friends who have been away from their families for a long time, and we all seem to suffer in the same way. Tiredness? Or worse, arising from our horrible way of living in crowds?'

'Then I notice,' he went on, 'that both I and others are much longer-winded than we use to be. Our letters and documents are much more wordy than the ones we wrote early in the war, and they are woollier. That is why our committees are so long. We go on talking because it is less exhausting than thinking.'

Perhaps once more he was being too hard on himself, for – whether or no – he was soon receiving appeals from the BBC that the series of talks he'd been commissioned to give was so 'meaty' and closely argued that he, rather than the harassed editor, must cut as required to fit into the allotted time.

What cannot be gainsaid was that his hectic war years, leading him to castigate himself for personal failings most of us accept as part and parcel of life, provided a solid foundation for his deeper thinking about social work practice and administration; ideas soon recognized as original if not revolutionary. But first, even before delivering his inaugural lecture, still imbued with the spirit and fellowship of the Society's war victims relief service, he single-handedly initiated a monthly newsletter to every member of FRS still working overseas. The reasoning behind this gigantic unlooked for labour of love was to such a man just plain common sense. He knew that some of his former colleagues received no letters from home at all; others more fortunate still felt deprived of news about Britain beyond their family circle. Roger decided therefore to keep them up-to-date of political, social and moral developments, a monthly letter maintained for almost a decade until he felt it was no longer required. A moment's reflection can estimate the work involved, with up to 150 addresses on his list.

A couple of snippets set the flavour:

> The *Church Times* had a leading article strongly condemning the marriage of a statesman (Sir Anthony Eden) who had already been a party to divorce, and indicating that this was a decline in the standard of public morality which would not have been tolerated a generation ago. The *Manchester Guardian* had a leading article roundly condemning the *Church Times* for prejudiced narrow-mindedness. This brought a spate of correspondence, and the *Guardian* finding room for only a part of it said that the letter writers, in the proportion of about 4 to 1, supported the *Church Times*. That perhaps is a commentary on the kind of people who read the *Manchester Guardian* and write letters to it.

> The appointment of Sir Oliver Franks as British Ambassador in Washington is of rather special interest to Friends. His wife is the sister of Tom Tanner who was Chairman of the FAU (Friends Ambulance Unit) until he was lost at sea in December 1942 on his way to visit the Unit work in the Middle East, India and China. Oliver Franks' mother is a Friend and he was himself born under the shadow of Woodbrooke where his father, Robert Franks, was one of the first members of the teaching staff. FRS members may remember that Oliver Franks came to stay for a month

in the Spartan conditions of the Mount Waltham training centre in the summer of 1944.

But whatever the serious context of anything Roger was writing, humour was never far away, as this final extract from these monthly letters illustrates:

> In a period of religious instruction the teacher asked a small boy who gave them food to eat, and the small boy said it used to be Ben Smith but now it was John Strachey. The teacher declined to accept this answer and gave the small boy another chance by asking about the lovely flowers and fruit, to which the small boy answered Tom Williams. As a final shot, the teacher asked who gave us warmth and light, and the small boy said Emanuel Shinwell. So the teacher asked the next small boy who gave the satisfactory answer *God*. But the first small boy hissed to the second small boy – *You bloody little Tory*.

As the Director of a university department struggling not only to establish itself but to be accepted as an academic discipline at all, Roger lost no time in setting out his programme. Convention had it, he said, that a student enrolled for a course of social studies, and having successfully completed the course graduated as a qualified social worker. Not so, he declared. The job of any social studies department was not to turn out social workers. It could not so easily be done. Social workers needed first of all a broad experience of life, something no university could give. Students possibly had it before they arrived, others acquired it during their studies, always hoped for but never guaranteed. Trainee social workers could at best only be pointed in the right direction, given education as distinct from instruction to facilitate the ability to make sense of whatever life threw at them, first their own life and then that of the persons they were seeking to help. And this ability – no matter how excellent the university training – was related to another mysterious if not mystical dimension – human personality in all its variation.

Why was it, he asked, that individuals sharing a common integrity and commitment differed often so considerably in their intuitive understanding and capacity to get alongside persons with backgrounds, evaluations and problems wholly unlike their own? In searching for an answer he gratefully acknowledged the contributions of Freud, Jung and others in the field of psycho-dynamics, but guarded against disproportionate discussion of such theories – a temptation not restricted to social work students! – by concentrating first of all on involving the undergraduates at the 'coal face' of social deprivation, what he called 'a bellyful of life fired at point-blank range', and then, in lectures, seminars and the like, using *that* in their search for deeper self-awareness and objective understanding of factors beneath the surface of individual and community need.

This same emphasis was made in his choice of student placements, such areas as Tiger Bay in Cardiff and the East End of London, both at the time notorious for their degree of poverty but also the chirpiness of often the most needy. More routinely he led his students on visits to local factories, mills, holiday camps for slum children, orphanages and old people's homes again with the primary aim of helping them and of course himself to see real people and situations in all discussion of social work theory.

All the time he sought to ensure that every member of his department, staff and students alike, should challenge not only the *status quo* of welfare policy and administration but the tendency if not already established convention for social workers to adopt the medical model of despotic diagnosis and arbitrary treatment, the patient or client viewed as little more than a body or case rather than a person capable and indeed ideally required to make a contribution to the healing process. Many years were to pass before this became the accepted wisdom in both professions.

Because other of his ideas were also years ahead of their time, some of the academic demands he made of his students were initially baffling. Nearly fifty years later one of the first group recalled her discomfiture at a title he set for her second essay – 'Relate the Parable of the Good Samaritan to your idea of Social Work'. What he wanted, despite his Quakerism and war relief service, was to kill stone dead the assumption that social work was professional do-goodism and necessarily exclusive to Christian motivation. 'It is a curious arrogance,' he argued, 'which leads us to appropriate as specifically Christian a virtue whose best known expression is attributed by Jesus himself to a non-Christian outsider.' And in so far, he went on, as anybody possessed this same spirit, there was nothing that differentiated Christians from Jews, Muhammadans, Hindus or atheists. It seems barely credible now that his advocacy of this self-evident truism was a necessary debating point at university level, never mind within the narrow confines of institutional religion. Yet even some Friends were among the dissenters!

Roger's distinctive style as thinker and teacher was nowhere better illustrated than at weekly seminars in the Wilsons' own home. Beforehand two students and possibly the guest speaker shared supper with the family. 'It was,' Camilla Case, a student, remembered, 'a simple, generous hospitality. There would not be much small talk, and at times there were silences which those unused to the Quaker tradition found rather difficult. I recall an old professor of physics trying to explain the meaning of his subject by rolling a ball down his leg – I'm not sure now what it was all about! But the memory of those fascinating evenings sitting round a fire is still very vivid even after an interval of nearly fifty years.'

No less unmistakable was the impression Roger made upon her at their first meeting; she already a qualified nurse but feeling intimidated by the university, both generally, and now as she stood waiting at his tutorial door. He immediately put her at ease, gave her every reason to believe he understood her apprehensions, and turned the occasion she'd dreaded into an exciting conversation. Here was, she concluded, an exceptional man. Shortly into the course she changed her mind. 'Exceptional' was too modest by half. Here was also a great man.

Contributing to this assessment was his world-wide vision, superficially grandiose but always geared to the 'nuts and bolts' of national, community and individual welfare. His students, confronted by social needs in city slum or urban wilderment, were encouraged to wrestle with the problems they found there as part of a wider situation notably of post-war Europe.

During his first long summer vacation he returned to Germany, and shared his reactions both at seminars and in a lengthy feature in the old *Manchester Guardian* (4 August 1947). He had seen worst conditions, he pointed out, in East London during the blitz, and in some hen-houses used by British evacuees in 1940/41, but what made the German situation more terrifying than anything he had encountered elsewhere including France and Greece was 'its scale, its comprehensiveness, and its apparent unendingness'.

There was something else about the German situation that was never far from his mind, a moral contradiction he saw at the heart of all human affairs, seats of government no less than scenes of unbelievable debauchery. On the one hand, while Europe was full of evidence of the ghastly corporate brutalities of Germans and their satellites, almost all the people he knew who'd had Germans quartered on them had spoken well of them as men – well-behaved, always 'correct' and quite often actively kind and helpful. But such individual decency appeared to have been totally unrelated to military duties involving the burning of villages or the shooting of hostages. About this gap between personal humanity and organized brutality there appeared to be no means of knowing where one would end and the other begin.

From Germany he moved on to Norway for in part a family holiday but primarily to report on indigenous Quaker activity and potential following the German occupation. Having been repeatedly told and now seeing for himself that Norwegians 'do not think easily or naturally in terms of ideas and principles' he urged that they should be encouraged 'to find their own framework for the basic experience which in Britain would be enshrined in the Society of Friends'. Their national characteristics, their Lutheran background, their educational and social systems all helped to produce a distinctive personality, meaning that Quaker orthodoxy as understood in Britain should not be expected. 'I come back to the point,' he concluded, 'I have made on a number of occasions in the last few years, that we English-speaking Friends have not been helpful to those who share with us an element of Christian experience, but who live in countries with such totally different ecclesiastical histories that the group expression of Quaker experience must find its own national form.'

As for the family holiday in the mountains, it was in itself a rare treat for them all to be together. Anthony was home from another Friends boarding school, having himself decided that this was the best option – proving this time a very happy one – to fulfil his aim or early childhood assumption from which he never for a moment deviated to attend his father's old college and work for the same degree.

Elizabeth, though attending a local school and living at home, nevertheless often felt an outsider, enamoured by neither all the family intellectual talk nor what to her seemed like the endless silence at Quaker Meeting. 'I wasn't,' she explains, 'a thinker, not a deep thinker' – this despite gaining A-levels in, as she puts it dismissively, 'Latin and French, one thing or another'! If deep within herself she felt secure, safe, in the love of her parents, there was still a sense of isolation and loneliness at home. Part of these feelings which even now she finds impossible to articulate without fear of being misunderstood were rooted in her suspicion that her family was somehow 'odd', contrast to the families with whom she joyfully stayed when her own parents were away on university or Quaker business.

On those occasions food seemed more interesting, and the father of the house appeared always to be there, unhurriedly involved, unlike her own father who kept disappearing either into a book, his study or on some duty or other. The major barrier was, she reiterates, her academic *dis*interest.

'When we were living at Cottingham,' she recalls, 'father was giving some talks on the radio, one about family life, and he asked the question, "What's wrong with the family?". He answered it by quoting what we used to say at home – "The way Pop treats the cat". Mother and I were particularly fond of our cat; she ruled the house, more or less, and we would let her sit on the kitchen table. But whenever Daddy came into the room she shot off the table. He was fond of puss but wouldn't let her get away with things as we did.'

What brought her greatest joy on holidays was the chance to invite a schoolfriend along. 'I had someone to talk with as opposed to just being with the family.' These oases of companionship, however, did little to relieve her settled conclusion that she was something of a family misfit.

Anthony on the other hand recalls his childhood as 'very happy', due in no small measure, he believes, to his early love of fishing which remains a passion. Yet he too has no recollection of being able to get really close to his father. Their relationship was always loving and welcoming, providing for the growing boy a sense of fundamental well-being, but as for any sort of openness and intimacy they appear rarely to have existed. Unlike Elizabeth, Anthony contentedly lived in his own world, a bit of a loner, at peace with his books and fishing rod, eager to share the intellectual and Quaker life of his parents.

From his earliest recollection he never doubted that his father was somehow 'different', possessing an importance reaching far beyond the family – his voice frequently heard on the radio, like his name in national and international Press, learned journals, and of course *The Friend*, not to mention his numerous public addresses and lectures, saw to that. Yet looking back to those days and the years since, Anthony is surprised and no less puzzled to realize how little he knew his father, how wide was the emotional and conversational gap between them, notably in the light of the easy free-for-all mutuality he now enjoys with his own children.

Love, warmth, trust and pleasure in each other's company he experienced with his own father in abundance, but as for that much rarer uninhibited meeting of minds and hearts it happened all too infrequently. Despite the undoubted longing on both sides!

One reason was unquestionably Roger's inability to make small talk with anybody, loved one, friend and stranger alike. Another was his shyness and lack of self-confidence, both open to misinterpretation as indifference or insensitivity, and even sounding patronizing when he sought only to praise. But the chief reason of all notably when the children were young was the demands of his work and his Quaker concerns, a comprehensive commitment which drove him on with a sense of divine calling and urgency. All too often his family not only found themselves taking second place but expected to understand why, and approve. In any case, the war meant that Roger was largely separated from his children for six years.

Margery totally shared her husband's vision and spirit, but sometimes wished he was able to find more time for the family. She was kept busy, too, apart from at home with voluntary welfare work, teaching French at the village school, and supporting Roger at the university. The fact of his preoccupations, even his non-availability at home in his study, in no way undermined what she and the children took for granted – his love and devotion as husband and father.

It was ironically only in the final weeks of their father's life that Elizabeth and Anthony, together or separately keeping vigil with Margery by his hospice bed, time paradoxically short but never more plentiful, came to know him on an altogether deeper level, and realized the measure of their loss in earlier times.

Perhaps Roger felt this too. Certainly he perceived the sacrifice and deprivation suffered by the families of zealots driven on by what they believed to be a divine imperative, and – himself suggesting a book should be written about it – set the tone of what he had in mind with David Livingstone's great mission to Africa while his wife Mary Moffatt and their numerous children were left at home almost penniless and finally dependent upon the charity of local Friends at Kendal.

This was more than a plea that charity should begin at home! He admired Livingstone and his achievements, but still saw the subtle inconsistency of men motivated by religion, moral causes, ego-centricity or naked lust for power imposing the price of their own single-mindedness upon their nearest and dearest.

To what extent Roger was thinking of himself is questionable; but there can be no doubt that at least sometimes he denied Margery and the children the one thing they cherished most – his undivided company.

Part of the reason was his zest for work coupled to his belief that life was a mission amounting in his case to a compulsion to use every fleeting moment in service to God and humanity. Another element in his constant busyness was his apparent inability to say No to virtually any request for help of one sort or another. They flowed in, outcome largely of the growing reputation that here was a man with something to say, something distinctive, penetrating and evocative. To be either politely formal or profoundly obvious was happily beyond him. Extreme ideologies, whatever their stage, local, national or international, he detested – one reason why, risking unpopularity not to mention character assassination, he referred to 'the ghastly and degrading trend' of McCarthyism.

On a different tack altogether, illustrating the comprehensiveness of his social concerns, was his acceptance of an invitation to serve as joint secretary of the Hull Council for Old People's Welfare, anything but a sinecure and demanding of his most precious commodity – time. So why did he agree to do it? 'We are all apt to get the impression that old people are a liability to the community while, in fact, they are the very opposite. Their wisdom and experience are of great value, especially to the young,' he explained.

Concurrently he was a member of the Advisory Committee of the National Assistance Board, a member of the local Hospital Management Committee and of the Mental Health Sub-Committee of the Leeds Regional Hospital Board, and also on the local Community Council which in conjunction with the Society of Friends ran a hostel for old people. Illustrating that the busiest of men can always find time for something more, he was one of three main speakers at the inaugural meeting of Christian Action at Oxford, the town hall packed and necessitating the repeating of each address at overspills in two nearby buildings.

Roger's theme, suggested by Canon L. John Collins, the movement's founder, was the inner nature of Friends Relief Service, the subject, six months earlier, of his 1949 Swarthmore Lecture, *Authority, Leadership and*

Concern – a study in motive and administration in Quaker relief work. In the foreword to the printed edition he issued a warning: 'Competitive commitment to the acquisition of visible possessions as such has become so embedded in our economic institutions that there is very little room to assert the reality of other aspects of human motivation; it may indeed be that the world's economic single-mindedness will prove ultimately self-destructive.'

This was one reason why, years later, he was so vehemently an anti-Thatcherite, not merely condemning her policies but the woman herself as advocating values that legitimized selfishness, greed and social divisions. He could barely spit out her name, making her unique in his life-long aspiration to love his neighbour as himself. The Falklands war was the last straw or rather, as he saw it, the inevitable outcome of Thatcherism gone mad. It would be an exaggeration to say that this gentle Quaker hated the woman, but beyond question he detested everything she stood for, and at times the distinction between her and her policies appeared not to count.

In the Swarthmore Lecture itself, admitting that in the Friends Relief Service, 1940–48, 'our action and our principles were always coming adrift', he focussed primarily on principles, the *spirit* of their implementation rather than the self-satisfaction of observing the letter of the law: 'The despotic master of an economic enterprise and the conductor of an orchestra may appear to hold pretty much the same sort of status in an organization chart; so may the "hands" and the musical performers. But, in fact, the relationship between the economic despot and his "hands" is very different from that between the autocratic conductor and his players from whom he cannot extract more than he can inspire them freely to give him. The difference is between authoritarian superiority and inspired leadership.'

Anticipating his interpretation of the Thatcher years, he went on: 'In political life, a government with a secure majority can either use its superior strength to dominate, or, without in any way relinquishing its responsibility, it can extract creative ideas from the opposition and from elements outside the narrowly political field. A sensitive government has an extraordinary knowledge of when to stop arguing and act and when to prolong the discussion in order to let thought and experience mature.'

His fear was that even well-intentioned authoritarianism fostered an I'm-all-right-Jack attitude within society, resulting in the kind of fragmentation that made inevitable a person or family being isolated and overlooked without anybody being any the wiser. At routine lectures to his students as well as at national conferences about aspects of social work he emphasized that meeting the plight of the needy should never be divorced from striving for a change in political structures, for one without the other was surely to perpetuate the client's inescapable dependency upon hand-outs.

'Far better to have a client who is a nuisance because he is struggling to make his own pattern of reality,' Roger told the British National Conference on Social Work at Harrogate, in 1950, 'than one who is not a bit of trouble to anybody because he touches his cap, does what he is told, is duly grateful – and comes back for more. The struggle to make a pattern may take a political or social or an economic form; or, especially among the chronic social casualties, it may take the form of a struggle towards spiritual conviction, vital and creative. We must take pains,' he challenged an all too prevalent concept from the days of Lady Bountiful, 'to see that our social work is not a drug either for ourselves or others.'

This same 'drug' of supposed charity or altruism in mind, he told a radio audience that in human affairs it was much easier to do harm than good, the corollary being that 'when you don't know the facts, have the courage to do nothing', a dictum he frequently addressed to himself having witnessed the devastation caused by 'half-baked' ideas no less than noble ignorance. 'Don't just do something,' he reversed the popular maxim, 'stand there'; stand there until the way forward more than placated a guilty conscience or induced a show of futile zeal.

Nearly fifty years later it's hard to believe that such ideas not only needed to be underlined to professional social workers, but also ran counter to assumptions within the profession itself. Rather like his insistence upon the *spiritual* dimension in social work which shocked many and infuriated not a few. Asked to review two publications about social work training and practice, he wrote that one 'demonstrates the dreadful lack of any deeply rooted common agreement among the universities as to what it is they are trying to do' while the other confirmed that existing university courses generally had not yet come to grips 'with the relation of the purposes of God to the purposes and abilities of man, a reflection of the agnosticism of university outlooks'.[1]

He concluded that university teachers would do well to re-think their courses in the light of the conviction of their practical colleagues that social workers must be required to grapple with the nature of the universe. 'What the Christian citizen is entitled to ask is whether, at any point, the social student is helped to come to a sense of the purposes of God, for without such a sense the best social work is not more than competent plumbing where plumbing is not enough.'

Among those rejecting such a perspective was Barbara Wootton whose books Roger generally admired, but not her latest, *Testament for Social Science*, which he was invited to review in *The Friend*. 'This is,' he told the editor, 'an extremely disappointing book, particularly bearing in mind the quality of her earlier books.' He went on: '*Testament of Social Science* seems primarily

---

[1] *The Friend*, January 1947.

designed to give her a means of attacking Christianity and to a lesser extent Communism because they stand in the way of what she conceives to be a relentless pursuit of scientific truth which is as valid in the field of human affairs as in the field of the physical sciences. Better done, the book would be more challenging. As it is, it is irritating partly because the tone of it is petulant rather than constructively critical.'

However, having reached this conclusion, he wasn't sure about the next step. Should the book be reviewed in *The Friend* at all? 'If one only gives it 300 words one can only be negative, which is a bit unfortunate in relation to an author of her repute dealing with the subject in a way offensive to Christians, and a very short review of this kind might suggest that we are on the defensive.' Just so. But a longer review pointing out the book's limitations would suggest that it was worth something, and 'it is not worth much'. So what to do? 'Hesitantly therefore because it may be the coward's way out – I know Barbara Wootton of course and should not enjoy particularly meeting her after doing a damning review – I suggest that you simply do not review it. But if you would like something let me know and I will make a draft.' The book wasn't reviewed.

Another insight into the wheels within wheels of reviewing was provided when Roger's advice was sought by the BBC about how best to present B. Seebolm Rowntree's long-awaited new book on *English Life and Leisure*: should it be with a series of talks or just one, on the Third Programme or where? Having agreed that the new book was not going to be in the same street as Rowntree's other works, Roger explained his personal dilemma: 'It would not be difficult to decide what to do about all this were it not for the fact that I know, and you can guess, how much BSR is looking forward to reviews and publicity for the thing. For two or three years past he has told the Rowntree Trustees at each Quarterly Meeting that the BBC had promised to review it on the day of publication, and it would be a fearful blow to him if this did not happen. I would grant you that BSR's personal feelings are hardly a relevant factor in deciding what the BBC ought to do about a work on its own merit, but I am not inclined to dissociate myself in quite that way. I think the thing is probably worth a single review, perhaps in the Third Programme, very soon after publication, but I do not for a moment think it would stand anything more than fifteen minutes, several of which might well be spent by the reviewer paying tribute to BSR's nearly sixty years of survey work.'

Clearly the feelings of an old man took precedence over a hurtful public assessment of his latest work. Accused of intrusive sentiment or academic compromise, Roger would have concurred – without the slightest sense of guilt. He knew that his own subjectivity affected the objectivity of his every judgment; the only area of uncertainty was the degree of his self-awareness and the integrity of his motivation.

His own book reviewing notably in *The Friend* was so frequent that he suggested his name or even initials should be omitted if too many of his pieces were wanted for the same issue.

All this extra work over and above his mainline responsibilities was, of course, of his own choosing, but not invariably so. When professional social workers, for instance, were seeking to establish their own Guild akin to a trade union to safeguard standards of practice it was understandable that they should look to Roger's drive and ideas for guidance, but this was surely no reason why – no matter how apologetically – they should bother him with such matters during a family holiday! It was, they explained, the lesser of two evils. The greater evil was the collapse of the Guild, leading them to the admission that 'members must take more responsibility and cease to depend so entirely on your energy and initiative'.

Such appeals happened not because Roger refused to delegate or sought to hog the limelight. The simple fact of the matter was that he was unmistakably so head-and-shoulders above his peers that they naturally turned to him for inspiration and leadership. To what extent he sometimes allowed himself to be exploited for the sake of their common goal is an open question. Certainly as far as *work* was concerned he appeared not to know the meaning of moderation. And having accepted an assignment he was incapable of being other than thorough in both preparation and execution.

This was typified by the lecture he gave to the Friends Historical Society, in January 1949, about the *Manchester Guardian*, a hugely enjoyed occasion but demanding mammoth research which yielded cameos of particular interest to Roger himself. One was about the great C.P. Scott being rejected by the Queen's College, Oxford (Roger's own) 'because he could produce no certificate of baptism'. Corpus Christi finally agreed to take him without a 'religious test' but sought to enforce its rule that all undergraduates must attend College chapel. The Dean and Scott eventually negotiated a deal to their mutual honour – he, Scott, would go to chapel except on Sundays and Saint's Days. In fact, having satisfied his principles, he attended chapel regularly and became a leading light in reorganizing the chapel singing.

Further endearing Scott to Roger was his courage when public fury burst over his head for his paper's opposition to the Boar War from start to finish, reminiscent of Roger's father's experience during the First World War, and requiring protection by the police from an incensed public.

The same courage on a different front was being exemplified by Roger's father in his devoted care of his wife, progressively incapacitated with dementia; a courage both inspirational and humbling. In one of her more lucid moments she told Roger how close they felt to him in all his work for God and international peace; and of how they hoped to move back to the north where she and her husband felt most at home, and could spend the rest of their lives together free of care, explorers still into the riches of God's grace.

No less touching was his father's constant insistence that the last thing either he or his wife wanted was to hinder him in all he was doing, activities they shared with him in spirit and supported with their prayers. Such herculean courage and self-disregard was paradoxically of great concern to the whole Wilson family, for they wanted to help but felt respectfully constrained by their parents' proud independence; proud but not unrealistic, a pride nourished by humility, strength made perfect in weakness. How else to describe qualities as indefinible as they were real!

Much of the talk whenever Roger visited was of Quaker gossip and humour which Roger with all his contacts appeared to have an inexhaustible supply: 'We were discussing the condition of one of our Yorkshire graveyards. A Friend expressed the hope that its name and purpose were clearly stated on the gate. Another Friend said that she had seen a Friends' graveyard with a notice saying that it was a 'Friends' Sleeping Place'; but she did not think this sufficiently distinguished it from a Meeting House.'

'One of my colleagues in FRS who was returning to civilian life had to buy a house to live in and had to go heavily into debt to do it. Within a few weeks he was unexpectedly appointed to another job. So, rather embarrassed, he went to the house agent and explained that he wanted to sell again. "That's all right," said the agent, "we'll easily get £1000 more than you gave for it." "Oh," reacted the ex-relief worker, I couldn't make a profit like that. I'm a Quaker. Make it £500."'

Roger's father loved such stories, and responded to them with a capacity for humour few suspected, a capacity sustained despite the sad domestic situation he faced every day without the merest suggestion of self-pity or complaint. His care for his wife was as gentle as it was patient and comprehensive, exemplifying his life-long sense of duty which in this case was given wings by the spirit of triumphant acceptance that governed their joint understanding of God's providence and grace.

Roger, like his brothers and sister, tried to make every visit a time of light relief for his parents. It wasn't easy. Conversation with his mother, never effortless, was now more difficult than ever. With his father it was more straightforward, a mutuality of enjoyment, talk about the ideals and causes that bound them ever closer as the years slipped by. But the fundamental situation was unchangeable, only to be faced and lived through, as the older man was prone to say, 'one day at a time'.

Roger could have said the same about his own daily pressures, but they so matched his enthusiasm that such an outlook never crossed his mind. Each day was rich in variety and opportunity offering more than enough personal fulfilment and sheer happiness to give his sense of humour, even when serious, full play. Invited to address a meeting of Hull businessmen about his work, he told them: 'University teaching has two facets – educating the young on the one hand, and on the other pushing forward the frontiers of knowledge. Some of us are perhaps better at one than the other; some of us enjoy teaching so much that we have given up thinking; others so enjoy thinking that they say university life would be all right if it weren't for the students. I stand,' he concluded, 'somewhere in between.'

But not 'somewhere in between' when it came to other matters! He went on: 'To many an academic, it is much easier to go on amassing knowledge than to pause and attempt to understand it. Some would say that understanding is no business of the university. I cannot agree. Knowledge is too important a social commodity to be allowed to float round in a detached sort of way . . . The danger of knowing without understanding is to feel at home among familiar labels of the local intellectual slot-machine but quite lost in any part of the world where the labels were different.'

Such speaking engagements, both local and national, involving long preparation and frequently longer journeys, Roger saw not as extraneous to his central responsibilities at the university but as inseparable from them, a coherent whole and single commitment. Little wonder, then, that his children though never doubting *who* their father was – an exceptional man and fearsomely busy – often wondered *where* he was; not unlike their mother who frequently found it necessary to track him down by appealing to his colleagues and friends for a last sighting! The man was a piece of quicksilver, intolerant of unpunctuality, viewing time-wasting as a cardinal sin, and demonstrating that by redeeming the fleeting moment he could manage twice as much work as the average busy person.

By now, the end of 1950, he was like Margery unreservedly settled at Hull, revelling in the challenge of his central academic interest – social work studies and practice – attracting to his department an annual increase of students, incidentally two to one in favour of men, a trend reversal he neither understood nor necessarily approved, and putting down roots in the local community. His neighbours showed towards him the same affection and admiration he felt for their north-eastern blunt openness; his university colleagues, grateful for his amiable personality as well as his outstanding gifts, respected, even revered, him; his widening reputation as a pioneering influence in social studies saved him from any approach of frustration at provincial obscurity or limitation. He had every reason to believe and indeed hope that the rest of his days might be centred in Hull.

His ever-growing personal correspondence, too, kept him in touch with the international scene. He wrote to Anthony, still at boarding school but soon to leave for Oxford: 'An old school pal of mine has been appointed Moscow representative of the *Sunday Times* – the only British paper to have been able to get a Moscow rep. appointed. So I wrote to him, saying that I thought the *Sunday Times* was a rotten paper, but that I looked forward to his dispatches.'

Enclosed with Anthony's letter was a copy of Roger's second talk of his series of three on the Welfare State, broadcast on the Third Programme, and published in *The Listener*, but surprisingly no referrence to a recent letter from the University of Bristol: 'My senate has decided,' wrote Professor Basil Fletcher, Director of the Institute of Education, 'to institute a second Chair in Education, co-equal to the first . . . I wondered if the possibility of filling a Chair of Education had ever crossed your mind. Perhaps it is a fantastic suggestion,' he anticipated Roger's likely reaction, 'and you are committed to a social studies line of work. But there are special educational opportunities in this region, and of a Christian kind.'

Roger, naturally flattered, was frankly bemused. He knew nothing about the teaching of education! Unhesitatingly he underlined this in his reply, to which came the immediate response, as concise as disarming: 'What's that got to do with it? It's *you* we want.' Indeed it was; and they left no stone unturned to persuade Roger that Bristol offered the greater opportunity for his gifts both to teach in a field he claimed to know nothing about and to develop his own strong social studies interest as part of the Institute of Education's own curriculum.

Ironically, as he found himself the focal point of a tug of war between the Hull Vice-Chancellor (still John H. Nicholson), more a much admired personal friend than his boss, and the combined pull of Sir Philip Morris, Vice-Chancellor at Bristol, and Professor Fletcher, Roger's dilemma was further confused by an invitation from the University of Edinburgh for him to become Director of the Department of Social Study and Training, an offer likewise out of the blue and – despite no immediate professorial Chair – mightily attractive for reasons Roger himself outlined: 'the distinction of the University itself, its attraction for good students, the fruitful possibilities in a Department which includes Diploma, Certificate and Mental Health students, and the chance of collaborating with a medical school . . . upon such bases it should be possible in certain conditions to develop a Department of distinction.'

Of the three, Hull, Bristol, Edinburgh, there can be little doubt that the last tugged strongest, not least because of the firm assurance of comprehensive support in his wish to establish a clinic for social work clients and research in co-operation with the medical faculty and the Department of Social Medicine. So why did he hesitate?

Niggling at the back of his mind was the awareness that at Edinburgh, in contrast to Hull, the subject of social studies, even after more than twenty years, had not yet won its place in the main stream of university departments, meaning – and this was the rub – that freedom to develop would involve a struggle at every step for the confidence of both Senate and Council. This in itself, it seemed to Roger, at least intimated a university too staid and inflexible to live at peace with fundamental change.

His frankness brought renewed assurances from the Principal and Vice-Chancellor, Sir Edward Appleton, who also mentioned 'a very real possibility of promotion to the status of Reader' though he readily acknowledged that with a professorship already on offer such an inducement was irrelevant and in any case for this particular candidate clearly superfluous. But about the central issue, the Senate's recognition through representation on its body of the Department of Social Study and Training, nothing could be guaranteed. Nevertheless, he enclosed a personal letter to Roger when formally offering him the appointment: 'I would like to add a further word, and that is to say how delighted those of us who met you would be to see you joining us. I think I can claim that we, here, are a happy ship, and that I think you would like us if you came!.'

No sooner had Roger settled for Bristol than he received a confidential express letter from the United Nations Educational Scientific and Cultural Organization inviting him to consider becoming the Director of a Division of Education and Welfare for Palestinian refugees. The salary, like the expense allowance, was attractive with tax concessions! If he could agree to secondment from his present job for twelve months, high level UNESCO representations would be made to the United Kingdom government and university authorities.

Roger, aware he could hardly request secondment from a job he hadn't yet even started, deeply regretted his inability to respond. One can only speculate what difference it would have made to the rest of his life if the invitation had arrived a matter of only weeks before, for the spirit of his work with war victims was still his motivation, ordering his priorities and making him largely indifferent to the fruits of worldly status and success. All he could honourably do in the circumstances was decline but promise ready co-operation if such an invitation was repeated in a couple of years or so.

This settled, he turned his undivided mind to the opportunities awaiting in Bristol.

12

Provincial Professor with World Vision

1951-1956

One of the appeals of Bristol University to Roger was its internationalism, its eagerness to take students from overseas not only to enlarge *them* educationally but also *itself* to benefit from the richness of their national traditions and culture.

Shortly before assuming his new responsibilities his own world vision had taken him and Margery to the United Nations Headquarters in New York at the invitation of the Friends World Committee for Consultation to the Economic and Social Council of the UN. Quaker House, essentially a private home as distinct from an office, provided, as Roger himself put it, for UN employees at all levels the sort of fellowship, emotional and intellectual, that binds individuals together as friends rather than business acquaintances, professional colleagues or people who want Quakers to do something. The common aim – of Friends and UN personnel alike – was how to translate desires for international peace into effective working shape, and how to relate the daily practice of politics to fundamental spiritual principles. Into this family setting came heads of important delegations who declared that the very *feel* of the place, apart from helping them to unwind and talk without fear, refreshed them as nowhere else in New York.

By now, and throughout the rest of his life, Roger found it impossible, though still a Socialist in outlook, to identify himself with the Labour Party or indeed any other political party in his own country or elsewhere; impossible because no government or opposition party was pacifist or likely to be in the foreseeable future. And this absence of what he called a 'resting place in the field of international affairs' was 'very frustrating to a person like himself who so completely shared the outlook, common to the Society of Friends, that Christian conviction should lead to personal and corporate responsibility in political matters'.

So he revelled in this Quaker House experience from which he emerged convinced that whatever the conflicting viewpoints about how Friends' representation at the UN was to be organized and administered – at the time a matter of lively debate – this was secondary to the recognition that a creative movement had taken place and must be allowed freedom to grow. 'Nothing would be more irresponsible,' he summed up, 'than for the Society to attempt to organize itself in so clear-cut a way that inspiration and imagination and leadership would be subordinated to the system.'[1]

This was uppermost in his mind when at Friends Yearly Meeting shortly after his return he spoke about a recent Quaker Mission to Moscow as 'the most striking event in the history of Friends for some time' and underlined 'that Friends have something to say that is worth listening to by busy statesmen, politicians, national and international civil servants – not generalities but real light on current issues, only graspable by experts'. Waffling on the other hand would receive only what it deserved – disregard or contempt. 'But it is clear,' he concluded, 'that our fellows expect us to give what we can; and if that has to be given spectacularly or confidentially by a few at the diplomatic level, let us remember that our service in our locality and our worship in our local meeting is the place where in the purposes of God it all begins and ends.'

A bonus of his stay at Quaker House was the opportunity to meet readers of his 'English Notes' published regularly in *The Friend* of Philadelphia, requested by the Editor in 1946 and maintained from then for a decade. What appealed was the Wilsonian mix of seriousness and humour guaranteed by its freshness to tease the mind into a re-examination of traditional ideas and assumptions.

Shortly before he actually assumed his new responsibilities at Bristol, further evidence of this writing industry was the publication of his book *Quaker Relief*,[2] an account of the Society of Friends' service for war victims, 1940–48. Running to 374 pages, it was well received by the religious and secular Press alike, *The Times* describing it as 'a well-written account of a fine service performed in unprecedented circumstances'; and the *Church of England Newspaper* as 'this wonderful record of humanitarian work at home and abroad during and after the war which both sociologists (of every religion) and students of international affairs will find of permanent value'.

Roger himself never doubted a main lesson of Quaker relief – it had no room for *stars*. All FRS workers had to be prepared to be nameless. 'In 1947,' he recalled, 'the French government offered decorations to two members of the Service in token of the work done in and after 1944. After hurried consultation it was agreed that it would hurt the French donors more to refuse than it would hurt the Quakers to accept. So a letter was sent to the French expressing our appreciation and our hesitation to accept on the ground that the work was done for a sense of obligation before God rather

---

[1] 'Friends and International Politics', p.8, reprinted from *The Friends' Quarterly*, April 1952.

[2] Published by Allen and Unwin 1952.

than to earn thanks of humanity. Back came the reply that the French government recognized that we would prefer our reward in the next world but that they were glad that we could, after all, accept it in this. We were therefore highly appreciative of the words used by Doctor Gunnar Jahn in presenting Friends with the Nobel Peace Prize in 1948, when he referred to Quaker Service as *from the nameless to the nameless*.'

Desirous himself of living in such a spirit, he now faced the unavoidable spotlight of being the professorial newcomer at Bristol. The University, largely through the influence of its Vice-Chancellor (Philip Morris), whose appointment in 1946 was itself as remarkable as the daring innovations he facilitated during the next twenty years, offered a perfect setting for Roger's impatience with an irrelevant *status quo*. Morris caught the newcomer's outlook perfectly when he said that the 'biggest single issue of modern times is that men and women will content themselves with an unthinking capitulation to what seem to be the insistent demands of the immediate present'. What he sought were educational institutions alive with the movement and enjoyment of human thought, communities 'groping for the wisdom that would make life more than its possessions and hierarchies' and universities 'becoming the nursing mothers of the men, women and values and ideas that are needed to sustain a free responsible society, guided by light and truth rather than by makeshifts and possessions'.[3] All those coming within the orbit of this brilliant educationist's vision and undemonstrative strength found it hard to believe that his Vice-Chancellorship at Bristol was his first university appointment.

Roger opened his inaugural lecture with characteristic self-mocking: 'When this university did me the honour of inviting me to accept a Chair of Education, it was clearly understood that, although I believed that Education was probably the most important thing men do, yet about Education in any particular sense I knew little. However, the appropriate officers of the University had absorbed at any rate part of the truth revealed in one of the great contemporary books on the subject, A.N. Whitehead's *Aim of Education*, for he asserts that the function of a university professor is to exhibit himself as an ignorant man, thinking. The University has made no mistake about the first part of the formula. Whether I can fulfil the second part must remain in suspense for some years yet.'

Also typically he early seized the opportunity to pay tribute to two of his own educators, one internationally lauded, the other barely known: 'Paton was my former headmaster; I know what Miss Helen Wodehouse (first Professor of Education at Bristol, and the first woman to hold such a post in a

---

[3] *A University for Bristol*, Bristol University Press 1985, p. 52.

British university) means when she speaks of the "succession of wise and kindly men who have cared for the helplessness of youth". For Paton, fine scholar that he was, established human relationships as firmly with a class of ten-year-olds on his annual visit to the junior school as he did with his Prefects: with no sacrifice of academic quality, what inspired his teaching was a quality of affection which as Bertrand Russell points out can be expressed by a great educator but not by a local education authority. Paton had his weaknesses; I doubt if he was much judge of a man. Fortunately young schoolmasters had a habit of choosing Paton. One of them was Gordon Cox of this city, a very great teacher of history who died lamentably young; he made learning irresistible.'

What followed was a meticulously-researched history of educational pioneers, a step-by-step guide to the wider acceptance of ideas once thought not only dangerous but harbingers of industrial and societal disintegration.

'Education seems to me,' he revealed the aim and motivation of his own teaching, 'to derive from the inspiration of the two great teachers of the Western World, Socrates and Jesus of Nazareth who were both executed by the societies in which they lived because they stimulated some of their contemporaries to profound and socially disrupting wrestling with the very nature of truth. The true educationist seems to me to live, however humbly and whether he knows it or not, in the tradition of Socrates and Jesus, helping the child to grapple critically with inert spiritual, intellectual and social institutions of the day, and so giving a pattern of his own to incoherent experience as it hurls itself at him. This is the way in which men in some measure step beyond contemporary society and make the future.'

Thus his call for teachers at all levels to be *radicals*: 'In our sort of society at any rate people are wanted who can devise change and who can adapt; who can invent and discover; who can criticize and who can see when criticism is sound and when it is shallow; the health of our society depends on widespread ability to create and to enjoy aesthetic achievement and to speculate and to worship. Yet these long-term social abilities are a standing threat to the orderly way in which things get done at any given time. Our kind of society depends precisely on this sort of tension being robustly maintained, and it is primarily the educators who have to hold the claws of the future against the innumerable parties demanding current competence, a position all the more difficult because the educator is also the instructor.'

This lengthy and cogently argued lecture, no less relevant today as when delivered, was skilfully lightened with Roger's brand of humour. He told, for instance, the story of a school inspector in the 1850s trying to get away from the sterility of formal composition by asking children to write on things they knew about. 'The racehorse,' one eleven-year-old responded, 'is a very noble animal, used very cruel by gentlemen. Races are very bad places. None but wicked people know about races. The last Derby was won by Mr I. Anson's *Blinkbonny*, a beautiful filly by Melbourne, rising four. The odds were 20 to 1 against her; thirty started and she won by a neck.'

When the inspector, the Rev. W.H. Brookfield, showed this to one of the school managers, the latter said, 'I am very sorry indeed for this. He was always a good little boy till now'. Brookfield commented: ' . . . notwithstanding the ominous "now", the intelligent and amiable appearance of the child and the good character I heard of him gave colour to the hope . . . that he may yet clear the treadmill.'

Within three months, on the other side of the world, Roger experienced a 'Brookfield' of his own. Attending a conference in Madras about the Role of Social Services in Raising Standards of Living, he was taken to a village some fifteen miles from Lahore to visit two schools, one for boys, the other for girls. 'The only sign of life I saw at either school,' he said, 'was an illicit scribble on a wall in the girls' school where a child had drawn a bird eating a mango. I congratulated the headmistress on it, and commented on it in the visitors' book. But I have a feeling that this was not popular!'

He arrived for the conference in early December, and was surprised to be met by a representative of the British High Commissioner who whisked him through customs and put him in a diplomatic car to be taken to stay with the Deputy High Commissioner, the High Commissioner himself, apologies were offered, being away in East Pakistan. Why this VIP treatment, he wondered? Was it to do with his chairmanship of the British delegation to the conference or perhaps the influence of his brother Geoffrey, Technical Director of the Colombo Plan, a scheme for the relief of backward countries within the British Empire? He was never sure.

No less surprising both during the conference and his subsequent seven or eight weeks travelling in India, Pakistan and Ceylon as it was then called was the warmth shown to Great Britain and the British. He illustrated this in one of his pieces for *The Friend* published in Philadelphia: 'As you probably know the tension is high between India and Pakistan, and the security and customs staff on both sides of the frontier are, in general, nosier than I have ever seen at work. Not only do Indians give Pakistanis a terrific searching and vice versa, but most European and American passport holders are also subjected by both Indians and Pakistanis to laborious questioning and form filling. The only people who sail through both sets of officials in a couple of minutes without a fuss or a check-up are the holders of British passports.'

He then described two successive meetings in Parliament House at Delhi. The first was the public opening of a UNESCO seminar on the application of Gandhian ideals to national and international tensions. Altogether it was a distinguished occasion and the audience was appreciative. Half-an-hour after that meeting had dispersed a new meeting convened to hear ex-Prime

Minister Attlee make a speech on his way through to an Asian Socialist Conference in Burma.

The Parliament House was crammed to bursting for him, and when he came in the whole audience rose spontaneously to its feet, and the clapping at appropriate points in the meeting was the most vigorous Roger had heard at any gathering in India. The contrast, he said, between the normal appreciation of the audience at the first important and distinguished meeting, and the quite spontaneous enthusiasm at the meeting of which Attlee was the sole attraction was, certainly to Roger, not only surprising but moving.

Even more surprising but, he thought, less significant was the occasion at the end of the Madras Conference when a student approached him and said he would be very much obliged if one of the British delegation returning to London would send him a picture of Mr Churchill whom, Roger concluded his piece for America doubtless to the horror of some of his readers, 'I regard as the most outstanding of our remaining imperial villains!'

As for the Conference itself he kept his usual detailed diary of astute observation, humour and contrasts:

Night after night as we went home we saw people sleeping on pavements, their only *home* . . . The security, elegance, intelligence, friendliness of our Conference went right alongside the savage brutality of life in an *under-developed area* caught up in the tide of world events . . .

Sunday meeting (Friends) at Upper Wood Street Calcutta, was shattering. We began at 10 with 4; by 10.20 we were 10 of whom one was reading a newspaper, one an illustrated magazine – both strangers – and one a book. I read the 19th psalm without comment, the only ministry. In talking afterwards one of the non-readers said he had come by mistake, since the Lord had guided him to come but had misinformed him about the kind of meeting it would be; and another who was very deaf said he thought all ministry was a mistake. We broke up at 10.30 but chatted until 11.30.

Lahore, first Sunday of 1953. Morning meeting was good, I thought. About 30 there, half and half, Indian and European. The Indians included the Home Secretary and the Europeans the German Legal Advisor to the Indian Government. The best thing about it was the quality of the silence. One young Sikh spoke quite unsuitably but the meeting absorbed it.

The next day he needed that quality of silence as the Head of Delhi School of Social Work, thoroughly demoralized, sought his counsel. She explained that the students, led by an ex-member of staff, had kicked up a frightful fuss about the frank honesty of her testimonials and also her insistence on a high standard of work. Consequently a decision had been taken early in December to close the school and send the students down. Questions were asked in Parliament and the Prime Minister himself agreed to look into the situation. He reported he was satisfied with the action taken. But now the Head couldn't get her committee to meet to decide what to do next. They claimed they were too busy!

Such an aspect of social work education was new to Roger – his time would come during the student sit-ins and the like in the late 1960s – but the same pastoral concern shown to the Head in Delhi was immediately needed on his return to Bristol.

'Your nephew,' he answered a frantic enquiry from Sydney, Australia, 'was not at Hull but here at Bristol last year, doing his Certificate in Education course. We all liked him very much indeed, and I saw quite a bit of him. I am not myself very much worried about his Communism. He is a Communist for the right kind of reasons, even if it leads him to keep pretty unsatisfactory political company. He is much too sound a character to be ultimately corrupted, and in the meanwhile I think he probably does his fellow Communists more good than they do him harm. He ought, I think, to make a really good job of teaching.'

The one thing he could not tolerate in students was under-achievement through laziness. He accepted that finally they must be responsible for themselves, and face their own nemesis, but if his ambition for them exceeded theirs his gentle prodding and probing was unrelenting, appreciated usually only in retrospect.

What he also couldn't bear was injustice to students and staff alike, whether located in the University's own administration or the result of impersonal bureaucracy elsewhere. 'But for Roger and Margery Wilson,' wrote a student from Botswana, 'I might never have completed my studies. I was admitted to the University of Bristol for a two-year course for the degree of Master of Arts in Education. The British Council awarded me a one-year scholarship on the understanding that my government would pay for the second year.

'I was three-quarters of the way through my first year when the government reversed its decision and I was faced with the indignity and disappointment of returning home without completing the course. Professor Wilson tried to negotiate with the Director of Education in Botswana or Bechuanaland as it was then called, but to no avail. Bristol University was not amused. I was determined to finish my course and decided to stay, even if it meant working vacations and at week-ends. Then Roger and Margery Wilson offered me free hospitality in their own home; and the British Council volunteered half the fees if my government paidthe other half. I got my degree!

'Apart from material help and professional guidance, Professor Wilson influenced my life in his humanitarian caring manner towards the disadvantaged, and his sympathetic and forgiving attitude towards everyone.'

This student, Gaositwe Chiepe, eventually became Botswana's Minister for External Affairs.

The Wilsons' home was likewise open to many, far more than most people ever suspected. One reason was that, as a staff colleague put it, Roger's left hand never knew what his right hand was doing. No less to the point he somehow found the needed funds, either from his own pocket or a small trust set up by his parents for such emergencies or by appealing to charitable bodies of which he appeared to know an inordinate number. If Roger had a failing in this area it was that at times he tended to overlook or under-estimate the extra work his open-house philosophy imposed upon his wife, largely, it must be said, because Margery herself so completely shared his spirit of hospitality, not hospitality as a social exercise or entertainment but rather of the kind that took people into their home for a week, a month, a year, as long as necessary.

'Generous hospitality,' recalled Wendy Robinson, 'was a wonderful part of our student life. Roger and Margery had regular open meetings in their home in Stuart House. We would all sit on every available bit of space and listen to someone who had been asked to come and speak informally about what life was really like for them in their professional work. I remember especially Eric James and Edward Blishen, so different as men, yet so alike in their capacity to stir mind and imagination.

'We really believed in those days in something called creative education. Roger, who always had a particular dislike of what he tended to call "stuffed shirts", had a real knack for getting the powerful to speak "off the cuff". It was all part of our realization that the best things in education are caught not taught. Margery's and Roger's hospitality is written in my heart for during a difficult time in my life they asked me to live with them in Stuart House. I have always said to them that since then the one sure, still point in a turning world was the absolute knowledge that there would always be boiled eggs and the Bible for breakfast at 8 o'clock sharp in the Wilson household. I mention this because I know how many students of all nationalities became part of the Wilson "extended family".'

Roger was sufficiently self-aware to know that injustice, deliberate or unintended, frequently asserted itself in most surprising places, not least a loving home where parents, as he put it, 'will always be a bit resistant to change'. The answer was for parents, like governments, to be pressurized to change, and the contribution of children in the home to this end was of immeasurable importance. And if, he told his students training to be teachers, the children were to do their job properly, they needed behind them the sensitive support of a wise school.

To what extent, if at all, Roger's own children wanted their parents to change is an open question, but certainly Elizabeth, since the family's arrival at Bristol, had taken on a new lease of life through the sensitive support of a wise school and teacher.

'I went to Bath High,' she recollects, 'where I met this music teacher who was fairly young, and we just clicked. Music suddenly became *the* thing in my life. I joined the Bath Bach Choir, and my whole life from then on revolved around music making. I used to stay the night at Bath after choir; then I did become very happy because I'd found something that I really wanted to do, and people to do it with.'

Paradoxically, though Roger rejoiced at Elizabeth's musical blossoming, and did everything possible to encourage it, she still felt restricted in sharing her new life with him, for musically he was a novice, content with occasional Mozart and Beethoven, while she continued to lack the aptitude or wish to more than skirmish his academic interests. What she profoundly appreciated was his enthusiastic and practical support when she decided to go to the Royal College of Music, in London, a time during which, feeling her worship could better be expressed through music, she joined the Church of England, with the full support of both parents.

Almost a decade later, her promising operatic career necessarily abandoned through a recurring throat infection, she likewise appreciated not only their sympathy but their hard-headed attention to all the implications. 'I went to all sorts of specialists,' she remembered those days, 'but nobody could help. I had the voice but not the stamina. Singing was the one thing I wanted to do.'

What in fact she did was to devote herself mainly to teaching, both singing and the piano, again with her parents' strong but non-intrusive support.

Non-intrusive – that was the key word. Indeed it could be argued that Roger's own children unconsciously demonstrated the independence of thought and judgment he saw as the essential outcome of education as distinct from instruction and training. For unless individuals developed the capacity to resist pressures to conform – for family or group approval, societal advancement, easy popularity, membership of the inner circle – they were, in Roger's terms, possibly knowledgeable but certainly not educated.

'If 100% success in the orthodox academic race is not *necessarily* the mark of a good teacher, what *is*?' he asked his students. Is it to teach children how to keep their heads and noses clean?'

This question of *What Are Schools For?* was never far from his mind. 'I must confess,' he told a packed lecture hall, 'that when I suggested this title I expected a snug little meeting of a score or two where we could talk together about our children, and where I could listen at least as much as talk. In face of this audience I'm at a bit of a loss because it's clear that I shall have to do most of the talking myself, and my wife said that if I did most of the talking you'd expect me to give some sort of answer. One of my children, on the other hand, when she saw the question took a pencil and increased the number of question marks to five. So there we are – you've got to listen while we look at one of the most difficult questions that anybody can ask.'

Of course it wasn't only the title that, unexpectedly to Roger, packed them in, but the honesty and openness of the lecturer, his apparent inability to be other than interesting and evocative by shunning easy answers as much as academic claptrap, illustrated by his reference to William Rathbone wanting to call his little book *Muddle Versus Method and Waste in Charitable Work* but being persuaded by pompous friends to call it *Reference to the Organization of Effort in Works of Benevolence and Public Utility*!

Roger somehow managed clarity in his lectures without sacrificing profundity. He seemed to have read everything which meant he was never short of stories and quotations from history, but the contemporary scene was his favourite source of illustrations. At his *What Are Schools For?* lecture, for instance, he spoke of a schoolmaster recently taken to court by five parents for caning a whole class for stamping on the stairs. As part of his defence his solicitor declared that parents complained about juvenile delinquency, cosh boys and lack of discipline, putting the blame on schools. But what were teachers to do, he asked, if they couldn't impose discipline?

'Well,' asked Roger, 'is that a fair point? Are schools places for discipline?' 'In a special sense, *yes*,' he answered his own question. 'But *not* for the kind of discipline of which either the solicitor or teacher was thinking. The caning may or may not have done the boys good or harm, but the other part of the punishment was to make them write out passages of the Bible instead of playing football! If *that's* the measure of that school's idea of its job, treating the Bible as an instrument of punishment thereby destroying both its spiritual importance and possible enjoyment of its superb language – I'm not surprised,' he concluded, 'there's trouble with discipline.' The teacher was found not guilty.

'Take care,' Roger often quoted Mark Twain's dictum, 'that your son's schooling doesn't interfere with his education.' Few occupations were more exacting, he warned, than that of a teacher who cared about education, for education was the stimulus to create rather than the inculcation of habit. But this meant an unending struggle with educational institutions which, like most social institutions, tended to standardize practice rather than to liberate the spirit. To reinforce this emphasis about which he felt passionately, he turned to what he called yet another wise observation of A.N. Whitehead: 'An education which does not begin by evoking initiative and end by encouraging it must be wrong.'[4]

---

[4] For a detailed discussion of this whole section, see Roger Wilson, *The Teacher: Instructor or Educator*, University of Bristol Institute of Education 1954.

This protest against outward conformity at the price of inward liberty was another of the themes to which he frequently returned usually in terms of the corporate versus the individual. While the former, he said, *tended* to be rigid, conservative and formal, the latter *tended* to be experimental, but they were not necessarily incompatible, and the key to spiritual life was the preservation of the creative tension between the individualist and the corporate ends of the spectrum.

'At its best, godliness is a sensitive understanding of the corporate life as the seed-bed, the store-house of experience, and of personal responsibility, and a reaching out beyond a traditional experience to make a world anew. Jesus was no anarchist. He rejected the formality of contemporary Judaism, but his teaching was firmly rooted in the corporate tradition of his people. Just as goodness is no quality once and for all achieved but a continuously emerging quality as evil is faced and rejected, so the fruitful relationship between persons and the societies of which they are members is not a static thing, but something which emerges in the interplay of challenge and restraint both of which come from God, the one leading to new creation, the other to the preservation of hardly-won insights.'[5]

These direct references to God, though sparse in his lectures and indeed his personal conservation, could so easily have been dismissed as special pleading, yet so much were they a part of the man himself that they were accepted not as Christian propaganda but as consistent with his customary scholarship. On those grounds alone did he wish his ideas to be considered.

Apart from this intellectual integrity, what also appealed was his willingness to tackle controversial issues current on the national and international scene. So, giving one of his regular *Christian Commentary* broadcasts, in early 1954, he felt compelled to return to what he called 'the new eruption of Senator McCarthy in the United States', a theme incidentally again exposing him to the flak of this gathering witch-hunt.

'This is the issue,' he said, 'of Communism and civil liberty – civil liberty, the right of people to think and talk and advise and act in the light of their own judgment and in conformity with their own conscience without being treated as necessarily either traitors or blasphemers. Senator McCarthy seems to be so terrified of Communism that civil liberty seems to cease to exist in his vicinity, and I think this is a matter about which Christians should consider how they may best protest, for a Christianity which fails to stand up for civil liberties may be socially powerful but will kill the spirit.'

His final thoughts on McCarthyism left no room for ambiguity: '... though I'm no Communist, that wouldn't prevent McCarthy calling me one

---

5 See *The Individual and the Community*, Friends House, April 1954.

and perhaps getting me fired, certainly preventing me broadcasting; and I might well finish up a Communist out of sheer desperation, driven to it not out of conviction but out of frustration at seeing better men broken by a clever rascal who was prepared to accept no honest difference of opinion about public affairs. In short, to fight evil with evil is much more likely to perpetuate evil than to cure it; and whatever McCarthy may be doing in his own country, he has done a tremendous lot to shake overseas confidence in the strength of reason, tolerance, goodwill and Christian forbearance in the USA.'[6]

The possibility of effective ideas in the short term proving to be detrimental to the individual and society as a whole reinforced Roger's conviction that new thinking should always go hand-in-hand with research at the 'coal face'. Answers, he used to argue, would never be found by those who sat in armchairs only, nor by those who sat in offices only, nor by those who laboured all hours of the working day in the field only. They would emerge from careful thinking based upon accurate and imaginative observation of the facts of practical involvement.

So, within eighteen months of his arrival in Bristol, it wasn't in the least surprising that, invited to become Chairman of a five-year community research programme, he should welcome the opportunity. Sponsored and funded by the Carnegie Trust, the Bristol Social Project was given terms of reference as concise as ambitious: To investigate and take part in the life of a developing community in Bristol in an attempt to establish practical means of tackling those stresses and strains which arise in such a community in the form of delinquency and other disturbances.

Apart from his commitment to research *before* the implementation of community action or political ideology of whatever colour, Roger's interest was related to his own experience of living for several years on a corporation housing estate in Manchester. What troubled the estate dwellers most was, he recalled, the quietness; they wanted a brass band, but not enough of them could play to get a band started! 'We also grumbled, quite rightly,' he said, 'about the shortage of convenient shops, the badness of the bus service, and the expense of getting to churches, cinemas, pubs and public libraries. A lot of the people on the estate were unemployed, and there was nowhere, not even a decent street corner, to meet their mates.'

He also mentioned how a good many people missed living close to Mum or Grandad while a good many others seemed glad to have escaped to a life of their own. Some liked their new neighbours, others didn't; some thought the language of other people's children was terrible, others complained that the estate was like a bloody Sunday school.

---

[6] From 'English Notes' published in *The Friend*, Philadelphia, 24.3.53.

In sharing these personal experiences by way of introducing the Bristol Social Project, he pointed out that far more was known about council houses, their gardens, roads, drains, than about the families living in them; about the price of making walls and ceilings sound-proof, but not the price people have to pay in nervous anxiety if their homes are not sound-proof. 'If,' he concluded, 'we knew as much about the *human* aspects of living on estates as architects know about houses and roads we might avoid some mistakes that are now made.'

But – again because of his own experience of living on a corporation housing estate in the 1930s – he didn't underestimate the difficulties facing the researchers, warning that to study 'the stresses and strains of a community' was like trying to 'elucidate the principles of navigation in a hurricane while experimenting with the engines under the gaze of television'.

The five-year Project altogether covered an eight-year period before a bulky report was produced, and significantly Roger saw it through from beginning to end despite some of the 'stresses and strains' being researched sometimes spilling over into affairs of the executive and various sub-committees. Beyond doubt all the members were concerned for the Project, but some of those more academically minded didn't always see eye-to-eye with residents from the two council estates themselves whose primary aim was understandably for action before what they sometimes suspected was procrastinating analysis. Desperate for a toddlers' club, an adventure playground and a community centre, they, together with representatives of local clubs, pubs, churches, and vested interests of one sort or another, were not easily persuaded that 'social research' was other than a snooping exercise by the authorities or an excuse for doing nothing.

Roger's own summary of the final report plus his own observations were published in *Difficult Housing Estates* as a Tavistock Pamphlet which incidentally further explains why he found the philosophy of Thatcherism so obnoxious. Everything up for grabs was fine for those with the required capacity, but what of those more limited, limping along and inadequate through no fault of their own? A helping hand as distinct from charity or patronage was not only a necessity but a right.

'The Bristol Social Project attempted therapeutic work with three specific groups,' Roger recorded; 'outstandingly aggressive adolescents, children of an age to use an adventure playground, and withdrawn unself-confident mums. In each instance the effort revealed the need for an educative approach far subtler and more difficult than is usually thought necessary, and threw up the difficulty of explaining complexities that were by no means obvious to the plain common sense of the neighbourhood. An experiment in the relatively simple care of a group of toddlers revealed what very limited responsible and reliable help can be expected from people of goodwill resident on the estate. They could manage physical organization but not responsibility for other people.'

Long before the Bristol Social Project started, let alone its main report and Roger's summary of its findings were published, his international reputation as an authority on social studies brought him an increasing number of invitations to visit the Third World. One, sponsored by the Ford Foundation of America, gained him a four-month secondment from January 1955, to serve as Consultant to the Pakistan Government on Social Services. Happily Margery was able to accompany him, though she spent much of the time visiting Quaker centres in India.

The Report he subsequently produced is not without interest or indeed significance for its time, but snippets from his personal diary better convey the flavour of his observations:

In Karachi went with Margery to TB clinic, swarming with people and notices saying *Don't Spit Everywhere*. A valiant effort is being made to do some intensive social work with some of the patients, but it's very difficult, especially as living is so frightfully crowded and wages are so low that there is no possibility either of isolation or rest.

In the afternoon I made a courtesy call on the UK Deputy Commissioner who put me up two years ago. He was very cordial and introduced me to the High Commissioner – an odd fish. As Geoffrey's brother, I get by. They say the Pakistanis get too much advice from long-haired academics from all over the world.

I talked with a man called a Probation Officer. But his job isn't what you might think it. He is a sort of superintendent of persons who have been designated 'disorderly persons' or 'dangerous disorderly persons' by the courts – most of them for moral offences. He's a police superintendent, and I don't see what he can begin to do in such a sink as Karachi.

On Wednesday I went to see the 'Remand Home', a bleak little block of buildings with a tiny compound surrounded by refugee squatters. They have fifty boys who eat, sleep, play and learn in a single room and two verandahs . . . As I went out two policemen came in with a boy tied to them with a rope. This is the ordinary way of taking malefactors about; they defend it on the ground that there is no mechanical transport to spare for malefactors, and that if one escapes, his escort is dismissed forthwith.

In a prison at Sukkur (in the Province of Sind) the set-up was particularly impressive because of the excellent sense of hard and intelligent work in the workshops, and also because of the obvious self-respect of the prisoners promoted to special responsibility – in striking and glistening yellow and white uniforms. About one fifth of the prisoners – 300 out of 1500 – were in for murder. Most of them are venerable, bearded characters whose appearance would lend quality to any university senior common room. They aren't vicious; they've just done their duty in relation to the demands of local blood-feuds. This is quite a problem here. Prisoners are classified into two main lots – *Casuals* of whom murderers are the great majority, and *Habituals* who are the real bad lads.

. . . A missionary in the Punjab who stuck around with us for the next ten days and was a major pain in the neck. I wouldn't have believed that anybody could live in a country for fifteen years and be so stupid and insensitive. There is a treatise to be written on missionaries, good and bad.

In part of his report Roger focussed on the problem of the blood-feuds. It had, he said, darkened life in the tribal territories, and having himself seen evidence of its terrible reality in Peshawer and the Tribal Territories themselves he stressed that its power would not be diminished by external fiat but only as the people felt the futility of the feuds. At the moment they believed that personal injury demanded personal or family vengeance in a never-ending chain, a fact illustrated at a hospital in a tribal area where half the surgical cases were the result of gunshot wounds despite only the most serious and complicated cases receiving in-patient treatment.

This blood-feuding also had devastating economic consequences for the entire area, for men subjected to such hazards felt little or no inducement to go out to work.

As Consultant of the Social Welfare Council, Roger advocated the progressive establishment of social welfare services throughout the Tribal Territories, with the caveat that quality should not be sacrificed for the sake of speed; and this became part of the Planning Board's five-year plan. But this evident success, coupled to the crossing of the t-s and dotting the i-s of the full report wasn't the end of the matter as far as Roger was concerned. Even before the report was delivered he was writing to the Pakistan Minister of Communications, a letter doubly interesting as illustrating Roger's secret diplomacy, his often unobstrusive method of getting things done:

Dear Doctor Khan Sahib,

It is with some hesitation that I ask if I may come to see you when you must be very busy, but I have recently paid a short visit to the Tribal Areas of the NWFP (North-West Frontier of Pakistan) on behalf of the Planning Board. There I saw what looked like a possible opening for a modest piece of Quaker Service in support of the Government of Pakistan's efforts to develop constructive policies. My ideas are quite unofficial and very rudimentary. They are not ready for detailed presentation, but before I return to the UK on May 5th I should like a very informal talk with you as Chief Minister Designate of West Pakistan, so that I may know whether you think there is any sense in trying to work out a firm scheme.

At the same time, when the Acting Vice-Chancellor of the University of Peshawar visited the Planning Board's Advisory Committee, Roger, encouraged by his friendliness, 'risked showing him my draft chapter on Tribal Areas' and asked for his comments. 'To my pleasure,' Roger recorded, 'he said it was the best summary of the situation that he had seen, and he went to some trouble to rectify some slight inaccuracies, the corrections of which would, he said, make it certain to carry weight on the Frontier. Thus encouraged I asked him about the prospects of a Western group of women health workers. He was not by any means damping. He said it would be easier in mild Malakand than in fiercer Khyber or Wazinstan. But he would obviously talk sympathetically about a specific proposition, and as he is himself a tribesman with a first-rate record of Frontier service he would be a very good friend. He hopes to come with his wife and boy to the UK for a longish leave in the autumn. I have pressed him to come to Bristol and will try to follow this up.'

Knowing nothing of this all-too-typical behind-the-scenes activity, this somehow finding time and taking the trouble to follow up leads when other men were justifiably relaxing after a hard day, some of his colleagues were astonished at his ability to get things moving, and for whatever reason one or two intended to be less than complimentary in calling him Mr Fix-it. The simple fact was that apart from always being wide awake to seize or create opportunities to further his concerns, his tenacity was matched by his diplomatic skills and was sufficiently free of egoism to know the difference between obstinacy and dedication.

If obstacles had to be overcome he left no stone unturned in pursuance of his aims while at the same time possessing the patience that waits with purpose. His consequent success was neither elementary nor fortuitous. When, for instance, the response from Doctor Khan Sahib was disappointing, he wrote a follow-up letter, dated 5 May 1955: '... as I leave for Bristol tonight I regret that I shall not have a chance to meet you, at least on this visit. A fellow-Quaker, Miss Joan Court, knows as much about the matter as I do, and since she worked with the Quaker Service Unit as a district mid-wife in Calcutta 1945–47, and has been with the World Health Organization in Lahore and Karachi since 1951, she is much better informed about the health services generally than I am. She herself leaves for the UK on May 18th, but if in the meantime you can spare half-an-hour she would welcome the chance to talk with you about our idea. She can be reached through ...'

Clearly nothing was left either in abeyance or to chance if yet another effort might still tip the balance.

Roger's report to the Pakistan government, like all his writings centred upon the Third World, indicate how early he perceived the danger of Western experts seeking to transfer their concepts and practice of welfare services without due regard for indigenous traditions and susceptibilities. What he advocated were social policies and their implementation that reflected cultural, religious and community considerations at all levels. A blanket imposition of ideas developed in the West, a panacea envisaged by some visiting authorities, not to mention occasional local politicians educated in the West, was not only misguided but likely to prove disastrous in demanding inappropriate training for welfare and health workers. By all means let overseas universities assist but only if the curriculum was geared to the circumstances to which graduates would return; and better still let training centres be established and supported in the Third World itself, making possible the placement of students in precisely those areas to which they would be appointed after graduation.

He also pointed out that the concentration of population in urban centres, particularly in the Muslim world, had resulted in a disintegration of the family unit, thereby undermining the social security and cohesion previously experienced. Husbands and sons, living in cities to find work, were compelled to leave other family members in their village homes, and in many cases the separation was near complete because of the illiteracy of all concerned. One of the most important ways to prevent such estrangement was, Roger recommended, the spread of education in reading and writing, a simple measure sometimes overlooked in grandiose schemes. If letters can be sent, if the possibility existed to communicate and give expression to one's feelings, much was gained already. The contribution of the West lay not in ambitious generalized policies but in the application of all the expertise available to prevent as well as tackle breeding grounds of human misery.

Before leaving for Pakistan almost the last thing Roger had done was to visit his father, now alone after the death of his wife some eighteen months before. Characteristically, though increasingly restricted by his own ageing and deafness, he remained as resolved as ever not only to safeguard his independence but in no way to hinder the activities of his children in their individual whole-hearted support of his predominant life-long causes – Quakerism and international peace. So Roger's farewell, anything but easy for either father or son, had revealed not the slightest reservation on the older man's part.

News of his death had reached Pakistan barely two months into Roger's itinerary, but – knowing his father's mind – he hadn't hesitated to complete his assignment.

Back in Bristol he plunged into a new series of lectures on a *Sociological Approach to the Study of Education*, centred on his perennial question 'What Are Schools For?' Helping children to handle ideas was, he suggested, to create tension with other institutional demands of society – parents who wanted safe jobs for their children, teachers obsessed with pass marks before pupils, employers who sought 'hands', politicians who wanted voters, churches who wanted adherents, pornographers who wanted customers. To yield to any of these institutional pressures, the parents' no less than the pornographers', was to fail in providing children with the encouragement to have ideas of their own and to handle the attempted coercion by other people.

He returned to this theme – it was never far from his mind – as part of his T. E. Harvey Memorial Lecture in 1958, and as usual was adept in the use of purposeful humour. He spoke of one of his post-graduate students being asked to write an essay on the nature of tension possible between teacher and parents. The essay turned on a letter received by a teacher known to the student which read:

> Dear Sir,
> It is none of your business how my son Arthur smells. Don't smell him, learn him.
> Yours faithfully

Then followed a masterly exposition of what schools should set out to do, presented, he said, under seven headings which 'try as I will I can put in no order of priority'. Schools should help children:

> To have the experience of observing the world in which they live.
> To have the experience of creating something authentic of their own.
> To have the experience of enjoyment.
> To have the experience of reflection.
> To have the experience of thinking.
> To acquire skills and attitudes which will make them useful citizens in straightforward and operational terms.
> To have the experience of worship.

'I think children in school,' he summed up his concept of worship, 'should be offered an opening to an awareness of the mystery of life and creation that calls for an attitude of spirit that I call worship as well as an insatiable scientific curiosity.'

What also concerned him was the way authorities – religious, political, societal, family – assumed that conventional definitions of right and wrong were sacrosanct. In arguing that current morality was possibly no more than the rationalization of what was convenient, he hardly endeared himself to some stalwarts of the *status quo* by pointing out that conformity in a structured situation by the exertion of enough force could give the impression that a regimented school or a prison was the embodiment of 'morality'. What he wanted to see encouraged was the choice of 'a harder rather than an easier course in pursuit of a sense of goodness'.

Making such emphases, Roger significantly never sounded like a pompous sermonizer but rather a professor of education. But his academic approach, apart from revealing his massive scholarship, was never devoid of a searching personal application. 'Teachers who make a real impact,' he told his students, 'have always been those who left not the faintest doubt of where they stood. Those who have left no mark were those who dissected issues without committing themselves, showed no feeling about them.' What he had in mind were classroom discussions about moral values without the teacher being explicit about the nature of his or her personal commitment on the moral issues of the day. Such essential openness was, he said, easy enough when an orthodox position was adopted; but what of other occasions when honesty implied not only unconventional commitment but an admission of personal deficiency?

The last thing he wanted was arbitrarily to impose his own moral standards on anybody else, least of all to insist that student-teachers and social workers alike should be subjected to some sort of moral as well as academic judgment as part of their training. But his listeners were never left in doubt about where *he* stood in the moral conundrums under discussion, any more than they could fail to catch his conviction that personal morality and professional effectiveness in both teaching and social work were inseparable.

As though to counter his own strong views or expose to rigorous intellectual scrutiny the Quakerism he didn't doubt impregnated everything he thought and articulated, he arranged regular debates between himself and one of the other professors whose religious agnosticism was an open secret throughout the university. Judging by attendances few occasions were more popular or appreciated, everyone involved fully aware that Roger's purpose was not to make converts but raise ultimate questions in the cut-and-thrust of discussion.

Almost invariably one issue raised was human suffering and the omnipotence of a loving God, an issue not only of academic perplexity but inescapable for Roger in his daily life as to his desk (particularly after his appointment, in 1954, as Chairman of the Friends Service Council, responsible for British Quaker social welfare enterprises notably in the Third World) flowed endless reports of desperate need.

In the second half of the 1950s, Africa already in turmoil and with Southern Rhodesia threatening Unilateral Declaration of Independence (UDI), Roger promptly responded to the proposal that he should visit Central Africa both to see Quaker educational and health units, and to explore possibilities of greater support for inter-racial reconciliation and peace.

A strong advocate of the visit was Professor Basil Fletcher, his former Bristol colleague who was now, since December 1955, in Salisbury to set up an Institute of Education for students of all races. Within such a highly charged situation he had no doubt that Roger's wisdom and moral authority would be invaluable.

13

Challenging Racism in Central Africa
1957-1961

Using the long summer vacation of 1957, Roger started his tour of Central Africa in Kenya, and as usual kept a detailed diary. Extracts indicate lengthy private consultations with the likes of Tom Mboya, Garfield Todd (Premier of Southern Rhodesia), Guy Clutton-Brock, an Anglican missionary hated by the whites for his uncompromising living of racial equality, and Sir Robert Tredgold (Acting Governor of the Federation), but primarily with countless obscure, though, as he perceived, influential Africans often in their own homes:

On Friday we pushed off to visit schools on the foothills of Mount Elgon. We got stuck in the mud and rocks two miles short of the school site. Several Africans with bikes helped, but having extricated the car we decided to let well alone and go on foot, two miles to the primary and intermediate schools. I got shoved into the top year (4th) of the primary school with orders to try out their English which I thought very good. In the intermediate school we dropped in for two religious knowledge lessons, both taken by unqualified teachers – one on Noah, plain dull, the other on Jacob, Leah and Rachel, where the bright boys ran rings round the dim teacher on polygamy and related questions and Christianity. It was a bad business. But the question is how to get good teachers who will go to these high, cold remote schools. The log book is full of references to teachers who 'elope' with the girls – and there is certainly not much else for either party to do.

At Kamusinga I talked to the whole school about our purposes in visiting Africa and then answered questions for half-an-hour. Then spent ¾ hour or so with each of the top classes, listening to them talk about the educational problems of Kenya and commenting on their questions. The quality of their questions is first-rate: Is the main purpose of education to enable people to make more money? What's the good of an education system that has no room for most children after the first four years? Why should a pass in English be compulsory in School Certificate, no matter how good the candidate is in other subjects (a very important point in a country where the possession of a

SC has a direct value on official salary scales)? Why should a nearby girls secondary school have dropped Swahili and made Latin compulsory? How should you deal with the tension that arises between home and school? Is it more important to go into teaching or trade and industry? Why can European teachers teach anything, but African teachers only their special subjects?

They weren't always willing to listen to the answers, but their questions had quality, edge and maturity. If they do in the end learn to consider possible answers, there should be no lack of capable people to man the responsible jobs of Kenya.

It so happened that when we got to Kaimosi (Friends Secondary School) there were four women teachers already there from the very school at which the Kamusinga boys had that morning alleged Swahili had been given up for compulsory Latin. The story seemed so fantastic I hadn't really believed it, and so I had no inhibitions in forthwith saying what the allegation was and asking what sub-stratum of truth there was. To my horror they said it was quite true, and they defended two lessons a week on the grounds that it helped them with their English, that it was good for their minds, and that it helped them understand another society. This is the sort of half-baked thinking that bedevils educational devotion.

The Copper Belt, Northern Rhodesia, isn't in the least what I expected. I'd expected a heavily industrialized sort of area like the stretch from Sheffield to Rotherham or Birmingham to Wolverhampton. In fact, it's about six brash little towns of 8000 Europeans or so and 60,000 Africans, quite separate from each other – both towns and people – set in slightly rolling country covered with trees.

Roan Antelope Copper Mine, Ndola. I don't think I had before quite grasped the dilemma of either industry or government in these parts. They pay Europeans much more than they are really worth because they had to pay that to get started. But it wouldn't ever be economic to pay everybody on that scale, and therefore they don't *want* to pay Africans the rates which Europeans get at present. But not to pay Africans European rates is to discriminate. It's a very difficult situation indeed – and of course not many people *want* to pay Africans properly anyway.

At Kitwe I spent twenty minutes with the secretary of the European Miners Union. He is not an engaging character, fortyish, South African (?); I asked him to do the talking but he was incoherent in defence of European interests. He must be a trying man to deal with since he asserts but neither sees points nor constructs an argument. He speaks for the European technical mine worker who has status and money here that he won't get at home, and who is quite unaware of any issues other than his own income and status, both of which are threatened by forces he doesn't understand.

At Mindole girls intermediate boarding school, Kitwe, the European staff were nice women, but they didn't introduce me to the one African member of staff who was about the place.

The Chief Counsellor to the Gwembe Tongo tribes (Hezekiah Habanyama, an old student) says that after a lot of thought and wrestling he can support on its economic merits the Kariba Dam scheme (20,000 of some of the most primitive tribes of the territory are to be moved to make way for it). I had a couple of hours talk with him about it all. He says that in his own experience over the last three years racial relations have certainly improved; unofficial European members of official committees take African opinion seriously and courteously. But this is in a rural area where for several reasons things are better. From what I have seen of the urban areas, where white town councils are in control, there's precious little approach to co-operation. I don't think any town council has any African members and the difference between white and black amenities is shocking. In Lusaka, for instance, the European and the African hospitals are side by side down the same road. The tarmac stops at the European hospital; for want of 100 yards more tarmac an African ambulance has to bump down a dusty, pot-holey road on the last lap. It's the damned down-right short-sighted lack of generosity that is so awful. Things *do* get better bit by bit – but the lack of urgency or warmth is staggering.

Hezekiah H. lives in a simple white-washed thatched house picturesquely perched on a high bank above a river bed. He took me to his home where his wife gave me mid-morning tea. She is a delightful person of some education but very shy. She ought to come to the UK with him before long, as I feel that they could be influential people in Northern Rhodesia.

Talked for half-an-hour with the Secretary for Native Affairs, a most intelligent and impressive civil servant; and for an hour with the Director of African Education – a kindly but ineffective chap on the edge of retirement . . . finished this morning with a short talk with the broadcasters. They seem to be using Africans progressively and constructively.

Basil Fletcher met me in Salisbury. On Monday from 8 to 10 he took me round the university and its site; the architecture is 1951 Exhibition style, with modifications. I don't think it is all equally successful though the halls of residence are delightful.

On Tuesday I began with a visit to the *Capricorn Society* for a brief talk about their work and prospects – very perplexing. Should they form a party to push for their inter-racial contract? Something must be done to escape from the white superiority assumptions of even liberal orthodoxy. But will it split the progressive forces? . . . Then for a half-hour talk with Garfield Todd, Premier of S. Rhodesia, ex-missionary from New Zealand; a very pleasant informal man, first-rate exponent of policy, who gives the impression of really wanting to bring Africans in but is hampered by what the white electorate will stand . . . I wish I had known as much as I knew a week later as a basis for questions. I told him I was going to St Faith's for the week-end. He shook his head and said it gave him a lot of anxiety. But he didn't say why, and I didn't know how to frame a question.

. . . taken by Dudley Robinson, Assistant Director of Native Agriculture, and also Clerk of Salisbury Friends Meeting, to Msengexi, about fifty miles south west of Salisbury; a few miles out stopped to give a lift to a young chap who turned out to be a South African working as a land inspector on the surveying of European farm sites. He tended to talk most of the time and in a very loud harsh voice with great assurance about what could and could not be done with the land. After he had said enough to hang himself D.R. very quietly and penetratingly asked him what research stations he had visited and what technically expert Land Development Officers he had talked with. He was too stupid to see what this was leading to for a bit, but by the time we dropped him he was saying that there was quite a lot he didn't know. D.R. says there are an awful lot of chaps in this territory doing jobs they know nothing about – and probably cursing Africans when things go wrong.

Friday began with a talk to the thirty or so students in the Department of Education, about twenty-five Europeans, four Africans and one Indian. They asked fair questions. The one that put me on my mettle was about teaching morals in schools; honesty was obvious, but had a chap any right to take a view on another chap's ideas about race relations? Talking to some of them afterwards – the Africans sloped off – I gather that there is a *lot* of tension about race relations, and as the course is more than a little chaotic there is a good deal of unhappiness.

In the afternoon the Professor of Social Anthropology took me to Harare and Highfield, two suburbs where Africans live . . . they're not slums by any means, and Highfield consists of houses which the Africans can in fact buy on a long lease. But the whole system is wrong as can be and leaves me sick and frightened and angry.

I hired a Morris Minor, picked up Guy Clutton-Brock who was in Salisbury, and drove down with him to St Faith's, about 115 miles in about 2½ hours: St Faith's is a lot of things – Anglican mission, church, a village of perhaps 70/100 families, a primary school (200 children), an upper primary boys boarding school (150), a clinic run by Mollie Clutton-Brock for spastics and polio-crippled children (residential), a farming community and an adult education centre. There are at present about 10 Europeans helping in one or more of these activities, living very simply in a way which makes relationships with Africans absolutely easy – in the same sort of way as contacts between residents and neighbours in a good British settlement are entirely easy.

The thing I saw was the discussion group which has now been running for five years or so. I addressed it on Saturday evening for 25 minutes on various forms of adult education in Western Europe. This was followed by rather more than 2 hours of excellent questions from the 70 or so who were there, about 55 Africans and 15 Europeans. The Africans were all land workers or village characters except for perhaps 5 teachers – cattle man, carpenter, plumber, miller, store-keeper, assistant manager, tractor mechanic etc.; it was disciplined discussion of a high order, with Africans and Europeans participating absolutely unselfconsciously and all sitting unselfconsciously on the same benches and chatting freely over cups of tea at the end. *This is the first easy and unselfconscious inter-racial gathering I'd landed in in the Federation*. It shows what can emerge from common commitment to a real job. What I don't know is how near to the surface political tensions are . . . St Faith's provides whole week-ends of this kind from time to time with up to 200 Africans and Europeans participating . . . All this is very impressive. But one can see why G.C-B. is a highly controversial figure. He has the ruggedness of the pioneer rather than the diplomatic skill and capacity to explain of the persuader.

At Umtali I addressed the local branch of the Rhodesian Teachers Association – all European though many of them are engaged in African not European education. I tried to bring home to them the existence of Africans who are credible and valued members of British universities. Some don't know it; others have forgotten it; others are glad to have an outsider say what they would like to say themselves.

I had a talk for an hour and a half with Sir Robert Tredgold, Chief Justice and Acting Governor General of the Federation . . . His own views are very liberal and I think he does everything a Chief Justice and an Acting Governor General can to forward them, but of course he cannot be as forthright as a politician. He's much interested in the development of adult education, but I doubt if he quite appreciates that – precisely because he is mixed up with the government set-up – political Africans can't accept his leadership.

Suggestion made that the sole African woman student at the university should live not as she was in a separate wing of the hall occupied by African men but with white students. Rejected. I saw the African student on the Sunday morning; she was so distressed she was talking of leaving the university. Agreed that it isn't easy for a lot of S. Rhodesians quickly to treat Africans as human beings, it's the downright hypocrisy and cruelty of their defence of the attitude that is so desolating.

Nairobi. On Sunday we went at 10 a.m. to the European-type Meeting in the Boy Scout headquarters; about 20 there including 2 Africans and 1 Sikh.

Then back to Ofafa to the African-type Meeting – several lusty hymns, some prayers, some admissions, and other bits including a sermon by me, translated by an African tax-collector, followed by an additional sermon by the senior layman who put in the bits about the blood of the Lamb which I'd left out. There were about 70 there, with perhaps 12/15 women, with their toddlers and children at the breast – coming, going, feeding, smacking and loving, all seemed very uninhibited and there was usually a bit of discussion about what to do next and who to call on for what. The Africans were probably middle-class. But if the British may be equated with the imperial Romans, the setup was pretty unsophisticated and muddled Godliness.

. . . went to see Tom Mboya – a surprisingly unimpressive figure, though quick, intelligent and easy to talk to. His main point is that Multi-racial government is a vague phrase; what do white Kenyans really mean by it? T.M. is not prepared to accept anything less than government on the basis of equal universal suffrage; but he recognizes that this can't come at once, and is prepared to move that way by stages. Until that goal is reached he wants no relaxation of Colonial Office control, for he does not trust the European population of Kenya . . . Tom Mboya's basic difficulty is that an African nationalist movement has arisen with him as leader before there are anything like enough Africans to take responsibility. If the Colonial Office could hold on for 25 years this wouldn't be so serious. But the Colonial Office is faced with a European Kenya nationalism which also can't wait very long. Is there enough good sense all round to keep the situation manageable? It's doubtful.

Tea with group of African Friends in home of one of them . . . they wanted to know why British Friends didn't think it was their job to evangelize East Africa. We said that this was their job, not ours, though ours might be to help with training teachers and leaders. The ambivalence about their attitude to the British is frighteningly persistent.

From Thursday at 9 a.m. until Sunday afternoon the East Africa Yearly Meeting (full of tribal tensions and different language groups from an area covering 100 or more square miles) was in progress at Kigama Intermediate School. We attended quite a bit of this, and I spoke for half-an-hour plus half-an-hour translation on the Friday morning. Most days there were about 1200–1500 present, sitting around the slight amphitheatre of the lie of the land, with some but not much shade from a few large trees and some low bushes.

On Sunday there must have been 4000 present, the men soberly dressed and wearing long trousers, the women very gay, all with bright head scarves. There is much ignorance among them, but the whole is impressive and could be better used. I think George Fox must have been familiar with meetings of this sort in the 1640s and 50s.

When not at YM we lazed or wandered around the campus which is very beautiful or went for meals to other of the Mission houses. The hospitality was *very* generous and people were *warm and loving*; but the place is bursting, it seems, with tensions of personality and policy. It surely typifies one aspect of the problem of mission policy – how to hold teams together.

Following another busy academic year at Bristol, Roger returned to the Southern Rhodesian capital for a pioneering interracial residential conference at the university on 'Adult Education and Citizenship'. His own lecture to the mixed audience dominated by white influence lacked neither controversy nor courage.

Asserting that 'adult education is dangerous', he quoted William Temple: 'Are you going to treat a man as what he is or as what he might be? Morality requires, I think, that you should treat him as what he might be, as what he has it in him to become . . . Give him the full development of his powers; and there will no longer be that conflict between the claim of the man as he is and the claim of the man as he might become.'

Having pointed out that Temple was on a police list of suspicious persons in the 1914–18 war because of his involvement with the education on the lowest levels of society, Roger concluded with the reminder that in a rapidly changing world the question of how the tensions of Central Africa were to be resolved was for the seminars of the conference, not for the visitor who could only proclaim his conviction that adult education, no matter how dangerous to present structures of society, was an important road towards maturity.

Returning to Bristol, he immediately took up the cudgels on behalf of the Conference's proposals for racial justice by writing to the Colonial Secretary (Lennox-Boyd): 'I am not one of those who ever thought the problem of Federation was obvious or easy, either way . . . But if you did indeed say that "Freedom from fear of millions of Africans was as worthy an object as the physical freedom of a few dozen agitators" (as reported in the previous day's *Manchester Guardian*), one can't help deducing a singularly superficial approach to a fundamental problem, and it gives your critics very adequate grounds for thinking that you and the Europeans led by Welensky[1] are at

---

[1] Sir Roy Welensky, Prime Minister of the short-lived Federation of Central Africa (the two Rhodesias and Nyasaland)

bottom in agreement that what you want is a white man's country with a well-fed, docile African population.'

Having then referred to some of the Nyasalanders he had met at the conference and also in their homes, learning of their determination to have nothing to do with any Federation programme, opposition for which they were now, he feared, doubtless behind bars, he appealed: 'Of course Nyasalanders are nothing like as ready as West Africans or even Kenya Africans to take political responsibility. But the tide won't wait and to respond like Canute is merely provocative.'

These forthright comments, noted seriously not least because by now Roger was a highly-regarded member of the Colonial Office Advisory Committees on both Education and Social Development, led to him being invited to meet Lennox-Boyd at the Colonial Office, just the two of them; and during their exchanges, as frank as they were friendly, the Colonial Secretary said he would be interested to see any observations on the Central Africa scene that might come from Sir Robert Tredgold with whom Roger was still in touch.

Seeking the Acting Governor General's permission to share his latest letter (dated 20 May 1959) Roger said that in particular 'I should like to pass on to the Colonial Secretary your observations on South African'. 'One thing I can say with confidence,' Sir Robert had written, 'is that the talk of Southern Rhodesia joining the Union is largely bluff. Apart from more creditable reasons, the prejudice against the Afrikaner is strong enough to prevent this, except as a measure of desperation. In addition to pure prejudice, the fear of such practical disabilities as bi-lingualism weigh very heavily.'

Permission granted, Roger forwarded the whole of Sir Robert's letter to Lennox-Boyd; and also, bearing in mind the clear impression he'd received from the Colonial Secretary that he'd welcome comments from senior people generally in Southern Rhodesia from whom he felt separated by the etiquette of Colonial Office/Commonwealth Relations Office, Roger perhaps broadened the definition of 'senior people' by including details of racial injustice provided by Friends working in the field.

He maintained the same hard information when Lennox-Boyd was succeeded by Ian MacLeod at the Colonial Office. In a typical letter (dated 18 November 1959) he said how glad he was to hear about the release of one of a trio of his former Nyasaland students, all subjected to prolonged internment, and his hope for the early release of the other two whose only 'crime' was to express the impossibility they each felt of playing a responsible part in the next stage of territorial development. He then provided details of their prison conditions, all authenticated by reports from Friends on the spot.

Like an angry bulldog – and Roger was often angry about Central Africa at this time – he wouldn't let go or be put off by well-meaning assurances that did little to address his concerns.

Yet whatever these disputations, it goes without saying that Roger's responses were not restricted to such political in-fighting. No less pronounced were his immediate practical concerns about students from the Third World who found English weather incompatible with sustained study or rational thought at all. Time and again he handed his discreet secretary the necessary funds to provide shivering students with thick underwear, supplemented as required by blankets, water bottles, scarves, gloves, pullovers, anything to guarantee the maximum degree of comfort possible. The secretary alone knew the source of such caring.

Inevitably more known about were the testimonials he provided for overseas graduates returning home in search of suitable employment. The spirit of colonialism persisted long beyond political change, safeguarding the unwritten law that 'blacks' were incapable of real responsibility. Time and again he sought to counter any suggestion of racism at whatever level, and was the opposite of patronizing in pointing out the proven qualities of his students during their studies at Bristol.

Few things did more to tempt him to despair than well-intentioned individuals whose sincerity did nothing to redeem their unconscious support of institutionalized discrimination by race and colour. Hence the enthusiasm with which he attended a Conference for Diplomats, in July 1958, one of a series at Clarens, a village on Lake Geneva, organized by the American Friends Service Council. He and Margery attended several, but for the initial one he officiated as Chairman.

For the session on 'Colonialism', however, he vacated the Chair to give himself greater freedom to speak! Replying to the Russian delegation's attack on 'British Colonialism' he pointed out that Britain was actively assisting her colonies to attain independence, whereas the countries bordering Russia had been absorbed into the USSR and sunk without trace. Predictably the Russians were furious, and later that day approached Roger to ask if they could talk with him; they wanted to ask him a question. He prepared to be savaged. 'Would you tell us, please,' they interrogated, 'are *trousers* singular or plural?'

That same year, in both January and March, he attended a School of Social Studies at the Hague, viewing such opportunities as a means of pushing for what he perceived as simple justice for emerging nations in the Third World; simple not simplistic, for he recognized the problem of entrenched assumptions among former rulers, and didn't doubt that the required change of attitude would be hard won by persistence as much as perspicacity.

'Economic and social development,' he told the Hague conference, 'means change. Settled patterns of behaviour are disrupted. Those responsible for initiating change have an objective in mind: personal economic gain, a material rise in the general standard of living, a more just pattern of human relationship, the removal of political or economic bondage, the growth of national power or embodiment of a particular way of life.'

But to his mind there was something more basic, something reinforced by his recent experiences in Central Africa, and no more popular with people resisting change as those fighting for it. The broad objective is, he said, 'to enable people to use growing economic wealth in such a way that they enhance the quality of their non-material values and do not become spiritually and morally debauched or corrupted by material things'.

He did not expect a ready response to this emphasis from the Africans he had recently seen in the squalor of their shanty towns or working for a pittance without reference to their worth or potential; understandably their preoccupation was survival. But in addressing a European conference on social planning, with many of the delegates concerned about the Third World, he felt it essential to draw attention to what he believed to be the very heart, let alone the ultimate means, of human progress.

'Responsibility,' he said, 'means a sense of inner security in which a choice is exercised within an integrated personality. It involves trust in oneself, it even involves the preparedness to be for some time in an, in itself, insecure situation which can only be borne creatively when the person himself has the inner security mentioned. Responsibility means exercising choices which depend on taking a long view as well as a short view, which depend on being able to see oneself both as a person and as a member of society. Responsibility means – bearing the tension involved in making choices.'

About such 'choices' – and again he had the Third World particularly in mind – he underlined that what appeared to be mistaken or even illogical sometimes proved to be the most fruitful way to obtain results. In Pakistan, he once more illustrated from his own recent experience, no schools of social work existed and therefore no trained social workers were available, despite appalling need. Yet following the establishment of the first school and graduation of the first students, it was recommended that these trained social workers should be used not where the need was greatest but only in the area surrounding the school. In this way they could supervise the practical work of the next intake of students, thus increasing the number of social workers. In this instance, *the priority for more trained workers was greater than the relieving of suffering itself.*

Increasing the flow of trained personnel both *in* and *to* what he called low-income countries had already landed him in a degree of controversy. The absence in Britain of a coherent and directed course of studies for people who would become engaged in social development, policy and practice in the Third World was because, Roger claimed, the universities were terrified 'that this sort of thing was non-academic and cuts across their work in Ancient History, the oddities of Middle/High German, and the finer aspects of Brain Surgery, all of which were regarded as reputable university activities'. His irony was not entirely lost, and eventually, with Roger enthusiastically involved behind the scenes, a one-year training course for social workers from the Third World was initiated at the university of Swansea, forerunner of a similar development at Bristol in the early 1960s.

His support of this Swansea initiative, growing out of his work primarily in Pakistan in the early 1950s, illustrates that in all his international travels Roger was anything but a fly-by-night 'expert' or conference speaker who having occupied the centre of the stage with an exhortation as inspirational as scholarly immediately withdrew, unmindful of any personal involvement in the follow-up programme his 'expertise' had advocated as essential.

His sustained practical interest after the Adult Education and Citizenship conference in Rhodesia helped in the establishment of the Central Africa Institute of Education, its finances guaranteed for five years by a substantial grant from the Joseph Rowntree Charitable Trust.[2]

Such interest, however, was not restricted to eye-catching schemes which inevitably brought a degree of personal kudos. No less pronounced was largely secret evidence of his continued concern for his still-interned Nyasaland former students; along with colleagues in his own department he renewed subscriptions for journals for them, and – fed with up-to-date information from a Friend prison visitor – constantly brought their plight to the attention of British and African authorities. Needless to say, his correspondence about them revealed the extent to which he knew them as individuals, their personalities, politics, strengths and weaknesses. Whatever else the recipients of his appeals for justice and humanitarianism could say, he could never be dismissed as not knowing the facts.

Equally authoritative was his readiness to admit his ignorance and *ask* for help, admit it, incidentally, without practised humility. His openness much preferred to poke fun at himself. Addressing a conference for teachers on 'The Teaching of Personality Development', he began with an apology: 'Not only did I not read psychology in my degree, but I have not subsequently read my way properly into the subject. I am by no means sure that I understand a good deal of what has been said this week-end; indeed, I can best illustrate my condition by telling you of one of Mr A's experiences as an expert on

---

[2] Roger's long involvement with two of the Joseph Rowntree Trusts is discussed on pp. 255–58.

electronic circuits. He and his colleague were constructing one of those electronic machines which translate from one language to another, and to test its efficacy they decided to feed in a phrase from the Authorized Version for translation into Russian and back into English. They fed in: "The spirit is willing but the flesh is weak". When it came out again, it read: "The whisky is agreeable but the meat is bad".'

After such an opening his listeners were eager to follow his closely argued and brilliant paper on their possible fear of depth psychology in relation to their success as teachers: 'All new insights may well involve disintegration, and it is, I suppose, as terrifying an act of faith as a teacher can commit to lead his students into an area of possible disintegration in the conviction that this is a road to fuller life. Certainly this is the sort of situation which keeps some of us awake at nights from time to time, but from which very often there emerges exhilarating new life. We must not ignore or deny the dangers, but neither must we be inhibited by them.'[3]

What he feared was that potentially good teachers battling in adverse situations would lose heart or worse still write themselves down as incompetent. The criterion of success was, he said, not what happened in the first five years of a teaching career but in the last thirty years.

He was no less forward looking – causing a few eyebrows to be raised by his professional colleagues never mind some fellow Quakers – in his thinking about the needs of adolescents. When others of his age-group and respectability were appalled at the mini-skirt of the 1960s going ever higher and the shoulder-length hair style of boys ever lower, he told a national conference: 'It is conceivable that in the matter of tension between adolescents and the rest of the community it is you and I who are wrong and not the adolescents.' As though this wasn't enough, he went on: 'I get tired of the complaint about the clothing of adolescents. Why should they not be allowed to dress as they like. So far as boys and men are concerned they look infinitely more interesting than the Chairman and myself! I really do not see why we should not allow them this freedom to dress as they like. I would like to see the development of thoughtful sensitive research into the need and nature of adolescents in our sort of society.' He had in mind not simply 'the delinquent, the abandoned, the handicapped fringe' but 'the able, self-respecting, confident enquiring active youngsters' who were a positive asset to the community. Instead of condemning dress and hair styles, adults should be asking how better they could support young people in their search for self-identity.[4]

---

[3] Reprint from *The Sociological Review*, July 1958, pp. 119, 123.

[4] See Annual Conference 1960 Report of National Association for Maternal and Child Welfare, p. 66.

To anticipate, three decades later, then into his eighties, the same flexibility marked his approach to the behaviour and needs of the young. The gathering sexual revolution found this man of cast-iron principle neither judgmental nor despairing. On the contrary, he brought to the undermining of traditional moral values or evaluations the same spirit with which he had faced change of whatever kind throughout his life – *what was God trying to say in this situation*? Was it about a new understanding of human sexuality and relationships, of the shallowness of previous conventions and standards? A blanket condemnation of all pre-marital sex was out of the question, just as surely as the drift toward promiscuity was as destructive and sacrilegious as ever. In the turmoil and uncertainty, few things were more revealing of this old Quaker's inner life and faith than his confidence that at the centre of the whirlwind it was possible to hear the still small voice of God, perhaps with new truth, a deeper insight into the mind of Christ.

14

The Congo Experience and a New Professorial Chair

1962–1964

Roger's characteristic openness was never more evident than in his encouragement of pioneering ventures to channel youthful idealism. To the very last moment before leaving for the Adult Education and Citizenship conference in Central Africa he was exploring the possibilities of an idea emanating from the Colonial Office and supported by the United Nations Association of Great Britain – the formation of a Commonwealth Youth Trust to organize periods of voluntary service in under-developed member countries. And immediately on his return he agreed to chair a small informal group to get the project off the ground.

Unaware of this development, the Bishop of Portsmouth wrote to the *Sunday Times* proposing an altogether more ambitious scheme to aid not only members of the Commonwealth but any needy country the world over. Happy to see their own aims superseded, supporters of the embryonic Commonwealth Youth Trust promptly threw their weight behind this new plan which eventually evolved into the now internationally acclaimed Voluntary Service Overseas.[1] Roger's only regret was that his existing commitments plus others already promised compelled him to decline an invitation to serve on the committee of this far more extensive enterprise.

Many of these additional commitments were, not surprisingly, related to Roger's own initiatives within the Institute of Education at Bristol and within Quakerism. But others, totally unexpected and indeed unwelcome, were the outcome of Roger's international reputation as an educationist and authority on social welfare theory and practice.

---

[1] The letter signed by the Bishop of Portsmouth was actually written by Alec Dickson who – having been asked by the British Council of Churches to help during the 1956 Hungarian uprising – saw for himself the impact of Western students in refugee relief. The following year he visited Sarawak where his brother Murray was Director of Education, and was confirmed in his belief that untrained young people could give valuable voluntary service.

In early June 1961, back in Bristol after a series of committees and consultations, he popped into the university on his way with Margery to Quaker Meeting, to glance at his in-tray. The deep pile included a letter from the Ministry of Labour passing on, it explained, an inquiry from the United Nations in New York about his interest and possible availability for a twelve-month assignment in the Congo.

As top Social Affairs Advisor he would be based at Leopoldville to determine the needs, priorities and development of social welfare programmes; advise on the organization of emergency and long-term assistance; advise on the formulation or simplication of social legislation; assist in the organization of training courses for multi-purpose workers; and set out guide lines for the fullest utilization of self-help methods in resolving social and economic problems.

His reaction was negative, confirmed by his wife's. He was already fully occupied at Bristol. No less pertinent, he was too wise a diplomat not to perceive that long absences from his department, no matter how justified and supported at the university, imposed an inordinate amount of extra work on his colleagues. The last thing he wanted was to exploit their loyalty, any more than he wished to compromise his own to the Institute of Education. And there was, he readily admitted, something else. *He simply didn't want to go to the Congo.*

This emphatically settled, he and his wife proceeded to morning Meeting, the pair of them wholly united in putting the proposed upheaval behind them. Spoken ministry during the otherwise corporate silence turned on the need to be open to a call for service whenever it came. Walking home together afterwards, first Roger confessed, and Margery offered her independent endorsement, that for him the Congo was inescapable. Never more serious in their lives, they nevertheless saw the funny side of this complete change of mind for reasons they could neither explain away nor doubt.

Knowing their man, the Vice-Chancellor and Roger's departmental colleagues were immediately supportive. The Congo in any case was no easy number, and anyone prepared to confront such a maelstrom of uncertainty and danger was either mad or exceptionally clear-headed. They knew as well as Roger that the Congolese army of some 28,000 men had mutinied a week after the country had achieved independence, on 14 July 1960, since when Belgian paratroops, against the wishes of the new government, had been sent in to safeguard Belgian nationals, and tribal conflicts were growing accompanied by threats of secession in several sections of the country.

Despite the United Nations response to appeals for help from the Congolese, the situation had continued to deteriorate, and now – mid-1961 – with Katanga, rich in minerals, notably copper, cobalt and uranium, having seceded, a bloody civil war could engulf not only the Congo but adjacent newly emerging nations. If Roger's colleagues were supportive they were also sympathetic; not surprised that such a man was prepared to face this assignment but almost pitying, whatever their admiration, that he should feel constrained by imperatives beyond their own rationality or experience of faith.

Having satisfied himself that the work he would leave behind could be willingly shouldered within the Institute of Education, Roger then set about finding out precisely what he would be expected to do in the Congo, not only *what* but *how*. Hard experience in Pakistan plus his two more recent visits to Central Africa had taught him that to define social policy and create an administrative system to implement it was relatively easy. More problematic was to find suitable indigenous personnel to do the work and then set-up a means of adequate training.

As he sought for clearer guidelines, the waters, as he himself put it, were further muddied by the offer of another job. The American Friends Service Council, encouraged by what had already been achieved by Quaker influence at the United Nations Headquarters in New York, asked whether he could make himself available to take over this role of widening opportunity. If he could not accept for a lengthy period, the cable read, would he at least guide the programme in the immediate for what could prove to be 'the most significant General Assembly in UN history'?[2]

As much as he had enjoyed his brief time at Quaker House in 1952, and not for a moment doubting the importance of such work, he found no difficulty in declining. In doing so, however, he explained that what this Congo business had led both him and Margery to realize was that, though they had no wish to leave Bristol, 'we could contemplate doing some job for Friends or others if required and given adequate notice – which ought not to be less than a year. But *if* we were to go it would probably be fairest to resign.' He concluded: 'This doesn't mean that we should be around the necks of Friends for ever since by 1966 I shall be sixty anyway, and could retire to the life of a perpetual committee member.'

Meanwhile in the Paris Office of the United Nations he was being briefed about his Congo assignment by both the UN Head of the Social Affairs Division from New York and the Social Affairs Advisor to the Congo, the latter described by Roger as 'full of ill-disciplined insight, an irresistible prophet, a difficult colleague'. Everything he heard led him to the conclusion that the Congo situation was 'a real dog's dinner of major proportions, and I don't feel any sense of exhilaration in contemplating it. But I think that there is probably something I can do about it, and there is nobody else in sight'.

---

[2] A letter amplifying details was dated 13 July 1961.

He reached Leopoldville in September 1961, fourteen months after Independence. On the very day of his arrival, only a month following the formation of the first substantial Congolese government established under the auspices of the United Nations, fighting flared up in Katanga, increasing the flow of refugees from one tribal area to another in search of UN protection.

The two immediate issues were how to deal with the Katangan leader (Moise Tshombe) and how to create effective working relationships with totally inexperienced government ministers and ministries of the new country. To this newcomer both issues 'looked like great black curtains threatening to envelope us, yet with no method of getting hold of them or controlling them'. He wasn't a bit surprised that the UN High Command from top to bottom was perplexed and depressed.

Then news arrived of an impending unexpected visit by Dag Hammarskjøld, the Secretary General, and to Roger's astonishment spirits rose remarkably; but not his own. In the face of such impenetrable darkness – political and moral – he could see not the slightest justification for optimism. He even thought of not going to the airport as part of the UN senior personnel welcoming party, frankly admitting that apart from not being 'much of a one for ceremony' there seemed to him far more important things to do. 'But I did, to my everlasting thankfulness,' he reflected on the whole experience.

As the most recent arrival (just two weeks), Roger took his place at the very end of the line of Congolese cabinet members, military and civil dignitaries, and top UN staff. It was, he recalled, a very hot afternoon and surely pretty trying for Mr Hammarskjøld, after fifteen hours or so of flying, to emerge from a cool plane into the blazing airport apron without sunglasses.

'Mine must have been about the 100th hand he shook, but his hand was still cool and his eyes – the brightest blue eyes I had ever seen – were still bright with just the flicker of a twinkle as he saw what was in store for him – a dais for a salute. He somehow symbolized and personalized the courage and strength of the healing forces in the world and I understood *why* those who knew him already had taken such heart from his prospective arrival.'

Early the next morning Hammarskjøld met twenty-five or so of the senior civilian staff, explaining that he didn't want to make a speech but rather to listen to them talking about their difficulties; he would take part in the discussion only as points came up on which he wanted to comment.

'And he did just that,' Roger recalled, 'but he contributed in such a way that, out of our perplexities and incoherence, he indicated what he thought was the way we should be able to make progress. He shifted the focus of the occasion from griping to constructiveness without ever making a speech and without ever indicating that he thought some of the stuff was footling – as it was, for we weren't more than average in ability.

'It was a masterly piece of sinewy leadership; and though subsequently I came to believe that his actual proposals were based on wrong assumptions I had a still higher regard for his integrity, his intelligence, his stamina and his power to hold and lead men. I think even the most cynical of us left that two-hour meeting with some new sense of the scale in importance and feasibility of the job, and a new sense that we had a moral obligation to the emergent Africa, however incompetent.

'On the following night was a party for all, the great and the small. Hammarskjøld could have stood with the ambassadors, the generals and the UN high-ups. But he'd seen them at his meetings, and on this occasion he was to be found talking with the back-room boys, the company commanders, the people whom he wouldn't meet in any other way.'

'By the week-end, four days after his arrival,' Roger sought months later to analyse his reactions, 'morale was good. Consequently when the news of his death began to circulate as rumour at midday on the following Monday the effect was cataclysmic. Mr Hammarskjøld had conveyed a sense that the Congo was not abandoned and that under his ministrations the new Congolese government and the UN between them could do what was required to assure peaceful progress. The important phrase here is *under his ministrations*. The inspiration was personal; with his death the sense of direction seemed to disappear completely. Looking back, I am still quite uncertain how we recovered, for my chief recollection is of two or three weeks during which I found myself again and again during the day doing nothing for minutes at a time and on the edge of tears. And nights were always restless and sometimes nightmarish.

'But it was part of the moral stature of the man that we *did* pick ourselves up again and get back on to our feet and work towards the goals that he had so powerfully and yet unpompously shown us.'

'For myself,' Roger attempted a summing up of this whole episode which left a permanent mark on his life and to which he often referred, 'I began to see how over the preceding years he had swung the UN from an instrument dominated by the great powers to a piece of world machinery in which the small countries with their interest in peaceful change could exercise real influence. It was Hammarskjøld more than any other single person who has turned the world into something a bit more complex and a bit more hopeful than a ring for the exercise of rivalry between great powers with the little chaps holding their coats. And if we now have rudimentary but perceptible beginnings of a political world society, the credit is Mr Hammarskjøld's.'

High praise indeed, especially as Roger's personal association with Hammarskjøld covered an aggregate of hours over a period of days. So why;

why the immensity of this impact and influence on a man not given to hero worship or blind to the foibles of the great? Part of the answer must lie in Roger's own assessment of the man:

> Hammarskjøld's strength lay in his personal integrity, his first-rate mind, his courage, his steadfastness, his conviction that there was no safety for the world in reliance on the past, and that there was light and hope if people worked hard enough looking for it with imagination and resource.
>
> He was a man of great spiritual strength though I think he had little use for ecclesiastical establishments. He travelled with a little French book of devotion, and on the night before he was killed he had put a marker in a passage which said that though men often reflected that they seemed to get caught up in small things yet if the small things were laid on them by God they were invested with the grandeur and importance and eternity of God himself.

Another clue might be the two men's capacity for justifiable anger and their way of dealing with it. Ralph Bunche, great servant of the UN, observed that it was typical of the Secretary General to contain himself throughout an interview and express his anger afterwards, and, he added, his anger was fierce; as was Roger's in like circumstances, and also expressed *afterwards*, as we'd already noticed, to his uncomplaining wife serving as a verbal punchbag.

Equally if paradoxically, the other side of this same coin, the two men exemplified habitual tranquillity in the face of sometimes outrageous provocation. Indeed, witnessing this imperturbable inner peace that characterized their lives, people beyond their intimate circle might have found it impossible to believe that either man was capable of fiery indignation at all, let alone eruptions of wrath in the face of implacable injustice.

There can be no doubt that Roger's Quakerism resonated to Hammarskjøld's spirituality, devoid of dogmatism, positive and sure, but free of the aridness of certainty; certainty but not certitude. Shortly before his arrival in the Congo, Hammarskjøld wrote in his diary: 'I don't know Who – or what – put the question, I don't know when it was put, I don't even remember answering. But at some moment I did answer Yes to Someone – or Something – and from that hour I was certain that existence is meaningful and that, therefore, my life, in self-surrender, had a goal. From that moment I have known what it means "not to look back" and "to take no thought for tomorrow".'

A decade or so earlier he had said that God does not die when we cease to believe in a personal diety, but we die on the day our lives cease to be illuminated by the steady radiance, renewed daily, of a wonder the source of which is beyond all reason.

So although the two men's understanding of and participation in institutional religion was different their shared Christian discipleship was beyond doubt, providing similarity of aims and motivation. They were both servants of peace and workers for world peace. They both ordered their priorities against the touchstone of ultimate reality, what they saw as the eternal values of the Kingdom of God. Both were devout but not remotely sanctimonious, delightfully confirmed by a sense of humour sufficiently 'wicked' to reveal their humanity.

Yet still the measure and permanence of that fleeting encounter in the Congo on Roger remains something of a mystery. It appears disproportionate unless – and this can be no more than conjecture – Hammarskjøld's visit focussed not only his personal charisma and idealism but his authority to get things done in global terms; and Roger, sharing the Secretary General's impatience with bureaucracy as a hindrance to action, wished for a similar wider platform on which he could serve his dream of world peace and social justice. Whatever the final explanation it seems safe to assume that Hammarskjøld was Roger's *alter ego*, the nearest approximation to the dedication, status and strong gentleness that reflected the potency of meekness, the spirit of the servant master, and finally the glory of life.

At a memorial gathering in the hall of a Leopoldville secondary school, largely for UN staff (some 650), the chief co-ordinator of UN operations in the Congo[3] explained that the book he held was the only one Hammarskjøld brought with him, the well-worn French commentary on the life of Christ from which he was accustomed to read each night in the very little time he kept for himself. The marker was his oath of allegiance to the UN:

> I solemnly swear to exercise in all loyalty, discretion and conscience the functions entrusted to me as Secretary General of the United Nations, to discharge these functions and regulate my conduct with the interests of the UN only in view and not to seek or accept instructions in regard to the performance of my duties from any government or other authority external to the Organization.

There was, the UN chief continued, no need to speak of Hammarskjøld's greatness; rather to be reminded of his care for persons, his warmth and his inner life. Then as the company stood in silence, there was, Roger detailed in his diary, 'a recorded playing of a Sibelius symphony during which extracts from two of Hammarskjøld's speeches were superimposed on the music – one in French, expressing the principles of the Congo operation, the other his

---

[3] Mr Linner, a Swede, like Hammarskjøld himself.

refusal to resign from the Secretary Generalship because it wasn't the Soviet Union that needed the UN but the small nations. It was all beautifully done, and when one considers the pitfalls of Protestantism, Catholicism, Jews, Hindus, Buddhists, secularists and so on the appropriateness was the more remarkable. For a little one felt better.'

Writing to his colleagues at Bristol, Roger added, 'I met Hammarskjøld on three occasions on the days he was here and was newly impressed with some new facet of his personality each time. One didn't feel lonely or helpless with him around. Who personifies the world that cares now?'

This letter to his colleagues significantly included greetings to the Institute's 'char-ladies', with the suggestion that the new intake of students should be told how hard these valued members of staff were compelled to work 'to clean up the carpet from the coffee stains of their predecessors; it might make a difference. But I doubt if they'd believe it!' Little wonder these 'char-ladies', a bunch of colourful characters, 'worshipped their professor'; one of them, famed among them as a poet, never missed a chance – end of academic year or Christmas party – to write a song of eulogy about him, praise sprinkled with earthy humour. If Roger now wondered who would care on the world scene, they never doubted his care about them, stained carpets or whatever.

Despite his sense of desolation at Hammarskjøld's death and the mystery of the circumstances surrounding it, Roger wasted no time in getting down to work, first to grasp what he called 'the peculiar wretchedness of the ex-Belgian Congo'. This vast land, the size of the whole of Western Europe, had been governed, as he saw it, by a centralized authoritarian regime whose monolithic competence had been safeguarded by allowing virtually no Africans to carry or learn how to carry major responsibility. In consequence, at the withdrawal of Belgian personnel, there were far too few Africans capable of exercising the necessary authority.

The whole pattern of colonial administration had been one of governors and governed with an unbridged gulf between. The upshot was that the new Congolese government, having only seen representatives of the old authority give orders, no discussion, no explanation, and expect to be obeyed, acted on the assumption that this was what being-in-power was all about. Any tendency to consult or seek the advice of UN experts was seen as weakness. Conversely, if UN experts sought to offer advice they were accused of interfering beyond their terms of reference, and firmly put in their place. And whereas in neighbouring Kenya and the Rhodesias coherent political argument had gathered momentum for five years or more, in the Congo it had never started, leaving a chasm between two distinct groups and ways of life. 'All this gives one a feeling,' he early recorded, 'of loneliness and of helplessness amounting almost to paralysis.'

Only 'almost', for Roger's diary indicates to what extent he set about bridging the chasm, creating relationships of mutual trust, confidence and respect. It was neither easy, quick nor painless, but once more his sense of humour no less than his self-evident interest in people proved winsome and often created lasting friendships. The following extracts from his copious observations are chronologically correct though – written at irregular intervals – not always precisely dated:

22.9.61 Half of Leopoldville's African population (1,400,000) is under fifteen years of age, two-thirds of it under twenty-five. Half the males between the ages of sixteen and twenty-five have no regular jobs. The African townships burst with uncontrolled willing young humanity absolutely apart from the European villadom. When you look at the townships from the high inside of a bus and see the incoherence you feel – at least I do – why Congolese politicians seem to be so often entirely inconsistent and unstable. Life is just like that where they grew up – shouting, swarming, pushing, drinking, whoring. And out of it all the Europeans have produced an extraordinarily comfortable life.

At the level of daily life, the outstanding feature this week has been the sight of hundreds of women and children with tins grubbing about under trees for caterpillars, under any trees anywhere. And, heavens, the place fairly crawls with the things. You tread on them on pavements, they go at tremendous pace and in enormous hordes – they fall out of trees into your hair. The local populace boil them with salt, pepper and spices. It gives them animal protein which they can't afford otherwise.

7.10.61 I lunched today with the British Council man here. Somehow the conversation got around to burglary and its type and quality here and in British Guiana where he was before. He thought the standard higher there; for example, when he and his housekeeper were both away, burglars broke in and collected the WC, cistern, pipes and all, and sealed off all the pipes, a proper job. This seems to me a very effective pattern of technical assistance.

In the latter part of the week I ran into a fantastic piece of muddle – two ministries are charged with exactly the same responsibilities in the field of community development which is my responsibility. Nobody has noticed this for the past two months – possibly because neither does anything, but there are all the seeds of a major row in this, and my French just isn't good enough for situations of such tension and such speed, especially as the trouble will be within UN as well as within Government. It's certainly taken me nearer to the springs of feelings in these parts, but I wish it didn't come into my dreams too.

It looks as if the UN simply had not got enough able and disinterested civil staff with enough experience of the crooks of the world to be able to get and keep control. It'll be perfectly easy in the days to come to present the whole affair as the sort of incompetent muddle that was the First World War, as compared with the vastly superior planning and operational techniques of the Second. It *is* a muddle and often pretty cheerless. One feels as if one lived in a house riddled with dry rot in which one may fall softly and helplessly through the floor any day. On the other hand it might catch fire; or like so many situations it may be nothing like as dangerous as theory would lead one to believe.

16.10.61 Is it worth hanging around in this morass? I don't know. Somebody's got to, while enough Congolese learn how to govern. There are those who can, without doubt. And I have a feeling that, in spite of my limited French, some of them are beginning to trust me. My main *job* is to try to get them to cut their ideas down to size that they might be able to manage and then try to help them to see how they translate ideas into operations and training. It's not exciting.

28.10.61 I was moved by an incident just after I left the transit hostel where I had been for six-and-a-half weeks. It was worked by two shifts of domestic staff, two on each shift, alternating weeks of nights and days. All four of them, at one time or another, had invited me to supply them with black-market cigarettes or liquor, or had asked me for financial loans till their wages were paid, and they had all accepted my refusals without sulking. I think we had real confidence in one another, but I was surprised by what happened next.

The senior, Jerome, is a very good laundryman, and so, after I left, I took my laundry along to him. The next day he came to my office, a hot half-a-mile away, in his free time, to say that he had spilled a thermos of tea and some of it had gone over my pyjamas and a handkerchief, and he couldn't get it out. He reckoned the damage was about 200 francs (25/-) and when I collected the laundry from the other shift I would find 200 francs in an envelope. He gets 300 francs a month. I said, of course, that accidents happened and that he needn't bother. All the same the 200 francs *were* there when I went to collect the laundry later, and I had to work quite hard to get the other shift, Leo and Emil, to keep it until they could give it to Jerome. And when I came to look at the pyjamas and the handkerchief I can barely see what happened and would never have noticed.

17.12.61 We spent two days in Stanleyville. The UN local representative had asked us not to go, as conditions (extensive floods) were so bad and we should be in the way. But we said that we must see for ourselves and that we must support our minister. So we turned up to sharp disapproval. 'No food' – 'we've brought our own'; 'no electricity' – 'we've brought candles'. 'No security in a hostile population' – 'we'll take the risk'. 'No transport' – 'we'll walk or rely on our Minister'. Having convinced them that we could take it, it then turned out that they *had* found rooms for us in military quarters and they did put two officers' messes at our disposal; we preferred our own raw rations.

We spent the first afternoon finding the Provincial Minister of Social Affairs who turned out to be Lumumba's[4] brother. He hadn't a clue about policy or action, and was mainly concerned about how to get a new suit for his marriage to a (2nd?) wife on Saturday week . . . Next morning was very hot indeed and we spent a long time trying to locate blackmarket waterproofs for the African members of the party . . . Once on the launch we spent the rest of the morning looking at both banks. In some places we passed *over* houses, elsewhere people on roofs or in upper floors, with furniture and animals. Of course it *is* a river population and floods as such are not strange or frightening. But these are worse than the previous known worst in 1909.

The only moment of light relief was a sudden shout to stop by our Minister who had just noticed a woman standing in the doorway of a hut off the road. 'That's my divorced wife,' he said, 'I didn't know this was where she lived.' So we went back and there was a restrained family reunion.

I've not much doubt that Welensky (only one thug among a lot, and most of the UN people are *not* politicians, let alone thugs) with or without the knowledge and connivance of the British Government, has been backing Tshombe in all sorts of ways. And I haven't any doubt that the Salisbury capitalist lobby has been putting the screws on very tight indeed.

It's all so stupid for Tshombe will *have* to come in before he can then negotiate how far he can get some sort of devolved power. And the fighting will simply make the process more bitter, particularly if the whites now quit in a body, thus creating exactly the chaos which they've said they feared. It has been clear here for months that if Tshombe would really negotiate he would get very reasonable terms and be no danger to anybody in the short-run. What really frightens UN now is that they may win the military battle and have civil chaos and scorched earth on their hands. But it's not UN's fault. It's the fault of all those who have encouraged Tshombe to think that his next step was not with the Congo.

Christmas Eve, 1961 Leopoldville. Sitting on the verandah at 5 o'clock this afternoon, sweating gently, drinking tea, and watching lizards climb higher up the tree trunks to keep up with the sinking sun, I was fooling about with the radio, trying to get either news or good robust African carol singing, when I hit on King's College Chapel, faint but recognizable; the first time I've ever got the BBC direct. Sheer sentimental nostalgia cheered me up a bit, for this last couple of weeks have been about as shame-making for the British of

---

[4] Patrice Lumumba, Congolese Prime Minister, 1960–61.

my acquaintance as were the weeks I spent in India/Pakistan just before Suez. It's difficult to know which is worse, the insensitivity of the Tories or the sheer ineptitude of the Government. And basically this situation isn't a difficult one in its main outlines.

The British Government seems to have made three howling errors. First, it seems to have assumed that the rest of the Congo is indifferent to the Katanga issue which wouldn't be difficult if it wasn't for the UN. Second, it seems to have assumed that the local UN high-ups don't know what they are doing, either politically or militarily. Third, it seems to assume that Tshombe, and whoever is behind him, is reasonably easy to negotiate with. One would have thought that all of these assumptions would have been blown sky-high since September.

It's only the presence of the UN as a potential or active agency that has held off civil war of the most futile kind in Katanga, since probably neither side could have won, though Tshombe could have held southern Katanga with the support of mercenaries and Welensky whose cynical crookery seems almost certainly established, with or without the connivance of the British Government, and blessed by Lord Salisbury and his commercial interests.

It doesn't feel like Christmas, even though I did sleep under a blanket for the whole of last night. But I'm struck again by a query about the whole symbolism of international religions. In a place like the Congo I don't know whether there ever is a time of year when new hope breaks through darkness. The days don't get shorter and darker and then longer and brighter. They stay the same. We sang 'See amid the winter snow' in church this morning. To us in Europe this all means something very deep in our experience. But here where the stuff vegetation seems to grow without cessation to a positively obscene degree, one feels that hopes and fears must take quite different forms.

7.1.62 The last fortnight has been rather overshadowed by tension between my colleagues and me in the UN Social Affairs Section and the Secretary General of the Ministry of Social Affairs. He says he wants help which will build up into action on policies which are already determined. The fact, in my view, is that there are no policies, only quite vigorous and attractive sketches which omit all foreground and imply different foregrounds anyway.

Just before Christmas this all came out in a rather offensive letter asking us to confine ourselves to what we were asked to do and not complicating life by unearthing factors which were, in his view, irrelevant.

Then just after New Year's Day he made a fearful row about a meeting which two of my colleagues had had with officials of Leopoldville province to discuss the possibilities of a practical field project some 150 miles from Leopoldville. He was absolutely furious at what he thought was our interference in what we hadn't been asked to do, crossing every sort of administrative and policy wire, and telling his staff what to do. At the end of ¾ of an hour – during which I was astonished by what seemed to me the lucidity of my own French! – he was a little quieter. I've gone into this long and dreary domestic story because in fact it illuminates a whole lot of the Congo's troubles.

S., like many other senior Congolese, is humiliated by his own and his country's inability to cope. They know they need help, but they haven't learnt how to accept it, and we, corporately, haven't learnt how to give it in these very painful and delicate conditions. The UN in New York goes on pretending that this is an extended but basically conventional operation of Technical Assistance, to a government that knows what it wants and that has some sort of machinery.

Self-respect demands that the Congolese believe this, and that we act as though we believed it, too. In fact intelligent Congolese know it's not true; but they can't admit it nor can we assent it. And neither they nor we are skilled enough to find ways of working that get round these emotional blocks. So the Congolese make UN neo-colonialism the scapegoat for all the things that go wrong or don't happen. They can lose their temper, but we mustn't lose ours. This is proper, for we have the security that they haven't got. But it's exhausting especially as nothing happens at the end of it, except that we're still here, and that doesn't look or feel like a useful outcome of energy spent.

The operation here is messy, inefficient, ill-co-ordinated but not wrong-headed. The directives from New York at the Technical Assistance level show no grasp at all; but they may be troubled by money. And anyway few of us on the spot know what either New York or we *ought* to do.

21.1.62 I have been in Elizabethville for five days; a preliminary look that there might be a useful job for a small Quaker team on the spot.

Elizabethville is 1000 miles south east of Leopoldville. The UN maintains contact by air with a number of chartered planes that strike the outsider as very ramshackle and badly under-crewed – two only to do everything. They carry supplies for the most part – I travelled with a ton of raw unwrapped meat in the cabin, whoof – but have crude seats for 15 passengers in the tail. The freelance pilots are said to divide their time between ferrying UN supplies and gun-running for the Katangese mercenaries. This does not seem to me unlikely.

The whites are frightened both of UN and of Africans. The African communes, untouched almost by the fighting, are heavy and dejected. There's no life in them, and this is extraordinary for the feature of African townships everywhere, East, West and Central, is their incredible vitality.

The only place bursting with life is the refugee camp, 40,000 people squatting in little huts in less than 100 acres. Conditions of life and hygiene are dreadful, but there's vitality, a vast amount of it devoted to feuds within the camp and to looting in the European city.

Urquhart (UN civilian representative in the Congo) looks as if he's walked off a mortuary slab. He's exhausted but has done a good job. The other senior UN man is Dumontet, French, very calm, seemingly mild but quite fearless and a man of peace. The morning I left he had been invited to go to the *house* of the Minister of the Interior, and the most virulent of Tshombe's group. One isn't often invited to people's *houses*, and the previous evening Dumontet was being urged to take a bodyguard. No, he said, the only thing to do in this situation is to meet people wherever they ask you, whatever they ask you, without surprise and without precautions.

7.2.62 The main news from my part of the Congo was the arrival of Margery, straight from talking about the World Council of Churches conference in Delhi to nineteen meetings in twenty-one days, from Canterbury to Belfast and Bridgwater to Middlesbrough.

I had to get up at 3.15 a.m. on Tuesday in order to pay my third visit to Elizabethville. Quite a lot has happened since my first $3\frac{1}{2}$ weeks ago. For one thing, my suggestion that there would be a useful job to be done by a couple of appropriate Quaker workers in investigating the nature of the rehabilitation needs of Elizabethville produced a first-class couple on the ground within a fortnight. This was a remarkable performance, especially as the team is remarkably strong. Walter Martin, senior Friend in East Africa, is French and Swahili speaking (Swahili is the local language of Elizabethville); Laurence Naish is French-speaking with ten years of Madagascar political and social change behind him. Apart from the Congo itself, they couldn't have better introductory experience, and it is plain that in their twelve days in Elizabethville they have already established a range of contacts with Africans in the communes, with ministers, with UN and with European residents that will be invaluable.

One of the most difficult problems here is the real position regarding the Balubas, the very able minority tribe, anti-Tshombe, who since September have quit the African communes and have been living, 45,000 of them, in a makeshift camp of 100 acres on the edge of Elizabethville where they are a political, health and criminal menace to the whole place. How to get the camp closed? How to start?

Walking down the main street of Elizabethville, Walter noticed the carved wooden animals for sale. 'Wakamba surely,' he said, identifying a Kenya tribe who do this. So he talked to the African in charge in Swahili, found that they had common acquaintances on the Ofafa housing estate in Nairobi, that the chap lives in one of the communes and finished up with an invitation to visit him. This was followed by two or three further conversations, followed again next day by Walter being stopped in the street by Wakamba who wanted to greet *him*. Now these chaps live in the communes, talk the same vernacular, but are *not* involved in the tribal feuds. They can give a most useful cross-bearing on the essential local tribal issue. They won't necessarily be right, but at least they won't have the same perspectives as the people tribally committed. But they wouldn't say anything to anybody except a chap like Walter whose knowledge of their own home base reassures them.

They (Walter and Laurence) were equally skilful in establishing a cross-bearing via a Nyasalander and a Rhodesian African whom they found among the officials of the bank they use . . . I sidelight – they asked the Nyasalander if Nyasaland was better prepared for independence than the Congo? 'Yes,' he said, 'here I count as an educated man; in Nyasaland there are many better educated than me.' Interesting, for Nyasaland education isn't all that generous. Anyway Martin and Naish have really built themselves in with a splendid range of contacts and I think will do a fine job.

I wrote a week or so ago about our troubles with our ministry. Twelve days ago the atmosphere changed absolutely – and we got the go-ahead with every encouragement. Why, why, why? This is the sort of thing that happens in the Congo, and I'm not sensitive enough to be able to make sense of it. I don't know any Europeans who are, and the Congolese I can ask don't know either, or more likely can't say because they aren't as aware as we are of the apparent illogicality of the situation. To them coherence and continuity lie in some factor not apparent to us.

13.5.62 Leopoldville. The most interesting thing I did before we went away for 3½ weeks leave early in April was to visit S. Kasai with half-a-dozen other UN people to see whether it would be feasible to repatriate anything up to 20,000 of the Balubas in the 'refugee' camp at Elizabethville who claim that this is their *home*.

Our job on our mission was to find out if, after already taking 100,000 back, the locality, the local government and the local hereditary chiefs would be prepared to take another 20,000 or more from Elizabethville. Without exception they said yes, and most were prepared to take about as many as the current population of the village. It was a very effective demonstration of what clan loyalty means – for good in this instance but of course equally for ill in the political context of the Congo today.

For the 3½ weeks leave, Roger and Margery took a ferry across the Congo to Brazzaville and from there flew what he called the 'short 1500 miles' to Salisbury, Southern Rhodesia. The resident representatives of the American

Friends Service Council (Lyle and Bicky Tatum) entertained them for the week-end providing an opportunity for Roger to see at first-hand any developments of the inter-racial trends set down at the Adult Education and Citizenship conference some four years before.

Indeed their first engagement was at University College for degree celebrations, and apart from interviewing numerous students who wished to do post-graduate work at Bristol Roger was encouraged that, despite three-quarters of the University's under-graduates being white, an African was president of the students union, elected by the whole student body. Outside the university, however, things were not so promising. Black students continued to be ruled by segregation, change of any sort barely perceptible. To counter the prohibition of black and white students swimming in the same civic pool, the Principal of the university had had a pool built in his own garden and made it available at any time to students of whatever race, but though appreciated this did little either to heal the hurt of apartheid or satisfy the growing political protests of its victims.

An altogether different ethos awaited Roger and Margery in Nyasaland where their son Anthony, social development officer, and his wife Anne were waiting to greet them at Blantyre. That same evening, Monday, Roger and Margery drove to Zomba to stay for a couple of nights with Augustine and Mary Bwanaussi, he an old Bristol student and now Minister for Internal Affairs. The most interesting meeting of their time together was a frank discussion between all their host's African ministerial colleagues and a young European lawyer who was both a member of the Malawi party and also a minister. 'We talked about the Congo,' Roger recalled; 'the two most talkative Africans were the Minister of Education and the Minister of Justice. They simply see Tshombe as a stooge and the UN as an incompetent and half-hearted support to the Central Congolese government. They find it quite impossible to see the complexities of the Tshombe line, fail to recognize the UN Congo Organization as the agent of 104 nations at some odds with each other, and have faith in the efficiency of swift military suppression of Katangese aspirations.'

At midday on the following Monday they met their daughter Elizabeth at Blantyre airport, straight from London, and immediately set off on the 450-mile drive to Mzuzu, the administrative centre of the northern province, where Anthony and Anne had their home. Almost 200 miles into the journey they stayed overnight at Lilongwe to meet a couple of Roger's old students at Bristol, and entertain them to dinner. One was the first African to become a senior provincial inspector, concentrating on raising the quality of primary teaching; the other an educational field worker trying without a car to supervise 100 schools, an illustration, explained Roger, of 'the economic position'.

This in mind Roger noted approvingly an extract from the minutes of an Administrative Council he and Margery attended of a local government unit in Northern Nyasaland: 'The Council has found that many people do not pay licences for their dogs. Some say that as the country shall have a new Government there is no need in the new Government to pay licences for dogs. After long discussion on this subject the council resolved that members of the Council should try to explain to people that anyone who does not pay licence for his dog shall be liable to a fine, and explain to them that the new Government may licence dogs at a higher rate then the present Government. No Government can run without money. Therefore people should be encouraged to pay their dogs' licences. Also they should be strongly informed that the new Government means hard labour and self support.' Roger felt constrained to add the comment: 'The Congolese would do very well to absorb some of this philosophy.'

After the delights of a family Easter at Mzuzu, Anne expecting her first baby, the atmosphere of the country as a whole relaxed and excited as the fruits of independence were confidently anticipated, Roger and Margery possibly needed a reminder of the grim reality that awaited them in the Congo; and they found it with a vengeance during the final few days of their leave, in Johannesburg where Roger particularly wanted to talk with local Friends about their work among both the families of political prisoners and for the prisoners themselves on release. Nothing could have conveyed the evils of apartheid more vividly nor underlined the near despair of many Friends in the face of what Roger described as 'the familiar story of the rigidity and brutality of the segregation'.

It was the bewilderment of *good* people caught up in a system of blatant injustice and suffering through colour that wrung his heart and challenged his faith. Hating what was being done by their government in their name they themselves didn't know what to do, how to challenge the military might that buttressed policies they detested but with which their very impotence appeared to collude if not approve. There was no obvious answer, and Roger endeared himself to the Friends with whom he talked by not suggesting otherwise.

On 1 May, loaded with apples, he and Margery returned to the Congo taking just under four hours for the 2,000 miles from Johannesburg to Brazzaville, only the final three to four hundred miles over the Congo. The weather was stiflingly hot and humid, making tempers short, Roger mentioned, 'both in UN and government, and between all of us'. Furthermore policies were just as vague and confused as ever, creating a feeling of general gloom.

The most dramatic work with which he was immediately involved was with two lots of refugees – from Rwanda over in the far west between the Congo and Uganda; and in the Baluba camp at Elizabethville which the UN chief ordered should be closed as quickly as possible. This clear directive, cutting through long dreary arguments about trains and bridges and boats and aircraft, not to mention the political in-fighting and pressure groups concerned about loss of jobs for camp personnel, aimed at closing the camp completely by the end of July. The implications meant stopping food distribution, withdrawing the armed guard, and bulldozing what was left of the crude shelters. Belubas refusing to move would become responsible for themselves.

Into this quite unpredictable and dangerous prospect Ruth Bitten and Tony Cashmore, representing Friends Service Council, set about projecting themselves as a sort of Citizens Advice Bureau. Roger didn't hesitate to go with them to review the whole situation. The Quakers urged that as the refugees had demonstrated their wish to be evacuated to Albertville where they declared they would be among their own people and out of the reach of the Katangan police, the UN 'cannot abandon all responsibility for their welfare'.

In a report to Friends House, London, dated 13 August, Tony Cashmore included the observation: 'Roger Wilson has made a very deep impression on those with whom he worked; I was extremely grateful to have Roger's backing and comments, pushed in in odd moments during his hectic last days here, but cool and collected nonetheless.' Cashmore also passed on how 'very regretful of losing Roger's wisdom and experience' was the man in charge of UN operations in Leopoldville (Robert Gardiner).

As for Roger himself – sharing the Quaker workers' fears of possible epidemics among the refugees, rats taking over on a broadening front, and with no one appearing to want to be responsible for anything – he used some of his 'hectic last days' in the Congo to write detailed hand-over reports.

To his successor (Professor Rose) he included the suggestion that 'an occasional outburst of anger when one is obstructed by remediable unhelpfulness does not seem to come amiss', outcome of what on another occasion he called 'fruitful states of tension'.

To the UN in New York he was equally pungent: 'We have felt ourselves getting a bit closer to some sort of understanding of people and situations over the last three months, but our perplexities grow rather than diminish. I think we have won some measure of confidence among those we have worked with, but it is difficult to know what this is worth in a setting which needs administrative order before confidence can have executive significance. And I'm not sure the UN operation has adequately applied its mind to this over-riding problem of the pattern of government in the Congo. It has been preoccupied on the one hand with Katanga and political crises, and on the other with technical detail . . . This isn't a very cheerful ending; but it isn't a cheerful prospect. A policy of drifting into tolerable chaos may be the right thing – but it's more costly than the UN budget can stand.'

With such a man on the spot, deeply involved at a personal level but with the ability of a visionary to stand back and formulate strategy, it was hardly surprising that Roger's UN departmental bosses in New York viewed his imminent departure from the Congo as little short of calamitous. 'We have so few men of your standing,' they wrote; and asked whether 'we can look forward to a further assignment for you in due course?' In fact, they further appealed, a Pakistani government minister was recently making inquiries as to the possibility of Roger returning to Pakistan for another term as Social Welfare Advisor. If this was out of the question so soon after the Congo they were sure that they would 'be able to offer an assignment that would demand from you the sort of service you wish to give to an international organization'.

The New York UN Office tried again only days before Roger actually left the Congo; left it, as his hurried reply indicated, 'with more than a tinge of unexpected regret', though he felt constrained to add, 'I shall be glad to be doing my own job in a fortnight'.

Even before departing *for* the Congo, in again declining a strong invitation to lead the Quaker Programme at the UN in New York, he had hinted at the possibility of leaving Bristol, a prospect neither he nor Margery cared to contemplate. Encouraged by this crumb of hope, Colin W. Bell of the American FSC returned to the subject within weeks of Roger's return. 'It would be a matter, I believe,' wrote Bell, 'of great satisfaction throughout the Quaker world if it transpired that you are able to shoulder this task.'

The *task* was to lead a permanent staff of four or five in further developing a 'Quaker Presence' at the UN, not necessarily to suggest solutions to questions before the Assembly; not necessarily to tell delegates what the Quaker point of view was on any given question – for who, commented a prominent Friend, can say what the Quaker point of view is on *any* subject, much less as related to the terribly difficult and complex matters before the UN? In short, the main job was simply to make friends, deeper relationships, and in so doing create an atmosphere in which solutions could be found.

Bold claims were made about this 'Quaker Presence'[5]: 'People all over the world know about Friends. We are universally beloved and respected – perhaps we don't deserve this reputation but it exists. It is a fact; it is truly amazing – phenomenal – how often UN personalities have had previous contact with Friends and are therefore willing to seek them out to talk over their problems, and to talk frankly and freely.'

---

[5] See, for instance, Thomas R. Bodine's *Report on Quaker UN Program to the American Section*, Friends World Committee for Consultation, Washington, 1 February 1964.

Roger, not doubting that all this was true, would be inclined nevertheless to view some of it as hyperbole; but about the work itself at the UN he needed no persuasion of its importance. Hence his response that in principle both he and Margery felt that they must regard themselves as available. There were, however, unexpected complications, all bearing on his present job and his freedom to consider the nature of other commitments.

On his return from the Congo he had been somewhat surprised at the nagging *persistence* of his interest in the principles and practice of UN Technical Assistance in parts of the world where self-evidently it was desperately needed. This did not mean, he explained to the American FSC, that he wished to tie himself to the UN; other considerations apart it needed criticism as well as support! But it did mean that he would welcome 'being freer for middle-length leave of absence than could be granted to most British university academics'.

Another part of the 'unexpected complications' was the uncertain outcome of current negotiations to re-organize the Institute of Education so that, with the appointment of a third professor of education, it might be possible for Roger 'to move sideways to look after our operations in overseas education and in the field of social work' while also leaving him free to be away for substantial periods.

Friends House in London had already asked him and Margery if they were willing to be nominated as visiting Friends at Quaker House in New York next autumn, and having replied in the affirmative they envisaged being there, from the middle of November until near the end of January 1964. This would give them opportunity to get the feel of the place and see what might be involved in accepting the UN Quaker Programme Directorship, plus the chance for discussion about the whole enterprise with the American FSC. In the meantime, he assured them, 'if you find the right Director for three, five or ten years, you should not feel any obligation to the Wilsons'.

Confirmation of Roger's autumn arrival, still nine months away, immediately set in motion the organizing by American Friends of a series of large public meetings at strategic points across the country aimed at combating, they explained, the adverse criticism of the UN in particular and of 'world order under law' in general, largely a product of prejudice and ignorance. Hatred of the UN was, they said, being fanned rather vigorously these days, and the Congo operation notably was being associated with the most derogatory stories. 'Your recent experience and capacity to put it in a wider perspective,' they enthused, 'would constitute a message which is greatly needed.'

This concern about misrepresentation of the UN Congo operation was also causing anger among UN personnel in the Congo itself. From Leopoldville Roger received an appeal that he should talk on the BBC to correct what was seen there as 'a great hindrance to intelligent interest in the development of the Congo story' as presented by the British media. He had in fact already broadcast on the Home Service, promptly followed by a suggestion that he should give a much longer talk on the Third Programme, but finding time was the problem; since the beginning of the new academic year, he replied to Leopoldville, he'd been so appallingly busy that he'd had no chance to do anything beyond keeping his work at the university going and addressing twenty-six or so meetings between Bristol and Aberdeen, addressing them precisely about the Congo!

Even so, he sought to respond to the Third Programme, providing what was an analysis of his key impressions: At the core of the de-colonialization process and the sensitive area of offering technical assistance in low-income countries was the way the colonizing power – for political reasons – and the indigenous leaders – for emotional reasons – conspired to understate the element of crisis which was unavoidable when an authoritarian power gave way to the quite different dynamics of power among people hitherto under authority. Behind the order-giving which they had experienced only on the *receiving* end were complex processes by which policy was hacked out, apart from the moral stamina required to see it through.

In consequence, 'we technical assistants made all sorts of sixth-form assumptions that were meaningless to bright boys in the lower school. We thought in terms of getting something done when the real problem was to help our Congolese colleagues to grasp the very idea of government'. The concomitant feature was no less perplexing. 'Those of us on technical assistance missions for a short time or a year or two wanted *to get something done* for the sake of our reputations. But this was neo-colonialism, going faster than our indigenous colleagues could at that time manage. Alternatively the long-term personnel whose careers were in international organizations could easily drift into rootless ineffectiveness.'

He concluded by frankly admitting that neither he nor anybody else as far as he knew had any real answers; and far too many people had stopped, if they had ever started, asking the right questions. What bothered him, he told the BBC, was that this kind of honest talking might prove offensive not only to the Congolese but some UN personnel. All he could hope was that he sounded neither outrageous nor self-righteous.

This temptation to do things – anything, needed or not – for the sake of personal or institutional reputation was one that Roger himself demonstrably overcame. In the early days after his return from the Congo he was approached by the American FSC for advice about their contemplated involvement in relief work for refugees fleeing unrest in Angola. He replied that from what he knew of the situation these refugees were being completely integrated with their Congolese fellow-tribesmen. 'I would myself take the view,' he summed up, 'that there is no useful place for the fresh initiative of a further agency.'

Work as an educationist, a technical assistant or anything else, as a means of self-justification or for personal kudos was to this busy man little short of criminal in the light of all that really needed to be done; if ignored would be left undone. Duplication of the good works of others by Friends was no less indictable, related, he suspected, to furious activity as a cover for the absence of real purpose.

In a different context he warned a conference of tutors about the danger of superficial assessment of their work: 'Examiners find it much easier to mark dead knowledge than living insight.'

Roger made a similar emphasis when some twelve months later American Friends once more sought his advice, this time about a proposal that they should participate in a community development programme for the Congo. His reply was made through Josephine Noble of Friends House, London, who explained that he was 'extremely busy at present as it is the end of term and the middle of the examinations. Therefore he has asked me to make a copy of his hand-written memo and forward it to you'. She also included his personal aside to her: 'I wish I could get FSC and AFSC to see that the Congo is far more like Normandy in 1945/46 than Algeria or even Elizabethville.'

As for his 'memo' – a detailed exposition under eight headings! – he made no attempt to hide his exasperation that AFSC, even if prepared to be involved, was anxious to keep the operation exclusively under its own umbrella. 'We *must* be *willing*,' he said, 'to consider lending personnel when a major job has to be done and where the contribution of the unpaid volunteer doing it for service motives is of untold significance. We have got to be willing to muck in when this makes sense. For AFSC or FSC to go in cold would involve a twelve-month prior investigation, and I do not myself believe that this would be a good way to help the Congolese. It does a job *for* them, instead of growing out of what they themselves feel. Far better to find that there is a youth group in some bush town which wants to rebuild its road to the river but needs the necessary moral stiffening to get started and keep going. This is why offers of personnel are far more valuable than projects planned by strangers.'

One way or another, no matter how absorbed at the university, he could not escape the Congo. If individuals or organizations were not appealing to him for advice, he himself felt constrained to write encouragingly to former colleagues in Leopoldville, address yet another public meeting, respond to a request from an Oxford student magazine for a resumé of his Congo experience, and keep the whole matter at the forefront of Quaker thinking. But to one particular invitation he answered with alacrity – alacrity tinged with sadness. The United Nations Association in Great Britain requested him to officiate at the presentation of a memorial plaque to Dag Hammarskjøld, to be placed at Meridian Hall, a residence for overseas students at Bristol University.

Roger's speech re-lived Hammarskjøld's last visit to the Congo and news that his plane had crashed en route from Leopoldville to Ndola, on a mission, Roger recalled, 'which the conventional say was beneath his dignity, but which he undertook, I think, because he could not tolerate the thought that there was fighting which he might be able to stop'. He concluded his moving tribute with the confident hope that all who lived at Meridian Hall or entered the building in international friendship would be refreshed by the spirit of a truly great man.

The impact of Hammarskjøld on Roger, apart from the Congo experience as a whole, undoubtedly initiated the explorations about the possibility of a third professor being appointed within the Institute of Education, and this was finally decided to take effect from 1 August 1964, leaving Roger himself free to occupy innovatively the new Chair of Education and Social Development. In a personal letter to colleagues throughout the university he explained that, first, the new arrangement would make it possible for the university in general and for himself in particular 'to give more attention to certain aspects of Technical Assistance to developing countries'; and, second, that he was looking forward to 'many more years of happy collaboration with those engaged in education within the area of the Bristol Institute of Education'.

All this was decided almost a year before it officially took effect, thus hitting firmly on the head his suggested Directorship of the Quaker Presence at the UN Headquarters; though not his promised brief involvement there with Margery from the autumn of 1963.

But first, following up a lengthy private conversation with an old associate of Oxford University Labour Club, Michael Stewart, by now Minister of Education and Science in Harold Wilson's 1964–70 Government, Roger was putting the finishing touches to a detailed memorandum on 'Socialist Initiative in the Non-financial Social Services'. (Roger revelled in telling the story that Mr Stewart was actually addressing one of the regular student guest nights in the Wilson's own home when he was called to the telephone to receive confirmation of his appointment as Foreign Secretary.) The memorandum, focussing problems that didn't get solved not because they were intractable but because of lack of communication between the various insular groups involved – professional social workers, local authorities and academics – was delivered a fortnight before Roger and Margery left for America, but its degree of effectiveness was apparently subjected to the Official Secrets Act, or something of the sort. Certainly there is no record of the meeting he requested with the Minister to hammer out his substantive proposals ever taking place.

More positive was the success attributed to the Quaker House visit and the USA country-wide meetings he addressed about the UN, but attributed not *unconditionally* by Roger himself. Almost immediately on his return to Bristol he typically analysed the whole experience from which there emerged a central evocative proposal. The fact was, since his first visit to Quaker House, in 1951, the UN world had moved on and was now vastly more sophisticated. Whereas within both the UN Secretariat and national delegations there had been little experience of dealing with refugees, technical assistance, human rights and so on, and a tendency to think in conventional 'power' terms symbolized by the veto provision of the Security Council, now international diplomats and UN personnel alike had developed enormous know-how of both peace-keeping and tackling humanitarian problems issuing from military conflict.

'No Friend, operating from Quaker House or elsewhere,' Roger concluded, 'can now expect to be able to keep up with UN experience and prod it in useful directions over as broad a front as was earlier possible. The Friends who do this work have got to have the ability and the time to develop their own expertise at which they have a right to be taken seriously. But they can't do this if the Society expects them also to pick up and play every ball that is thrown from London, Philadelphia or wherever.' From his own recent experience he mentioned the 'ball' of human rights thrown by a British Friend, another on economic affairs thrown by a Swede, and yet another, this time thrown by himself, on South Africa, all aimed at Quaker House staff while the throwers 'went home', leaving the 'catchers' not only ill-equipped to deal with such a wide range of 'declared interest' but with no time in the unequal struggle to develop their own personal lives.

His proposed answer? It might be more valuable for the permanent staff at Quaker House to be less impeded by generalized visitors of goodwill and instead to receive visits from *really* well-informed Friends who might stay for a month of concentrated work in their own specialist area. However, he also pointed out that 'the thing which gives the Quaker at the point of UN impact authority to speak is not simply his own experience, but the fact that there are other Friends in gaol for their conscience, conducting clinics in the desert, packing old clothes or offering uninhibited social, intellectual or spiritual fellowship in a Centre to a perplexed student who five years later turns up as his country's prime minister or ambassador to the UN'.[6]

Immediately it became known that Roger's new professorial appointment

---

[6] Part of a memorandum sent to Duncan Wood at Friends International Centre, Geneva, in June 1964.

was aimed at making him more readily available for international commissions, the UN, the World Bank, the Governments of Pakistan, Malawi, the Gilbert and Ellice Islands, and opponents of apartheid in South Africa started negotiations. His mind was rarely free of the needs of Central and Southern Africa. With the break-up of the Federation of the two Rhodesias and Nyasaland, the University in Salisbury became exclusively the University of Southern Rhodesia, meaning that the other two countries were required to start from scratch in creating universities of their own.

In England discussion centred upon an initiative from America that Friends world-wide should endow a professorial chair at the University of Zambia, formerly Northern Rhodesia, discussions in which Roger enthusiastically took part. But if the needs of Zambian higher education were admittedly great, another area of Africa with reputedly no such need continued to haunt him – the Republic of *South* Africa, superficially prosperous but heading, he didn't doubt, to self-inflicted destruction.

As far back as 1952 he was warning on the BBC of the inescapable bloodbath ahead unless policies of colour discrimination were corrected; warning but also suggesting ways of reconciliation within the reach of everybody. Having spoken of a Friend in Durban who was breaking all the conventions by getting his African, Indian and white friends into his drawing room at the same time, to discover a new respect for each other in face to face conversation, he went on: 'What can *we* do? Talk with Africans, talk with white South Africans, talk with white settlers, with them, not at them, and then with sympathy and understanding for the difficulties of all those on the spot, try to decide what you, as a Christian citizen of a colonial power, ought to do; and then, try to do it!'

In those far-off days his recipe for such an entrenched and intrinsic evil might have sounded simplistic to the point of folly, evidence of his failure to grasp the stranglehold of apartheid, but this would be to overlook his faith in the power of powerlessness and the ministry of the nameless to the nameless, a settled conviction that explained not only his policies but the man himself. Little wonder, then, that with his newly granted freedom within his university responsibilities, he should turn to South Africa for his first assignment.

15

More International Assignments 1964-1968

Roger's return to South Africa was, of course, totally outside the auspices of the Nationalist Government. Liberals were at best tolerated, never welcome. His arrival coincided with the start of Nelson Mandela's treason trial, contrasting the quiet dignity of the accused with the seething racism of a nation at war with itself, the vindictiveness of an all-powerful tyranny against the moral authority of its victims.

What immediately struck Roger since his visit two years before from the Congo was the 'oppressive proliferation' of public notices stating baldly and aggressively 'Whites Only', 'Non-Whites Only' at stations, bus stops, public lavatories, parks, public beaches, a development not only unthinkingly absorbed by the white minority but justified as advantageous for blacks and whites alike. To deter opposition from those alive to what was happening, any private criticism of the system was publicly silenced by the threat of a banning order, draconian restrictions in movement and association, the explanation, Roger learned, of how in the previous fifteen months the Defence and Aid Fund Committee for victims of apartheid had lost seventeen of its thirty-three members, either banned, detained, sentenced, exiled or fled the country. In such a situation, his *fact-finding* mission was to recommend how better Quaker resources internationally could be used to support opposition to apartheid and also relieve the sufferings of the growing number caught up in its iniquities.

He started by breaking the law himself. An Afrikaner journalist, Chairman of the Defence and Aid Fund until served with a banning order, visited Roger in the flat of a Quaker business man, another lawbreaker! The journalist explained that 'there just wasn't enough police to keep tabs on everybody, and the chances of being picked up were small so long as the banned person was not aggressive about his contacts'.

Roger early gained the impression that, unlike Nazi Germany, there was no widespread talebearing. Neighbour did not snoop on neighbours. Letters were opened and phones tapped, but not always. 'I am not sure,' he reported, 'who is entitled to meet in whose premises. Certainly Europeans are not supposed to go into African urban or rural areas without permission – though we did. There were Africans at Friends meeting in Johannesburg and also at Witwatersland University where they come for evening classes provided by volunteers among European students.'

To this end, Mrs Robert Birley whose husband, formerly headmaster at Eton, and now visiting Professor of Education at Witwatersland, counted herself an honorary student; and it was the Birleys who provided hospitality for Roger during his days at Johannesburg where he divided his time between educational contacts provided by Robert Birley and Quaker contacts made by local Friends. One fruitful outcome of his time with the Birleys was their subsequent co-operation in arranging practical assistance for Albie Sachs, subjected to endless banning orders, and finally compelled to leave South Africa, in 1967.[1] During Roger's 1964 visit, this hounded man, an Afrikaner lawyer, involved with the defence of many Africans in Cape Province charged with political offences, had only weeks before emerged from prison after five-and-a-half months in solitary confinement, without charge. By the time he arrived in Britain, after yet another experience of the 100-Day Detention Law, his financial situation was desperate.

Roger was impressed by nothing more than the courage of such individuals, more numerous he discovered, than the slumbering white national consciousness appeared to suggest. They challenged official State policy either by way of defying it and risking the consequences or ingeniously employed some legal device to circumvent administrative oppression. Of this minority group he found himself most in sympathy with those who vigorously sustained their opposition to apartheid despite their inability to believe that it would collapse from within or that the use of warlike pressure from without was to be welcomed. Some of them were constitutionally pessimistic, others optimistic. Yet what they shared was a repugnance to be either complacent or cataclysmic.

Positively, they worked on the principle that to labour with persistence and imagination in asserting legal rights for all, in opposing racial legislation and legal repression, and in serving humanity in every possible form across racial differences was never wasted in the sight of eternity, though they also had no illusions that apartheid could be overcome in the foreseeable future.

What gave Roger heart was, paradoxically, a visit to what he called a squalid township of 40,000 Africans, to see a new school created by a former South African diplomat (Patrick van Rensburg), exiled for his opposition to the regime, and his wife, a Sheffield graduate, whom he had met and married after his expulsion. She looked, Roger said, 'as though a desert wind would blow her through the back door though, in fact, she was a Yorkshire girl, as

---

[1] See *The Jail Diary of Albie Sachs*, Harvill Press 1966.

tough as boots'. Together in Bechuanaland (now Botswana) they had created out of virtually nothing but faith and hard work a thriving school at Serowe, leaving Roger, after his stay with them, at least as much concerned about their unspoken personal needs as the more obvious needs of the school.

Hence the proposal in his report that as well as receiving a large grant towards capital costs, and an annual sum for five years toward running costs, the van Rensburgs themselves merited £150 per annum, paid into a personal account, 'so that they may get a holiday and an occasional book, record or drink'.

Adding poignancy, never mind urgency, to Roger's many other recommendations was Nelson Mandela's address to the court before receiving sentence: 'During my lifetime I have dedicated myself to this struggle of the African people. I have fought against white domination, and I have fought against Black domination. I have cherished the ideal of a democratic and free society in which all persons live together in harmony and with equal opportunities. It is an ideal which I hope to live for and achieve. But if needs be, it is an ideal for which I am prepared to die.'

The sentence of life imprisonment reflected Roger's frankly confessed near despair not only about what was happening inside South Africa but about whether, as he expressed it, 'the rising tide of international disgust would be well organized and effectively directed or would result in squalid vilification and sporadic sabotage'. He was no less concerned that the giving of any support – which he saw as an international *obligation* – should be done in ways that were delicate enough not to embarrass the recipients in South Africa as would be the case if it became obvious that they drew large financial resources from outside. Anything spectacular that deliberately or otherwise drew attention to itself would be self-defeating.

Roger readily acknowledged that his suggested low-key approach was not the only one or necessarily the most effective. He applauded the frontal attack of Trevor Huddleston and his kind, not doubting its contribution within a comprehensive strategy of opposition, but having seen how the Nationalist government's answer to the appearance of cracks in the practice of apartheid was more aggressive legislation, increasing the number of victims at the fringe and adding to the weight of what he called 'administrative tyranny', he thought not in terms of seeking in open confrontation to dismantle the solid apparatus of apartheid but rather of giving priority to the more feasible task of aiding the system's growing number of casualties.

As the recommendations of his report were being widely discussed, Roger himself was also compelled to think about – as he put it to Professor Adam Curle, a Friend working as an educational consultant in Karachi – 'something quite different':

'From away back in the 30s,' he wrote in a letter dated 9 July 1964, 'British Friends were deeply concerned with the political struggle in India and played some part in conciliation between Delhi and London, symbolized by a silent meeting, on one occasion, at Friends House attended by both Gandhi and Halifax. Since 1947 they have been more or less – from time to time – concerned about the tensions between the successor states, but the contacts have always been closer with India than Pakistan. Now there is a feeling among some of those longest associated with this concern that we ought to be better informed about and have closer knowledge of the Pakistani interpretation, and from time to time it has been suggested that my association with Pakistan could lead to such contact. I have been doubtful about this for a variety of reasons, notably the length of the tie and the slightness of the contact anyway. But the concern on the part of Friends both in UK and USA won't lie down.'

Neither would it, as we shall see, lie down for Roger; but first – as well as being involved at the university and making himself available for both public and private meetings about his time in South Africa – he was preparing for a British government assignment from the Secretary of Technical Co-operation 'to undertake a survey in the field of adult and social education in the Gilbert and Ellice Islands', a vague appointment, he said, but inevitably so since nobody familiar with these islands in the Pacific was also familiar with the methods or implications of adult and social education.

He left London in early September flying via New York to attend an eleven-day Afro-Anglo-American conference on African universities and national educational development, largely about how best universities in Africa could contribute to the education and training of teachers. What really took hold of the some one hundred delegates was the difficulty associated with receiving and giving international aid, but otherwise, he concluded, we didn't get very far. The conference included six Quaker professors of education, three of them at African universities, and these three he arranged to take to dinner at Quaker House.

Fulfilling another part of his assignment to the Pacific islands he called in en route to Tarawa, administrative centre of the Gilbert and Ellice Islands, at Fiji to survey their educational programme. What bothered him were the segregated schools for Fijian, Indian, European and Chinese children respectively, officially justified by 'different vernaculars' but reinforced, he suspected, by European snobbery on the one hand and on the other by the reputed difference of academic pace and cultural background of Fijians and Indians; the Chinese were acceptable only in Catholic schools.

He was charmed by the Fijians themselves, many of them every bit of twenty stone, extremely good looking, and with the 'sheer distinction' to raise the level of any university senior common room by one hundred per cent.

'Maybe,' he noted their complete relaxation, 'it's just that they take life at their own pace – which is not considerable for the most part. They just don't set out to compete . . .' – until they play or watch rugby! One Fijian asked Roger where he came from? When he said 'England', the Fijian said 'that's somewhere near Wales, isn't it?' Fiji had just beaten Wales at rugby.

After nine days at Tarawa, about fifty miles north of the Equator, he extended his research to the outer islands, described by Roger as 'like a string of sausages, joined together by sandbanks at low tide but separated by fifty yards to three or four miles of water at high tide'. Only when the tide was just right – low enough for the captain to see the bottom but high enough to give him room to manoeuvre over sudden outcrops of rock or sand – was it possible to get the ship into the lagoons. To add to the captain's problems, he could only see the bottom when the sun was shining directly above and not across the water; and if the sea was so smooth as to be glassy he couldn't get his bearings right to locate the exact position of the reef since the sea wouldn't be breaking over it except at low tide, when the lagoon was too shallow to navigate.

All these details fascinated Roger, until the ship was compelled to anchor well out from the shore, meaning that passengers and goods had to be off-loaded 'for anything up to five miles out', the final half-mile with water 'up to their calves'. Taking one look at Roger, the locals decided he was too old to paddle, and called upon a couple of burly policemen to carry him ashore.

No less surprising was the honoured tradition throughout the islands – with no more than 4,500 inhabitants on any single string of the sausages, sometimes as few as four hundred – of the non-refusable request for anything that somebody else possessed, either money or goods – £5, bicycle, shirt, shoes, guitar, literally anything at all. It was, Roger commented, a bit like Christmas presents in reverse. You ask a person for what he has that you want, remembering of course that he at a later date could ask for what you possessed. 'It's vastly complicated, but unbelievably pervasive, and means that, apart from land, houses and canoes, there is absolutely no stability in personal property, be it Bibles, grass-skirts, suitcases or outboard motors. This knocks sideways all conventional assumptions about the incentives to work and is only one of the factors that complicates the problems of planning any sort of development.'

Going ashore was a mixture of village feast plus ceremonial concert plus talk with as many locals as were likely to have anything to say about dominant interests and aspirations. The talking was hard work on the *bottom*! Islanders lived in houses raised anything from a foot and a half to four feet off the ground, like a split bamboo platform with a permanent roof and removable sides for extra ventilation. 'It's a good clean arrangement, but,' testified Roger, not the tallest of men, 'there's never a ladder, and you have to scramble up as best you can and meet your host in good order and accurate Gilbertese greeting. And once you start talking – on mats! – the whole extended family comes and stands around the platform, and half of them move off with you to the next port of call where to their amazement you ask the same questions.

'My job,' he explained in his letters to family and university colleagues, 'is to find out from people in what sort of way they think of community development, adult education, social improvement and so on, with a view to formulating a policy which may enable them to cope better with the pressures of the outside world as these creep up on them. It's a puzzling sort of issue, for they have so little experience of the outside world that they haven't really *got* any general ideas about it. In this sense they are primitive. Yet in terms of the organization and use of things they have, they are remarkably mature, not least,' he noted approvingly, 'in their refusal to work very hard for rewards which are largely meaningless.'

One island (Vaitupu) impressed him particularly by its highly organized system of keeping the place clean and healthy with voluntary community work; and a women's committee which comprehensively ensured that every child on the island was looked after properly. Through an administrative oversight this island wasn't warned of Roger's visit but once details of his arrival and *why* started to circulate the islanders began to organize, quickened by an islander putting about his limited understanding of what a professor was, and pointing out that this was the first time such a dignitary had visited the island, let alone one sent by the British government whose previous senior visitor had been the Duke of Edinburgh.

Soon the whole island was ordered by the eighty-year-old chief to attend ceremonial lunches on two days, followed by a cricket match on each, one for men, the other for women, and then by a sort of dance cum concert. The feasts were, said Roger, fantastic, each family group bringing its own food, with 'old men', together with leading officials like the magistrate and the pastor, given places of honour. Outside was a group of twenty or so saffron frocked young women fanning the flies off the food for these distinguished guests, and a cohort of about twenty brawny young men stripped to the waist standing to attention in the sun.

The honoured group walked up the steps at one end of this community centre and shouted a greeting. The people rose and shouted back, everybody remaining 'standing to attention' as the master of ceremonies made a speech of welcome. He then blew a whistle, and the whole assembly sat on mats; then another whistle, and the pastor said grace; then a third whistle, and the brawny young men leapt into action, conveying to each honoured person a vast palm leaf of food – chicken, fish, pork, babai (soap-like root), taro (less soap-like root), pandanus, coconuts – accompanied by the saffron maidens who promptly squatted in front of the guests of honour, one to one, with waving palm fronds to keep the flies away.

As each eater finished the meal, the maiden signalled to one of the young men to take away the 'very considerable leavings', followed by another with basin and towel for finger washing. The final whistle gave permission for all the attendant maidens to troop out; and then they and the young men set about the remains, flies and all.

'My fly-swisher,' wrote Roger, 'was about fifteen stone, an eighteen-year-old who works in the island store and had an impressive amount of English. She turned out to be the island guide captain, an impressive person.' (Only later was he to realize how impressive!) More immediately obvious was the importance to the islanders of their hospitality. They killed the fatted calf and self-evidently enjoyed doing so, confirmed by their gifts following the speeches, on this occasion two pigs, four hens, eighteen eggs, some fifty pounds of fish, four hundred coconuts, vast quantities of 'those nasty roots', eighteen mats, three fans, one shark's teeth stick, two handbags made of palm leaves, and three hundred yards of shell necklaces.

The visitors reciprocated in a traditional way – recently modernized by providing talcum powder which periodically was sprinkled freely on male and female alike. 'I've sprinkled about two pounds in four nights of dancing,' Roger wrote home, 'and at the end – in the early hours – you distribute your other presents, sticks of tobacco and chewing gum in vast quantities.'

Each of his journeys from island to island was full of the unexpected as large contingents of islanders travelled with everything – enormous quantities of mats which served as mattresses and sheets, pigs, chickens, dogs, bicycles, sewing machines, palm leaf baskets of all kinds and sizes, and at least three canoes. In addition they always let out fishing lines, usually to no purpose, but on one of Roger's trips very successfully – the best part of a ton of 'great big tuna, barracuda, king fish, bonitos and what-not'.

There was so much excitement that nobody appeared to notice the deck pigs making a good meal of what had been caught. As for the chickens, they were liable to fly overboard as passengers disembarked with their possessions, compelling one of the crew to jump overboard in rescue, despite the chickens swimming 'very well considering'. More unforgettable were the deck passengers and their seemingly unlimited capacity for sleep; as indeed, he added, they have on land. 'Walk down a village street any time in daylight and there's at least one person on the floor in every house. And this, he lamented, 'is what we are trying to deprive them of – may heaven forgive us.'

Equally disconcerting was a church school's military-like march past, with drum beating, and 'eyes right', as Roger was put on a saluting base under the Union Jack. 'You can't be rude,' he commented, 'but neither can I be correct, even if I knew what correctness was – which I don't. So one slops through somehow; but it's terrible that agencies in the colonies still think that this is education. The missionaries are awfully nice young people who really ought to know better.'

Also lacking in know-how through no fault of their own were welcoming officials at another island (Marakei), recipients of a telegram alerting them to the imminent arrival of 'the High Commissioner'. A police guard of honour, a sergeant and four men, greeted him as he went ashore, springing about him as if on elastic and, he added, finishing up with a terribly disciplined salute. 'What should I do if I *were* the High Commissioner?' he asked. 'And what do I do, as I'm not?'

After five days back at Tarawa, thinking about what he had already seen and checking up on 'a whole lot of factual stuff', he was ready to begin the second part of his survey. This began at Ocean Island, a coral mushroom rising two hundred and fifty feet above the sea, and with a surface skin from thirty to seventy feet thick of phosphate, a mineral of enormous agricultural value. This vast quarry, virtually the entire island, provided employment for some six hundred Gilbert and Ellice islanders on an annual contract, but with the phosphate due to be worked out within ten to fifteen years the economic prospects were bleak particularly as nothing, absolutely nothing, observed Roger, had been done to prepare the work force for an alternative elsewhere.

'Now the government is panicking – as well they may,' he recorded, 'and that's largely why I'm here. I can see all sorts of things that should have been done fifteen years ago and could be started now. But the demoralization is so much a habit that it's probably too late. It's made me hopping mad, but not so mad as some of the more thoughtful people who work on the island. Basically I think there has been a gross failure on the part of the British Colonial Office to realize its responsibilities. I guess it's been bullied by the Australians to provide cheap phosphate, and the Australians-dominated phosphate commission is a singularly short-sighted employer.'

At another island (Abaiand) the ship on which he travelled was delayed longer than anticipated by a passenger finding 'that this was the moment to have a baby'; and the captain, called upon to be the midwife, wanted to remain within range of the island's hospital – no doctor. This was the second baby born on board in the last three weeks; just a bit difficult, Roger commented, bearing in mind how much the ship, only three hundred and fifty tons, 'bounced about like a saucer'. 'But I must say that the Scottish captain does a remarkably good job of all the ploys that come his way.'

Moving from school to school, island to island, Roger was struck by what he called 'the range of crazy incongruities' – children doing sums about trains, the nearest two thousand miles away; a notice saying *Spitting Is Anti-Social*; and a large shop trading in tinned pilchards – very expensive, when the traditional occupation of many islanders was fishing.

As for the people themselves as a whole he found them very attractive; not beautiful but extraordinarily comfortable, dignified and at ease. They didn't laugh as much as Africans, but still had a nice sense of humour. 'They have,' he said, 'remarkable physical grace; they are beautiful ball players. They are very courteous without being obsequious. It's a man's world, but the women aren't downtrodden. They play tennis, volley ball and cricket with the men. Nobody is ever aggressive so far as I can see. And whenever a situation is too difficult,' he returned to a favourite observation, 'they don't worry but go to sleep. The temptation is to leave them to it. But population growth and land limitation make this impossible, as does the exhaustion of their phosphate.'

To leave them to it? To what? Their excessive congeniality devoid of intellectual curiosity, economic ambition or political enquiry? To a bare existence once phosphate supplies were exhausted? To *sleep* as their first priority? 'My, what a gift they have,' Roger made no secret of his envy. 'I'm not bad at sleep myself, but I'm an absolute beginner by comparison. But they don't sleep,' he added, 'when it comes to games or canoeing.'

This enthusiasm for play and sporting activity was perhaps only matched or even exceeded by religious fervour, expressed in church at somewhat different levels. At a London Missionary Society Sunday service, finding it hard work sitting on the floor listening to a sermon in Gilbertese on Revelation, Roger was grateful for the diversion of a young gentleman, aged about seven, spending the first twenty-five minutes studying not only members of the congregation in general but a copy of *The Economist* in particular. After which his mother used it as a fan. 'Will he be the first finance minister of the islands?' Roger wondered. 'And will he explain that he got interested because his mother was the house girl of the Auditor General, and picked *The Economist* out of the waste paper basket to use as a fan in church where it came into its own for an alternative purpose during an incomprehensible sermon, even in Gilbertese?'

But at least, Roger further explained, it kept him quiet, unlike the general mass of children at the front. So after the benediction somebody complained that he couldn't hear the sermon because of the noise made by the children. Couldn't they, he appealed, sit with their parents? To which somebody else said that it would be much better if they had a story of their own and then left before the sermon. This brought an old man to his feet to prophesy that if the children were turned loose without their parents they'd eat the Sunday dinner – big laugh. On that happy note the discussion, as apparently was usual, was adjourned for further thought. Roger himself stopped for a few minutes to talk with the pastor, and as he left a boy in the next house was singing Jingle Bells at the top of his considerable voice. Such a finale seemed singularly appropriate.

His report pretty well finished in the final days of November, he left in a tiny plane once more for Fiji, twelve hours flying time away, to spend three days in secondary schools before boarding his plane for London, 'with,' as he put it, 'two nights and two days in the same place, thirty-six hours in duration, but by the calendar counting as one day. Work that one out'.

He wrestled hard and long putting the final touches to his comprehensive report, clearly bothered about the 'wisdom' of economic considerations taking precedence over the Islands' traditional values and way of life: 'Sustained and systematic hard work,' he wrote, 'has had no place in the traditional island culture. Fishing demands resource, courage, fortitude and endurance as well as complex skills. All these qualities are widely prevalent in relation to fishing where the effort is spasmodic and the reward immediate. There has been nothing in the past experience of the islanders which has required the sort of skills and discipline necessary to systematic economic and political development. The rewards for a systematic approach to the daily problems of living are not obviously more attractive than the pleasures of taking life as it comes, unsystematically and unreflectively.' An economist who had just visited the islands wrote to the Colonial Office: 'You don't want an economist, you want a magician.'

Having sought to strike a balance between economic necessity and values, as he saw it, of a higher order altogether, Roger characteristically set about ensuring that the Gilbert and Ellice Islands were kept at the forefront of Colonial Office thinking. For him to accept that his responsibility ended with the delivery of his report was as impossible as to allow dusk to gather on his fifteen-point recommendations, impossible despite the consuming tasks awaiting his return. For though now freed of much routine administration at Bristol he was still an integral part of the Institute of Education, involved at the highest level of policy making and new initiatives.

But before barely giving him time to turn round, the Ministry of Overseas Development pressed him to visit Ghana to attend the annual conference of its senior social development staff. He described the occasion as 'singularly interesting and illuminating', though also confessing it was difficult to know how to be critical – his appointed function – of the methods by which a development programme was being pursued when there was no disagreement with the development programme itself! To rock the 'boat' without adequate reason was not his style.

Unfortunately there proved to be plenty of other 'boats' to be rocked. Immediately he was back he made an early opportunity to confer with the Under Secretary of State at the Colonial Office about his more urgent recommendations, quickened by a further appeal from the Resident Commissioner of the Gilbert and Ellice Islands to push *his* critical staffing problems. Indeed, this appeal had been couched in such evocative terms about the apparent incompetence of the Colonial Office that Roger had sought and received permission to quote in writing the relevant sentences, to quote anonymously.

Not a little incensed by the harshness of the comments, Lord Taylor replied that 'we are doing our best to tackle this intractable problem'. 'Intractable my foot!' came the Resident Commissioner's reply when Roger passed on the message.

Roger himself, agreeing that the Under Secretary of State's reply didn't amount to much, promised to focus the Commissioner's concern about finding suitable staff at a forthcoming four-day conference at Oxford organized by the Colonial Office. 'What you say,' he added, 'about the heart-breaking effect of the sense of neglect which settles down on people carrying responsibility for administration in the Pacific seems to me very important, and needs continually presenting to the people concerned in Whitehall'; presenting, he felt constrained to say, not merely in the measured terms of a government diplomat!

To take up the cudgels of top people excited by his report and impatient for the implementation of its main recommendations was perhaps to be expected, though even here his persistence in refusing to take no for an answer was surely exceptional, but to battle just as hard, and often at much greater inconvenience to himself, for little people, individuals without authority or influence, was more revealing of the essential man himself.

The 'very impressive' guide captain on the island of Tarawa was a case in point. Seeking to establish a much needed children's library, and getting nowhere with local officials, she wrote in desperation to Roger. Unhesitatingly he launched a one-man campaign to secure the required books, finally winning the co-operation of the BBC in widening the appeal, and also, by personally addressing six-formers at a Bristol school, recruiting their support with magnificent results. Alas, having made arrangements to dispatch the books direct, he was politely rapped over the knuckles by the English Speaking Union for not working through official channels. He was suitably contrite for his inadvertent oversight.

Thus he continued both his ceaseless round of Colonial Office consultations and correspondence, and maintaining personal contact by letter with an army of individuals who – frustrated or beaten by the system – looked to him not merely for encouragement but to fight for justice on their behalf.

Not that he ever interpreted such a crowded personal programme as necessarily evidence of progress or conscientiousness. 'It is as easy,' he warned, 'to be as compulsively overbusy as to be lazy; indeed they may be the same thing if overbusyness is an escape from making the moral effort to think. Almost anything is defensible,' he went on, 'except laziness, and laziness in any of its forms is singularly easy to rationalize in a university setting.'[2]

---

[2] 'On Being A University Teacher', *Crucible*, January 1966, p. 15.

Easy or not, Roger himself surely found it impossible in the hectic aftermath of the Gilbert and Ellice Islands to escape from the moral effort of truly hard thinking about his next assignment. Concern about Pakistan still 'wouldn't lie down'. His letter to Professor Curle had brought a predictable invitation, pushed as an urgent necessity, for him personally to visit both to develop his old Pakistani relationships and assist to achieve peace in a deteriorating situation between India and Pakistan.

Within days of its receipt he also received a communication from American Quakers urging him to accept their invitation to preside over a conference in West Africa. 'It is evident,' they said, 'that there are many points where we feel your influence, personally presented, is quite indispensable.' To leave him in no doubt about the depth of their concern they added that they had sent a cable to the FSC in London 'indicating our feeling that the mission in West Africa as Chairman of the Conference there carries a heavier weighing with us than the possible mission to Pakistan.'

Not wishing to cloud the issue further, Roger didn't mention that his recent hospitalization – for surgery – had compelled him to cancel a two-month visit to Malawi, and as this had been intended as preparatory to a six-month visiting professorship at the newly established national university there he now felt doubly obligated to fulfil this arrangement.

In the end, a compromise of sorts was reached. With his commitment to Malawi sacrosanct, he would go to West Africa, and then as one of three Friends to Pakistan without proceeding with them to India. In fact, this programme, theoretically possible, proved to be far too tight, compelling him to exclude Pakistan altogether.

The West Africa Conference, for university teachers in that part of the Continent to consider the place of university graduates in the development of emerging independent countries, focussed a core problem both endemic and dangerous. Every one of these teachers was deeply concerned for the future of his country and willing, indeed anxious, to play a part in nation building. But none of them could subscribe to the one hundred per cent conformist line of one-party government which simplified issues beyond the point of tolerance to their integrity. Without exception every one of them had run into difficulties in proving to the powers-that-be that because they were not one hundred per cent *for*, neither were they one hundred per cent *against*.

This presented them, Roger heard re-echoes of the situation in the Congo, with two matters of discomfort: because they were not one hundred per cent *for*, they were not used at all when their expertise could have been helpful; and if they wanted actively to dissent, there were no established channels for doing so. Some of them, he said, *did* feel an intellectual and political obligation to dissent, but each had to find his or her own *personal* way of so doing, in most cases at some risk.

'It's a dreary business being a lonely dissenter,' Roger reacted as he listened to them sharing their different ways of protest, 'and to be a member of a dissenting group in a country which does not tolerate dissent is to become a member of a secret society. That is to say, dissenting doesn't become easy until it has been institutionalized. And because in Africa it isn't institutionalized either in traditional tribal society or in the new political nations which have taken over from the West certain aspects of party discipline and mixed them up with governor's rule, and got the worst of both – because dissent isn't yet institutionalized in most parts of Africa, it is dangerous to dissent; and change doesn't take place peacefully.'

Nyasaland, now Malawi, to which he would soon be heading, had already painfully illustrated this with some of his old Bristol students 'behind the wire'. In the light of such realities, accentuated by the consequences of dissent in West Africa, he wondered whether protest in the West was so fully institutionalized that its impact was negligible, even a self-generating comfort or conscience appeaser.

He returned to such a theme, shortly before leaving for Malawi, in giving a memorial lecture[3] at the Bristol Fabian Society in tribute to St John Reade, an alderman of the city with whom he had both co-operated and crossed swords notably on the Bristol Social Project. 'Too often,' Roger commented as though anticipating the 'sleaze' factor of the 1990s, 'drama is left to the rogues in public life. St John's integrity flashed and scintillated.' No less appealing was the alderman's attitude to legalized indifference or depotism. For him there were no sacred cows; nor was dissent hidden under a bushel. Furthermore, Roger emphasized, he had the ability to apply his dissenting ideas to great issues, but never at the expense of losing sight of individuals suffering an injustice at the hands of authority. And the awkwardness of toppling authority, Roger approvingly concluded, never troubled him in the least. Yet he was never anarchist. He knew and supported the role of administration; and – for all his gift for dissent – he was essentially a great builder, not just of bricks and mortar, but of ideas and of men and women.

Such qualities Roger himself never more obviously exemplified than during his time in Malawi. The first thing he noticed, and deplored, was the extent to which the educational services were being stripped of the best teachers. Of three Malawi graduates who had also done post-graduate studies with him in Bristol – in the mid-1950s – one had been a member of the first Cabinet after independence, but had left the country following the Cabinet crisis in 1964, and was now teaching science near Dar-es-Salaam;

---

3 'Equality, Fraternity and Dissent', delivered on 20 January 1966.

one had been appointed Ambassador to Washington and the UN, had eventually resigned, and was now on the staff of the University of East Africa; and the third, having become a senior officer in the Ministry of Education, was currently Ambassador to Washington.

Travelling the country, talking to endless people, seeing the hordes of Malawian children receiving either no education at all or schooling inappropriate to the needs of the country, realistically seeking to match resources and facilities for indigenous teacher training, he felt constrained to bring his spirit of dissent to bear in a politically, never mind educationally, delicate area. National pride following independence was sensitive to criticism, a fact he both understood and with which he sympathized, but the issues, as he saw them, were far too serious for less than frank analysis and bold recommendations.

The urgent need was, he said, to develop a pattern of schooling which was relevant to Africa's changing social ideas and aspirations, a pattern related to the prospective national economy which for decades, he thought, would have to be very unlike the national economies influenced by one hundred and fifty years of European and American educational values and aims. In other words, the criterion of *usefulness* must take priority over the *international standards* beloved of politicians, administrators and university establishments with their preoccupation of short-term prestige.

Little of this, if any, was appreciated by African leaders educated in the West, anxious to import such standards on a widening front – one reason why Roger himself was there! – and viewing Western culture as the goal, a trend encouraged by European missionaries and mission schools. But what this Quaker, the very embodiment of Western culture, saw as crucial for educational development in Africa was a curriculum that promoted active learning leading to the enlargement of reason, imagination, appreciation and compassion in terms of African environments and the riches of Africa's distinctive culture and traditions.

This in mind, he warned against the history of Christian missions being repeated, a comment open to misunderstanding but one he felt keenly. Organized education in English-speaking ex-colonial Africa suffered, he said time and again, from a fundamental weakness in that no aspect of it rested *in* or *on* any feature with deep roots in *African* culture. What bothered him, he made an observation still relevant forty years later, was the likelihood that without fundamental change secondary schooling for African children would be based on some sort of elitist system, excluding the vast majority.

His summing up could hardly have been more radical, or brave in the circumstances: 'The question is whether the rapidly developing countries get adequate value for their money for educational systems that seem to bear so little relationship to the societies in which they operate. My thesis is that they do not, and that there is therefore a case for considering the whole edifice – not in its extent, which is bound to grow, but in its content, objectives and methodology.'

His official working day in Malawi – he and Margery were living with Anthony and Anne in Blantyre – was from 7.30 a.m. to 3.30 p.m. after which, he wrote home, he became either a busy grandfather or attended academic committees which had the habit of going on from 4 p.m. to 6.30 p.m. before adjourning without coming to any conclusions. Clearly his wish always to be the chairman was not granted!

As for the grandchildren, now three of them – Kenneth, Frances and Martin – each born in Malawi where their father continued to work in the Ministry of Social Development, it has to be said that Roger (perhaps because unavoidably he saw them only occasionally) rarely at any time achieved in his grandchildren's life the same warmth of relationship enjoyed by Anthony with his paternal grandfather. Precisely why is hard to fathom. Part of the answer might be the grandchildren's perception of his eminence though he carried it so lightly that this, if at all, was no more than a minor factor. In any case, the spirit of his involvement should have been sufficient to reassure them.

He was not, of course, any more available than he had been to his own children, having little time for recreation even when the grandchildren were present. This could explain why they found him not so much always busy as seemingly disinterested in them and their affairs. The extreme opposite was, in fact, the case, but this never communicated itself as they grew up and left home for university, with all the attendant interests that theoretically should have brought each of them more intimately into his circle. It never did.

He loved them. He was proud of them. He revelled in their achievements; all obtained degrees, two were awarded PhDs and became professional academics, and the third, a free spirit, busked his way round parts of Europe before eventually using his rare skills as a mountaineer together with his engineering degree to set himself up as an abseiling surveyor in New Zealand. Yet somehow these feelings of love and pride and profound interest never convincingly manifested themselves to the grandchildren in ways they recognized or felt free to reciprocate with confidence – strange, for a man as approachable as he was understanding.

Reflecting on the matter, Anthony wonders whether the contrast between his relationship with his parents, secure and fond but not overtly emotional, and the much more relaxed interaction he and his wife enjoyed with their children meant that the children never felt the need, as he did, to make space for their grandfather, space in which tactile relationships were as crucial as cerebral ones. He doesn't know. The one thing he *is* sure about, and regrets, is that his children never really knew their grandfather, rarely progressed beyond an affectionate but formal relationship. Incredibly for such a voluminous correspondent he only very occasionally wrote to them or they to him.

Frances remembers as a teenager attending Quaker Yearly Meeting at Warwick accompanied by a girl friend who was, she said, astonished that Roger, coming across them, greeted his granddaughter no differently from herself, a complete stranger; and only when this was pointed out to Frances did she see it as rather odd!

Kenneth, perhaps closest of the grandchildren, offered another perspective: 'In part our relationship was a bit cerebral. But it was a warm relationship with happy hours around such things as playing chess. Roger always did play second fiddle to my Gran's hosting of us and attending to our birthdays as children, sensing her great pleasure in doing this and grandchildren's special relationship with their grandmothers. I certainly never felt he was cold or distant.'

Their mother, Anne, a formidable scholar in her own right whose research, like her books, Roger readily admitted he couldn't understand, reached the conclusion that though he spoke warmly *of* his grandchildren he couldn't be very warm *to* them. For a man of such genuine warmth this inhibition – doubtless reflecting the mores of his own childhood – deprived both sides, as with his own children, of a longed-for greater intimacy. 'I admired him most,' his daughter-in-law recalled, 'through his writings. He told me once that he was often nervous or afraid when facing some of his tasks.'

Anne went on to say that she was aware he learned nothing from her, but this was probably a misjudgment, for what cannot be doubted was Roger's openness and willingness to learn; one reason why many of his long-term colleagues whose admiration deepened with the years into affection found his strong views evocative, never offensive, never parochial or prompted by self-interest. Not a few of them, themselves eminent in their own right, felt for him a respect approaching reverence for his transparent genuineness and integrity. They thought him a saint.

Roger himself was suspicious of saints, sharing with George Orwell in his essay on Gandhi the healthy scepticism that saints should be judged guilty until proved innocent. Aware of how his own secret and public life fell short of his ideals, Roger made no pretensions to being innocent, let alone a candidate for canonization. And some of the people who loved him most were not thereby silent about either his failings or less attractive characteristics. They could hardly overlook – though often misunderstanding – his expectation of the limelight through other people habitually turning to him for leadership. Yet paradoxically, if he could not always be adjudged as innocent, he was possessed of that essential spirit of childlike innocence, a capacity for wonder and curiosity, of love of life, of pleasure in simplicity.

Quakers and others wanting their saints to be perfect or paragons must look elsewhere than to Roger. He himself would have reacted to the very idea of personal sainthood with a wicked and knowing twinkle, one of bemusement at the gullibility of human judgments or with the alarm of a man unfairly accused of devout irrelevance. In any case, he didn't aspire, let alone claim, to be a saint, not of the orthodox kind. In so far as sainthood ever crossed his mind he thought of the likes of Dag Hammarskjøld and Nelson Mandela and some of his unsung colleagues of the war years, Christian or secularist, Jew or Gentile, atheist or agnostic; for the sainthood he sought was wholly unselfconscious and rooted not in the cloister but the hard-nosed world in which, motivation frequently at variance with outward appearance, the attribution of sanctity was not necessarily meant as a compliment.

Included in Roger's own gallery of saints were two of his colleagues at Bristol – the Vice-Chancellor (Philip Morris), a Christian, and Professor Cecil Powell, Nobel Prize winner for his work in the world of physics culminating in the discovery of the pi-meson, and a disinterested agnostic. This high-powered trio were soul brothers, bound together not least by a spirituality as unmistakable as rarely mentioned directly among themselves. They had discovered that to attempt to articulate what none of them doubted was to obscure rather than clarify. 'Those who know don't say, those who say don't know.'

Roger could have been referring to either of them when he said of Philip Morris that there was nothing formidable about his personal relationships; he was kind and gentle, even when putting a penetrating question on some aspect of a matter that one had only half thought through.

Inevitably the three were united in their appreciation of humour, exchanging old chestnuts or revelling in, for instance, the latest discovery from Roger's catholic reading – the depth of Disraeli's romantic devotion to Queen Victoria. When Disraeli, regaled Roger, was asked in his last illness if he would care to be visited by the Queen, he replied: 'No, it is better not. She would only ask me to take a message to Albert.'

More fundamental still was the affinity of their motivation and aim at work. When Roger claimed that the quality and quantity of a university teacher's work, so difficult objectively to assess, were mainly found in the non-material sphere of internalized personal values, he had in mind the likes of these two old friends. And they complemented each other, drawing from Roger in one notable particular a spirit of envy, sometimes despair.

To what extent Morris was a DIY enthusiast is debatable, but Powell could turn his hand to anything. When the Wilsons acquired a country cottage little more than an hour's drive from the city centre, it was Powell, the eminent Nobel Prize physicist, who expertly built a garden wall, in contrast to Roger who barely recognized a trowel when he saw one. The nearest he ever came to practical work was in the garden where Margery's expertise achieved an annual miracle. Proud as well as privileged to be called the gardener's boy, he never progressed beyond cutting the lawn and hedges, and nurturing the compost heap and bonfire. For the rest, the garden, like all practical jobs, was safer with Roger deep in his study.

He wasn't so much hamfisted as born with an unlimited and quite perverse capacity to complicate the changing of a light bulb or the spreading of paint intended for the wall he was disfiguring. Horses for courses. Roger was definitely never intended to be a handyman.

Morris retired shortly after Roger's return from Malawi. During his Vice-Chancellorship the university had almost trebled in size over a span of twenty years; in the colleges of education associated with Bristol's Institute of Education for the training of teachers there were 5,000 students, as many as there were undergraduates in the university itself, and this, Roger had no doubt, was largely due to Morris. 'We always knew,' he said, 'that we were working with a far-sighted and liberal statesman – who was also a wiley tactician', notably at a time when society at large was changing not only rapidly but disjointedly.

Evidence of this was increasingly obvious within the university itself where rumblings of revolt were soon to develop into open warfare. But these portents, far from alarming Roger, who was sympathetic anyway to many of the students' complaints, were seen by him as indicators of educational success – the challenging of mindless loyalty to the *status quo*, the sharpening of values in furious debate about real issues, the need to justify authority rather than take it for granted with authoritative instructions.

What he deplored was the growing extremism, not, be it noted, of the ideas being advocated, but the militant irrationality of some of the advocates. If he understood their anger he deplored its unreasonableness, arguing as strongly as they that *volume* of protest was no substitute for *thought*.

Still, life must go on – lectures delivered, students tutored, academic and other assemblies addressed, his voluminous correspondence even more urgently maintained, for now individuals in Malawi, like others in West and South Africa, the Gilbert and Ellice Islands, the Congo and Pakistan, India and Sri Lanka continued to appeal to him for help and counsel. This largely secret ministry – for *ministry* it was, and fiercely demanding of time – frequently proved a life-line to otherwise bewildered and neglected persons.

These private letters were all of a piece with his public activities, some of them never mentioned by Roger himself. The new Vice-Chancellor (John E. Harris) wrote to him on 14 July 1967: 'I hope you have had at least a few of the tributes paid to you in person that were paid to me on your behalf as Public Orator at yesterday morning's ceremony. Everyone who spoke to me remarked on how felicitous and impressive the presentation speeches were and I know that the Graduates themselves particularly enjoyed them.'

Whether all his colleagues in fact were equally felicitous about a different occasion shortly afterwards is a moot point, revealed by another complimentary letter intimating that staff tranquillity is not necessarily a rule of life among academics: 'I hope this short note,' the writer could barely contain her jubilation, 'is not out of place, but I do want to say that your presentation of the BEd. entry case at Senate this afternoon was the best deployment of cogent argument, humanity and political skill I have met since coming to Bristol. I do not think I have ever seen opponents' guns so convincingly spiked. Certainly I felt, after you had finished, that the only room left for manoeuvre was in the batteries of prejudice and unreason – and that, I think, is how it turned out. It was,' she concluded, 'very pleasant to observe the victory of an advocate of reason and humanity.'

It does not take a postgraduate student in psychology to realize that such academic routs do not make for universal popularity. And Roger was no fool. The only reason he was held in high esteem virtually throughout the university, never mind elsewhere, was his graciousness in victory as well as defeat. Vindictiveness either way was not his style. If he could not always carry people with him in administrative or ideological debate, the last thing he wanted was their humiliation or alienation. As we shall see, if there was resentment amounting to bitterness and open hostility, he was the first to take the initiative in seeking reconciliation. Only once did such an impasse confront him; he continued to grieve over it for the rest of his life.

Roger's brilliance of presentation was typified in the opening sentences of an address he gave to a public meeting of the Bristol Council of Social Service, on 2 October 1967. He announced his text, not, he feared, from holy writ, but from a review of a book edited by 'our new Professor of Anatomy':

'The mass of nerve cells at the base of the brain is possibly the most intriguing and intricate cubic inch in nature; it affects almost every vital function of the body and energizes the mainsprings of behaviour – hunger, thirst and sexual drive, hoarding, exploration and predatory behaviour, as well as the maternal instinct, are all controlled from it.'

He then gave his own translation:

'Gluttony, drinking and rape, thieving, prying and murder, and the worst evils of possessiveness . . .'

Or try this, he said:

'The pleasures of the table, love and marriage, home and family life, science, art and invention, farming and sport . . .'

'The curtain that divides these two aspects of our deepest instincts is,' he informed his startled – but captivated – audience, 'perilously thin.'

Was his public talking always so colourful? Well, it all depended. He made no concessions to his students. They were there, he assumed, not to be entertained but to listen, to concentrate, to work, because of *their* intrinsic interest, not *his* ability to grab their attention and hold it. If their minds wandered or they were palpably disinterested, he was neither surprised nor distressed. That was their responsibility. His job was to share with them, mature postgraduates, themes he conceived as mighty and relevant to their future profession. The key one, indeed the one that coloured all his thinking throughout his entire university career, was, we have already noticed, the question *What Are Schools For?* He worried at it like a dog with a bone.

Before taking up a visiting professorship at the Harvard Graduate School of Education, from January to June in 1968, he packed a year's lectures into one term at Bristol, a series called 'Schools and Society', but essentially concerned about the same question – What are schools *for*? or if, he said, you prefer, What *are* schools for? Needless to say, he talked not from dog-eared lecture notes but from a mind of freshly minted ideas garnered by his own disciplined reading and thinking.

'I'm not asking an abstract question,' he assured his students, 'put up as an academic Aunt Sally. If teachers are underpaid, as many of us think they are, how would we define the job that they do in terms which would be convincing to the taxpayer? Most of the world's children don't go to school; they have less material wealth than us, but I don't know that they're any more miserable. Or make it more personal,' he appealed; 'teachers demand at least ½ the waking time of children for ¾ of the year over 10/14 years of very active life. What for – to teach them stuff 90 per cent of which they'll have forgotten within 5 years; to keep them off the streets; to turn them into cannon fodder; to bully them; to bore them?'

'Every time you make a demand of a child in school by way of subject or discipline or negotiations you are saying *something* about what you think schools are for. And incidentally,' he remained alive to what was happening at the grass roots of the university, 'it's a question that underlines a good deal of student criticism of the institutions of higher education – as you know probably better than I.'

Inevitably, the same basic theme – who *had* the power in saying *what* could not be left to chance in the curriculum or schools generally – was the substance of his visiting professorship at Harvard. Early on he took the opportunity of an academic engagement in New York to visit Quaker House, his old stamping ground at the UN headquarters. He found the staff 'very troubled' by its precarious budget, a problem belonging, he felt, to World Quakerism rather than American resources only. Nevertheless, with typical realism, he acknowledged that the Quaker UN Project would never be a money-jerker from the international body of Friends. It was 'too remote and too chronic' to touch the heart, and the head never contributed to funds except through some inspired individual!

What also concerned him was that, first, Friends in the USA should realize that the issues surrounding Quaker Peace Witness had become cruder and rougher; and, secondly, that though what he called 'the Quaker histories' had never paid their way they contributed to the Society's *total* life, just as knitting for refugees and talking with Ralph Bunche were all part of the peace testimony.

In the middle of his time at Harvard Roger found himself caught up in the nation's reaction to the assassination of Martin Luther King. The response in terms of memorial gatherings, he informed his colleagues in Bristol, was tremendous – 30,000 on Boston Common, 2,000 on Cambridge Common, 2,000 in Harvard Chapel plus annexes, even more at Yale (where Margery happened to be for what was a much better service than Harvard's); and the work in the School of Education at Harvard pretty well stopped for three days while students and staff talked about what could be done to push on with integrational activity that could have some meaning.

'But there is a strong sense,' he observed, 'that white America doesn't know how to talk with black America, and so much guilt that any cross-talk tends to become sentimental rather than intellectually and politically virile. So even concerned people don't really know where to go next.'

As for the postgraduate students as a whole, they were furious that neither the Education School nor the schools where they were doing their (teaching) practice provided any chance 'to think what this means'. With the horizon dominated by basic discipline and the technique of subject teaching, they complained that everybody within the educational system, teachers and pupils alike, were simply fodder for somebody else's expertise. Roger was inclined to agree, assessing that systems in the USA seemed to him much more dominant over persons than they were in Britain, but he made the proviso that 'my view may be corrupted both ways by distance'.

Mid-way through his time at Harvard, fulfilling a condition of his acceptance of the visiting professorship, he flew back to Bristol to take part in a Colston Symposium, ten days of lectures and seminars centred upon the theme he was pursuing in America. *En route* he called at the Overseas Development Ministry in London to be consulted, as he thought, about Malawi and the demand for teachers in Africa generally, but was invited to return to Fiji for two weeks – before the end of his Harvard assignment – to contribute what was now internationally recognized as his unique combined authority on educational and social welfare developments, at a seminar at South Pacific University. Amused at the very idea that he alone was indispensable for such an undertaking, he was honest enough to underline the difficulties of accepting the invitation rather than push his own strong inclination. He didn't go.

Harvard was too demanding and absorbing, providing contacts so extensive that he felt himself in the final weeks of his stay 'getting more understanding of *something* substantial in the American scene'. Not all of it was encouraging. 'There is a place in some way or other,' he said, 'for professional elite-ism. I can't define it, and I wish I didn't feel this as I have always regarded myself as being a profound non-elitist, but I emerged (from this latest American experience) feeling that society which had abandoned elite-ism is in for an incredible measure of nastiness. Nobody is prepared to say what is good for other people; nobody is expected to carry responsibility of taking that kind of leadership and decision making.'

Having himself – never mind his American students – profited so richly from this visiting professorship, he returned to Bristol hoping to set up some sort of interchange to enable staff at the Institute of Education to spend three months or so in America free from committees and administration, and 'able to do some thinking and writing'. Unlike himself! For on his own admission his time at Harvard, coupled to extensive Quaker activity, had left him time for barely more than his next appointment. And once home, with hardly chance to unpack, he was off again, this time to Helsinki to address an International Congress of Schools of Social Work – during his summer vacation!

His immediate impulse to turn down the invitation on the justifiable grounds of pressure of work was transcended not only by the persistence of the organizers but more by his own strong convictions about making social work training relevant to clients living within systems of political and economic injustice. What he sought was social work that prevented deprivation as well as tackled crisis situations.

No less contentious was his head-on discussion – guaranteed to raise the hackles of professional social workers – of to what extent, if any, members of the caring professions should be emotionally involved with their clients. Acknowledging the need for objectivity, he nevertheless argued that social work had its roots not in a theory but in an aspect of the mystery of life, the urge, as he called it, of men and women to care for one another; they were members one of another, no matter how often in particular situations and however recurrently in generalized action they denied it.

As for social workers seeing clinical detachment as a mark of professionalism, compassion as a barrier to objectivity, he underlined that persons should never be treated as objects, things, cases, and be expected to respond as persons, any more than social work could develop along the preventive lines he had advocated unless social workers challenged the social ills often too strong and intractable for the most vulnerable.

Bearing in mind the growing student revolt sweeping the Western world – and nowhere more militant than in Bristol! – it was hardly surprising that he seized upon a question thrown up in discussion of whether the education of social workers should include courses in how to achieve political, administrative and economic change. Was there a place for the dramatic protest, the strike, the sit-in, the innovation of force, perhaps starting at universities and colleges?

The immediate 'cut and thrust' this evoked led him to spell out his position, of particular interest in the light of the clearly worsening situation at Bristol, and soon to culminate in a twelve-day student sit-in at the Senate House: 'As persons seeking intellectual and moral growth towards social maturity, students have a right to be taken seriously as critics of the education they are offered. But this does not necessarily mean that they are right, in whole or in part. Their critical attitude may be a gesture of solidarity with students as a whole rather than a criticism of their particular professional education. Or it may have to do with the status, inside or outside universities, of social work educational institutions. But among teachers there can be no complacency about student attitudes – the post-student world is in no condition to justify self-righteousness.'

Also bothering him was that within the universities there had developed – on what he called the noble basis of the endless search for truth – a gigantic knowledge industry which seemed remarkably self-righteous and had so managed to professionalize the life of the mind that it was often hard to discern the university's other commitment to help the young to learn to *think* to some moral and social purpose.

What he couldn't stand were people who in situations of ideological conflict appeared to stand for nothing. This was immediately seen in three distinct areas.

Part of Roger's expertise known little beyond a close circle was the British judicial and penal system. For fourteen years he was a Justice of the Peace. In the long summer vacations at the university he ran Home Office courses for probation officers, social workers, and staff of remand homes and other residential welfare establishments. But in 1967 he began to have serious reservations about his continued participation in an administration which seemed, as he saw it, to make too little allowance for either the complexities of human behaviour or the inadequacy of formal legal procedures to deal with what were not formal situations.

He saw the same accused appear time after time, confirmed in their anti-social behaviour by terms of imprisonment. This led him more and more to urge that there should be remands for reports by probation officers before sentence, the corollary being extra work on the bench. Still, the value of proceeding in this way seemed to him abundantly justified.

'However,' he later recorded, 'to my horror, I found myself one day hesitating to support a remand by reason of the difficulty of finding time to take it. Plainly this would not do!' And as he rightly saw himself getting busier at the university in the three or four years leading up to his retirement, he resigned, prompted also by another reason.

Exasperated by the futility of sending offenders yet again to prison, with little if any possibility of being rehabilitated, with the entire penal system geared primarily to punishment, with virtually no attention to training or preparation for release, he thought he could perhaps best use his limited time not on the bench but as a prison visitor. He became Chairman of the Visiting Committee at Shepton Mallet prison.

For such a man there could be only one way of meeting this new commitment – personal involvement with both prisoners and their families; an involvement initially tolerated by the authorities but finally – no matter how admired and effective – deemed too unorthodox to be allowed to continue. The problem appeared to be Roger's casework, the readiness with which he approached outside social agencies if he felt they could help either prisoner or dependants, and this was considered a breach of confidentiality.

Roger's secretary throughout virtually the whole of his time at Bristol, Marie Taylor, devotee, colleague, friend and beloved of the Wilson family, described his work *in* the prison as 'the worst days of his life'. 'He returned,' she said, 'looking wretched and depressed in the extreme.' Summing up this three-year episode she said 'he was very glad in the end to leave the Visiting Committee; and when,' she added, 'I see and hear of Shepton Mallet now (long closed as too brutal a regime) I have no doubt he was right in trying to help in the way he did'.

Right or wrong, he had no choice. Necessity was laid upon him as surely as in his conscientious objection to war.

The second area, demonstrating the catholicity of Roger's concerns, also illustrated that his characteristic meekness sometimes found expression in the most pungent terms. On 30 August 1968, he wrote to the Soviet Ambassador in London:

> Comrade Ambassador,
> For fifty years I have been proud that, as a boy, I attended a great meeting in the Free Trade Hall, Manchester, to celebrate the Russian Revolution. Forty years ago, after graduating at the University, I used my first independence to pay a very stimulating visit to the USSR. Throughout the years I have hoped that Communism under the leadership of the USSR was saying something about social and political and economic relationships that would effectively challenge the conventional power brutalities of Western capitalism. Your country's action in relation to Czechoslovakia is,

however, conclusive evidence that Soviet Communism has nothing new to offer at all. The USSR is no worse than the USA, but neither is it any better or any different from the outworn imperialisms of Western Europe. Like the rest of the world you are obsessed with the crude and childish notion that might is right, that the only route to security is that of the bully.

Which brings us to the unsought but inescapable third area of Roger's concerns at this time, much nearer home in both nastiness and innuendo, testing all his skill as a peace-maker in an atmosphere of open warfare without guns. It centred on his beloved University of Bristol.

16

Revolutionary Approach to Retirement
1968-1971

After months of growing discontent, protests, token defiance of authority, demands for a greater say in how the university was run, hundreds of representative students – on 6 December 1968 – barged into Senate House, jubilantly ran up a red flag on the roof, and resisted every effort to turn them out, so starting the longest sit-in still at any British university. Recalling those twelve heady days, James Belsey, himself a Bristol undergraduate at the time, claimed that at least on paper Bristol was an unlikely hotbed of revolution: 'The university had Britain's highest proportion of undergraduates with a private education background, and its halls of residence were run on patrician, public-school lines. Only a year before, Sue Lawley had celebrated her dazzling success in ironing out her Black Country vowels by becoming the new, poshly-spoken president of the students' union . . .'

'But times were changing, and the sherry-party-and-smart-cocktail-dress ambience of the Lawley years was giving way to a noisier mood. Bristol's students,' continued Belsey, 'had become demo-happy. That summer they held a sit-in at the students' union building. But since it was theirs anyway, they didn't quite touch the revolutionary spot. They wanted nothing less than the ultimate symbol of authority, Senate House.'[1]

The official account of events was not surprisingly somewhat different: 'Apart from the flaunting of the Red Flag, and the clenched fist salutes among the crowd in the foyer,' wrote E.C. Wright, the university's deputy registrar and secretary, 'there was strong evidence of political motivations behind the sit-in leaflets found in the course of inspection quoting Marxist views of aesthetics, education and society.' The inspection by the Vice-Chancellor and five of his officers escorted by the police was to ascertain to what extent the occupied building was being damaged; such as there was proved to be superficial.

At the heart of the students' protest was their *demand* for a greater say on the Senate Council, a subject of negotiations for months but apparently

---

[1] 'Revolting Students Revisited', *The Guardian*, 7 December 1993.

getting nowhere. What they saw as a strategy of procrastination added to the explosive atmosphere and the questioning of authority by young people generally. In all the circumstances a dramatic protest of some sort was inevitable.

Roger hated the militancy with its occasional manhandling of university officials but its more usual verbal abuse and threats, evident at best, he thought, of vacuous idealism. If he had a blindspot in all his negotiations behind the scenes it was his persistence in believing that persons on both sides were essentially reasonable and therefore open to the possibility of reconciliation. While endorsing the university's policy of 'No negotiations with the sit-in' – during which rational discussion with the self-appointed leaders was largely academic anyway – he nevertheless sympathized, if not entirely with the students' ultimate aim, at least with their wish and right to contribute to the life of the university at every level of administration and policy making. Where he drew the line was in surrendering the university's final authority in such matters as the content of courses, arbitrary assessments by students of the performance of academic staff, and the total discontinuation of written examinations.

Eventually the high court granted orders and writs for Senate House to be cleared of occupying students, and this was done peacefully, the protesters resentful but gratified they'd made their point. But the whole episode, apart from doing nothing to resolve fundamental differences, left fractured relationships not only between staff and students but in both the senior common room and the students' union where deep divisions rumbled on for months.

Roger's more immediate concern was that one of his students, arrested at the sit-in, was due to appear in court to face a possible injunction prohibiting her not only from entering the Senate building but from the university as a whole. If the injunction was granted, he appealed to the Vice-Chancellor, its terms would amount to the rustication of the student, and was bound to be widely interpreted to mean that offending students were to be singled out and sent down, contrary to the spirit of the Vice-Chancellor's own statement that 'the university had no wish to be vindictive against particular individuals'.

What he sought was an unambiguous declaration in common sense terms that any disciplinary action would be taken only through the university's own procedures, and that the university's search for legal protection would not prejudice internal academic decisions.

In a sense he was back with his experience of the penal system, trying to balance punishment with the essential welfare of the offender. If he erred on one side, some of his academic colleagues erred on the other. But not a few of them came to the conclusion that during these weeks and months of set opinions and sometimes bruising encounters among and between staff and students his remarkable gifts for reconciliation and diplomacy were never better demonstrated. As one who shared these days with him remarked, reflecting the eight years of their professional relationship: 'I respected, admired and loved Roger Wilson more than almost any man I have ever encountered.'

As the university returned to some sort of normality, Roger was under no illusion. Resentments, like the crisis of authority itself, still lingered, festering, many of its causes unresolved. Half the trouble was, he believed, lack of any real communication, the exchange of partially-understood truths across a chasm of mutual good intentions. In all his discussions on both sides of the divide – among staff, among students, between staff and students – his essential aim was to foster a spirit of compassion throughout the university community; not, he hastened to add, as a matter of solid administrative slog or speech-day moralizing, but as the expression of intelligent and tender-hearted caring.

Anyone – staff colleague or student – under the illusion that Roger was too much a man of peace to plunge into the rough house of either the revolt or its tendentious aftermath was speedily disillusioned. To a lecturer critical both vehemently and publicly about student educational standards, he responded: 'If this is an accurate report of what you said, the conclusions which you draw imply a standard of reasoning that would be academically unacceptable if offered by our students. And I doubt if it would be acceptable, either, by yourself in its academic context.'

Nor were individual students privately left in any doubt about his opinion of the wild denunciations being made about some staff members and fellow students for no other reason than their refusal to support certain of the aims and most of the tactics of the revolt.

What he deplored were the misunderstandings, rumours and counter-rumours on both sides evoked by lack of information about each other. The key word for Roger was *involvement*, getting alongside friend and foe alike by providing a common meeting ground for the undermining of disinformation and the fostering of mutual trust. So, a strong advocate for a Communications and Relationships Committee set up by the Senate, he not only agreed to serve on it but urged the appointment of a senior official whose essential responsibility would be to keep the entire university including non-academic staff in touch with what was happening at every level of administration from the Vice-Chancellor to the humblest cleaner. At the same time he wanted roles more clearly defined.

'One of the puzzling aspects of university life,' he briefed the Lord Bishop of Bristol for a speech to be delivered in the House of Lords about student unrest, 'is that in the interests of the maintenance of academic freedom nobody can tell anybody else what to do. Nor is it really possible to dispose of or transfer anybody whose scholarship is impressive but whose capacity to meet the young in any significant way is small.' At least part of the answer was, he suggested, the appointment of individuals specifically for their ability to relate administrative continuity to grass roots stirrings.

Though slowly running out of steam, student agitation continued to the end of the academic year, and Roger, never one for turning away from unpleasant necessity, nevertheless found a measure of relief with thoughts of retirement! As early as May 1969, he wrote to the Vice-Chancellor with a revealing appeal: 'There is a long-standing custom that when a professor retires, a letter, signed by the Vice-Chancellor, Dean and some senior colleagues, goes to all academic staff, inviting contributions to a presentation which is subsequently made at a Senate House tea-party to which all contributors are invited.' Cannot this 'practice', proposed Roger, which made an undesirable distinction between professors and other academic and non-academic staff, be abandoned and replaced by 'a single annual farewell tea party on the retirement of long-serving staff who have served the university in any capacity'?

Contemplating retirement, both Roger and Margery had long decided where they wanted to live. At every opportunity they visited the borders of the Lake District and the Yorkshire Moors, what they called '1652 country', birthplace of Quakerism, hopeful of finding a suitable property, big enough for family visits and holidays, ideally with a garden extensive enough to satisfy Margery's aspirations.

They found it where she and the children had lived during the war in the tiny village of Yealand Conyers, three miles from Carnforth in Lancashire. The view from the front on a clear day took in conspicuously Ingleborough with its plateau summit; at the back was a bird sanctuary and a panoramic view stretching for miles of Morecambe Bay with its multitudes of wildfowl. Admittedly the property needed attention, but the eighteen months or so before retirement was ample time for renovations and in fact added to all the excitement and pleasure of anticipation.

First, however, Roger faced his final year at the university, the usual hectic round of lectures and seminars, implementing the lessons of the sit-in, and preparing the handover as head of his department: all grist to the mill. And if tying all these ends meant that overseas travel, apart from a brief visit to Malawi (as member of the Provisional Council of the University there), was virtually out of the question, he still found himself caught up in international affairs.

One of his former students (Tseliso Makhakhe), refugee from an illegal seizure of power in Lesotho, formerly Basutoland under British protection, smuggled a letter out to Roger saying he was in hiding and being hunted out. 'When you reply,' he warned, 'please avoid anything clearly controversial or objectionable to the fascists; write to my wife at the above address . . . We were looking forward to more sensible policies in every aspect of our life, especially in education and agriculture which have now sunk to a tragic state.'

Roger promptly wrote to the Commonwealth Office asking about possible ways of helping the victim and his family, but wasn't a bit surprised by the reply from the Under Secretary (Sir Jack Johnston) that 'although we hand on our responsibility for particular countries by making them independent, personal links and friendships and interests continue, as they rightly should, and make it all the more frustrating and saddening to have to stand by and honour that independence when our erstwhile dependents don't use their independence in ways we approve of. But the days of the gunboat are over'. Roger had no grouse with that, but he still somehow found a way to send money to the hounded family.

Within weeks he was called to London for a working lunch with the Rt Hon. Judith Hart at the Ministry of Overseas Development about a wide ranging discussion which naturally included his continuing concern to find enough suitable teachers for Africa. Anybody wondering what Roger meant by *suitable* was soon made aware of a quality he thought as important as academic qualifications. For teaching, he insisted, involved a tremendous commitment of faith; faith that this was God's world and that somehow or other there was more true understanding to be found, so that every child in every school 'should have the chance to meet at least some teachers who have more confidence in the wheat than the tares'.

The question of his own suitability on another front altogether appealed to his readiness to enjoy a joke at his own expense. In April 1970, he received a document from, of all places, the Imperial War Museum. A nation-wide appeal, this uncompromising pacifist was informed, had been launched for the private papers of men and women who had served their country with distinction in connection with the wars of the twentieth century. Would he consider depositing his papers in the archives of this national museum? Or – if this was too much to ask – would he be prepared to donate 'a microfilm copy of your collection'? Any contribution he could make 'would be greatly valued by the students of history who use the resources of this Museum'.

Did this represent a new military definition of distinctive service for monarch and country or merely crossed wires of administration? Either way, Roger's impish humour had a field day in declining the invitation.

What could never have crossed his mind was that soon he was to be caught in the cross-fire of another sort of war, one not of his making but leading to what proved to be, beyond doubt, his unhappiest months at Bristol, and perhaps of his whole life. It all started innocently enough. The headmaster of a comprehensive school near Bristol agreed to allow three lecturers of Roger's department to conduct a bold experiment with 'reluctant learners' in the school. Under the vigilant supervision of their tutors, selected post-graduates training to be teachers would involve themselves in unconventional ways governed primarily by pupil reaction. In other words, the trainee teachers would allow as far as possible the reluctant learners to decide both what was to be taught and how.

Roger had little doubt that the Local Education Authority, had they known about the venture, might well have frowned upon it; and certainly only this 'outstandingly able and courageous headmaster' would have risked it. But Roger applauded the man and the three lecturers for their initiative in tackling a problem as widely recognized as it was generally ignored. From this essentially innovative approach there emerged a book written by the lecturers. When Roger saw the proofs he reacted with warm approval though adding that 'perhaps some of the phraselogy did less than recognize the sensitivities of the school'.

The next he heard was of a major row brewing following the retirement of the headmaster. His successor was furious on two distinct counts – the first he had come to know about the book was when his wife had showed him a review of it in *The Guardian*; and though his school had not been identified by name he had no doubt that this would not finally safeguard its anonymity, a serious matter seeing that the school and certain members of staff were, in his opinion, criticized unfairly.

In the angry controversy that ensued, involving the headmaster and key LEA officials who shared his indignation, it became apparent that despite the original headmaster being aware that the three lecturers were keeping copious notes he had no idea they planned to write a book. Readily acknowledging this, the lecturers explained that they were so emotionally committed to the 'reluctant learners' that they had inadvertently overlooked the 'institutional implications and courtesies', an explanation accepted by Roger but still leaving an explosive situation.

At what he described as 'a very angry meeting indeed' between university and LEA leaders, Roger sought to defuse the situation by suggesting that 'as a token gesture' to placate the other side's sense of outrage the three lecturers should not be sent into Bristol schools for a year. 'I think,' he said later, 'it was an instance of the meaning of *atonement* and a generous one.'

The three lecturers, however, could hardly have disagreed more. They accused Roger not only of humiliating them but of bringing the entire 'relucant learners' initiative into serious jeopardy. Indeed, one of them felt so bitterly unforgiving about it that he rejected Roger's every appeal for reconciliation, the last one shortly before Roger died.

Reflecting on how the matter had developed to such an impasse, Roger continued to feel that in all the circumstances he could have done nothing differently, nothing, that is, apart from correct the now obvious oversight of not informing the original headmaster about the intended book, his successor of its pending publication, LEA officials about the project from its conception, never mind its actual inception, and crucially of ensuring the presence of the three authors at the meeting to resolve the divide. But hindsight did nothing to salvage the wreckage of bitter if largely innocent misunderstanding. The lecturers within Roger's authority felt themselves let-down. One thing alone was beyond dispute – Roger's lasting grief over the estrangement from three valued colleagues.

The other extreme of affection, respect and indebtedness marked all the arrangements made within the Institute of Education and the university generally to honour Roger on his retirement. A Symposium was addressed by three high-powered academics who each dealt with an aspect of Roger's central concerns during his twenty-one years as Professor of Education and latterly of Social Development too. Happily their cogent not to say sometimes turgid expositions were at times relieved by personal reminiscences and reflections.

The Vice-Chancellor of the University of Leeds (Lord Boyle of Handsworth), formerly a Tory Minister of Education, welcomed the chance to pay tribute to a man with whom, despite his politics, he shared a large measure of affinity about basic values and educational aims. For a start, he said, they shared a similar heritage: 'My father brought me up firmly on the principle that right and wrong were important in life, but that it was up to me to decide for myself what they were, to discover, as we would say nowadays, a scale of values with which I could feel identified – and that nobody could take this decision for me.' Re-echoing a constant theme of Roger's, he added: 'I should find myself very ill at ease in, as it were, trying to proffer unsolicited advice on morals and behaviour to students'.

Introducing his contribution, the Director of London University's Institute of Education (Lionel Elvin) claimed that during Roger's professorial tenure Bristol had been 'one of the happiest as well as one of the best places for the training of teachers under university auspices'. He continued: 'Coming from outside Bristol, I can bear witness to his standing in national discussions; he is the embodiment of good sense carried to the point of wisdom.'

The third contributor (Freda Gwilliam) transcribed one of Roger's grouses from his Congo days: 'Many a development has foundered because the *expert* or *consultant* has been given too short a time for his mission; he has had to try to report results to satisfy those who sent him, but long before changes could be expected to be understood, accepted and adapted to the situation.' Roger's achievements firmly in mind, she quoted from a prayer by Sir Francis Drake on the day he sailed for Cadiz: 'It is not the beginning but the continuing of the matter till it be thoroughly finished that yieldeth the glory.'

For their own farewell tribute the student body invited one of their number, Doctor Teame Mebrahtu, postgraduate from Eritrea, to speak on their behalf but also, he claimed, for the three hundred and eighteen former students from overseas who had come under Professor Wilson's influence and with whom in many cases he was still in touch. But though, as he said, he appreciated that Roger was an educator of world stature, he wanted first to underline what the professor had done 'for me as an individual' as evidence of his fatherly care and concern towards his students generally. Consequently the students had decided, in seeking to honour such a man, that nothing could be more appropriate than to set up the *Roger Wilson Children's Trust* for the educational needs of deprived pupils.

Roger delivered his final lecture before retirement on June 11th, 1971, sixty minutes littered with personal reminiscences and Wilsonian philosophy:

I was hearing yesterday about a child of ten who was invited by her father's students to go with them to see a travel film. She turned to her father who was standing by and asked if it would be all right. He said *yes* and they set off. On the way one of the students said, 'Joan, do you always ask your father?'. She said '*Yes, I try to; it gives him a feeling of authority*.'

Now that was twenty years ago, when it was much more common than it is now to be tender about the feeling of authority of either fathers or teachers. This, I think, is the most noticeable change so far as I am concerned over the last twenty years, and it has all sorts of implications that are not obvious on the surface. At its best this dethronement of hierarchical authority liberates intelligence where it exists and floats creative ideas where they are hatched, and that is a supremely good thing. In so far as it can elevate brightness on the surface at the expense of wisdom in the depths it is not so good.

. . . those on whom authority rests need to be able, on the one hand, to listen, and on the other hand, as a result of listening, to learn; and it means, I think, that those with new insights and a critical approach to what exists need to learn how to wait while establishments gear themselves to change.

I believe that the dethronement of authority as such means for all of us entry into a new ethos of uncertainty with a consequent need to live with uncertainty without engendering reaction or irrational impatience or contempt, and this is what all of us have got to bring ourselves intellectually and emotionally to understand.

Twenty years ago, as some of you have heard me say more than once, students were students, teachers were teachers, schools were schools, and subjects were subjects. None of this is any longer true. There's a tremendous differentiation which means that people are doing different things – every one of which seems to me to be a move in the direction of more penetrating enquiry or exploration into some facet of education, whether it's curriculum or human relationships or the nature of institutions . . .

This differentiation has, I think, all been in a good cause; and I see it going on, and I think this is right. But its counterpart is a dangerous slide into fragmentation – we are all so concerned to do different things whole-heartedly that the responsibilities of our corporateness are liable to be forgotten; we are liable, as it were, to exploit the institution which provides us with a working base.

I think hierarchical diminution is right in the interests of liberating thought about ideas. But if hierarchical authority as such is to be diminished, then mutual and interdependent understanding has got to grow without bogging down in formal procedure.

Insistence on formal procedures can be the worst impediment to maintaining the vitality of spontaneity, destroying the place for catching life where it bubbles; there needs to be on the part of all of us a capacity to be able to listen to other people, and listening doesn't mean hearing the noises. It means understanding what is being said and then being able to wait for the growth of what may come from understanding.

I think all of us, wherever we stand in the hierarchical structure, however strong or weak, need to remember that this week's ideas are not necessarily better or worse than last week's and that there can be wisdom in memory as well as a bloody-mindedness in staying put.

Somehow or other insight and understanding and compassion need to be pulled together into our institutional life which must evolve an administrative element. At the moment we don't know how to do it.

When I was born there was no health insurance, there was no unemployment insurance; secondary education had only just come above the horizon as a public responsibility. There were no votes for women. I can remember as a small boy seeing children in the streets with no shoes because they hadn't got any shoes.

At the level of public opinion, during the First World War as a small boy in a family which was known to have pacifist convictions, I had to be moved away from the windows in our bedroom because it was anticipated that the crowds might well come and break windows. This is a commentary on the extent to which war was then an accepted institution; it is an area in which in these days there has been a tremendous change in public attitude, as well as in many other major issues.

Many people may feel that nothing has been sufficiently fundamental to make real change. But the truth is that this change has come through the process of hard thinking, related to a growing compassion of feeling and a willingness to think and work politically and socially, while being prepared to wait until attitudes change.

Thinking – and knowing how to wait. And I would be very sorry if, as we look at our educational institutions, we underplay the importance of thinking and being able to wait as we move into an era in which we recognize increasingly the value and significance of feeling and caring.

I think one of the most interesting developments of the last couple of decades has been the way in which it has been the schools of the country who have picked up the great areas of compassion . . . The question is whether we as teachers can help boys and girls and students to keep their minds on these issues so that we are able with them to think our way through to finding answers to problems which our society sets itself because of its ambivalence about objects and concerns, about its priorities and methods, a society in which we are able to create possessions so much more easily than we are able to know what to do with them.

I am reminded of one observation of Beatrice Webb, one of the architects of contemporary social thinking who, in terms of the study of history and statistical material, was thought to be a pretty dry as dust kind of political academic or academic politician. She commented, the world is moved by passion and not by statistics; but that it is by statistics that the world is moved aright. We have got to get the mixture right, of thinking, intellectual clarity and a readiness to recognize the reality and the value of other ways of knowing if we are to produce a world that is fit to live in. You have my very best wishes. Goodbye.

17

Retirement Priorities

1971–1979

Retirement, like old age, held no fears for Roger. He was fond of quoting Margery Fry of the famous chocolate family who said that old age was intermittent; at eighteen she sometimes felt eighty, at eighty she sometimes forgot she was not eighteen. But what really appealed to Roger was her forthright reaction when visiting an approved school, where grace before dinner was commanded in parade ground bellows: 'Stand up; fold your hands; bow your heads . . . raise your heads; put your hands down; sit down'. 'If I were God,' she told the principal, 'I should be furious.'

Another member of Roger's gallery of saints – a secular saint! – was William Frend whose biography he reviewed in *The Friend* (23 July 1971) shortly after his retirement. 'Frend was quietly and unfailingly at the heart of every radical and philanthropic concern of any importance – civil and religious liberty, political reform, slavery, education, housing, flogging in the army; he was not a pacifist but never doubted the stupidity of violence; he was mediator between extreme wings of reform movements; he went round with the subscription lists for the families of agitators in gaol.'

'No man,' Roger summed up the reason for his admiration, 'was more steadily, widely, modestly, effectively and undramatically "right" – and withal trusted by all with whom he worked, and they were many and of all classes. Years before Frend's death, in 1841, Charles Lamb addressed him:

> Friend of the friendless, friend of all mankind
> To thy wide friendships I have not been blind.'

Lamb could have been writing about Roger himself, an assessment justified already by the spirit of the former Professor of Education's *professional* life-style, but soon doubly so by the nature of Roger's *retirement* priorities. One thing was immediately apparent – though grateful for the past, he had no intention of living in it. Replying to a request to say what he thought about the future of the BBC, a request from the Corporation itself, he replied: 'It's just thirty years since I left the BBC, and all my contemporaries have retired, on the whole disappointed. It's for the next generation to decide what and how they want to fight the invasion of commercialism. In short, I have an attitude, not a policy.' Typical of the man, he then took the trouble to enclose a foolscap of handwritten notes about his hopes and fears for the BBC.

Settling in at Yealand Conyers, Margery busy with the garden, Roger seeking to justify his role as her assistant, he early turned his mind to the possibility of leading visitors to the area on Quaker pilgrimages to Pendle Hill and its surrounds. Even before he could fully understand, Roger had heard the story from his parents of a young man standing on the summit of Pendle Hill, gazing over the moor and the fell with its struggling becks, and seeing a vision of a great people to be gathered in for God, a people not dependent upon ecclesiastical intermediaries but responding within themselves individually to the *Light that lighteth every man that cometh into the world*, the inner Light, the Quakers' *that of God in every man*.

Introduced to George Fox's Journal at an early age, Roger soaked up its history no less than its message, was captivated by both, and visited Pendle Hill at the first opportunity. During that youthful pilgrimage to the cradle of Quakerism, he was conscious of walking on holy ground, and this sense of awe in the place never left him; indeed, it grew with the years, making him impatient to facilitate a similar experience for as many people as possible. The comparative freedom of retirement gave him his opportunity.

Over the next almost twenty years he led countless pilgrims including many from the USA to Pendle Hill, Firbank Fell, Preston Patrick, Brigflatts, and Swarthmoor Hall, home of Margaret Fell, wife of George Fox, and eventually the acknowledged centre of Quaker life and activity in the North, with soon growing significance for the Society of Friends both nationally and internationally. At each historic place Roger, having delivered a potted account of its meaning for Quakers, provided ample time for unhurriedness – to take in the loveliness of the scenery, to share appropriate readings from Fox's Journal, to centre down and allow the stillness to lead to corporate worship.

The emphasis was simplicity, after the fashion, said Roger, of the 'unsophisticated, intelligently critical, unorthodox Christians' who eagerly awaited a 'spark from heaven' and received it from the ministry of 'a dynamic travelling preacher' named George Fox whose only authority was his own experience of the love of God in Christ; essentially the language of the heart which Roger for all his learning saw as the spirit and appeal of Quakerism. Within a couple of years, he told the groups of pilgrims, the fire spread throughout the country and was set on its way to Ireland, the Continent and across the Atlantic, spread by torches 'lit on Firbank Hill' and borne in the face of great hardship and dreadful suffering by some sixty men and women travelling for the most part in pairs who became known as *The Valiant Sixty*.[1]

Roger's thoughts often turned to Ireland, particularly the troubles in the North. How could it be otherwise? His Quaker faith made inescapable his involvement in the political ebb and flow of current affairs, but Northern Ireland was, he concluded, too complex for amateur dabbling, let alone his readily-admitted ignorance no matter how worthy his intentions. Yet – as with Pakistan years before – his concern about what was happening in the Province simply would not lie down. He saw clearly enough what was required or needed to be reinforced – a Quaker Presence not unlike the one at Quaker House in New York for UN personnel, a home rather than an office where people of whatever religious or political persuasion could find freedom to talk with the assurance of confidentiality.

There were, of course, indigenous Quakers in Ireland, of two distinct traditions, one liberal with its emphasis on silent waiting in worship, the other evangelical, by no means averse to silence but making generous room for gospel preaching and singing, and characterized by its grave suspicion of the Pope!

Roger wondered whether Anthony Trollope had better captured the spirit of Ireland or of English arrogance when he wrote to his brother from Ireland, in 1848: 'Revolution here means a row. Some like a row, having little or nothing to lose . . . I think there is too much intelligence in England for any large body of men to look for any sudden improvement; and not enough intelligence in Ireland for any body of men at all to conceive the possibility of social improvement.'

Only the year before, 1847, following the disastrous Irish famine resulting from the failure of the potato harvest in the previous autumn, Friends at London Yearly Meeting had unwittingly illustrated that noble aspiration was no safeguard from Trollope's superficial judgment of Irish affairs: 'When the adversities of our neighbours, their poverty and distress have the effect of softening our hearts . . . they are made a means of good to us, and we are prepared to feel the force of the words, "It is more blessed to give than to receive".'

'Could a better example be found,' Roger reacted, 'of smug insensitivity?' So it was not in the least surprising that despite his concern for the deteriorating situation in Northern Ireland refusing to leave him alone, he felt personally unqualified to accept the urgings of some Friends that he with Margery should take up residence in the proposed Quaker House in Belfast.

---

[1] See Ernest E. Taylor, *The Valiant Sixty*, Ebor Press 1988 edition, foreword by Roger C. Wilson.

For a start he wasn't convinced that the name Quaker would necessarily open doors in Northern Ireland, not least because Roman Catholics considered the Society of Friends to be part of the Protestant Church and therefore incapable of listening without bias to both sides.

No less crucial, he wondered whether Irish Friends saw a place for a Quaker from England making a real contribution? This answered affirmatively, he further asked who was likely to want to talk with such a Quaker? Moderates, no doubt, but what about the IRA? Would its members be susceptible to impartial talk from outside or were they so emotionally motivated that only something quite different could touch them? Merely to ask such questions persuaded Roger that – never mind his concern refusing to lie down – he was not the man for the undertaking.

The whole matter was further explored by a group of Friends meeting in London, on 22 December 1971, Roger not among them, but later that same day a letter was written to him by Cyril Elliman, Personnel Secretary at Friends House: '. . . I gather from discussions which took place when you were here last week that you are quite concerned about the situation in Northern Ireland and Friends involvement there. This leads me to ask if you would consider it right for us to lay this concern upon you and Margery. I know you must perhaps be weary of my letters to you but I do hope that you will give this suggestion serious thought. It is difficult to say whether it would take six months or two years, but were you able to do this you know we would give all the support necessary to enable you to do it.'

A final paragraph concluded with a vain hope that the programme could be so arranged that 'it would not interfere too much either with your other commitments, or keep you too long away from your newly established home'. The Chairman of the Community Relations Committee later added his support to this appeal: 'What we need is a grey-haired Quaker to talk to the various groups'!

Roger wasn't persuaded – not yet. His ignorance of what was happening at the grass roots in the Province, summed up by himself as nothing better than 'second-hand', disqualified him from any authoritative role. Yet Friends whose judgment he respected kept urging, gently but persistently. His response was, devoid of any 'committee label or responsibility', to spend a few days in Northern Ireland. What he sought was to listen to Friends on the spot, to people at the university, and perhaps 'the Home Office men'. He went in the early days of 1972.

On his return he was, as he put it, 'pretty well persuaded' that he *ought* to be in a Quaker delegation to the Home Office in London about Northern Ireland, though with the proviso that the occasion should be seen as 'exploratory rather than commitment to proposals' and that 'every effort will be made to get somebody from Northern Ireland' as part of the delegation.

What particularly concerned the Quakers were such matters as internment without trial, the modification and supervision of any interrogation of internees to eliminate possible ill-treatment, and the need for special training for peace-keeping procedures. These were the immediate issues, but basic to everything was, for the Quakers, the question of whether the British Army or any other group using violent methods could ever produce conditions in which a lasting solution could be found?

The discussions, both at the Home Office and on a widening front within the Society of Friends, reinforced the idea of a Quaker House in Belfast, but left Roger himself neither more convinced that he was the man for the undertaking nor less capable of escaping his concern.

Within weeks he was back in Belfast on another personal fact-finding tour during which a fortuitous conversation with a stranger eventually proved to be decisive. This contact was not associated with any political party or partisan group. The stranger's sudden notoriety in the local Press followed a particularly gruesome explosion in a crowded restaurant which as a surgeon kept him in the operating theatre with one victim after another, prompting him to make an impassioned public appeal for peace and a statement suggesting a possible way forward about which, Roger noted, Jo Grimmond for one had claimed there had been far too few.

One immediate result was an approach to the surgeon by representatives of the IRA who assured him of their wish to explore the possibility of getting talks going across the whole spectrum of Northern Ireland's political and religious thought. His clear impression was that these officially unofficial spokesmen for the IRA wanted to emerge from the isolation that led to the violence they didn't know how to stop, but at the same time he was appalled at their narrow understanding of the basic issues that so bitterly divided the community.

Having unhurriedly consulted with the surgeon, and listened to numerous other individuals on either side of the divide, Roger returned to Yealand Conyers with added enthusiasm for greater Quaker involvement, but still not sure about to what extent this necessitated his personal presence in the Province. There was another major obstacle to his commitment to Quaker House. 'I felt very much,' Margery recalled, 'that we shouldn't do it.' She smiled. 'I didn't feel that we shouldn't go, but I didn't particularly want to.'

Naturally she didn't. There was – a mighty deterrent in itself – the garden, a veritable wilderness when they arrived at their retirement home, but already showing signs of the glories within Margery's plans. This apart, she loved their new setting, enjoyed every aspect of village life, and was already deeply dug in to aspects of the community. Serendipity was never far away. Virtually across the road was the ancient Quaker Meeting House which she attended two or three times a week for various reasons as well as on Sundays for worship. She started painting again, inspired by the scenic beauty at every turn. Her whole life was one of peace and pleasure, with freedom to choose – to address groups about Quaker history in 1652 country; to do much of the secretarial work in arranging the pilgrimages led by Roger; to make new friends and entertain old; to potter, to read, to *be*, without the pressure of freely-accepted but still fiercely-demanding obligation – duty.

'If I had refused,' she returned to the subject of Northern Ireland, 'Roger wouldn't have gone.' Not that they *did* immediately, he surely sharing Margery's reluctance to be uprooted so soon after retirement, the pair of them able to indulge their love of walking in the fells, she as enthusiastic as ever to point out to him by name the rich variety of wild flowers and also expertly identify the wide range of birds. There was simply no time to remove themselves to Northern Ireland, certainly not before being absolutely sure that 'necessity was laid upon them' to put aside their existing Quaker activity on both a national and local level.

It was, in fact, not for some months, the early part of 1973, that Roger, assured of Margery's habitual whole-hearted support, finally accepted that for six months they should take up residence in Belfast at the flat adjacent to the new Meeting House and soon known as a place for confidential if not clandestine meetings and discussions.

His work took him into some strange places and company. A member of the IRA wanted the word spread that a recent attack had been a mistake not deserving of retaliation! One of Roger's Quaker colleagues, long known and trusted by both sides as a worker for peace in the hostile territory of Derry, quietly responded: 'I love you as a person but hate what you are doing.' The IRA man confessed that the first time he killed a person he felt bad, the second time pretty bad, the third time he couldn't have cared less.

Roger, privy to many such occasions, recognized them as essential if the Quaker peace witness was to be effective, but most of his work, less under-cover though still often secretive, was with groups and individuals on both sides of the divide, a gulf *fixed* and seemingly unbridgeable. The depth of bigotry of good people frequently within the churches, within Quakerism, made them blind to even the possibility of reasonableness beyond their own convictions and fears.

Significantly, he was quickly widely perceived not as an interfering outsider dabbling in matters he knew nothing about, but as a servant of peace with the authority to speak as a life-long opponent of war. People resistant to his pleas for greater understanding and the spirit of reconciliation, the vast majority, found his statesmanship no less than his humility formidable. The man himself, in all his personal relationships both open and secretive, silently bespoke his Quaker ministry, but if more cerebral individuals demanded a didactic approach his knowledge of the convolutions of Irish history won respect if not always agreement.

The effectiveness of this Quaker presence was paradoxically its hiddenness. To the flat at the Meeting House came people of all shades of opinion, nationalists no less than loyalists, anxious to pick over the bones of what they conceived to be a just and lasting peace for all sections of the community. This Quaker hope of seeking to foster a meeting of partisan hearts and minds also found expression at the Maze prison in a waiting room for visiting families where light refreshments were provided and facilities created for children to play, which was part of Margery's involvement.

Surprisingly to some people, Roger thought that Ian Paisley was both the biggest man around the place but potentially the worst, with a very great deal depending upon how he used his undoubted charisma and abilities. Making the distinction between Paisley and Paisleyism, he perceived that the latter was a dangerous stumbling-block to progress; on the other hand, Paisley represented a lot that wasn't Paisleyism, and if he could use this constructively the struggle would be nearly won or at least set in the right direction. If he devoted himself to Paisleyism, however, the outlook was gloomy!

'To us,' Roger further reflected, 'the awfulness of the tragedy lies particularly in the fact that the divide crystalizes itself in *religious* terms. So that cultural and political differences which are real but negotiable are interfused with the profoundest of mythological religious differences and sectarian forms that are as resistant to mutual understanding as any human experience in the world's history. Northern Ireland presents us all with the terrible experience of having allowed Christian symbols to drift into use as the justification for secular fears and aspirations that lead to economic and social discrimination on a grand scale, to the desolation of mass intimidation throughout the population on all sides, and to both deliberate and incidental murder on a dreadful scale. The symbols are taken from our religious history.'

'Let's be clear,' he concluded, 'the actual number of adult men and women of violence is probably very small, perhaps not more than 3/4,000 on both sides together, but embedded in a sea of fear and intimidation that enables them to operate from a base of secrecy and that worst of all provides a setting in which children can grow up believing that hatred of their fellows embodied in violence is the natural order of things. As a Catholic priest said to me: throughout the world there's a wave of violence, and to the young in Northern Ireland there's a semblance of a cause on both sides.'

After six months of strenuous activity, Roger – now almost sixty-seven years of age – accepted that the time had come for him and Margery to move on. There was, he felt, little more they could add to what they had either set in motion or supported, but perhaps more importantly he saw the urgent need for Quakerism as a whole to be made further aware of Northern Ireland as a personal and corporate responsibility. Familiarity with news bulletins and headlines of the latest atrocity, if not actually breeding contempt, was nevertheless possibly dulling sensitivity and active concern.

So although Margery returned to her beloved garden, this in no way reduced their commitment to Northern Ireland. Roger addressed endless private and public meetings about their experiences in the Province, and – apart from still serving on Friends Service Council and the Watching Committee to tackle emergency centres of need – frequently consulted with the Northern Friends Peace Board in its preoccupation with the situation in Northern Ireland.

Additionally he continued to tackle complex issues head-on, exploiting every contact to focus burning concerns of the people in both Protestant and Catholic back streets in Belfast. Alive, for instance, to all the feuding and divisiveness associated with whether political prisoners like the Price sisters should be transferred to Northern Ireland to complete their sentences, he wrote to the Prison Department at the Home Office, on 7 November 1973: '. . . The particular point is this: I came to know – as Chairman of the Visiting Committee at Shepton Mallet – that it was not unusual for the Prison Department to transfer Scottish prisoners to Scotland (and vice versa) when humanitarian and cultural considerations justify this. Is there a comparable pattern of transfer between England and Northern Ireland?'

Characteristically, he added: 'You may feel that you cannot properly give me this information; but to save burdening you with writing a letter I will ring you toward the end of next week.' Clearly this gentle Quaker wasn't called Mr Fix-it for nothing, not least for his tenacity in helping weary administrators tempted to answer awkward questions by ignoring them!

After living in an atmosphere of violence, with the constant threat of personal physical danger, Roger and Margery were relieved to return to their own home, in itself as peaceful as the silence of the surrounding lakes and fells. But such peace for each of them was never dependent upon *where* they were, any more than its maintenance was contingent upon freedom to escape the burdens of added unsought responsibility.

Meanwhile Roger, his preoccupation undimmed with the affairs of Northern Ireland, and as busy as ever, listened sympathetically to an appeal from Lady Mary Morris, widow of Charles, knighted for his services to education notably as Vice-Chancellor at the University of Leeds. As a social worker of vast experience, she was, she explained, disturbed by the growing number of drop-outs and push-outs from society in South Lakeland, her retirement home, and wanted Roger's help to establish a Council of Voluntary Action to tackle this and related social problems.

He agreed to serve as Chairman, and, with support speedily recruited and harnessed, the venture was soon an authoritative co-ordinating voice for numerous local independent bodies concerned about deprived children, the mentally-handicapped, the mentally-ill, and less articulate groups like the homeless and old age pensioners, many of the latter, it was discovered, too proud to admit their often appalling circumstances. But primarily this newly formed South Lakeland Council of Voluntary Action pioneered services for alcoholics, people little understood and largely ignored by official welfare agencies, and also for the carers of ageing parents or other dependents, carers whose own needs, frequently more desperate than those for whom they cared, were also being largely overlooked by statutory agencies.

If in his resolve to translate verbal concern into practical helpfulness Roger was sometimes an abrasive Chairman he was never discourteous, even less offensive. As one member of the Council put it: 'Roger was a wonderful bully in a very nice way', a judgment endorsed throughout the years by all sorts of committees and similar administrations grateful for his expertise in getting through an agenda expeditiously and to real purpose.

Another major asset was his national and international standing which he didn't hesitate to exploit in opening doors to officials and organizations he believed might be able to help. Added to his skill as a negotiator this frequently resulted in sizeable sums of money being made available and – perhaps more important – the whole-hearted support of authorities at both local and governmental level. So the work originally centred in a back-street office in Kendal was transferred to a main thoroughfare property, by courtesy of the Local Authority. And to this new centre came such numbers of needy people that soon a paid worker was required to organize the volunteers in staffing the place for longer hours on more days of the week.

Roger's only reservation – if it can be called a reservation – at the rapidity of the progress was that with the work among alcoholics firmly established and still growing, it was deemed wise to link it to a national movement, in itself a step he supported, but not its corollary, the transfer of part of its administration, notably financial, to Carlisle. The resultant controversy about which district should receive how much grant from central funds finally proved intolerable, and in 1979, after five years as Chairman, and with the whole enterprise recognized as an indispensable part of South Lakeland welfare services, he resigned, a mere seventy-three-year-old, with his enthusiasm, if not his patience with squabbling councils, undimmed.

Significantly, when *a decade and a half later* the still thriving organization again moved its headquarters to yet more capacious accommodation, it was decided to call its growing collection of books the *Roger Wilson Library*.

Unquestionably a major reason for Roger's sustained enthusiasm throughout his life, never mind his retirement, was the rich variety of experience he either initiated or welcomed as a fortuitous gift. In the first three months of 1975, for instance, he returned to Ireland on five occasions, once to Dublin, the rest to the north. His many contacts included representatives of the Northern Ireland Office, Provisional Sinn Fein, and the Ulster Community Action Group which might be described, he commented, as the political wing of the Ulster Defence Association.

He emerged neither more hopeful nor less. 'To become involved in the present and future of Northern Ireland is,' he said, 'to become engaged in a game without rules and with a variety of objectives.'

His main hope focussed on the Centre for Neighbourhood Development which incorporated ecumenical and secular co-operation at the grass roots, and where confidence would grow simply because neither side felt dominated, bullied, manipulated or used by the other. The Friends' essential contribution would be to ensure 'a well-understood and accepted foundation in principles of non-violence and inclusiveness which stemmed from a religious testimony' and to inspire 'respect on both sides of the conflict because of the reputation for fairness that Quakers have acquired'.

These returns to the Province, part of the concern that nagged relentlessly, were also doubtless related to another matter that increasingly occupied his mind during the final months of the previous year, 1974. 'I was born in the first decade of this century', he explained 'just old enough to appreciate the jingoism of the First World War and the 1918 khaki election, well able to be sickened by the appalling complacency of most of us in the face of the dreadful incidence of unemployment and misery between the wars. The change in the public temper in respect both of war and of unemployment is tremendous – and is,' he suggested, 'largely due to the steady refusal of small bodies of campaigners who refused to keep quiet about moral values – the *No More War Movement*, the *Peace Pledge Union*, Seebohm Rowntree, James Maxton, Beveridge, Eleanor Rathbone and Family Endowments.

'The advertisers and the salesmen loom larger in our lives on possessions but the compassionate virtues have not been crushed to the ground. It is within our power to stand up for compassion – and I think that we shall have to do this within the coming winter when I guess there will be very high social tension, with much misery and possibly violence by some of those who can find no other way of dealing with their feelings. In these circumstances it seems to me an obligation on Friends to testify to their faith.'

The national circumstances giving rise to these remarks were the mining dispute, the three-day week and gathering inflation, compounded by 'the sudden use of their economic power by oil producers'. He amplified his ideas in *The Friend* (9 August 1974): 'The question for Friends,' he wrote, 'is how, together and separately, we can set ourselves, from our own sense of peace, to be of service to the miserable whose trouble is that they have too little or believe that they have not enough, or exclude themselves from worship. I don't know the complete answer, but here are some beginnings.'

There followed the practical, if idealistic, suggestions of an earnest man, springing from the principles by which he himself sought to live. He ended: 'It comes back to the need to ask ourselves what sort of people are we? Do we sit in our corner like Little Jack Horner? Or do we set out, like George Fox, to shake the country for ten miles round by showing that human nature can be liberated by compassion rather than imprisoned by possessions?'

For Roger such questions were inescapable and constantly posed to himself throughout his life. Whether sharing the Quaker campaign in the late 1930s about *Simple Living* or wrestling with his conscience about how best to handle his own unsought prosperity, he kept asking the same penetrating questions and – surely evidence of freedom from self-righteousness or assumed infallibility – sometimes changing or qualifying his answers.

If he was essentially a man of principle, he was never less than vigilant to the danger of the *letter* of the law killing or contradicting its *spirit*. Few things within Quakerism, let alone society at large, bothered him more than the possibility of past insights becoming ossified in authoritative statements and granted mindless obedience.

In what sense, then, was he a man of principle? The answer goes to the heart of his understanding of Christian discipleship in its feeling for others.

18

Man of Principle or of Principles?

The most cursory examination of Roger's life indicates his suspicion of rigidity in belief and behaviour. Inflexible rules, whatever their devout motivation, had no room in his interpretation of Christian responsibility. Take, for example, his life-long commitment to total abstinance.

Before he and Margery had their own television, Roger was very keen to see England play in the European cup finals. Down the road lived a couple of old age pensioners who *did* have a TV. After the game, anxious to be generous hosts, they produced a bottle of port, explaining that this, a rare treat, had been kept for 'a very special occasion'. Roger felt that to have refused would have been tantamount to slapping the old couple in the face. He and Margery accepted without hesitation.

Again, as a young Socialist he made no secret of his disbelief in private education, seeing it as a barrier to the provision of the highest standards of schooling for every child. Indeed, he argued vigorously against privileged institutions of every kind which on financial grounds alone kept people in – or out! Yet when circumstances within his own family indicated that not only private education but boarding school was the best option available, he saw no justification despite heavy breathings of conscience for making his son a sacrificial offering on the altar of his own principles.

During his leadership of Friends relief work among war victims he was, as we have seen, constantly called upon to walk a moral tightrope in desperate situations offering only varying shades of grey. Those who worked closest to him never doubted that he was a man of cast-iron principle, his integrity intact at whatever cost, but this did not save him from controversial decisions, some of them causing great distress to those like his father and mother who loved and respected him most.

On many occasions he found it necessary to be utterly unbending, as when Montgomery issued his order of no fraternization with the enemy in immediate post-war Europe; but there were other occasions when Friends no less sincere than himself were troubled by his willingness to push ahead in situations demanding from their perspective unacceptable expediency.

No one doubted his absolute opposition to war – the war machine – yet he used military transport, petrol, accommodation, food, hospitality in the officers' mess; travelled on military trains without either official papers or even a ticket, dodging inspectors and the like; accepted from the *only* source of supplies available, the military, anything needed by Quaker relief teams for their work among refugees, displaced persons, prisoners (including known collaborators despised by virtually everybody else), the sick, the naked, the hungry, nationality irrelevant.

Little wonder, then, he advised any colleague bothered by not knowing precisely how to apply personal principles in unending emergency situations to do what he or she honestly believed was right, without drawing attention! What else, in circumstances that simply would not wait for reassuring consultation and official sanction? If he warned that '*to be all things to all men* – a biblical injunction! – was to risk finishing up being nothing to anybody', he also told his relief teams that 'to avoid the army may be to avoid danger but to renounce opportunities'.

Fenner Brockway pin-pointed the inescapable moral dilemma: 'People sometimes congratulate me on sticking to principles, but I have chosen the easier path. I have never wanted to be in government because not even a Labour Government will do things I feel are fundamentally important. But this has allowed me uninhibited action without responsibility, with freedom to express principles more realistic in the future than the present. To be in a pressure-group is child's play compared with participation in administration tackling day-to-day problems which inevitably compel compromise.'[1]

Compel *compromise*? Was this how Roger saw the countless occasions throughout his life when the choice was not between a convenient black or white but a questionable shade of grey? Even if this is part of the answer it still doesn't remotely explain a man whose *refusal* to compromise, often landing him in hot water, was universally recognized and respected. We must look deeper; deeper for the core conviction that regulated everything he did – at Oxford, in the cotton mills, at the BBC, during the war, at Hull and Bristol, as an international consultant in matters of educational and social welfare notably in the Third World where 'compromise' was functionally indispensable.

Roger indicated the flexibility of his own approach to principles of conduct in one of his regular BBC West of England broadcasts in the 1950s ('A Christian Looks at the News'): 'If Christianity were just a series of rules or the ritual performance of forms of worship there need be no arguments. In fact the Christianity which springs from the teaching of Jesus is a continuous assessment of the habits of fallible mortals by the probing, loving, forgiving, renewing Spirit of God.'

Now if Jesus himself was condemned for not being a man of principle –

---

[1] *Towards Tomorrow*, Granada 1977, p. 269.

consorting with quislings and harlots; ignoring the rules of Sabbath observance ('the Sabbath was made for man, not man for the Sabbath') and much else – it is hardly surprising that anyone refusing to set Jesus' teaching in stone but rather interpreting it by way of 'a continuous assessment' is likely to find himself at best misunderstood or at worst accused of hypocrisy. The latter was never applied to Roger, the very idea was palpably unthinkable, but that he sometimes raised a few eyebrows . . .

Example: A young Friend working with delinquents accompanied them to the pub as a means of getting to know them and – he hoped – being accepted by them. Roger passed on words of encouragement, and found himself having to defend the man against charges of not keeping himself 'separate from the world'.

Example: Roger was utterly opposed to gambling, no one could doubt it, yet as Chairman of the South Lakeland Council of Voluntary Action he sanctioned an application to the Local Authority lottery scheme for a grant to establish an adventure playground. A Quaker, happy herself with the application, nevertheless confessed to 'taking the mickey out of him like anything because Roger's principles were pragmatic'.

So was this it – he was simply a pragmatist? Or was it more likely that his principles were subjected to 'a continuous assessment' in the light of a more fundamental principle, one from which he never deviated – *the principle that people were more important than principle*?

Thus if his refusal to compromise meant that war victims and the like would be left without food, shelter, comfort and hope he never hesitated – *people* must come first. In this sense he was, before everything else, a man of principle, one of that all too rare company of men and women who, rejecting moribund tradition, risk being misunderstood in their 'continuous assessment' of how better to interpret and apply the teaching of Jesus in current economic and industrial developments.

Never was this more needed than in the unrest amounting at times to anarchy sweeping Britain in the mid and late 1970s. And Roger was by no means isolated in his concern within Quakerism. 'Some Friends (and I have been one),' confessed the Chairman of the Society's Social Responsibility Council (David E.C. Eversley), 'have wondered if the SRC was being used by the Society as a ragbag for its conscience . . . We therefore suggest that in the present situation we need to lift the level of debate from the generalizations with which we have contented ourselves for too long to a new level where we do not shirk *a fresh look at the fundamental principles of a new Christian Social Order*.'

London Yearly Meeting (1975) issued a Minute which only twenty or so years later seems plain common sense, not the voice-in-the-wilderness declaration it appeared at the time:

'We live in a part of the world where the dominant motivation is material self-interest, justified by the concept of personal freedom. In these circumstances the rich get richer, and the poor for the most part become comparatively poorer. This offends our moral sensibility, and at the practical level the process of material growth cannot in any event go on indefinitely. We must find some way in which we in the West can change our dominance in setting the style of the world's living from one motivated by self-interest into one in which material resources are made available according to need . . .'

The Minute accurately reflected the feeling of Yearly Meeting, but if at the same time its conciseness and clarity, never mind its emphasis, bespoke Roger's mind and skill in distilling the sense of Meeting this was hardly surprising because by now he was Chairman (1975–77) of this most influential annual gathering of Friends, the essential purpose of which he immediately underlined as either *corporate* responsibility or nothing: 'On the one hand the gathering can count on the help of specially well-informed Friends, familiar with intellectual and operational aspects; on the other it is at Yearly Meeting that there is an important role for the individual Friend with no special knowledge or expertise who can yet help the Society to cut its way through complexities and reach forward to the first principles of Truth.'

He concluded: 'At their best, Friends can make Yearly Meeting very, very good. At their worst they can make it horrid.'[2]

Looking at Roger's crowded programme both before retirement and no less after, a stranger might wonder why there never appeared to be any let-up. Was this a man frightened by or ashamed of idleness, so accustomed to being busy that even to slow down was interpreted as evidence of weakness or indulgence, an affront to his Puritan upbringing? Indeed, was 'never having a minute' essential to his self-image as well as his reputation for redeeming every spare moment in service of one form or another?

No doubt, he *was* fully occupied. To his endless Quaker commitments were added 'incidentals' like membership of the Court of Lancaster University, the board of governors at Charlotte Mason College of Education, sustained consultations with both national and local government welfare services, and the same specialist contributions to such bodies as the Educational Award Scheme, recruiting teachers for overseas, and the Council of Social Responsibility, preoccupied with identifying and allocatating funds to areas of deprivation.

He was, of course, also still involved with the South Lakeland Council of

---

[2] *Quaker Monthly*, May 1975, pp.81–84.

Voluntary Action, still leading groups of Quaker pilgrims in 1652 country, and still – in some ways the greatest time consumer of all – disappearing into his study to deal with a never diminishing international personal correspondence.

On the other hand, whatever his personal feelings, he never hesitated –once persuaded the time was right – to pass on responsibilities he had carried sometimes for many years. A case in point was his trusteeship of the Joseph Rowntree Charitable Trust.

Writing of his long association – in a pamphlet 'Money and Power: Reflections as a Trustee' – Roger first of all quoted a conclusion reached by Joseph Rowntree (1836–1925) that 'the observation of a life-time has led me to believe that any considerable amount of wealth more often proves to be a curse than a blessing'. Accordingly, Roger continued, JR throughout his life gave away a great deal of money in carefully considered ways. But when very large commercial prosperity came to him shortly after the turn of the century, he founded three Trusts, endowing them with shares in the Company amounting to about half his total property.

One, the Village Trust, was to initiate and support good housing policy and practice; one, the Social Service Trust, was to enable political and social campaigning that – however well-intentioned – was not legally charitable; the third, the Charitable Trust, aimed at financing literally anything that was legally charitable.

Roger attended his first JRCT in the early days of the Second World War, a gathering at York he described in typical robust style: 'This was held at the station hotel while bombers and fighters droned overhead. I suppose A., at about 50, is the next youngest incumbent of the concern. 'I was welcomed as being capable of carrying on after all the others were dead. I said I thought my chances of death greater than theirs at the moment!'

Roger was struck by two main impressions: the meeting as a whole was pretty disorderly, possibly because the chairman 'gets so at sea'; and he wasn't half as embarrassed as he expected in discussing the private affairs and needs of contemporaries he knew who needless to say never had a better champion. He summed up: 'Afterwards I had my hair cut by a man who thinks retired staff officers get too much and tommies too little. I agree.'

From then on Roger remained a Trustee for as long as the Trusts had been in existence when he joined, thirty-seven years, many of them (1950–1965) as Chairman of the Charitable Trust. In 1950 he was also appointed to the Social Service Trust, and used his concurrent responsibilities to bring their complementary functions together notably in such fields as race relations and Northern Ireland.

Roger whole-heartedly shared the central aim of the Trusts to search out the fundamental causes of what was wrong rather than simply alleviate distress, avoid providing palliatives without contributing to permanent solutions.

Hence, when Alec Dickson's vision of Voluntary Service Overseas looked like being indefinitely bogged down by bureaucratic deadlocks, a Trust grant of £2000 enabled it to break through into action by sending its first twelve volunteers overseas regardless – and VSO never looked back or needed a further grant from the Trust.

Likewise with many other grants for projects sprinkled throughout the story of Roger's life – Patrick van Rensburg's educational and training enterprise in Botswana; an educational unit in the University of Malawi; Friends' educational and social ventures in Kenya; the inter-racial University of Central Africa in Salisbury (Harare); the pioneering Quaker delegation to Russia, in 1951; Quaker House at UN headquarters in New York; the Northern Ireland peace witness; these and countless other ventures testifying to Roger's perception of need and its priorities.

That he had a reputation for always being able to find money for charitable causes is hardly surprising, not because he was a Trustee – the very idea would indict both him and his fellow Trustees – but because, having ferreted out the precise and often hidden nature of a need, he found it impossible to dismiss the matter with pious platitudes. Records clearly illustrate that having shared with fellow Trustees details of a project or a situation or a person desperate for financial aid, he then went out of his way not to influence let alone manipulate them in reaching a decision. So scrupulous was he that sometimes the case under consideration perhaps merited greater support than he personally was prepared to give. In any case, with the likes of Jo Grimmond, Richard Wainright, both Liberal MPs, two or three Rowntrees, and William Morrell, of Westminster Press, also on the Social Service Trust, and heavyweight Quakers on the Charitable Trust,[3] every application for assistance rightly required more than a single Trustee's enthusiasm.

Where indisputably Roger did make a considerable impact as a Trustee was in his standards of administration! Recalling the Charitable Trust meeting at which Roger had been appointed Chairman, Eric Cleaver, Secretary at the time, said that he was taken aside afterwards, into one of the dark aspidistra'd corners of the station hotel, what he called 'the one valuable feature of the place', by the new Chairman who whispered: 'Eric, we must run down the "ad hocery". We must have documents, agenda notes, supporting memoranda, preparatory papers. Can you see to it?'

The Secretary's response was 'to run the stuff off myself on a borrowed Roneo'. Then it was his turn to make an appeal. Leading the Chairman into,

---

[3] At the time of Roger's retirement these were: Joyce Blake, Alfred W. Braithwaite, Donald Court, William R. Fraser, A. Nicolas Gillet, Christopher J. Holdsworth, Gillian Hopkins, W. Grigor McClelland, Roger Morton, Christopher J. Rowntree, Michael H. Rowntree, and Lucie A.E. Shaw.

as he put it, 'the same penumbra' at the hotel, he said: 'Roger, how can we get out of this place? I and some of the newly-appointed Trustees are finding it spiritually embarrassing.' *This place* was, in Roger's own words, 'an absolutely splendid room on the first floor looking out over the Minster', somewhat opulent for a body of high-minded Quakers dispensing charity! In no time they were out, meeting in a Friend's flat, with a couple of schoolgirls earning extra pocket money by serving morning coffee and afternoon tea.

'I remember,' Eric Cleaver further reminisced at the time of Roger's retirement as a Trustee, in 1977, 'B.S. Rowntree saying in about late 1949, with a wry, dry humour, peering steely-eyed at the assembled Trustees over his gold-rimmed quartermoon spectacles, that a body such as this, to be effective, should have *just one* member who was a little mad. Everybody looked anxiously at everybody else! But mercifully the BSR gaze had not come to rest on any particular member present . . .'

Cleaver went on: 'I have found myself wondering sometimes whether BSR may not have been saying something profound. It is the privilege and sometimes the responsibility of an indepentent Trust, if it is to be truly *independent*, to look on occasion at unlikely and even "mad" ideas, even the impossible, if only for the reason that not many other bodies are likely to do so. In this way and along a route which at times can be tiresome and laborious, a Trust, particularly a Quaker one which is enjoined to look for new light from unexpected sources, can develop a mind of its own and a life of its own. I hope that Roger will not mind me saying that in this as well as in other ways he gave the Trust life!'

Was Roger 'mad' or the dispenser of 'mad' ideas? Well, yes – in the sense of never allowing strictly cerebral considerations to make final decisions or discouraging omens to regulate enthusiasm or insuperable barriers to be viewed as anything more than inducements to Quaker ingenuity. He *was* mad in his sometimes 'irrational' optimism, his refusal to take No for an answer against all the odds, and above all in his implicit belief that God's strength was made perfect in weakness; in the power of the powerless.

What, however, gave him greatest pleasure was Eric Cleaver's view that the character of the Trust began to change under Roger's chairmanship: 'It became an integrated group of Friends who were also friends, able to question and to disagree but also to reach a consensus enabling the Chairman to discern the true *feeling of meeting.* One had the unmistakable feeling that these and related developments were what the Founding Fathers to whom so much was and is still owed would have wanted.'

The reason, in Cleaver's opinion, was not hard to seek: 'Roger's readiness to be consulted – and, no less, to consult – was always generous. On occasion, the latter could be over-generous!', he spoke of his own dealings with the Chairman.

Roger's philosophy in his long association with the Trusts was explained during an interview about it some four years before he died.

'An active Friend,' he said, 'expects to be in a minority most of the time.'

'Is that a good or a bad thing?'

'It's a good thing.'

'Why?'

'Because by and large you're highly critical of power structures and more concerned to liberate people.'

This is, he also made clear, what a good Quaker ought to be concerned in, competence and ethics – social concern.

Social concern and the liberation of people were uppermost in an address he gave shortly after ceasing to be a Trustee, reflections to mark the fifieth anniversary of Friends Service Council, at a celebratory gathering at Friends House, London, on 4 November 1977. Quoting Dag Hammarskjøld, 'In our era, the road to holiness necessarily passes through the world of action', he summarized what he called 'fifty tumultuous years' as a boiling cauldron and series of cataracts in which Friends had had 'some active part to play, not simply being swept along, but trying to make something useful out of the currents and trying to do a bit of rescue and rehabilitation work on the way under the guidance of God and in the life-giving power of Jesus Christ that we have seen at work down through history'. To illustrate his interpretation of what this meant, he referred to two Friends (William Sewell and his wife) offering in the early 1920s to serve as Quaker missionaries, as teachers of science, in the West China Union University, but being unable to assure the kindly and perplexed selection committee that though they were converted they were without an evangelical urge.

'Their concern as Christians was,' said Roger, 'to be good teachers, but not with the motive of using science to attract students to the Christian faith.' He went on: 'We're not in a business that can be evaluated in terms of success, but in terms of an integrity that frees both us and others to seek divine guidance, whether our friends put it that way or not.'

By way of encouragement after admitting that 'within our work there is failure and many dark corners', he concluded with two quotations, one from the Talmud – 'We are not required to finish the task but neither are we permitted to lay it down'; the other written in 1831 by a Quaker from Sheffield (Hannah Kilham) on her way by sea, which she hated, to Sierra Leone to pioneer work on a written form for African languages: 'It is *life* only that can lead to life and no forms are available without it. Seek the life in all things and cherish it by all authorized means.'[4]

---

[4] The whole address was published in *Quaker Monthly* in the June, July and August issues of the following year, 1978.

At about this time Roger received two contrasting invitations which he saw as complementary, one offering relaxation and undiluted pleasure, the other nothing but sustained hard thinking about the world's greatest single danger. He accepted both.

The first took him with Margery to Palestine to lead a group of Quaker pilgrims. With a Jewish girl to guide them to holy places, they shared appropriate Bible readings, but otherwise, contrast to other groups listening to expositions, the Quakers observed their tradition of silent worship, only occasionally broken by ministry from one or other of the pilgrims. They sat by the Sea of Galilee, ascended the Mount of Olives, lingered in the Garden of Gethsemane. Bethlehem particularly proved unforgettable. The Quakers stood in the field of the Shepherds, sharing the astonishment of the first gazers at the Star. On such occasions, and they proved numerous, Roger exercised his role as leader by never intruding. On the contrary, he himself welcomed this opportunity to replenish his own spiritual resources, aware of the new commitment awaiting his return – membership of the Quaker Nuclear Energy Group to examine the moral and ethical implications of the choices facing the world in this area.

In agreeing to serve, he had made it clear that, being neither a scientist nor an economist, he wouldn't be able to contribute to the technical debate about the efficiency, safety, dangers or cost of nuclear energy; nor was he expected to. He was there, along with three other lay persons and eight scientists and engineers, all Quakers, to wrestle with the terms of reference from Meeting for Sufferings 'to carry forward the thinking on this issue and present a report[5] on the spiritual and moral issues on which the judgment of the Society should be sought'.

At the heart of the matter was, of course, the existence of nuclear armaments and the possible use of reactors to provide basic ingredients for more weapons. As Roger put it in introducing or sharing the deliberations of the group at various open Quaker debates, 'acceptance of nuclear armaments was a far greater spiritual and moral offence than the problem of nuclear power for civil purposes as such'.

The twelve members of the group, meeting regularly for twelve months, early saw that the problems of the production, use and distribution of all forms of energy, reaching to the very roots of their convictions about the nature of human societies, rich and poor the world over, what they are and what they should be, represented essentially a spiritual issue – 'how we, as citizens of the rich world, can seek, find and follow the guidance of God in the

---

5 *Nuclear Energy – What are the Choices?* (published in 1979 for London Yearly Meeting by Quaker Home Service).

responsible use of natural resources, the wise employment of high technical skills and concern for proper relationships with the third world'.

In seeking the 'guidance of God' in this spiritual minefield, the group not surprisingly came up with clues rather than conclusions about the way forward, clues as free of pious jargon as rooted in the real world:

'We would remind Friends that whether we like it or not we live in a society that relies on technology for the sustenance of life, and with world population at its present levels our technology cannot be abandoned without risk of major disaster. While small groups of people may attempt to *opt out* from this society even they depend in some measure on present technology, and such a retreat is not available to more than a small minority. It would be comforting to be able to say "Nuclear Power – No Thanks", but it would also be comforting to say "Coal mining, factory farming, chemical plants, motorways, pesticides, production lines, oil tankers, advertising – No Thanks".'

'There are risks in any technological process, and the risks associated with the use of nuclear power for civil purposes are such that this course could be accepted only with caution, but if the alternative were the failure to sustain the energy needs of the whole world, a limited nuclear power programme is an option that cannot be lightly laid aside.'

The guidance of God?

The Quaker Energy Group offered four choices for the seeking of further light:

Choice 1. It is possible to encourage the rapid development of nuclear energy, in the belief that dangerous aspects will be effectively dealt with as they are recognized.

Choice 2. It is possible to accept a further development of nuclear energy with the utmost caution, as a necessary measure to bridge the gap between the effective exhaustion of fossil fuels and the harnessing of long-lasting or renewable energy resources.

Choice 3. It is possible to take the view that the critical point is not so near as to require decision now, particularly if this critical point can be postponed somewhat by intelligent conservation and the exploitation of alternative sources.

Choice 4. It is possible to urge our government to say No to any further development of nuclear energy.

In harmony with the Society's understanding of God's guidance, the next step was for more hard thinking, more open debate, more corporate centring down and responding to 'sense of Meeting'.

Throughout his life, Roger made no secret that persons wanting to be told what to think or what to do were sure to find Quakerism an alien experience.

During all this additional activity involving long hours in his study as well as frequent attendence at the Nuclear Group's meetings in London, Roger never overlooked his priority of putting persons, individuals, first. By post, phone or visit he kept his old associations and friendships in good repair. And this inevitably meant that – at his age! – he found himself attending funerals, more often than not to give an address or pay a tribute. He was once asked if he found this easy? 'Very easy,' he replied, 'there's so much good to say.'

So it proved at the memorial service for Darlow Humphreys, Friend, friend and colleague at the Institute of Education. Fifteen years later a colleague of both men, Professor Roy Niblett, still vividly recalled the occasion. 'It does strike me,' he wrote, 'that some of Roger's qualities of intelligence, ability to say much in a few chosen words, as well as grasp a situation are shown in this little extract from his address about Darlow Humphreys: "It was the most over-subscribed Department in the country; the whole of its student population had to be *inducted* into and *shepherded* out of the Department every year; their need for school practice involved keeping on good but not subservient terms with 100 schools, six Local Authorities and a number of H.M. Inspectors, the demands incessant . . . the Department grew and grew".'

Having thus focussed the man's work, Roger then epitomized his integrity by quoting a poem by the Russian Yevgeny Yevtushenko, lines spoken, Roger explained, by Humphreys himself at his retirement farewell to students:

Telling lies to the young is wrong,
Proving to them that lies are true is wrong,
Telling them that God's in his heaven
and all's well with the world is wrong.
The young know what you mean. The young are people.
Tell them the difficulties can't be counted,
and let them see not only what will be
but see with clarity these present times.
Say obstacles exist they must encounter
sorrow happens, hardship happens.
The hell with it. Who never knew
the price of happiness will not be happy.
Forgive no error you recognize,
it will repeat itself, increase,
and afterwards our pupils
will not forgive in us what we forgave.[6]

---

[6] *Yevtushenko: Selected Poems* (Penguin Modern European Poets, 1971), p. 52. Reproduced by permission of Penguin Books Ltd.

19

The Faith of a Quaker

1980-1988

The beginning of the new decade demanded of Roger some hard thinking about his personal faith. Invited to give the James Backhouse Lecture at Friends Yearly Meeting in Australia, he chose for his theme one growing out of a series of desolating experiences in the second half of his life.

Until middle life he was, as he put it, 'a traditional Quaker, feeling totally secure in the Society's congregational religious fellowship, recognizing that there were some parts of the package that were not particularly congenial, but that they did not stand in the way of my total emotional sense of being at home in the Society. I had,' he admitted, 'not *had* to think'.

Then came, in 1961, the first of the dark experiences that challenged his faith to its foundations. 'The death of Hammarskjøld was,' he told Australian Friends, 'the most desolating and frightening experience of my life, far more frightening than being in the middle of the blitz in wartime London. Though he had thrown no light on how I should do my professional job, he had thrown up a protective fence between me and chaos, providing as it were a filter that would allow me to deal competently with as much of the encircling nastiness as I had spirit to manage, while in some undefined way he would bear the burden of the unmanageable. With his death I was back in the dark, dangerous, impenetrable jungle.'

Two years later, that experience still by no means wholly understood or resolved, he and Margery were back in America attached to Quaker House at the UN headquarters with the specific role of talking with Friends and others across the country about the moral and political issues raised by the Congo confusion. 'We were,' he recollected, 'in the UN restaurant when the first reports of the attack on President Kennedy began to come through, and in a New York taxi when his death was confirmed. Over the next few days I saw Americans in the throes of the frightening desolation I had experienced in the Congo. It was,' he went on, 'in this experience, as in some sense a detached observer, that I began consciously to formulate and interpret my own Congo experience.'

Four and a half years later, just as he was about once more to return to the USA, as visiting professor at Harvard, came the news of the killing of Martin

Luther King. Joining the thousands of people in the open air on Cambridge Common, mostly youngish, black and white, for a form of memorial service, he found 'a strange sense of reassurance as we sang "We shall overcome . . .". We remained for a time in silence and then shook hands with those round about and went our ways with a refound confidence that in death Martin Luther King had proclaimed an eternal message that would endure though, heaven knows,' Roger added, 'the muddiness of American waters has not cleared much since'.

Only three months later, while he and Margery were still in America, Robert Kennedy was murdered. 'So in the space of seven years,' he reflected, 'I had been close to the violent deaths of four men, each of whom, in life, had filtered the raw reality of the world's politics so that men and women were sheltered in facing its pressures rather than paralysed by its chaos. None of the deaths solved problems, but two of them, after the shock had receded, confirmed and renewed the quality of vision that the men had revealed to their associates during their life-time: the Kennedy deaths remained unredeemed tragedies, illustrating the frail charisma that hovers over the world of power politics, more concerned with the manipulation of human affairs than with the changing of human perceptions.'

Such experiences, however, though stored in his mind and frequently re-examined, might well have remained dormant but for two others, what Roger called 'provocative encounters', in 1976.

The first centred upon his membership of a group including Bishops, Moderators and Mothers Superior which met for a week in a retreat house in the grounds of Windsor Castle to consider 'both how bishops and the like in other churches in fact exercise their responsibilities as leaders and how they should do so'. The organizers said that they particularly wanted a Quaker in the group. The Quakers said they did not have that kind of animal. The reply came that any Quaker would do, and Roger, as Chairman of Yearly Meeting at the time, was nominated.

It proved to be what he called 'an eye-opening occasion for me'. Why? 'I had not previously appreciated,' he said, 'the truly awesome load of complex responsibility borne by contemporary bishops – spiritual, ecclesiastical, political, scholarly, pastoral, social, ecumenical, ceremonial and more – which led to a situation in which we had "forgotten how to talk about God", said a member of the group, a Roman Catholic abbot, Basil Hume, who was called away half way through to become Cardinal Archbishop of Westminster.

'So far as I was concerned,' Roger confessed, 'this struck home, bishop though I was not. Born and brought up in a very active Quaker home, thoroughly involved in the service side of the Society's life, not infrequently led to take part in the verbal ministry of my Meeting, I was yet a Quaker by tradition who shirked the proper commitment of a Christian to try to think and talk about God, not really because I was too busy, but because I did not have to.'

The second provocative encounter came only weeks later in more familiar surroundings. A session of Yearly Meeting was opened by Jocelyn Burnell, a young but already distinguished radio-astronomer who with research colleagues was working on the frontiers of knowledge about the universe, in areas of great uncertainty where growth of understanding was dependent on clear statements of truth as currently reached.

'If we are to travel forward in the life of the spirit,' Roger quoted Jocelyn Burnell, 'we have to provide ourselves with personally written "travelling documents" that will help us to find where we stand from time to time, that can be rewritten as we learn more, and that we can share with others as we seek "to know one another in the things which are eternal".' She then spoke of some of these things of which she *was* sure, and some of which other Friends were sure while she was not.

Thus, 'stabbed into reflection', as he put it, first by the Roman Catholic Archbishop and then the Quaker radio-astronomer, Roger found himself thinking on a new level about 'the meaning of Jesus for me'.

In sharing his answer, Roger focussed issues about which he felt strongly and were not without controversy within the Society: 'Christianity is about the meaning of Jesus in our search for God or, put the other way, in God's search for us as co-workers in the establishment of his Kingdom. Some of us are so haunted by the conventional significance of verbal terms that we repudiate the label Christian at all. Others of us are so clear about the meaning of Jesus for us personally that we are pained when others do not share it. This divisiveness is a pity, for I believe that the phrase of Don Cupitt, "one Jesus, many Christs", is a pointer in the right direction.'

Hence his openness, his ready acceptance of Universalism, the belief that no one world religion monopolized the truth. But for all his flexibility, the growing influence of Universalism *within* the Society of Friends bothered him. He welcomed Universalists and was grateful to learn from them, but not at the price of Quakers repudiating the Christian label altogether, ignoring their historical roots which he saw as inseparable from the life and teaching of Jesus of Nazareth. Not for a moment did he doubt that the spirit of the 'many Christs' was at work in the world in the broadest sense, often in the most surprising places, granting validity to the claims of Universalists, but this could never justify the Society of Friends repudiating its *Christian* label, its faith centred in the Jesus of history.

That Roger's own faith was Christo-centric was self-evident to all who knew him, though perhaps not his attempts to be more precise about what he believed. In providing an answer he first sought to avoid misunderstanding by saying what he did *not* believe:

I don't believe Jesus was divine.
I don't believe in the phraseology which regards
him as Saviour, Redeemer. Coming to Jesus, for
Christ's sake, have no real meaning.
I don't believe in the bodily Resurrection.

He then went on to say what sort of Jesus didn't help him:

1. One who was God or in any way removed from an understanding of what we have to face as ordinary men.
2. One who came to save the world as if it was doomed to perish. Not my idea of God!
3. One who came to atone; again not my idea of God.
4. One who in any way was supernatural; i.e. contrary *to* nature, not merely explicable.

More confusingly he did not believe that God created the universe. Rather he felt compelled to conceive of a creator God entering history by endowing the earliest members of humankind with the self-conscious ability to think and – at least in part – with an element of spiritual *apprehension*, a word, he explained, 'to signify a form of knowledge or experience garnered at a much more fundamental level than that gained by intellectual processes'. The ability to think enabled men, women and children alone of all living things to say 'I'.

'It is,' he continued, 'this very late arrival of self-consciousness in the world that enables us alone to know that we know and so to be able to interpret experience, to be able to choose whether to foster or exploit, to enjoy or reject, to define purpose in terms of value judgments, to wrestle as it were as citizens of a spiritual world with the temporal and material world of which we are, in our evolutionary animal existence, an exploitive, competitive part. This self-consciousness is an inexplicable gift of God which offers us the key to citizenship in that other world – his Kingdom.'

To interpret experience! 'To me,' he explained, 'religion doesn't begin in belief. It begins – and ends – with the experience of being loved, of being expected to love, of being forgiven and of being expected to forgive. Belief comes in the middle, as the attempt to systematize experience.'

Not that Roger underestimated either the importance or power of *belief*. With Voltaire he never doubted that 'those who make us believe absurdities can also make us commit atrocities'. It was simply that he saw the danger of belief not facilitating but becoming a substitute for experience, as though intellectual orthodoxy was a guarantee of authenticity and wholeness. And even in the interpretation of experience he felt it necessary to issue a warning:

'That reason can think critically about experience was the great intellectual re-discovery of the Renaissance, and man found a great sense of release in being able to examine himself. So far, so good. But then he found his reason so interesting, and its own working so much more easy to analyse, that he forgot about his actual experience, and lost himself in the logic and structures of his own thinking. And so for the last 400 years our philosophers have been busy thinking harder and harder about thought, and have neglected the discipline of relating thinking to actual experience which is the basis of action.'

All this granted, there emerged from Roger's own attempts to 'systematize experience' a hard core of belief.

His belief in God gave him the unshakeable conviction that goodness, truth and love are the ultimate realities; that behind all experience, no matter how dark, is 'the wise love of One whom we may call Father'.

This love he saw in the death of Jesus as the eternal heart of God. 'People tend to think of it (the cross) as a single episode concerning God . . . But we are still crucifying humanity, causing God pain.' To this he added, doubtless a reminder to himself: 'So long as people's religion is Christo-centric to the exclusion of God and his presence in all men, so the cross may arouse emotions but it will not be a stimulus or a challenge.'

Though rejecting the bodily rising of Christ, he believed in the Gospel of the Risen Life: 'It was the experience of resurrection – which to me is to be understood in spiritual rather than any kind of physical terms – and the encounter with the risen Jesus that compelled Gospel writers to look backwards to interpret his life, teaching and crucifixion in the light of the compelling experience that freed them to construct a fresh vision of how God comes into the daily life of men and women; fresh because while the Old Testament is a sustained account of how understanding of this theme developed through Jewish history, the search had become clogged by the weight of hierarchical authority.'

About life after death he was unambiguous: 'My feeling is not for subjective immortality but for one which is wholly objective or at least assumes nothing with regard to conscientious consciousness, for there seems no reason to believe that human self-consciousness is any more than a purely contingent attribute, like the physical side of us ourselves'.

However, after all his wrestling to articulate his beliefs, what he did and didn't believe, Roger summed up his personal creed in just a few words: 'Jesus shows us what it means to love and be loved, to forgive and be forgiven, to bear creatively the pain of wrestling with the cosmos,

. . . To hope till Hope creates
from its own wreck the thing it contemplates.

(Shelley, 'Prometheus Unbound')

This is freedom and *I know Jesus as liberator.*'

He added a sort of postscript:

'To me Jesus means that, in commitment to God as Love, there are ways of both enjoying and standing up to the temporal hurricane of the cosmos and so having a toe-hold in the Kingdom of God, even though for much of the time I am a thoughtless vandal, yet forgiven again and again and again.'

Roger never doubted that Truth was never static but alive, too much alive not to move forward in new ways consistent with itself. Indeed, once it stopped pulsating into new forms it encouraged the notion that conformity was synonymous with commitment, as though orthodoxy was the sole approach to God. Where there was *no* vision the people perished, but Roger was no less persuaded that where there *was* vision but no daring the people slowly died of boredom.

Thus his insistence that at its best Quakerism 'is a statement about membership in a Christian community which not merely allows but encourages originality that goes beyond its own conventions because its members have some inkling of the disciplined originality of Jesus himself'.[1]

'Jesus the Liberator' – this was his creed. Others found meaning in Jesus the Saviour, Jesus the Deliverer, Jesus the Redeemer, but for Roger *Jesus the Liberator* pin-pointed the essential discovery of his own spiritual explorations. His Quaker upbringing had, he said, made a strong emphasis on the *inward* aspects of religious life and an active repudiation of the sacraments and ceremonies of other denominations, though at Oxford he had come to have a very high regard for a good deal of Anglican litany – but not the creed!

However, what he called the great variety of formulations within inherited religious institutions were at one extreme concerned with fear and propitiation, and at the other with love and forgiveness, not as words or formulae but as the most fundamental of all human experiences. 'And while intellectuals may be able to handle these experiences in abstract terms and conceptualizations, I believe,' he declared, 'that it is in the language and experience of religious worship and religious history that they are most abidingly symbolized and embodied.'

This was, Roger believed, the safeguard against individualism or egocentricity mis-identifying itself as concern or conviction. As much as he argued that there was no stereotype of religious experience, that each seeker must find reality for himself, articulated in a personal vocabulary or perhaps not at all in words, he also advocated the necessary corrective or affirmation of corporate worship: 'Those with a live spiritual experience can never be either quite comfortable or quite respectable because the spirit of Jesus will always be reaching out to truer understanding, and so long as the Society of

---

[1] 'Plato Offered Ideas: Jesus Offered Himself', *The Friend*, 7 October 1966, p.1179.

Friends remains neither quite comfortable nor quite respectable in the name of Jesus Christ, it will have its part to play.'

On another occasion, addressing Friends in America at the Pendle Hill Conference Centre on 'Quaker Responsibility in the Modern World', he was even more explicit: 'The *central* responsibility of the Society of Friends is to maintain a vital worship from which new men go out to serve the world.'

Yet if such worship was essential, there was also something else to steer the believer's personal search for meaning away from arrogant or pompous individualism; the relation, quite simply, between belief and behaviour, the degree to which believing, no matter how verbalized, turned the believer not only in the way of emulating but actually of manifesting love, joy, peace, long-suffering, patience, goodness, what the New Testament called the fruits of the spirit. This granted, the inner light was trustworthy. This denied, 'truth' revealed its own barrenness. 'The only way to see Truth,' said Roger, 'is to live in the power of it,' to test its validity against the words of Jesus of Nazareth – 'by their fruits you shall know them'. Did a man's faith in God make him more human, turn his face toward wholeness, make him better able to cope, grant him corrective insight into his selfishness, quicken his compassion, teach him to distinguish between 'straining at gnats and swallowing camels', set his mind on the priorities of the Kingdom of God? Here surely was *the* touchstone of truth against which all orthodoxies and heresies could be judged. And far from fostering self-righteousness it induced a spirit of healthy humility. For who, searching his own heart, could possibly overlook his need of forgiveness, Roger reiterated, 'again and again and again'?

He concluded his James Backhouse lecture with two quotations, one well-known from Albert Schweitzer's *Quest for the Historical Jesus*: 'He comes to us as One unknown . . . And to those who obey him, whether they be wise or simple, he will reveal himself in the toils, the conflicts, the sufferings which they shall pass through in his fellowship, and, as an ineffable mystery, they shall learn in their own experience who he is'; the second almost inevitably from Dag Hammarskjøld's *Markings*: ' . . . I came to a time and place where I realized that the Way leads to a triumph which is a catastrophe, and to a catastrophe which is a triumph, that the price for committing one's life would be reproach, and that the only elevation possible to man lies in the depths of humilation. After that, the word *courage* lost its meaning, since nothing could be taken from me.

'As I continued along the Way, I learned, step by step, word by word, that behind every saying in the Gospels stands *one* man, and *one* man's experience. Also behind the prayer that the cup might pass from him and his promise to drink it. Also behind each of the words from the Cross.'[2]

---

[2] Dag Hammarskjøld's, *Markings*, Faber & Faber 1964, p.169.

Though grateful to quote Hammarskjøld, Roger never stopped searching for new forms in his own distinctive style to express his personal faith. Christian discipleship was total commitment or nothing; nothing more than second-rate conformity to second-hand beliefs, the difference between 'a good adjustment' and 'holy obedience'. For most people, he suggested, the words 'a good adjustment' meant something, while 'holy obedience' nothing. Between the two, Quakers were almost sure to experience 'a good deal of tension' simply because 'an organization which starts to give shape to the new always tends towards securing the familiar and therefore to disapprove of the new'.

He himself, though firmly rooted in the old, was constantly reaching out to the new, outcome of his inner spiritual security that enabled him to question everything and spurn nothing as too unconventional or risky. Consequently he had a reputation – neither cultivated nor cared about by Roger himself – for being both a deep-dyed traditionalist and an original thinker, one reason why people wanted to hear what he had to say and listened with heightened expectation. Once it became known, for instance, that he was to deliver the Backhouse lecture in Adelaide, invitations poured in from that side of the world. Margery saw the itinerary subsequently arranged for them in consultation with the Friends World Committee, and simply wondered how so much could be fitted into so short a time; short despite eventually covering four-and-a-half months!

En route to Australia they spent ten days in Jamaica, then to Costa Rica to Honolulu to Fiji to New Zealand, everywhere meeting Friends informally, visiting centres of Quaker welfare services, addressing gatherings both public and private, and broadening their own experience of Quakerism in the only parts of the world they'd never previously visited.

After Christmas in New Zealand – which each agreed, England apart, most appealed as a place to live – they travelled on the second day of 1981 to Australia for almost two hectic months visiting every key centre including Tasmania before – on the way home! – taking in Singapore, Hong Kong, Sri Lanka, and finally Greece where at the Epidaurus amphitheatre in Athens, site of the Temple of Asclepius, the God of healing, Roger, reminiscent of his schoolboy days, recited word perfect Shelley's 'Isles of Greece' and was heard, as Margery recorded, 'absolutely perfectly everywhere'.

Home once more, if there was any degree of routine to their lives it was more in the ingredients than a regular daily pattern. True, Margery worked in the garden, now sufficiently glorious to warrant open days to the public for good causes; and Roger still constantly disappeared into his study to maintain his heavy personal correspondence. But – now in their late seventies – for the first time in their lives they felt a new degree of freedom to please themselves

– to walk for miles on the fells, take a picnic to the lakes or moors, share favourite scenic places with visitors, participate as much if not more than ever in community activities in the village.

Roger's continued membership of Meeting for Sufferings entailed a monthly trip to London, with matters discussed to be pursued in between. Not to attend Yearly Meeting was out of the question; apart from its intrinsic significance and interest it was a chance to greet old friends whose number was shrinking! Furthermore, it would be surprising if he didn't enjoy receiving the veneration of a Quaker elder statesman. Richard Rowntree described him as 'probably the Friend personally known to more members of the Society in this country than any other, partly because of his leadership of Friends Relief Service during the war and later on his clerkship (chairmanship) of London Yearly Meeting and his very longstanding service as a member of Meeting for Sufferings'.

All of which would carry general agreement. But there was something else far more revealing of the man. 'Roger often recounted,' Richard Rowntree continued, 'how at the time of his wartime service he felt as a broadly liberal humanist that he could get through life without any of the conventional Christian beliefs in Jesus; but that in the light of experience he had come to find that he needed Jesus without being able to account for the mystery of his relationship with God, and during the last twenty years of his life his main concern was to share this experience in different ways with Friends.'

Happily, in a personal letter to Richard Rowntree, in 1989, Roger further attempted to spell out what he meant by the mystery of his relationship with God:

> Creedaly, our personal spiritual needs are very different and we shall draw from Jesus our own psychological threads. Paisley understands the Crucifixion as his route to salvation from the wrath of an offended God. I understand the Resurrection as illumination about and reassurance of a loving God. Both the ends are within the historical range of the Christian church. There is no single Christian tradition and the simplest pointer to the range of interpretations is the question, Why four Gospels? Because each of the authors was offering his own 'slant' – a poor word – for the particular audience for whom he was writing.
>
> About twelve years ago I was travelling back north from Woodbrooke (with two women Friends) . . . We fell into more general conversation and one of them said she needed Jesus because she didn't understand God, the other said she needed God to understand Jesus.
>
> We need both a background and a foreground in the religious life, but held together as a whole. God is at best a mystical experience, at thinnest a philosophical idea; Jesus is the historical witness to the meaning of God in

a thoroughly real historical situation – or rather two situations, the gifted challenging life of a travelling neighbourhood pastor in Galilee or the powerful prophetic life and death in Jerusalem, each/both of them brought to eternal illumination in the experience of the resurrection, and emerging in the history of the church in the pastoral witness of Paul, Savonarola, George Fox . . .

There's room for those who need theology, provided they don't forget the person of Jesus (for all his elusiveness) and for the universalists, provided that they are prepared to anchor it in some appropriate human, historical witness. (What do the universalists do about the God of Islam? And let's beware of comparing the worst of anybody else's faith with the best of our own tradition.)

For Friends as a body I think we must have Jesus – and as many Christs as a congregation of individuals may need, each for their own illumination. And we ought to encourage one another to reflect hard and deeply enough about Jesus, to see whether we want a Christ each for our own self (I don't think I do – but I *do* need Jesus). I'm a universalist in knowing that there is an infinity of ways in which God enters human experience. I'm troubled when I feel under pressure to restrain my declaration of the Jesus witness as a bond of unity which keeps the Society within the church – as puzzling to us as it is to the others (denominations).[3]

Eight years before writing that personal letter, in fact within only five months of delivering his Backhouse lecture and the like half way round the world, he was fulfilling an invitation to exercise his prophetic judgment before a gathering of more than 650 Friends at the historic Burlington (NJ) Meeting House to celebrate the 300th anniversary of Philadelphia Yearly Meeting, his prophetic judgment about the present and the future of Quakerism.[4]

'To get some clues on the present,' he declared, 'I turned to the 35 or 40 epistles which yearly meetings around the world exchange with one another annually', and discovered the puzzling feature that while membership of the Society was tending to decline, the number of attenders was tending to increase. 'Why don't they join?' he asked.

By way of an answer he referred to a radically minded group of young Friends who, while remaining in the Society, were highly critical of its intellectual aridity, intimated by the attitude of an elderly Friend to a young

---

3 Printed in *The Seeker*, Autumn 1991, pp. 22–23 shortly after Roger's death.

4 Published in shortened form in *Friends Journal*, 15 November 1981, pp. 4–8.

one: 'I heard thee say in meeting, "I think". Now thou shouldst not have been thinking.'

Roger made clear that this was at a time of passionate controversy within The Society of Friends about whether the true character of Quaker worship was in silent waiting or in vigorous doctrinal ministry with emphasis upon such themes as the Blood of Christ and the Atonement.[5]

But bold *thinking*, he insisted, was perennially demanded of Quakers, for only then would they find positive and mutually supportive faith, not – needless to say – to encourage endless devotional navel gazing, but to enter into the agonies of the world without being overcome by them.

An aspect of such *agonies* he had hoped never to experience again confronted him within months with the outbreak of the Falkland's conflict, in 1982. He was, of course, still a pacifist, though to what extent his constant travails on this front had modified – or were still modifying – his conviction about the Quaker and war reveals a man more concerned about obedience that dogma.

To such matters we now turn.

[5] He analysed this whole matter in a Presidential Address of painstaking research to the Friends Historical Society, in November 1988, published as a pamphlet *Manchester, Manchester and Manchester Again*, obtainable at Friends Book Centre, London.

20

Dilemmas of Quaker Pacifism

A helpful starting point is an address Roger gave at William Penn House, London, with the title heading this chapter. In assessing its significance, bear in mind that it was delivered six years *before* his retirement (1971) and four years *after* his Congo experience (1961), though, as we shall see, it pointed the way to the position he was advocating shortly before he died.

'I am,' he began, 'neither a theologian nor a philosopher, but I can try to say what it *feels* like to be a pacifist when one is intensely interested in what goes on in a world which is not pacifist. That is to say that being a pacifist, one declines to take part in one aspect of corporate life of nation states, not because one is not interested but because one is intensely interested.

'Some religious pacifists approach a resolution of the dilemmas that pacifism involves by withdrawing as far as possible from the world. Quakers on the other hand tend to be very active in the world . . . In practical terms the obligation of the pacifist in the presence of aggression and evil is to try to change the evil mind into the good. It may not work in any particular situation. But to engage in destruction with outward weapons is to terminate the dialogue in the arrogance of one's own power, and this is a denial of the reality of God and his power. War is the ultimate in destruction, and at this point the orthodox Quaker says "No". But he does not walk out of the world, either to suicide or a monastery. He tends to be intensely and actively concerned with politics, with social questions, with scientific advance, with education and international affairs. The "No" is not lightly said.'

So far so good. Nothing unexpected. Little with which the Quaker pacifist would wish to disagree. But then he moved on to perhaps more controversial matters in trying to answer *What Problems Does Pacifism Not Solve*?

1. 'At its most painful, at the personal level. In 1939–40 my friends, disliking war at least as much as I did, were fighting, killing, dying to preserve a way of life which respected my right to be a conscientious objector to military service.'

2. 'The war was about something – the evil of Nazism, the destruction of the Jews. War was an active response, much more satisfying in one way than rescuing refugees. How does one *know* that one is identifying oneself with those who hate Nazism etc.?'

3. 'Nobody now defends war; is it not better to come in 100% and help to create the institutions of a better world? Organized international force,' he recalled the Congo, 'with the appearance of military force and the functions of the police.'

4. ' . . . in a world which still believes in power (though it exercises it with some sophisticated restraint) is it not more honest to be interested in the politics of governments and yet to contract out at the personal level? For example, if an active Quaker were invited to join the Cabinet, he would *have* to resolve this problem operationally. Can those of us who are *not* cabinet ministers avoid living with the issue unresolved?'

He then came to what for him was the nub of the matter by asking *At what point does the Quaker make his assertion*?

'The tendency of those of us who know enough of the international world at first-hand talk its language; while a larger part of the body of the Society takes the view that Quakers shouldn't touch this dirty work of international power politics and its military weapons. We try to carry this by ourselves, as persons, keeping clear of the rewards or temptations of seeking or holding *power* but offering a framework for the consideration of ideas that are moving in this same direction. But is this shirking of responsibility? Or is there a place in the world for those who maintain personal loyalty to a principle while participating in discussion of modalities at a more earthy level?'

He answered for himself: 'Yes – but only just.'

Roger's experience in the Congo of an 'organized military force with the appearance of military force and the functions of the police' he later amplified as '200 unarmed Nigerian police, a magnificent force who kept order simply by the quality of their bearing and presence among a restless population, who nonetheless basically *wanted* peace'. Significantly, he went on: 'Elsewhere, 1000 miles away, my work was protected by an armed Indian contingent who had used their arms against an active minority. I found no real difficulty in working in that setting.'

Interestingly, such ideas were a re-echo of views first put forward at a National Peace Council in 1933 by Lord Clifford Allen whose uncompromising opposition as a pacifist to the 1914–18 war led to his imprisonment from which he emerged already an invalid and to an early death at the age of forty-three. With the authority of such proven commitment he startled delegates by suggesting, first, that what pacifists ought to do was to unite and press the British government to take a bold step at all international meetings in proposing that all countries should disarm completely within ten years; and then that there should be formed an internationally controlled force strong enough 'to provide the security necessary for international peace'.

That, he said, was what he meant by pacifism; not a tightrope dance of logic about whether force should be used, or when; not a negative advocacy for resisting war; but something quite different, namely testing out the possibility of using reason and initiating bold proposals, hitherto considered impracticable, not because they were undesirable but because no one would propose them. 'The choice is,' Lord Allen concluded, 'between an armed anarchy and an armed society. Both are evil. But I suggest that the armed society is less evil; that a good society, though armed, is on the way to becoming an unarmed one . . .'

The reaction was predictable, not least within the Society of Friends! Carl Heath insisted the idea wasn't new; it had been around when he was appointed secretary of the National Peace Council, in 1909. In a letter to Roger's father he quoted an American professor who said that such an international force would – 'Look like *war*. Smell like *war*. Taste like *war*, and feel like *war*.'

Whether Roger's father, who of course heartily agreed, replied to Carl Heath isn't clear, but certainly Roger did, in a memorandum dated 21 January 1934. In tracing the thinking of this particular Quaker pacifist it is invaluable:

'No, I am not myself an advocate of the international force, but I do believe that it may be the next practical step. I still think that the Quaker testimony is the right one, but it can only be justified provided it *is* part of a whole testimony against the economics of national and imperial competition which breeds war.

'The arguments against the international force are very unfair in one way. They assume that the pooled force has fighting as its object, and is exactly on a par with a national force. This seems to me quite a distortion . . . "If you want peace, prepare for war" is only a logical absurdity when two or more parties are playing the same game. It may be just as wrong morally, but it is logically watertight to say we'll give one authority all the force that is necessary, provided everyone else scraps their arms.'

Roger summed up – remember it is 1934: 'I stick to Quaker principles because I believe that the only security which is ultimate, which is an end in itself, is a free security, built on trust, but if anybody else does not get that far but is making a genuine effort to get a very long way, I am not going to abuse them.' What, however, of his ultimate position?

Only months before he died, the Gulf war raging, he surely left little room for doubt: 'In meeting on the Sunday before Christmas, and in our daughter's parish church on Christmas Day, I wept, lost in the maze of how to find a way through the splendour of Christmas mythology and the darkness of Gulf guilt for all that we citizens of the world have done to allow us to get into this mess.'

'As a politically aware citizen,' he again recalled his experience of unarmed and armed troops in the Congo, 'my niche was in the UN as a whole. As a Christian pacifist I identified myself in terms of the Quaker declaration of 1660 – We utterly deny all outward wars . . . for any end or any pretence whatsoever. And this is our testimony to the whole world.

'Under conscription I would again be a CO, aged 84. If I had the mobility and the stamina actively to join mass demonstrations against war, I would do so – as I have done in the past. But minority *ad hoc* demos of Christian pacifists do nothing to help a Foreign Secretary, working within the ambivalence of UN resolutions, who has to take decisions today or tomorrow on which peace or war may depend. I have therefore written to the Foreign Secretary to say that while I am a Christian pacifist who thinks we have blundered into a dreadful, guilt-ridden mess, what I hope he will do is to summon up all the statesmanship he can to use the potential of the UN, even though this may depend on the reluctance to use organized force.

'The majority of mankind are *not* pacifists. CND, Greenham Common and many other demos, including Quaker proclamations, have played, and do play, their constructive part in changing national and international perspectives over time. But they don't make any difference to the way a Foreign Secretary reaches a decision, today, here, where we are. I want to encourage him to use the UN to the very limits of its strengths, for all its clay-bound feet, come war or some sort of peace.'[1]

That piece was written when he was already seriously ill. Eight months later he was dead. The time in between, living with terminal cancer?

Behold the man.

---

[1] Lancaster Monthly Meeting Newsletter, January 1991.

21

A Quaker's Attitude to Death
1988–1991

In late 1988 Roger needed surgery for a prostate problem. Buoyant that the operation had been so successful, he reacted with characteristic impish humour when a villager expressed concern he looked so *drained*. 'You could say that,' his eyes twinkled.

In no time, it seemed, he was able to resume his normal routine – disappearing into his study each morning, lunch at midday, a short snooze (habit for many years), and then visiting, receiving visitors, a car ride to one of the Lakes, or walking his beloved fells, perhaps not so far, but far enough to stretch his younger companions.

Walking with Roger was a mix of lively debate and long silences, the latter predominant as the upper fells offered relaxation by a tarn or a view too 'splendid' – one of his favourite words – for comment. If during his convalescence he made any concessions it was to give up his membership of Meeting for Sufferings, reaching back almost fifty years.

But by the summer of 1989 it was again necessary for him to enter hospital, this time for exploratory prostate tests; he was by all accounts an excellent patient, too interested in what was going on around him to be over-concerned about himself.

Eventually an appointment was made for him to see a specialist at a Manchester hospital. Assured there was 'nothing to worry about', Margery phoned their daughter Elizabeth with the news. On hearing the name of the hospital, Liz was immediately suspicious; and a medical consultant friend of hers confirmed that no one was referred there unless cancer was suspected.

As for Roger himself, he felt in a sort of limbo, ignorant of any diagnosis and offered only a prognosis of mutterings. What he wanted was to *know*, for someone, he said, to tell him *straight* of his condition. Liz arranged for him to see her consultant friend, and was present when her father was told he had cancer.

The next time she visited her parents at Yealand, Margery, driving her from the station, warned her that 'she would see a big difference'. She replied that she wasn't surprised. After all, he did have cancer! 'But he hasn't got cancer,' her mother reacted, leaving Liz fearful she'd spoken out of turn.

Immediately on seeing her father alone she confessed. 'Oh,' he responded, 'you think the symptoms are cancer?' 'But you know,' she said, 'my friend *told* you you had cancer.' 'Well, yes,' he replied, 'I think it must be cancer.'

From that moment his acceptance of the total situation could hardly have been more unflinching or triumphant. Liz testified: 'He just coped absolutely magnificently, always ALWAYS cheerful; and when people asked how he was, he had his own phrase, not the usual "As well as can be expected" but "I'm getting along".'

He was still planning, looking forward, not least to his Diamond Wedding anniversary, in four months' time. But first there was the family reunion for the Wilson clan, held frequently over the years, giving expression to the sustained closeness of Roger to his brothers and sister, their children, grandchildren, aunts and uncles, in-laws, nieces, nephews and cousins plus exceptional friends like Oliver Franks. One special year the number topped a hundred. On this occasion, notwithstanding the death of some and the failing health of others too far away to travel, a more modest thirty or so were expected at the Quaker Guest House in Grasmere.

On the day the holiday was due to commence, the family of Roger and Margery gathered at Yealand for lunch, supposedly to sort out the cars for travelling together to Grasmere. The weather was dreadful: hurricane force wind. Liz casually suggested they should take the opportunity to visit a nearby spot beloved of her parents offering a panoramic view of Morecambe Bay. Margery dissented. She was in favour of the suggested family photograph, but why not, she asked, sensibly outside their own front door? Liz was adamant, sufficiently so for Margery to realize that 'something was going on'.

Roger was testily insistent he could not manage the walk from the road, unenlightened that arrangements had been made for the farmer to unchain the gate of his field to allow the full journey by car, all part of the plot.

By the time they arrived at Summer House Hill her father, Liz recalled, 'was as gauche as anything yet smiling and laughing at waiting photographers and representatives of the Press'. One picture shows him holding his stick aloft, sort of, thought Liz, saying Hi, epitomizing his spirit and the jollity of the occasion. Then came the essential point of it all, the revealing of a slightly premature Diamond Wedding gift from the children – a bench-seat for viewing the bay simply inscribed 'Roger and Margery Wilson, June 1991'. In celebratory mood the family then made for Grasmere.

During the following days Roger's infectious gaiety was barely credible. Gaiety? An amalgam of joyousness and peace somehow enhanced by a steely-eyed realism. No need for anyone to pretend, to feel conversationally inhibited. Roger knew he was dying. His courage heartened and released everybody else. Sometimes he was able to join the family group. Otherwise individuals sat with him in his room; talking; reminiscing; anticipating. If anything, his always profound interest in people appeared to have quickened, intensified. Spasms of pain both found him and left him entirely free of either self-pity or self-centredness.

At low points he was grateful to sit by the window. Looking – across the fells; at gamboling lambs . . . birds . . . flowers; looking in a new way, enjoying at a new depth; just looking. He wished he'd learned the art much earlier.

And exploring silence. This life-long Quaker once confessed he didn't find easy even the silence of worship! Now he was content to be still, to listen, to receive in greater abundance the gift of wonder.

Towards the end of the holiday a doctor had to be called one night; and it soon emerged that Roger would require some form of hospital care, a decision reinforced by the journey home. Roger himself accepted the situation; Margery less so, conscious that his break from home would almost certainly be terminal. Within days his condition left no choice.

Roger was admitted to a hospice at Lancaster run by an order of Roman Catholic nuns. Soon the Sister in Charge was telling Margery and the children that it was 'absolutely a privilege to have him in the hospice'; never before had they nursed anyone so close to death yet so accepting of it. He joked with the nurses, took an interest in them and their families, and followed everything going on around him in what was described as 'a quite incredible way'.

If he had any regrets it was that he wished he'd had greater opportunity to 'look around' that last spring, 'the most beautiful spring there'd ever been'. Certainly he'd been taken by the family to favourite spots and spent more time, unlike before, silently gazing. 'He had the view of Ingleborough, of course, from his study window,' Liz reflected, 'but I think he should have stopped earlier from being driven on to do this writing and reading and I don't know what else, ninety per cent of it,' she presumed, 'Quaker work'.

A further remembrance brought a smile. 'He was always speaking at other people's memorials. Somebody said it was a pity he couldn't speak at his own.'

After five weeks in the hospice Liz even thought it possible he might be able to return home. His pain was under control. His energy, like his humour, appeared irrepressible. By every indicator, he wasn't afraid of death or indeed of dying. He was calm, open-eyed about his situation and prayerfully adjusted to it, but such was his love of life, the enthusiasm with which he greeted each new day, that a hospice seemed singularly inappropriate. He, a terminal patient, was comforting rather than being comforted. Visitors entered his presence with heavy hearts but left feeling uplifted often for reasons they didn't altogether understand. His bedside, assumed a place for whispered commiserations, was marked by explosions of laughter.

And mercifully his mind remained clear, as sharp as ever, able to recall recent events no less than distant memories! He and notably his brother Geoffrey reminisced about their childhood, but if he was happy in recalling the past he had no intention of escaping into it; the *eternal now* remained his preoccupation. Little wonder, then, that the nurses including the nuns loved him, *sought* opportunities to be with him, respected his Quaker faith despite on their own admission knowing next to nothing of The Society of Friends. He was to them a unique hospice patient. Proving that in the midst of death we are in life!

Understandably *they* associated his courage, humour and concern for them with, first, his faith in God and, secondly, his belief that death was the door through which he would soon pass into the more immediate presence of his Maker. About the first there could be no doubt. About the second he still believed only in life after death in *this* world, in the resurrection experience, the constant presence of the risen Christ. The former alone was enough to guard the serenity of mind and heart he exemplified during what proved to be his final days; no morbidity; no complaints; no earthly clinging; nothing negative. If pain wasn't always under control and his mind too exhausted to remain rational, let alone cogent, his essential identity was unmistakable. The nuns and nurses were unanimous. Here was a man of God. Unaware of his history or reputation, knowing him only in this hospice situation, they spoke simply of his transparent and radiant *goodness*, his freedom from fear, his thoughtfulness and kindness.

In any assessment of a man's life, the manner of his coming to terms with death is surely crucial. Roger's attitude was summed up in what he called 'remember the Hammarskjøld: "For all that has been – THANKS; for all that will be – YES"'.

During these final months and days his children came to know him on an altogether deeper level. Being confined to bed, Liz smiled, he wasn't able to disappear into his study. His sickness made him constantly available, and his openness, like his approachableness about anything, generated a new intimacy. In the circumstances this was hardly surprising, but it was a mutuality engendered by far more than the nearness of his death. 'I suddenly realized,' said Liz, 'that here was a man I'd never *really* known'; loved him, respected him, realized that he was outstanding, special; but never really known him for all that he was.

Anthony felt something the same, though he placed his emphasis not so much on getting to know his father as on coming to recognize and enjoy more fully the richness of his personality. But whichever way they recalled those final months and days, they rejoiced that they felt closer to him than ever before; not the closeness of sympathy and sentimentality almost inseparable from such circumstances, but of love and respect bordering on veneration.

Apart from his hitherto busy life, half the reason for their not knowing him better sooner was, of course, his disinclination ever to talk about himself and his achievements. If his integrity refused to 'hide his light under a bushel', he nonetheless, as we have seen repeatedly, rarely allowed his right hand to know what his left hand was doing. From *that* standpoint no one other than Margery knew what he was up to, for any *display* of virtue for its own sake was to Roger obscene. In this sense much of his life was hidden, and if to this is added the long hours he felt compelled to spend in his study, it is hardly surprising that even his children only discovered the greater measure of their father within the confines of his terminal illness and from the tributes that poured in from far beyond Quakerism at news of his death.

The end came quickly. Overnight from being his perky self he drifted in and out of consciousness, aware of his family's presence, grateful too for other visitors. He slipped peacefully away on 31 July 1991, three days before his Diamond Wedding anniversary.

'What a lovely surprise he must have had,' Margery commented, not for a moment doubting that he and her theologian father, meeting for the first time, were already enjoying animated discussion. Perhaps about Roger not believing in the After-life! Who knows? More certain was Roger's endorsement in death as in life of words spoken by George Fox:

> Sing and rejoice, ye children of the Day, and of the Light; for the Lord is at work in this thick night of darkness that may be felt. And Truth doth flourish as the rose, and the lilies do grow among the thorns, and the plants a-top of the hills, and upon them the lambs do skip and play.
>
> And never heed the tempests nor the storms, floods nor rains, for the Seed Christ is over all, and doth reign. And so, be of good faith and valiant for Truth.

Index